The Presentation of Authorship in Medieval German Narrative Literature

1220–1290

SEBASTIAN COXON

CLARENDON PRESS · OXFORD

OXFORD
UNIVERSITY PRESS

Great Clarendon Street, Oxford OX2 6DP

Oxford University Press is a department of the University of Oxford.
It furthers the University's objective of excellence in research, scholarship,
and education by publishing worldwide in

Oxford   New York

Athens   Auckland   Bangkok   Bogotá   Buenos Aires   Calcutta
Cape Town   Chennai   Dar es Salaam   Delhi   Florence   Hong Kong   Istanbul
Karachi   Kuala Lumpur   Madrid   Melbourne   Mexico City   Mumbai
Nairobi   Paris   São Paulo   Shanghai   Singapore   Taipei   Tokyo   Toronto
Warsaw and associated companies in Berlin   Ibadan

Oxford is a registered trademark of Oxford University Press
in the UK and certain other countries

Published in the United States
by Oxford University Press Inc., New York

British Library Cataloguing in Publication Data
Data available

ISBN 0-19-816017-8

Library of Congress Cataloging in Publication Data
Data available

1 3 5 7 9 10 8 6 4 2

Typeset by Florence Production Ltd, Stoodleigh, Devon
Printed in Great Britain
on acid-free paper by
TJ International Ltd,
Padstow, Cornwall

To Kate and Jacob Felix

ACKNOWLEDGEMENTS

I have been fortunate in the help that I have received in writing this book. My first debt of gratitude is to Nigel Palmer for his expert advice and guidance over the years. I have also benefited greatly from the critical observations of Almut Suerbaum and Mark Chinca (my D.Phil. examiners), and in the final stages also Timothy McFarland. I was only able to undertake a research degree in the first place due to the generous support of D.W.D. Shaw, John Ashton, and the Trustees of the Pirie-Reid Scholarship Fund. A Michael Foster Memorial Scholarship later allowed me to spend an invaluable year (1995–6) at Cologne University where I had numerous instructive discussions with Peter Dieckow, Franz-Josef Holznagel, and Ursula Peters. More recently, Somerville College, where I held a lecturership in 1999–2000, provided me with ideal working conditions for revising my text. I should also like to thank Wolfson College, Jill Hughes of the Taylor Institution Library, the Committee of the Oxford Modern Languages and Literature Monographs Series, and finally Peter Coxon, who helped with the proofreading, and Kate Preller for her constant encouragement and patience.

SC

CONTENTS

LIST OF ILLUSTRATIONS

LIST OF ABBREVIATIONS

AASS	Acta Sanctorum quotquot toto orbe coluntur [. . .], edd. Johannes Bollandus *et al.*, Antverpiae etc. 1643–1867
ABäG	Amsterdamer Beiträge zur älteren Germanistik
AKG	Archiv für Kulturgeschichte
ATB	Altdeutsche Textbibliothek
BNL	Bibliothek der gesammten deutschen National-Literatur von der ältesten Zeit bis auf die neuere Zeit
BSB	Bayerische Staatsbibliothek
Bull. du Cange	Bulletin du Cange: Archivum latinitatis medii aevi
CCM	Cahiers de civilisation médiévale
DHB	Deutsches Heldenbuch (edd. Jänicke *et al.*)
DTM	Deutsche Texte des Mittelalters
dtv	Deutscher Taschenbuch Verlag
DVjs	Deutsche Vierteljahrsschrift für Literaturwissenschaft und Geistesgeschichte
EdF	Erträge der Forschung
EG	Etudes Germaniques
FMLS	Forum for Modern Language Studies
FMSt	Frühmittelalterliche Studien
GA	Gesammtabenteuer (ed. von der Hagen)
GAG	Göppinger Arbeiten zur Germanistik
GGN	Nachrichten von der Königlichen Gesellschaft der Wissenschaften zu Göttingen. Philologisch-historische Klasse
GRM	Germanisch-Romanische Monatsschrift
HAB	Herzog-August Bibliothek
HMS	Minnesinger (ed. von der Hagen)
IASL	Internationales Archiv für Sozialgeschichte der deutschen Literatur
JOWG	Jahrbuch der Oswald von Wolkenstein Gesellschaft
KDIHM	Katalog der deutschsprachigen illustrierten Handschriften des Mittelalters
LB	Landesbibliothek

MF	Minnesangs Frühling (edd. Lachmann/Haupt)
MGH	Monumenta Germaniae historica
MGH SS	Monumenta Germaniae historica: Scriptores
MHRA	Modern Humanities Research Association
MMS	Münstersche Mittelalter-Schriften
MTU	Münchener Texte und Untersuchungen zur deutschen Literatur des Mittelalters
NF	Neue Folge
NGA	Neues Gesamtabenteuer (ed. Niewöhner)
ÖNB	Österreichische Nationalbibliothek
PBB	Beiträge zur Geschichte der deutschen Sprache und Literatur (Halle/Tüb.)
PL	Bibliotheca patrum latinorum, ed. J.-P. Migne, Paris 1844–64
RF	Romanische Forschungen
SBB-PK	Staatsbibliothek zu Berlin—Preußischer Kulturbesitz
SM	Sammlung Metzler
StB	Stadtbibliothek
StLV	Bibliothek des litterarischen Vereins in Stuttgart
UB	Universitätsbibliothek
^{1}VL-^{2}VL	Die deutsche Literatur des Mittelalters: Verfasserlexikon, edd. Wolfgang Stammler/Karl Langosch, 5 vols., Berlin/Leipzig 1933–55; 2nd revised edn. by Kurt Ruh *et al.*, Berlin 1977 etc.
WdF	Wege der Forschung
WW	Wirkendes Wort
ZfdA	Zeitschrift für deutsches Altertum und deutsche Literatur
ZfdPh	Zeitschrift für deutsche Philologie
ZfdWf	Zeitschrift für deutsche Wortforschung

INTRODUCTION:
THE AUTHOR IN THE TEXT

PRELIMINARIES

Authorship is the most fundamental and provocative literary theoretical issue of all. When in the late 1960s, for example, Roland Barthes declared 'the death of the author' in order to assert the priority of language and the role of the reader, he merely ensured that authorship would remain a primary concern of theorists and scholars for the next thirty years.[1] The most enduring contribution to this lively debate belongs to Michel Foucault, whose exposition of the historical variability of the 'author-function' ('fonction-auteur')—authorship being attributed to different kinds of texts at different moments in the course of Western civilization—effectively issued a challenge to literary historians in every field.[2] As a result, a number of key points on the massive trajectory that Foucault sketches, such as the seventeenth and eighteenth centuries, have been reconsidered in greater detail in recent years,[3] and scholars from a variety of disciplines have banded together to compile their own overviews of the changing landscape of authorship from antiquity to modernity.[4] The Middle Ages, a period that Foucault is inclined

---

[1] Roland Barthes, 'La Mort de l'auteur', in *Roland Barthes: Oeuvres complètes*, ed. Eric Marty, 3 vols., Paris 1993–5, ii. 491–5: 'la naissance du lecteur doit se payer de la mort de l'Auteur' (495). For critical discussion of this axiom of post-structuralist thought see Seán Burke, *The Death and Return of the Author: Criticism and Subjectivity in Barthes, Foucault and Derrida*, 2nd revised edn. Edinburgh 1998; Maurice Biriotti/Nicola Miller (eds.), *What is an Author?*, Manchester 1993.

[2] Michel Foucault, 'Qu'est-ce qu'un Auteur?', in *Dits et écrits: 1954–1988*, edd. Daniel Defert/François Ewald/Jacques Lagrange, 4 vols., Paris 1994, i. 789–821: 'Dans notre civilisation, ce ne sont pas toujours les mêmes textes qui ont demandé à recevoir une attribution' (799); 'Toutes ces opérations varient selon les époques, et les types du discours' (801); 'elle ['la fonction-auteur'] ne s'exerce pas uniformément et de la même façon sur tous les discours, à toutes les époques et dans toutes les formes de civilisation' (803).

[3] The best work of this kind is by Roger Chartier in his monograph *Culture écrite et société: L'ordre des livres (XIVᵉ–XVIIIᵉ siècle)*, Paris 1996, pp. 45–80.

[4] Felix Philipp Ingold/Werner Wunderlich (eds.), *Fragen nach dem Autor: Positionen und Perspektiven*, Constance 1992; *Der Autor im Dialog: Beiträge zu Autorität und Autorschaft*, St Gallen

to underestimate,[5] has also come under increased scrutiny. Central topics in this context include the theories of authorship underlying Latin scholastic writing,[6] the classificatory function of authorship in manuscript transmission,[7] and the practical and ideological circumstances surrounding vernacular authorial activity.[8] There is clearly a need for more work to be done on these areas, and interest in the issue of authorship shows no signs of abating in (international) medieval studies. This is further evidenced by recent scholarship in English on the texts of writers such as Dante, Chaucer, and Langland,[9] and by a number of French and German collections of essays which explore a wide range of European vernacular and Latin works.[10]

The principal objective of this study is to shed further light on authorship in the Middle Ages by examining its 'presentation' in German narrative literature between 1220 and 1290, that is to say the medieval poetic practice of addressing the question of the authorship of a text within the literary work itself. As we shall see, the works of the two outstanding individual writers of this period, Rudolf von Ems (active c. 1220–55) and Konrad von Würzburg

1995. See also Seán Burke's literary theoretical anthology: *Authorship: From Plato to the Postmodern. A Reader*, Edinburgh 1995.

[5] Foucault, 'Qu'est-ce qu'un Auteur?', 799f.

[6] Alastair J. Minnis, *Medieval Theory of Authorship: Scholastic Literary Attitudes in the Later Middle Ages*, London 1984, 2nd edn. Aldershot 1988; Jan-Dirk Müller, 'Auctor–Actor–Author: Einige Anmerkungen zum Verständnis vom Autor in lateinischen Schriften des frühen und hohen Mittelalters', in *Der Autor im Dialog*, edd. Ingold/Wunderlich, 17–31.

[7] Thomas Bein, '*Mit fremden Pegasusen pflügen': Untersuchungen zu Authentizitätsproblemen in mittelhochdeutscher Lyrik und Lyrikphilologie*, Berlin 1998 (Philologische Studien und Quellen 150), 193–233.

[8] Joachim Bumke, 'Autor und Werk: Beobachtungen und Überlegungen zur höfischen Epik (ausgehend von der Donaueschinger Parzivalhandschrift Gᵟ)', *ZfdPh* 116 (1997), Sonderheft 87–114.

[9] Burt Kimmelman, *The Poetics of Authorship in the Later Middle Ages: The Emergence of the Modern Literary Persona*, New York, NY 1996 (Studies in the Humanities 21); Kathryn Kerby-Fulton, 'Langland and the Bibliographic Ego', in *Written Work: Langland, Labor and Authorship*, edd. Steven Justice/Kathryn Kerby-Fulton, Philadelphia, Pa. 1997, pp. 67–143. The European literary landmark of the *Roman de la Rose* has also proved fruitful in this context; see David F. Hult, *Self-fulfilling Prophecies: Readership and Authority in the first 'Roman de la Rose'*, Cambridge 1986.

[10] Danielle Buschinger (ed.), *Figures de l'écrivain au moyen âge: Actes du Colloque du Centre d'Etudes Médiévales de l'Université de Picardie, Amiens 18–20 mars 1988*, Göppingen 1991 (GAG 510); Walter Haug/Burghart Wachinger (eds.), *Autorentypen*, Tübingen 1991 (Fortuna vitrea 6); Elizabeth Andersen et al. (eds.), *Autor und Autorschaft im Mittelalter: Kolloquium Meißen 1995*, Tübingen 1998.

(active *c.* 1257–87), together with the genres of the later heroic epic and the secular short story (or 'Märe') offer many different poetic responses to the issue of authorship. Such disparate attitudes towards the figure of the author are generated by both literary and oral spheres of influence, and are a function of the complex process of development of literature in the vernacular at this time.[11] In terms of the approach adopted in this book emphasis will be placed throughout on close readings of individual texts. For the sake of as precise a description as possible of the literary phenomena thus encountered, recourse will be had to terms current in modern literary studies, and especially to those pertaining to the concept of the narrator. These will only be used, however, once their relevance for medieval narrative works has been established. Each analysis will also include at least a note on the transmission of the text and on any textual variation as it affects the internal literary presentation of authorship. The main purpose of this is to ensure that the reader does not lose sight of the material reality of medieval book culture in which details relating to authorship were liable to be changed or even lost in the course of manuscript transmission. Furthermore, textual variants can prove to be illuminating points of comparison and can, on occasion, facilitate the comprehension of particularly intractable passages.

The main body of this introduction falls into three parts. The first will review the main issues involved in the critical discussion of authorship for the Middle Ages, and will also include an exposition of the various ways in which authorship was taken into account in the production of medieval (German) manuscript books. The second will then introduce the phenomenon of the literary presentation of authorship properly, with specific reference to the works of the most distinguished German narrative poets of around 1200: Hartmann von Aue, Wolfram von Eschenbach, and Gottfried von Strassburg. In the examination of these authors' works the question of the relationship between the presentation of authorship and the appearance of a narrator in the text will be especially important. Finally,

---

[11] See also Rüdiger Schnell, '"Autor" und "Werk" im deutschen Mittelalter: Forschungskritik und Forschungsperspektiven', *Wolfram-Studien* 15 (1998), 12–73, esp. 58–73; Jan-Dirk Müller, 'Aufführung–Autor–Werk: Zu einigen blinden Stellen gegenwärtiger Diskussion', in *Mittelalterliche Literatur und Kunst im Spannungsfeld von Hof und Kloster: Ergebnisse der Berliner Tagung, 9.–11. Oktober 1997*, edd. Nigel F. Palmer/Hans-Jochen Schiewer, Tübingen 1999, pp. 149–66, esp. 156–61.

in a third part, key socio-cultural developments that occurred in
Germany over the course of the thirteenth century will be discussed
with the aim of establishing a broader historical framework of reference for the sustained close textual analysis that follows.

I. AUTHORSHIP IN THE MIDDLE AGES

It should be acknowledged at the outset that in certain quarters of
medieval studies the topic of authorship is viewed with suspicion.
This position is championed by Bernard Cerquiglini (1989) as
part of an uncompromising critique of traditional philological practices, and it has been espoused wholeheartedly by the subsequent
advocates of a 'New Philology' (1990).[12] For Cerquiglini the notion
of author depends entirely on technological and legal developments from the sixteenth to the nineteenth centuries and as
such is misplaced in a discussion of medieval textuality: 'L'auteur
n'est pas une idée médiévale' (25). Undoubtedly, the presupposition of a single fixed text as the inviolable property of its author is
largely incompatible with the variance of a manuscript culture
and the well-documented medieval practices of pseudepigraphy
and 'plagiarism'. But Cerquiglini goes too far. Typically, in spite of
the privileged status he accords Foucault and his description of the
modern construction of the author, Cerquiglini fails to account for
the latter's implicit acceptance of other, earlier, concepts of authorship.[13]

Such a dismissal of authorship may be compared with the work
of Paul Zumthor (1972) and Hans Robert Jauß (1977) regarding the
'alterity' of the Middle Ages.[14] Zumthor's idea of an abyss ('abîme
infranchissable' 19) between modern and medieval worlds also rests
on the impact he perceives in the invention of printing. Here too,
medieval vernacular literature is understood as belonging to an

---

[12] Bernard Cerquiglini, *Eloge de la variante: Histoire critique de la philologie*, Paris 1989, esp.
17–29. For the 'New Philology' see the five articles assembled and introduced by Stephen
G. Nichols in *Speculum* 65 (1990), 1–108. For further discussion of this movement see the
Sonderheft of issue 116 (1997) of the *Zeitschrift für deutsche Philologie*.
[13] Cerquiglini, *Eloge de la variante*, 13, 25. For productive attempts to incorporate Foucault
into the discussion of medieval authorship see Hult, *Self-fulfilling Prophecies*, 62f.; Müller,
'Auctor–Actor–Author', 17; Bein, *Authentizitätsproblemen*, 443–9.
[14] Paul Zumthor, *Essai de poétique médiévale*, Paris 1972; Hans Robert Jauß, *Alterität und
Modernität der mittelalterlichen Literatur: Gesammelte Aufsätze 1956–1976*, Munich 1977.

impenetrable age of textual instability in which the individual author operates under severe constraints: 'Pour l'époque archaïque, antérieure à 1100, c'est la notion même d'auteur qui parfois semble se dérober. [. . .] Le rôle de l'individu dans la genèse de l'oeuvre nous apparaît mal, et sans doute, les contemporains lui attribuèrent-ils peu de valeur' (68).[15] Nevertheless, Zumthor's qualification of 1100 falls some way short of Cerquiglini's radical programme. Furthermore, Zumthor concedes that positive evidence of a medieval awareness of authorship—such as instances of authorial naming—exists after this date, however restricted in scope he actually deems this material to be.[16] Thus, careful postulation of medieval 'alterity' by no means invalidates authorship as a legitimate object of investigation. Recognition of the potential otherness of this period might indeed be profitably integrated into our work to safeguard against an unwary application of modern values and presuppositions, and yet the possibility of aspects of medieval authorship which seem more familiar to us is not to be rejected out of hand either.[17]

In modern English and German usage 'author' and 'Autor' commonly operate as generic terms that encompass a variety of literary activities. In the Latin Middle Ages the word *auctor* had an additional function.[18] The sense of the author as 'originator', be it the founder of a city, chief perpetrator of a crime or composer of a book,[19] was invariably secondary to that of the author as 'authority' with juridical connotations of responsibility (*auctor* signified 'guarantor' in ancient and medieval common law). Indeed, *auctor* figured prominently in the scholastic sphere as the designation for those writers of classical and late antiquity whose works made up the sum of learning, as in the *Dialogus super auctores* of Conrad of

---

[15] Zumthor is followed in this by Jauß, *Alterität*, 14–18.

[16] Zumthor, *Essai*, 66.

[17] For critical assessment of the notion of 'alterity' see Peter von Moos, 'Gefahren des Mittelalterbegriffs: Diagnostische und präventive Aspekte', in *Modernes Mittelalter: Neue Bilder einer populären Epoche*, ed. Joachim Heinzle, Frankfurt a. M./Leipzig 1994, pp. 33–63, esp. 59ff.

[18] Marie-Dominique Chenu, 'Auctor, actor, autor', *Bull. du Cange* 3 (1927), 81–6; *La Théologie au douzième siècle*, Paris 1957 (Etudes de philosophie médiévale 45), esp. 353ff.; Müller, 'Auctor–Actor–Author'.

[19] This list is given by Honorius of Autun (*c.* 1090–1156) in the prologue to his commentary on the Song of Songs: 'Auctor est aequivocum.[. . .] Est autem auctor civitatis, id est fundator ut Romulus Romae; est et auctor sceleris, id est princeps vel signifer, ut Judas Christi mortis; est quoque auctor libri, id est compositor, ut David Psalterii, Plato Thymaei' (PL 172, 348).

Hirsau (c. 1070–1150).[20] Similarly, the attribution of a text to a recognized 'author' served to institutionalize and authenticate its contents,[21] and this concept of authorship also lay behind thirteenth-century scholastic controversies in which opponents were denounced for insolently claiming the status of *auctores* for themselves.[22]

The complex relationship between the two levels of meaning of *auctor* is illuminated by Alastair J. Minnis (1984) with specific reference to the prologues of scholastic commentaries on scriptural texts.[23] Minnis shows that by the thirteenth century the aspect of divinely sanctioned authority no longer presented an obstacle to attempts to grasp the individual literary and moral activity of human authors such as David and Solomon. This was due partly to an increased interest in the literal sense of the Bible, and partly to a new critical idiom, based on the Aristotelian concept of the four causes, which facilitated a (literary) theoretical distinction between God as primary efficient cause—the unmoved mover—and the human author as secondary efficient cause—inspired by God to produce the text. Consequently, scholastic discussion of types of literary activity became progressively refined. Bonaventure (c. 1217–74), for example, formulated a scale of possible literary functionaries from *scriptor* (scribe) to *compilator, commentator,* and *auctor*.[24] Terms such as these were used to describe the roles of minor participants in the production of biblical books as well as to qualify the instrumental position of the human authors *vis-à-vis* God.

Bonaventure's scheme is determined by the degree and mode in which a writer combines foreign material with his own, and this is

---

[20] Ernst Robert Curtius, *Europäische Literatur und lateinisches Mittelalter*, Berne 1948, esp. 56–60, 65ff., 263–7; Minnis, *Medieval Theory of Authorship*, 13ff. There is some evidence to suggest that a second word, *actor*, was occasionally deployed to differentiate the non-authoritative writer; see Chenu, 'Auctor, actor, autor', 82f.; Minnis, *Medieval Theory of Authorship*, 25f., 157.

[21] The third related word *aut[h]or* was understood by medieval grammarians to reflect the particular sense of 'authenticity'; see Chenu, 'Auctor, actor, autor', 85f.

[22] Müller, 'Auctor–Actor–Author', 29.

[23] Minnis, *Medieval Theory of Authorship*, esp. 73–159.

[24] Bonaventure makes this statement in the context of an assessment of Peter Lombard's authorship of the *Sentences*: 'Aliquis enim scribit aliena, nihil addendo vel mutando; et iste mere dicitur *scriptor*. Aliquis scribit aliena, addendo, sed non de suo; et iste *compilator* dicitur. Aliquis scribit et aliena et sua, sed aliena tamquam principalia, et sua tamquam annexa ad evidentiam; et iste dicitur *commentator*, non auctor. Aliquis scribit et sua et aliena, sed sua tanquam [sic] principalia, aliena tamquam annexa ad confirmationem; et talis debet dici *auctor*' (*Opera omnia*, i. 14f.). See also Minnis, *Medieval Theory of Authorship*, 94–103, esp. 94f.

in line with medieval scholastic doctrine which reserved creativity for God.[25] Even an *auctor* is not a free agent, obliged instead to remain within the bounds of pre-existent tradition ('scribit et sua et aliena'). Of course, theory and practice do not necessarily coincide, and while the idea of poetic creativity in an absolute sense appears only to have been accepted from the fifteenth and sixteenth centuries onwards, much work remains to be done on just which guises vernacular authorship could assume outside of the theological sphere.[26]

The medieval German courtly narrative tradition which developed from around the mid-twelfth century centres on another kind of literary activity that might seem to impinge on the freedom of the poet. Hartmann von Aue (active *c.* 1185–1205?), Wolfram von Eschenbach (active *c.* 1195–1220?), and Gottfried von Strassburg (active *c.* 1200–20?) all worked on the basis of Old French originals, and later thirteenth-century authors, including Rudolf von Ems and Konrad von Würzburg, often still professed their works to be translations of French and Latin source-texts.[27] On closer inspection such 'translation' is revealed to be more of a process of adaptation, performing a cultural transfer similar to those which Rita Copeland (1991) has identified at the heart of vernacular translations of Latin academic texts.[28] As a discipline Middle High German translation–adaptation is generally thought to be grounded in Latin school poetics.[29] Vernacular literary culture and the sphere of Latinity are interconnected in so far as a large number of the courtly narrative poets were clerically educated. Yet we must exercise caution on this point for it will ultimately determine our view of the literary standing of the medieval German narrative. Ernst Robert Curtius's flagship work (1948), for instance, is representative of a widespread critical approach which so subordinates vernacular literature to

[25] Thomas Cramer, '*Solus creator est deus*: Der Autor auf dem Weg zum Schöpfertum', *Daphnis* 15 (1986), 13–28.

[26] Walter Haug, 'Innovation und Originalität: Kategoriale und literarhistorische Vorüberlegungen', in *Innovation und Originalität*, edd. Walter Haug/Burghart Wachinger, Tübingen 1993 (Fortuna vitrea 9), 1–13, esp. 7–11.

[27] Carl Lofmark, *The Authority of the Source in Middle High German Narrative Poetry*, London 1981 (Institute of Germanic Studies: Bithell Series of Dissertations 5), esp. 48–120.

[28] Rita Copeland, *Rhetoric, Hermeneutics, and Translation in the Middle Ages: Academic Traditions and Vernacular Texts*, Cambridge 1991 (Cambridge Studies in Medieval Literature 11). For the varying significance of translation for medieval German literary history as a whole see the essays collected in *Wolfram-Studien* 14 (1996).

[29] Lofmark, *Authority of the Source*, 90–5.

Latin tradition that sight is lost of the former's own significance.[30] Vernacular authorship was not limited to 'downloading' forms and structures from Latin, in spite of the fact that the suggestions of autonomy that can be found in vernacular writing have often been underplayed in the critical literature.[31]

Walter Haug (1985) has done more than any other scholar to draw attention to this imbalance and promote the notion that medieval German literature was sufficiently complex to have fostered its own literary theoretical discussion: 'Hingegen soll hier [. . .] auf das geachtet werden, was bislang eher vernachlässigt worden ist, darauf nämlich, wie die vulgärsprachlichen Schriftsteller in Zusammenspiel und Auseinandersetzung mit der lateinischen Poetik die spezifische Position und Funktion ihrer Werke theoretisch zu fassen suchten' (7f.).[32] Notwithstanding the controversy that surrounds Haug's principal thesis of the rise of fictionality in the twelfth-century Arthurian romance,[33] his methodology forms an essential backdrop to the approach adopted in this study. In many cases vernacular narrative texts of the period 1220–90 contain evidence of a greater degree of literary theoretical awareness than might otherwise have been expected. The passages in question may be elucidated with reference to Latin (and Old French) material but only in part; medieval German texts should also be seen to function in their own right.

Vernacular authorship can be characterized further by taking the external circumstances of medieval literary composition into account. The role of patronage is paramount in this context, as Joachim Bumke (1979) has shown.[34] Only the most privileged in medieval society could afford the production of extended narrative and had the necessary (political) contacts to procure source-texts.

---

[30] *Europäische Literatur*, esp. 41f., 387–91. For further assessment of Curtius's central tenets see Peter Dronke, *Poetic Individuality in the Middle Ages: New Departures in Poetry 1000–1150*, 2nd edn. London 1986 (Westfield Publications in Medieval Studies 1), 1–22; Mark Chinca, *History, Fiction, Verisimilitude: Studies in the Poetics of Gottfried's 'Tristan'*, London 1993 (MHRA Texts and Dissertations 35. Institute of Germanic Studies: Bithell Series of Dissertations 18), 1–7.

[31] See the second phase of Minnis's argument in *Medieval Theory of Authorship*, 160–210.

[32] Walter Haug, *Literaturtheorie im deutschen Mittelalter: Von den Anfängen bis zum Ende des 13. Jahrhunderts*, Darmstadt 1985, 2nd revised edn. 1992.

[33] Joachim Heinzle, 'Die Entdeckung der Fiktionalität: Zu Walter Haugs "Literaturtheorie im deutschen Mittelalter"', *PBB* 112 (1990), 55–80.

[34] Joachim Bumke, *Mäzene im Mittelalter: Die Gönner und Auftraggeber der höfischen Literatur in Deutschland 1150–1300*, Munich 1979; (ed.), *Literarisches Mäzenatentum: Ausgewählte Forschungen zur Rolle des Gönners und Auftraggebers in der mittelalterlichen Literatur*, Darmstadt 1982 (WdF 598).

The authors may be supposed to have been materially dependent on their patrons, so that a loss or change of patronage might prove disastrous for them. Literature was evidently a means of cultural and social representation for the aristocratic patrons and their courts,[35] and we must accept that their wishes, rather than those of the author, may have determined the choice of a work's story material. This is not to say, however, that the literary interests shared by the primary recipients could not provide authors with the space to develop their own poetic themes.[36]

In comparison with the patrons there is, as a rule, little documentary evidence relating to the biographies of twelfth- and thirteenth-century poets of vernacular narrative.[37] Medieval German literature includes texts in which poets describe their own circumstances, but the information preserved in this way is lacking in detail and unverifiable, and the literary context itself raises serious questions. Scholars continue to work with sociological authorial types, such as the court cleric, yet these attempts at categorization are frequently beset with the same methodological dilemma.[38] Ursula Peters (1991) argues incisively that authorial 'types' are misleading for they are liable to gloss over complexities and our imperfect knowledge of the historical situation.[39] Furthermore, these types are invariably based on material from within the literary texts themselves, a critical practice which is in danger of failing to distinguish between 'biographische[n]

---

[35] For a historian's view of the princely courts of this period see Peter Johanek, 'Höfe und Residenzen, Herrschaft und Repräsentation', in *Mittelalterliche Literatur im Lebenszusammenhang: Ergebnisse des Troisième Cycle Romand 1994*, ed. Eckart C. Lutz, Freiburg, Switzerland 1997 (Scrinium Friburgense 8), 45–78.

[36] For an introduction to the recent, and at times controversial, discussion of the relationship between textual poetics and external circumstances see Joachim Heinzle, 'Literarische Interessenbildung im Mittelalter: Kleiner Kommentar zu einer Forschungsperspektive', in *Literatur im Lebenszusammenhang*, ed. Lutz, 79–93.

[37] The most celebrated evidence of this kind concerns the lyric poet Walther von der Vogelweide (active *c.* 1190–1230?) who is attested for 12 November 1203; see Hedwig Heger, *Das Lebenszeugnis Walthers von der Vogelweide: Die Reiserechnungen des Passauer Bischofs Wolfger von Erla*, Vienna 1970, esp. 86: 'Sequenti die apud Zei[zemurum] Walthero cantori de Vogelweide pro pellico .v. sol. longos' (II, 54f.).

[38] Haug/Wachinger (eds.), *Autorentypen*; Jürgen Schulz-Grobert, '"Autoren gesucht": Die Verfasserfrage als methodisches Problem im Bereich der spätmittelalterlichen Reimpaarkleindichtung', in *Literarische Interessenbildung im Mittelalter: DFG-Symposion 1991*, ed. Joachim Heinzle, Stuttgart/Weimar 1993 (Germanistische Symposien Berichtsbände 14), 60–74. See also Zumthor, *Essai*, 67.

[39] Ursula Peters, 'Hofkleriker–Stadtschreiber–Mystikerin: Zum literarhistorischen Status dreier Autorentypen', in *Autorentypen*, edd. Haug/Wachinger, 29–49.

Autorexistenz' and a 'Szenerie der Autorbilder, Autorrollen und Autorstilisierungen' (31). At this point in our study it suffices to observe that although the historical validity of such authorial 'scenery' is often difficult to assess, it is entirely appropriate to approach this material with a view to its 'internal' poetic forms and functions.

Indeed, as L. Peter Johnson (1993) points out, the presentation of authorship, encompassing devices such as the naming of the author and references to patron and source, is an increasingly prominent feature of the medieval German courtly narrative tradition.[40] For the 'classical' period 1170–1220 this would appear to reflect a new literary situation. In stark contrast to the genres of 'Spielmannsepik' and heroic epic, whose overriding anonymity was perhaps a function of their dependence on the cultural common property of oral tradition, the reworking of French source material in German may well have been regarded as a special activity meriting the stamp of the author's name.[41] Similarly, the explicit integration of details concerning foreign source and circumstances of production may have served to underline and record the deliberate programme of cultural and social representation that lay behind this whole literary enterprise.[42] The influence of literatures in other languages should not be discounted either. The impulse for German authors to name themselves could only have been strengthened by their French source-texts which featured corresponding passages;[43] and it is possible that both Old

---

[40] L. Peter Johnson, 'Die Blütezeit und der neue Status der Literatur', in *Literarische Interessenbildung*, ed. Heinzle, 235–56, esp. 253. For a collection of Early Middle High German data see Ernst Hellgardt, 'Anonymität und Autornamen zwischen Mündlichkeit und Schriftlichkeit in der deutschen Literatur des elften und zwölften Jahrhunderts. Mit Vorbemerkungen zu einigen Autornamen der altenglischen Dichtung', in *Autor und Autorschaft*, edd. Andersen *et al.*, 46–72.

[41] For more on this 'nominal function' see Zumthor, *Essai*, 65f.; Hult, *Self-fulfilling Prophecies*, 31f., 102; Laurence de Looze, 'Signing Off in the Middle Ages: Medieval Textuality and Strategies of Authorial Self-Naming', in *Vox intexta: Orality and Textuality in the Middle Ages*, edd. Alger N. Doane/Carol B. Pasternack, Madison, Wis. 1991, pp. 167–78.

[42] In both Germany and France this also included non-narrative 'Sachliteratur'; see Helga Unger, 'Vorreden deutscher Sachliteratur des Mittelalters als Ausdruck literarischen Bewußtseins', in *Werk–Typ–Situation: Studien zu poetologischen Bedingungen in der älteren deutschen Literatur. (Hugo Kuhn zum 60. Geburtstag)*, edd. Ingeborg Glier *et al.*, Stuttgart 1969, pp. 217–51; Max Grosse, *Das Buch im Roman: Studien zu Buchverweis und Autoritätszitat in altfranzösischen Texten*, Munich 1994, pp. 47–121.

[43] The best-known French examples are found in the works of Chrétien de Troyes: *Le Chevalier de la Charrete* 24f.; *Le Chevalier au Lion* 6804f.; *Cligés* 43, 6664; *Le Conte du Graal* 61–4; *Erec et Enide* 9–12, 23–6. For more on the presentation of authorship in Old French see Michèle Gally, 'L'Amant, le Chevalier et le Clerc: l'auteur médiévale en quête d'un statut', in *Images de l'écrivain*, ed. José-Luis Diaz, Paris 1989 (Textuell 34/44: 22), 11–28;

French and Middle High German were shaped in this respect by the
resurgent Latin literature of the eleventh and twelfth centuries.[44] By
the end of the 'Blütezeit' (c. 1220) and the beginning of the so-called
post-classical period explicit authorial self-presentation had become
the norm in courtly epic, and this appears to have been a distinctive
feature of narrative literature. In the vernacular German lyric of this
time authorial naming remains exceptional and only occurs more
frequently from the second half of the fourteenth century.[45] Where
authorial self-consciousness comes to the fore in love poetry
('Minnesang') and gnomic poetry ('Sangspruchdichtung') the focus
tends to be on the act of performance rather than the activity of literary composition.[46]

Apart from the appearance of authorship as a theme in medieval
literary works, the manuscript books containing these texts could
also reflect an interest in authorship. Of course, to the primary recipients of a work, who in all probability knew the identity of the poet,
any further authorial record may have seemed superfluous. With the
exception of the acrostic—of which more will be said in the next
part of this introduction—codicological representation of vernacular authorship was scarce in the twelfth and early thirteenth
centuries. Poets of around 1200 could not reckon with the colophons
used in medieval manuscripts of Latin works or anything resembling
the title-pages of the later printed book.[47] In order to secure a trace
of their authorship for posterity vernacular writers had to create a
space within the literary text itself; and even then passages such as
the prologue and epilogue of a narrative were vulnerable, not only
because of their physical location as textual extremities but also
because the data they contained was subsequently often perceived
to be irrelevant.[48]

Michel Stanesco, 'Figures de l'auteur dans le roman médiéval', *Travaux de Littérature* 4
(1991), 7–19.

[44] Curtius, *Europäische Literatur*, 505ff.; Paul Klopsch, 'Anonymität und Selbstnennung
mittellateinischer Autoren', *Mittellateinisches Jahrbuch* 4 (1967), 9–25; *Einführung in die
Dichtungslehren des lateinischen Mittelalters*, Darmstadt 1980, esp. 83–94.

[45] Wilfried Wittstruck, *Der dichterische Namengebrauch in der deutschen Lyrik des Spätmittelalters*,
Munich 1987 (MMS 61), 397–462; Bein, *Authentizitätsproblemen*, 154–79.

[46] Thomas Bein, 'Das Singen über das Singen: Zu Sang und Minne im Minne-Sang',
in *'Aufführung' und 'Schrift' in Mittelalter und Früher Neuzeit*, ed. Jan-Dirk Müller,
Stuttgart/Weimar 1996 (Germanistische Symposien Berichtsbände 17), 67–92.

[47] For precisely this aspect of the modern printed book see Gérard Genette, *Seuils*,
Paris 1987, esp. 38–53.

[48] Bumke, *Mäzene*, 23f.

Nevertheless, in the course of the thirteenth and fourteenth centuries several codicological features privileging the author emerged in the manuscripts of vernacular texts, and in particular in the transmission of the medieval German lyric.[49] Most famously, the collections of songs known as A ('Kleine Heidelberger Lieder-handschrift', *c.* 1270–80), B ('Weingartner Liederhandschrift', *c.* 1300), and C ('Große Heidelberger Liederhandschrift', *c.* 1300) arrange large numbers of texts in accordance with their authorship to produce extensive compilations of authorial oeuvres.[50] In each codex the choice and order of the authors betray a further program-matic concern with issues such as literary status (A), an emphasis on the early Minnesang (B), and social hierarchy (C). The demarcation of one authorial corpus from another in A is primarily achieved by means of a scribal inscription, in red and blue lettering, of the name of the respective author.[51] In B and C rubrics act in conjunc-tion with full-page pictures of the authors (25 and 137 complete illustrations respectively).[52] Aside from their obvious structural function these pictures were of considerable material and aesthetic value, and lent eloquent expression to an exclusive aristocratic culture. This is especially evident in C which contains a far greater range of iconographic motifs than B and depicts the authors engaged in numerous courtly activities such as hawking (fol. 7^r), playing chess (fol. 13^r), and jousting (fol. 52^r) to name but a few.[53]

The fascination with the figure of the author in these German lyric manuscripts is remarkable, if not quite unparalleled in a wider European context. Many Provençal *chansonniers*, for instance, featured

---

[49] Burghart Wachinger, 'Autorschaft und Überlieferung', in *Autorentypen*, edd. Haug/Wachinger, 1–28; Franz-Josef Holznagel, *Wege in die Schriftlichkeit: Untersuchungen und Materialien zur Überlieferung der mittelhochdeutschen Lyrik*, Tübingen/Basle 1995 (Bibliotheca Germanica 32), esp. 49–88; Bein, *Authentizitätsproblemen*, 201–24. For an account of compar-able French evidence see Sylvia Huot, *From Song to Book: The Poetics of Writing in Old French Lyric and Lyrical Narrative Poetry*, Ithaca, NY 1987, esp. 39–80; Cynthia J. Brown, 'Text, Image, and Authorial Self-Consciousness in Late Medieval Paris', in *Printing the Written Word: The Social History of Books, circa 1450–1520*, ed. Sandra Hindman, Ithaca, NY 1991, pp. 103–42.

[50] For detailed description and analysis of all three see Holznagel, *Wege in die Schriftlichkeit*, 21–280.

[51] See facsimile edn. by Carl von Kraus, fol. 1^r, 4^v, 5^r, 5^v etc.

[52] The illustrations in C are conveniently assembled in Ingo F. Walther (ed.), *Codex Manesse: Die Miniaturen der Großen Heidelberger Liederhandschrift*, Frankfurt a. M. 1988.

[53] Hella Frühmorgen-Voss, *Text und Illustration im Mittelalter: Aufsätze zu den Wechselbeziehungen zwischen Literatur und bildender Kunst*, ed. Norbert H. Ott, Munich 1975 (MTU 50), 57–88; Holznagel, *Wege in die Schriftlichkeit*, 66–88.

not only names and pictures but also short biographies of the authors (*vidas*) or statements of the supposed personal background to specific songs (*razos*).[54] However, in French and Latin codices other principles of compilation (generic; alphabetic; thematic) were more common. It is generally thought that the preoccupation with authorship in the transmission of the German lyric reflects the enduring social and cultural status of the art of Minnesang—after all, earlier practitioners included the Hohenstaufen Emperor Henry VI with whom C opens—as well as a respect for formal mastery of the lyric, and a keen interest in German literary tradition on the part of those who commissioned the manuscripts in the first place.[55]

Outside of the domain of the lyric the aspect of authorship plays a decidedly lesser role in the compilation of manuscripts, which is not to say that there is no comparable evidence at all. Shorter texts in verse couplets by Der Stricker (active *c.* 1220–50?), for example, are codified and assembled together from the end of the thirteenth century;[56] and an attempt appears to have been made *c.* 1250 to collect several of Wolfram von Eschenbach's works by adding *Titurel* and two dawn songs to a manuscript of *Parzival* (Munich, BSB, Cgm 19).[57] Rubrics identifying the author of narrative and non-lyric texts are more unusual as well. One notable case is that of the tripartite superscription (*titulus*) heading a fourteenth-century copy of Wolfram's *Willehalm* (Vienna, ÖNB, cod. Ser. n. 2643, dated 1387, fol. 66ᵛ), which repeats several lines in the vernacular in first red and then blue ink:[58]

Hie hebt sich an marcgraf wilhelmes buch das ander. das getichtet hat der von Eschenbach herr wolfram der edle meister.

---

[54] Elizabeth W. Poe, 'The *Vidas* and *Razos*', in *A Handbook of the Troubadours*, edd. F. R. P. Akehurst/Judith M. Davis, Berkeley, Calif. 1995 (Publications of the UCLA Center for Medieval and Renaissance Studies 26), 185–97.

[55] Wachinger, 'Autorschaft und Überlieferung', 12f.; Holznagel, *Wege in die Schriftlichkeit*, 57–61.

[56] Hans-Joachim Ziegeler, 'Beobachtungen zum Wiener Codex 2705 und zu seiner Stellung in der Überlieferung früher kleiner Reimpaardichtung', in *Deutsche Handschriften 1100–1400: Oxforder Kolloquium 1985*, edd. Volker Honemann/Nigel F. Palmer, Tübingen 1988, pp. 469–526.

[57] Wachinger, 'Autorschaft und Überlieferung', 6; Holznagel, *Wege in die Schriftlichkeit*, 50 note 136.

[58] This manuscript situates Wolfram's text between its prequel (*Arabel*) and sequel (*Rennewart*) by Ulrich von dem Türlin and Ulrich von Türheim respectively. For a reproduction of the rubric see Josef Krása, *Die Handschriften König Wenzels IV.*, transl. from the Czech by Hans Gaertner and the author, Prague 1971, p. 43. See also Burghart Wachinger, 'Wolfram von Eschenbach am Schreibpult', *Wolfram-Studien* 12 (1992), 9–14, esp. 13f.

(Here begins the second book concerning margrave Willehalm. It was composed by that man of Eschenbach, lord Wolfram the noble master.)

before ending in Latin and in gold:

Hic incipit liber secundus margrauij wilhelmi quem compilauit et composuit magister wolframus de eschenbach.

(Here begins the second book [of the story] of margrave Willehalm which was compiled and composed by master Wolfram von Eschenbach.)

Elsewhere a relatively substantial number of superscriptions concerning authorship are contained in collections of shorter verse-couplet texts: 61 texts in 7 manuscripts are attributed to Der Stricker in this way.[59]

Pictures of the author in the transmission of (non-lyric) vernacular literature are equally rare.[60] Those that do occur are related to an iconographic tradition extending back to antiquity, in which authors are depicted in a number of set poses: writing at a desk, dictating to a scribe or pupil, or dedicating their work to a patron. In the Middle Ages author portraits based on these models were predominantly used for writers of only the most authoritative and sacred texts, such as the Evangelists, and thus they often included the motif of divine inspiration as well.[61] Such essentially Latinate author portraits are absent from the 'Weingartner Liederhandschrift' and are relatively scarce in the 'Große Heidelberger Liederhandschrift' where the emphasis is very much on the authors as lovers and representatives of a courtly aristocratic culture. Of the 137 illustrations in C, for example, solely 3 (Bligger von Steinach [fol. 182^v]; Reinmar von Zweter [fol. 323^r]; Konrad von Würzburg [fol. 383^r]) depict the author dictating to a scribe.[62] With the exception of the

---

[59] Franz-Josef Holznagel, 'Autorschaft und Überlieferung am Beispiel der kleineren Reimpaartexte des Strickers', in *Autor und Autorschaft*, edd. Andersen *et al.*, 163–84.

[60] Wachinger, 'Autorschaft und Überlieferung', 7–11.

[61] For representative examples see Horst Wenzel, 'Autorenbilder: Zur Ausdifferenzierung von Autorenfunktionen in mittelalterlichen Miniaturen', in *Autor und Autorschaft*, edd. Andersen *et al.*, 1–28, esp. 18–22, 24f.

[62] Frühmorgen-Voss, *Text und Illustration*, 59–62; Joachim Bumke, *Ministerialität und Ritterdichtung: Umrisse der Forschung*, Munich 1976, pp. 87f.; Holznagel, *Wege in die Schriftlichkeit*, 83. For more on the suggestion that differing degrees of orality and literacy are represented in these pictures see Michael Curschmann, '*Pictura laicorum litteratura*? Überlegungen zum Verhältnis von Bild und volkssprachlicher Schriftlichkeit im Hoch- und Spätmittelalter bis zum Codex Manesse', in *Pragmatische Schriftlichkeit im Mittelalter: Erscheinungsformen und Entwicklungsstufen*, edd. Hagen Keller/Klaus Grubmüller/Nikolaus Staubach, Munich 1992 (MMS 65), 211–29, esp. 221–6.

opening historiated initial in codex B of the *Nibelungenlied* (St Gallen, Stiftsbibliothek, cod. 857, *c.* 1250–60, pag. 291),[63] literacy and authority are prominent motifs in those few author portraits that appear elsewhere in manuscripts of Middle High German texts.

Two of the most important thirteenth-century works in this context are Thomasin von Zerklaere's *Der welsche Gast* (dated 1215) and Eike von Repgow's *Sachsenspiegel* (*c.* 1225–35). The transmission of each is characterized by an extensive cycle of illustrations that may well have formed part of the orginal authorial design but is only preserved in later manuscripts with often a significant degree of variation.[64] In the Gotha codex of *Der welsche Gast* (Gotha, Forschungsbibl., Cod. Membr. I 120, *c.* 1340) the illustration of the dedication of the work to the German tongue (fol. 8ᵛ) is affirmed as an author portrait by the Latin inscription *causa efficiens* ('efficient cause') above the kneeling male figure; at the same time the very inclusion of this scholastic, originally Aristotelian, term radically elevates the standing of Thomasin, the vernacular author.[65] All four of the illustrated manuscripts of the *Sachsenspiegel*—the 'Bilderhandschriften' of Heidelberg (H), Oldenburg (O), Dresden (D), and Wolfenbüttel (W)—feature at least one pictorial representation of authorship.[66] In the three complete codices the work opens with a depiction of the author, either as he sits at his desk, writing implement in hand (O fol. 6ʳ), or as he presents his work to two kings

[63] Joachim Heinzle, *Das Nibelungenlied: Eine Einführung*, revised edn. Frankfurt a. M. 1994, pp. 110f. The most accessible reproduction of this initial is probably the cover of Heinzle's book itself. A further comparable historiated initial is to be found on p. 411 of the codex.

[64] Wachinger, 'Autorschaft und Überlieferung', 10f.; Horst Wenzel, 'Die Beweglichkeit der Bilder: Zur Relation von Text und Bild in den illuminierten Handschriften des "Welschen Gastes"', *ZfdPh* 116 (1997), Sonderheft 224–52, esp. 247.

[65] Thirteen manuscripts of *Der welsche Gast* include illustrations; see Hella Frühmorgen-Voss, *Text und Illustration*, 35–44; Friedrich W. von Kries (ed.), *Der welsche Gast*, vol. iv. The picture in question is the second in the cycle of 120 which is best preserved in the Gotha manuscript, and appears to relate to lines 87–90 of Thomasin's prologue: 'Tiusche lant, | enphâhe wol, | als ein guot hûsvrouwe sol, | disen dînen welschen gast | der dîn êre minnet vast.' For reproductions of this picture see von Kries (ed.), *Der welsche Gast*, iv. 11; Wachinger, 'Autorschaft und Überlieferung', 27. For more on the term *causa efficiens* as it relates to the scholastic discussion of authorship see Minnis, *Medieval Theory of Authorship*, 75–84.

[66] The sigla and dates of these manuscripts are as follows: Heidelberg, UB, cod. Pal. germ. 164, *c.* 1300–15; Oldenburg, LB, CIM I 410, dated 1336; Dresden, Sächsische LB, Mscr. Dr. M 32, *c.* 1350; Wolfenbüttel, HAB, Cod. Guelf. 3.1 Aug. 2, *c.* 1350–75. For an overview of this material see Ruth Schmidt-Wiegand/Wolfgang Milde, '*Gott ist selber Recht*'. *Die vier Bilderhandschriften des Sachsenspiegels: Oldenburg, Heidelberg, Wolfenbüttel, Dresden*, 2nd revised edn. Wolfenbüttel 1993 (Ausstellungskataloge der Herzog August Bibliothek 67).

(D fol. 3ᵛ; W fol. 9ᵛ); in all three the author is shown to be divinely sanctioned in his enterprise through the close proximity of the Holy Ghost in the shape of a dove.[67] Several further author portraits that functionalize quite different iconographic models occur at later points in the text, whereby the author is portrayed as a teacher, brandishing a rod at a pupil (H fol. 1ʳ) and, intriguingly, as the hapless victim of assault as he sticks out of the leaves of his own book like a bookmark (D fol. 91ʳ; W fol. 85ʳ).[68]

The intrinsically authoritative nature of both *Der welsche Gast*, an extended moral treatise, and the *Sachsenspiegel*, a law book, as vernacular versions of traditionally Latin text-types, made it possible for the respective authors to be represented in this fashion. The link with literacy and Latinity is crucial, and this is further demonstrated by the inclusion of an author portrait of Wolfram in the Vienna codex of *Willehalm* mentioned earlier: just as Wolfram's subsequent status as a canonical vernacular author overshadows his own self-presentation as an illiterate layman, and hence he is deemed worthy of a scribal inscription in Latin as well as in German (fol. 66ᵛ), so he too can be pictured as a learned author at a desk, bearded—a traditional sign of wisdom—and with writing implements in hand (fol. 313ʳ).[69]

The broader cultural associations of these kinds of author portraits, and the specific cases outlined here, are especially important for this study, as they form the background to the remarkable visual representation of authorship in the transmission of Rudolf von Ems's works. Rudolf's position in the history of the author portrait in medieval German literature is unique, for the manuscripts of his texts contain at least five of such pictures, including the earliest

---

[67] For high-quality reproductions of these pictures see Schmidt-Wiegand/Milde, *Die vier Bilderhandschriften*, 35 (O fol. 6ʳ), 59 (W fol. 9ᵛ). They are also discussed by Ulrich Drescher, *Geistliche Denkformen in den Bilderhandschriften des Sachsenspiegels*, Frankfurt a. M. 1989 (Germanistische Arbeiten zu Sprache und Kulturgeschichte 12), 88–98, plates 1 (W fol. 9ᵛ) and 2 (O fol. 6ʳ); Drescher points to the existence of a comparable historiated initial in another *Sachsenspiegel* manuscript (the so-called 'Harffer *Sachsenspiegel*', in private possession, dated 1295): ibid., 90, plate 4a.

[68] See also Ruth Schmidt-Wiegand, 'Text und Bild in den Codices picturati des "Sachsenspiegels"', in *Text–Bild–Interpretation: Untersuchungen zu den Bilderhandschriften des Sachsenspiegels*, ed. Ruth Schmidt-Wiegand, 2 vols., Munich 1986 (MMS 55/1–2), i. 11–31, esp. 14, 30, ii. plates 3 (H fol. 1ʳ), 20 (W fol. 85ʳ), and 149 (D fol. 91ʳ); Schmidt-Wiegand/Milde, *Die vier Bilderhandschriften*, 49 (H fol. 1ʳ); Wenzel, 'Autorenbilder', 6f., 23 (W fol. 9ᵛ, 85ʳ).

[69] See also Krasa, *Handschriften*, 45; Wachinger, 'Wolfram von Eschenbach am Schreibpult'.

extant example (Munich, BSB, Cgm 63, *c.* 1270–80, fol. 1ʳ). As we
shall see in Chapter 2, this body of material is not only indicative
of the socio-historical context in which Rudolf first composed the
works in question, but it also provides us with an opportunity to
observe the extent to which the external, secondary devices of
scribes and illustrators interact with primary (authorial) strategies of
self-presentation when the literary composition becomes a manuscript book. The codicological representation of authorship is less
spectacular in the transmission of Konrad von Würzburg's works,
and in the genres of the heroic epic and the secular short story.
Nevertheless, a number of relevant scribal superscriptions and
colophons crop up here as well, and these too will be drawn on in
later chapters. Methodologically speaking, evidence from manuscripts will be included wherever possible in order to lend an
additional dimension to the principal discussion of the present book
concerning the internal, literary presentation of authorship.

II. THE LITERARY PRESENTATION OF AUTHORSHIP

Thus far the 'presentation of authorship' has been loosely defined
as the medieval poetic practice of addressing the issue of the authorship of a text within the literary work itself. But what kinds of
constructions and themes does this practice involve? Let us now
consider this question in greater detail with reference to the well-
known narrative works of the 'Blütezeit', where three aspects of
authorship are routinely signified: first, the author's name, as in
Hartmann von Aue's *Iwein*:

> er was genant Hartman
> und was ein Ouwaere,
> der tihte diz maere. (28ff.)

(He was called Hartmann and came from Aue; he composed this tale.)

second, the activity of literary or poetic composition, as in Gottfried
von Strassburg's *Tristan*:

> die rihte und die wârheit
> begunde ich sêre suochen
> in beider hande buochen
> walschen und latînen

und begunde mich des pînen,
daz ich in sîner rihte
rihte dise tihte. (156–62)

(I began to search diligently for the correct version and truth in both kinds
of books—French and Latin—and I took great pains to shape this composition in accordance with his [Thomas's] version.)

and third, the broader circumstances of production, including references to other participants, as in Wolfram von Eschenbach's
Willehalm:

lantgrâve von Düringen Herman
tet mir diz maere von im bekant. (3,8f.)

(Landgrave Hermann von Thüringen made this tale about him [Willehalm]
known to me.)

These examples are found in the prologues of their respective
works, which is entirely typical. The presentation of authorship in
medieval German narrative literature often forms part of extended
passages of commentary (prologues, epilogues, excursuses) that have
come to be regarded as repositories of thematic meaning and
vernacular poetological reflection. Of course it is also precisely at
these points that the storyteller or narrator is most visible, and this
raises the question of the relationship between the presentation of
authorship and the 'I' or enunciating subject in the text.

In modern literary studies the narrator has long been recognized
as an integral feature of narrative texts.[70] Wayne C. Booth's contribution (1961) to the terminology in this field has been especially
influential, not only in his concentrated use of phrases such as
'dramatized', 'unreliable' and 'self-conscious' to qualify various
manifestations of the narratorial figure, but also in his formulation
of the 'implied author', that is to say, the authorial persona which
the reader infers from the work as a whole and which is located
somewhere between the textual narrator and the real author.[71] This
threefold distinction continues to enjoy a certain theoretical prominence. In a more recent paradigm for narrative analysis, narrator,
implied author, and real author are all deemed to operate as different

[70] Käte Friedemann, *Die Rolle des Erzählers in der Epik*, Berlin 1910 (Untersuchungen zur
neueren Sprach- und Literaturgeschichte NF 7), repr. Darmstadt 1965; Franz K. Stanzel,
Theorie des Erzählens, Göttingen 1979 (Uni-Taschenbücher 904).
[71] Wayne C. Booth, *The Rhetoric of Fiction*, Chicago, Ill. 1961, esp. 71–7, 149–65, 205–40.

'transmitters' ('Senderinstanzen') within a hierarchical structure of various levels of communication.[72]

The sticking point is whether or not notions of a fictional narrator are appropriate in a discussion of medieval texts. Since the 1960s numerous studies have sought to answer in the affirmative for Middle High German narrative tradition. This positive response is most illuminating in research which deals with the respective workings of orality and literacy and the vital developments in vernacular narrative stimulated by the encroachment of the latter on the former throughout the Middle Ages.[73] The shift to written composition may be supposed to have increased the distance between two fundamental aspects of the vernacular poet's activity: the preparation of his material and the actual (oral) performance. Poets consequently became more aware of their own authorial role and created a narratorial figure to represent the situation of storytelling to an audience in the text itself; an internal communicative situation which could both refer to and influence the external real one. Crucially, such a disparity between author and narrator lends itself to sophisticated uses of irony which are generally viewed as characteristic of the medieval romance.[74]

Objections have been raised on the basis that in practice narrator and author are far more likely to have coincided in the courtly epic of the twelfth and thirteenth centuries than in the modern European novel.[75] Indeed, in numerous cases the presentation of authorship within a text appears to undermine the division between narrator and author. Several of Hartmann's key works, for instance, contain passages in which the first-person voice of the narrator is explicitly

[72] Cordula Kahrmann/Gunter Reiß/Manfred Schluchter, *Erzähltextanalyse: Eine Einführung in Grundlagen und Verfahren. Mit Materialien zur Erzähltheorie und Übungstexten von Campe bis Ben Witter*, 2 vols., Kronberg/Ts. 1977, 2nd revised edn. of vol. i. Königstein/Ts. 1981.

[73] Robert Scholes/Robert Kellogg, *The Nature of Narrative*, New York, NY 1966, esp. 51–6; Rainer Warning, 'Formen narrativer Identitätskonstitution im höfischen Roman', in *Identität*, edd. Odo Marquard/Karlheinz Stierle, Munich 1979 (Poetik und Hermeneutik 8), 553–89, esp. 573–89; Michael Curschmann, 'Hören–Lesen–Sehen: Buch und Schriftlichkeit im Selbstverständnis der volkssprachlichen literarischen Kultur Deutschlands um 1200', *PBB* 106 (1984), 218–57; Dennis H. Green, *Medieval Listening and Reading: The Primary Reception of German Literature 800–1300*, Cambridge 1994; Günter Butzer, 'Das Gedächtnis des epischen Textes: Mündliches und schriftliches Erzählen im höfischen Roman des Mittelalters', *Euphorion* 89 (1995), 151–88.

[74] Dennis H. Green, *Irony in the Medieval Romance*, Cambridge 1979, pp. 213–49; Bumke, 'Autor und Werk', 104ff.

[75] Johnson, 'Blütezeit', 238f.

identified as that of the author, as in the well-known digression in
Erec concerning Enite's horse:

> ouch tuot daz mînem sinne kranc,
> daz ich den satel nie gesach:[. . .]
> 'nû swîc, lieber Hartman:
> ob ich ez errâte?'
> ich tuon: nû sprechet drâte. (7485f., 7493ff.)

(My ability [to tell you] is undermined in that I have never seen the saddle
[. . .] 'Be quiet a moment, dear Hartmann: do you think I can guess what
it is like?' As you wish: now speak quickly.)

However, the fictional context should advise us that this 'Hartman'
is not to be equated with the author's historical biographical self.
The poet rather is 'playing himself',[76] and functionalizes the theme
of authorship—by the inclusion of his own name—in order to
dramatize the internal textual scenario of the storyteller in supposed
dialogue with a member of the audience.[77] Significantly, there is a
large body of evidence in the lyric poetry of the day of a comparable interest in complex role-play,[78] and Hartmann's own lyric
poetry documents that this could also involve explicit references to
authorial identity.[79]

In broader terms Hartmann's intrusive storyteller in *Erec* represents an important innovation in medieval German narrative
tradition. As is widely recognized,[80] the potential of this new dimen-

---

[76] Leo Spitzer, 'Note on the Poetic and the Empirical "I" in Medieval Authors', in
Romanische Literaturstudien 1936–1956, Tübingen 1959, pp. 100–12; William H. Jackson,
'Some Observations on the Status of the Narrator in Hartmann von Aue's *Erec* and *Iwein*',
FMLS 6 (1970), 65–82, esp. 72; Paul Herbert Arndt, *Der Erzähler bei Hartmann von Aue:
Formen und Funktionen seines Hervortretens und seiner Äußerungen*, Göppingen 1980 (GAG 299),
132–81; Butzer, 'Gedächtnis des epischen Textes', 164f.

[77] Cf. also *Erec* 9169f.; *Iwein* 7015–74. A similar strategy is employed in the dialogue
with Frau Minne earlier in *Iwein* (2971–3024).

[78] Rainer Warning, 'Lyrisches Ich und Öffentlichkeit bei den Trobadors', in *Deutsche
Literatur im Mittelalter: Kontakte und Perspektiven. Hugo Kuhn zum Gedenken*, ed. Christoph
Cormeau, Stuttgart 1979, pp. 120–59, esp. 122–33; Jan-Dirk Müller, '*Ir sult sprechen
willekomen*: Sänger, Sprecherrolle und die Anfänge volkssprachlicher Lyrik', *IASL* 19 (1994),
1–21; Peter Strohschneider, '"nu sehent, wie der singet!": Vom Hervortreten des Sängers
im Minnesang', in *'Aufführung' und 'Schrift'*, ed. Müller, 7–30.

[79] 'Maniger grüezet mich alsô |—der gruoz tuot mich ze mâze vrô -: | "Hartman,
gên wir schouwen | ritterlîche vrouwen"' (MF 216,29–32). See also Elisabeth Lienert,
'*Hoerâ Walther, wie ez mir stât*: Autorschaft und Sängerrolle im Minnesang bis Neidhart',
in *Autor und Autorschaft*, edd. Andersen *et al.*, 114–28.

[80] Joachim Bumke, *Wolfram von Eschenbach*, Stuttgart 1964 (SM 36), 7th revised edn.
Stuttgart/Weimar 1997, pp. 1–7, 128–51; Michael Curschmann, 'Das Abenteuer des
Erzählens: Über den Erzähler in Wolframs "Parzival"', *DVjs* 45 (1971), 627–67; Eberhard

sion was subsequently exploited fully by Wolfram von Eschenbach whose extremely conspicuous narrators in *Parzival* and *Willehalm* are also coupled with bold statements of authorship:

> ich bin Wolfram von Eschenbach,
> unt kan ein teil mit sange,[. . .]
> disiu âventiure
> vert âne der buoche stiure.
> ê man si hete für ein buoch,
> ich waere ê nacket âne tuoch,
> sô ich in dem bade saeze,
> ob ichs questen niht vergaeze. (*Parzival* 114,12f.; 115,29–116,4)

(I am Wolfram von Eschenbach and know something about singing [. . .] This tale of adventure goes without the aid of books. I would rather not have a stitch on, just as if I were sitting in the bath, than allow people to regard it as a book—as long as I hadn't forgotten the bath brush!)

The presentation of authorship in passages like this appears to fulfil a specific function in Wolfram's work.[81] Repeated assertion of authorial identity is fundamental to the make-up of narrators who— to an unprecedented and unsurpassed extent—stand on the threshold between fiction and reality.[82] The remarkable nature of this concept is underlined by its resonance throughout the thirteenth century, leading to the instigation of a veritable Wolfram-role in later works,[83] as well as pictorial depiction in the famous *Willehalm* fragments of Munich, BSB, Cgm 193/III (datable to the 1270s).[84]

So far we have been concerned only with the issues raised by passages where the storyteller or narrator is explicitly named as the

Nellmann, *Wolframs Erzähltechnik: Untersuchungen zur Funktion des Erzählers*, Wiesbaden 1973; Christian Kiening, *Reflexion–Narration: Wege zum 'Willehalm' Wolframs von Eschenbach*, Tübingen 1991 (Hermaea Germanistische Forschungen NF 63), esp. 43–59, 151–68; Ulrike Draesner, *Wege durch erzählte Welten: Intertextuelle Verweise als Mittel der Bedeutungskonstitution in Wolframs 'Parzival'*, Frankfurt a. M. 1992 (Mikrokosmos 36), esp. 456–62; Klaus Ridder, 'Autorbilder und Werkbewußtsein im 'Parzival' Wolframs von Eschenbach', *Wolfram-Studien* 15 (1998), 168–94.

[81] Cf. also *Parzival* 143,21–144,4; 184,27–185,9; 337,23–30; 416,20–30; 433,1–434,10; 827,1–30; *Willehalm* 1,1–5,14; 237,3–14.

[82] Michael Curschmann, 'The French, the Audience, and the Narrator in Wolfram's "Willehalm"', *Neophilologus* 59 (1975), 548–62; Bernd Schirok, *Parzivalrezeption im Mittelalter*, Darmstadt 1982 (EdF 174), 7–27.

[83] Hedda Ragotzky, *Studien zur Wolfram-Rezeption: Die Entstehung und Verwandlung der Wolfram-Rolle in der deutschen Literatur des 13. Jahrhunderts*, Stuttgart 1971 (Studien zur Poetik und Geschichte der Literatur 20).

[84] See facsimile edn. by Ulrich Montag, fol. A₂ʳ, 1ʳ, 1ᵛ. See also Curschmann, 'Pictura laicorum litteratura?', 220f., plate 4.

author. But passages also occur in which the author is referred to in the third person, and consequently, where a distinction between narrator and author sometimes becomes manifest in the text itself.[85] This kind of presentation of authorship is an element in the prologue of Hartmann's *Gregorius*:

> Der dise rede berihte,
> in tiusche getihte,
> daz was von Ouwe Hartman. (171ff.)

(The man who composed this text in German verse was called Hartmann von Aue.)

These lines are typical of many authorial namings,[86] conventional 'signatures' which may owe their third-person form to Latin literary tradition, but fulfil a new pragmatic function in the context of the vernacular.[87] Poets such as Hartmann probably read out their own works in the first instance and must have been aware that their texts would subsequently be recited by others. While the first-person narratorial voice naturally lent itself to appropriation by the actual reciter, the use of the third person in prologues and epilogues preserved an independent space for the lasting identification of the author.[88]

The impression of objectivity created by the third-person presentation of authorship aligns it with the scribal devices of the superscription (*titulus*) and colophon. However, this construction is still very much part of the literary text and therefore as liable to be used as an element of a poetic strategy as the first-person presen-

---

[85] Warning, 'Lyrisches Ich', 122–5; Kiening, *Reflexion*, 52ff.

[86] Cf. *Der arme Heinrich* 1–28; *Gregorius* 3989–99; *Iwein* 21–30; *Die Klage* 29f. See also Käthe Iwand, *Die Schlüsse der mittelhochdeutschen Epen*, Berlin 1922 (Germanische Studien 16), 138–44; K. Dieter Goebel, 'Der Gebrauch der dritten und ersten Person bei der Selbstnennung und in den Selbstaussagen mittelhochdeutscher Dichter', *ZfdPh* 94 (1975), 15–36.

[87] Scholars often cite Conrad of Hirsau's definition of a *titulus* in this context: 'Quod de pagina liminari requiris, differentiam tituli, proemii, prefacionis et prologi sic distingue:[. . .] sed inter prologum et titulum hoc interest, quod titulus auctorem et unde tractet breviter innuit, prologus vero docilem facit et intentum et benivolum reddit lectorem vel auditorem' (*Dialogus super auctores* 121ff., 125–8). See Gustav Ehrismann, 'Duzen und Ihrzen im Mittelalter [4]', *ZfdWf* 5 (1903–4), 127–220, esp. 142ff.; Olive Sayce, 'Prolog, Epilog und das Problem des Erzählers', in *Probleme mittelhochdeutscher Erzählformen: Marburger Colloquium 1969*, edd. Peter F. Ganz/Werner Schröder, Berlin 1972 (Publications of the Institute of Germanic Studies University of London 13), 63–72, esp. 70ff.; Manfred G. Scholz, *Hören und Lesen: Studien zur primären Rezeption der Literatur im 12. und 13. Jahrhundert*, Wiesbaden 1980, pp. 1–9.

[88] Green, *Irony*, 213–22.

tation of authorship. In other words, in terms of the appearance of the text on the manuscript page such internal third-person references to the author are still written in black ink and not red. Consideration of the relevant passages in Hartmann's works also allows us to make the observation that the two different modes of first-person and third-person presentation are not mutually exclusive. In a text such as *Iwein* it is entirely feasible for the author to be named in the third person in the prologue (21–30) and identified with the narrator in the course of the main body of the narrative (2971–3024, 7015–74). Moreover, one and the same passage may address the theme of authorship from complementary perspectives, as is the case with the prologue to *Gregorius* where third-person identification of the author (quoted above) is preceded by a first-person authorial statement.[89] The literary presentation of authorship emerges as a composite phenomenon whose analysis requires a flexible methodology; differences between the various textual manifestations are not to be glossed over in the interests of a single critical paradigm.

As has already been outlined in this introduction the codicological representation of vernacular authorship in Germany only really becomes apparent in the course of the thirteenth and fourteenth centuries. The significant exception to this rule lies in the employment of acrostics in works from the twelfth century onwards.[90] This artifice had an extensive tradition in religious writings, and the covert but irrevocable link that it forged between text and authorial identity in such works in the Middle Ages may have been motivated by the promise of devotional benefits.[91] In one sense, the acrostic—like the superscription and the author portrait—is integral to a work as a manuscript book and preserves a record of the authorship of a text without forming part of the main body of the narrative. Yet acrostics are singular among such devices in that they were invariably devised by the author. As an alternative means of self-naming, acrostics were an irreducible part of the fabric of the text and could

---

[89] 'Mîn herze hât betwungen | dicke mîne zungen | daz si des vil gesprochen hât | daz nâch der werlde lône stât: | daz rieten im diu tumben jâr' (1–5). See also Haug, *Literaturtheorie*, 134–7.

[90] Scholz, *Hören und Lesen*, 139–52, 158–65; Green, *Medieval Listening*, 131f.; John L. Flood, 'Offene Geheimnisse: Versteckte und verdeckte Autorschaft im Mittelalter', in *Autor und Autorschaft*, edd. Andersen *et al.*, 370–96.

[91] Gérard Gros, *Le Poète marial et l'art graphique: Etude sur les jeux de lettres dans les poèmes pieux du Moyen Age*, Caen 1993, esp. 47–88.

operate as an authorial hallmark or 'seal' (*sphragis*), simultaneously discouraging later scribes and writers from interpolating foreign passages.[92] Thus, acrostics represent another form of the literary presentation of authorship and may be regarded as a further, if subsidiary, aspect of the primary object of this enquiry.

The best-known acrostic of this kind is found in Gottfried's *Tristan*:

> **G**edaehte man ir ze guote niht,[. . .]
> **D**er guote man, swaz der in guot [. . .]
> **I**ch hoere es velschen harte vil,[. . .]
> **E**z zimet dem man ze lobene wol,[. . .]
> **T**iur' unde wert ist mir der man,[. . .]
> **Ê**r' unde lop diu schephent list,[. . .]
> **R**eht' als daz dinc ze unruoche gât,[. . .]
> **I**r ist sô vil, die des nu pflegent,[. . .]
> **C**unst unde nâhe sehender sin,[. . .]
> **H**ei, tugent, wie smal sint dîne stege,[. . .]
> **T**rîb ich die zît vergebene hin,[. . .]
> **I**ch hân mir eine unmüezekeit [. . .] (1–45)

Unbeknown to the listener, whose understanding of the authorship of the work depends on what the narrator reveals in passages such as the prologue (1–242) and the so-called literary excursus (4587–972),[93] Gottfried's authorship is also imparted to the reader of the work through a cryptographic sequence of initials which spans the whole of the fragmentary text. In the opening lines of *Tristan* (quoted above), the first letters of the names of the poet (G) and the central characters (T, I) bracket a certain DIETERICH, generally assumed to be Gottfried's (unidentified) patron.[94] The use of such an acrostic is telling in itself as it reflects the author's consciousness of the text as a book and presupposes a readership, thereby placing the vernacular work squarely in the sphere of literary culture. Acrostics are not employed in the works of either Hartmann or Wolfram, and this may be seen in part as a function

---

[92] Klopsch, 'Anonymität und Selbstnennung', 20f.

[93] For further discussion of the numerous excursuses in *Tristan* see David A. Howard, 'The Relationship between Poet and Narrator in Gottfried's "Tristan"', Ph.D. thesis, University of Cambridge 1973; Rüdiger Schnell, *Suche nach Wahrheit: Gottfrieds 'Tristan und Isold' als erkenntniskritischer Roman*, Tübingen 1992 (Hermaea Germanistische Forschungen NF 67), 13–56.

[94] Bernd Schirok, 'Zu den Akrosticha in Gottfrieds "Tristan": Versuch einer kritischen und weiterführenden Bestandsaufnahme', *ZfdA* 113 (1984), 188–213; Gesa Bonath, 'Nachtrag zu den Akrosticha in Gottfrieds "Tristan"', *ZfdA* 115 (1986), 101–16.

of their self-definition as authors, which differs considerably from that of Gottfried. For instance, bookishness is ultimately held in check in Hartmann's self-presentation in *Iwein* as a knight who can read:

> Ein rîter, der gelêret was
> unde ez an den buochen las,
> swenner sîne stunde
> niht baz bewenden kunde,
> daz er ouch tihtennes pflac [. . .] (21–5)

(A knight who was educated and read around in books—when he could not use his time better it was his custom to compose poetry—[. . .])

and the very suggestion of literacy runs contrary to Wolfram's central authorial role in *Parzival*: 'I cannot read a letter' ('ine kan decheinen buochstap' 115,27). In Gottfried's *Tristan*, on the other hand, the occurrence of the device of the acrostic is entirely consistent with the profile of highly literate authorship that is offered by the narrator at the outset when he is at pains to emphasize the archival research he has undertaken.[95]

The differences between Hartmann, Wolfram, and Gottfried have only been touched on here as this exposition has primarily been concerned with the basic types of construction used to present authorship in medieval narratives. The three outstanding authors of the 'Blütezeit' will, however, recur as points of reference in this study, for poets of later generations (such as Rudolf von Ems and Konrad von Würzburg) often built upon the poetic forms and techniques of one or another of their celebrated predecessors.

III. THE 'POST-CLASSICAL' PERIOD OF 1220–1290

Attitudes towards the German vernacular literature of 1220–90, a period which is often taken to mark the start of the later Middle Ages,[96] have changed dramatically over the last twenty to thirty years. One sign of this is the recent revision of Helmut de Boor's literary history (1962) by Johannes Janota (1997) who marginalizes De Boor's thesis of a poetic 'decline' in the course of the thirteenth century in parallel to the waning of the universal powers of empire

---

[95] Chinca, *History, Fiction, Verisimilitude*, 47–53.
[96] Joachim Heinzle, 'Wann beginnt das Spätmittelalter?', *ZfdA* 112 (1983), 207–23.

and papacy.[97] De Boor's view is representative of an earlier stage in scholarship when awareness of the tremendous literary quality of works such as *Parzival* and *Tristan* gave rise to disparagement of the following, so-called post-classical phase of medieval German literary tradition whose poets were routinely labelled as epigones. A change of approach was advocated by Hugo Kuhn as early as the 1950s,[98] and value judgements have largely been replaced now by the concern to understand the literature of 1220–90 in its own right. It has subsequently become clear that this was a time of development crucial to the establishment of an autonomous tradition of written literature in German.[99]

The first thing to note about this phase of medieval German literary tradition is that it is informed by a process of social diversification. As Joachim Bumke (1979) has described in his study of patronage, vernacular literature gradually came to be commissioned by individuals from a wider range of stations.[100] Secular princes continued to take the lead in fostering literary activity in German, but from the first decades of the thirteenth century onward we also have evidence of the participation of emperors and kings, as well as greater and lesser ecclesiastical officials, counts, ministerials (*ministeriales*), and cities. Both Rudolf von Ems (active *c.* 1220–55) and Konrad von Würzburg (active *c.* 1257–87) figure large in Bumke's collection of data, and their respective careers seem to exemplify a number of his central points.[101]

All but one of Rudolf's five extant texts can be directly linked to historically documented individuals who differ considerably in social status: his first work, *Der guote Gêrhart*, was written for Rudolf von Steinach (attested 1209–21), a ministerial of the bishop of Constance; the composition of his second, *Barlaam und Josaphat*, depended in

---

[97] The full title of the volume in quesion by Helmut de Boor runs: *Die deutsche Literatur im späten Mittelalter: Zerfall und Neubeginn. Erster Teil 1250–1350*, Munich 1962 (= Helmut de Boor/Richard Newald [eds.], Geschichte der deutschen Literatur von den Anfängen bis zur Gegenwart 3:1). The problematic subtitle 'Zerfall und Neubeginn' has been dropped in the fifth and latest revised edn. by Johannes Janota (1997).

[98] Hugo Kuhn, *Minnesangs Wende*, Tübingen 1952 (Hermaea Germanistische Forschungen NF 1), 2nd expanded edn. 1967.

[99] See the programmatic statement on this issue by Joachim Heinzle, *Wandlungen und Neuansätze im 13. Jahrhundert (1220/30–1280/90)*, 2nd revised edn. Tübingen 1994 (= Joachim Heinzle [ed.], Geschichte der deutschen Literatur von den Anfängen bis zum Beginn der Neuzeit 2:2), 3f.

[100] Bumke, *Mäzene*, 248–93.

[101] See also Heinzle, *Wandlungen und Neuansätze*, 25–31 (Rudolf), 33–42 (Konrad).

some measure on the Cistercian abbot Wido von Kappel (attested 1222–32); his third complete work, *Willehalm von Orlens*, was commissioned by the powerful Hohenstaufen ministerial Konrad von Winterstetten (d. 1243)—in association with another ministerial Johannes von Ravensburg (attested 1246–64) and count Konrad II von Öttingen (d. 1241/2?)—who held important offices at the imperial court and acted as adviser to the young kings Henry VII (1220–35) and Conrad IV (1237–54); finally, the *Weltchronik*, Rudolf's last work, was written for King Conrad of Hohenstaufen himself.[102] Thus, the course of Rudolf's literary career is marked by a shift from more regional environments to one of the most prestigious courts in Germany. In both stages he is employed by ministerials (*ministeriales*), that is to say members of an originally unfree social grouping that only began to commission literature in the course of the thirteenth century,[103] although on closer inspection the respective socio-cultural contexts bear little comparison. Whereas Rudolf von Steinach's patronage reflects an emergent interest in vernacular literature outside of the courts of the lay princes, when Konrad von Winterstetten employs Rudolf von Ems at the Hohenstaufen court, it is against the background of an illustrious, imperial tradition of literary production and reception. In the twelfth century this had meant primarily Latin literature, but Emperor Henry VI (1190–7) also appears to have cultivated love poetry, and within twenty to thirty years the Hohenstaufen court had also become a flourishing centre for vernacular lyric and narrative composition.[104] Konrad von Winterstetten, who is named as patron by both Ulrich von Türheim (active *c.* 1230–50) and Rudolf von Ems, played a leading role in this cultural milieu, promoting courtly literature for the entertainment of an elite circle of lords and ladies. It also seems likely that he commissioned works such as *Willehalm von Orlens* for the benefit of the young kings in his charge.[105] Rudolf evidently

---

[102] Bumke, *Mäzene*, 251f. (*Willehalm von Orlens*; *Weltchronik*), 261f. (*Barlaam und Josaphat*), 274f. (*Der guote Gêrhart*). See also Edward Schröder, 'Rudolf von Ems und sein litteraturkreis', *ZfdA* 67 (1930), 209–51.

[103] Bumke, *Mäzene*, 272–83.

[104] Id., *Höfische Kultur: Literatur und Gesellschaft im hohen Mittelalter*, 2 vols., Munich 1986 (dtv 4442), ii. 639–54.

[105] See also Helmut Brackert, *Rudolf von Ems: Dichtung und Geschichte*, Heidelberg 1968, esp. 220–30. Rudolf's *Alexander* is the only one of his works in which there is no mention of a patron. It is possible that this text was also commissioned at the Hohenstaufen court, by Konrad von Winterstetten for King Henry VII or by the latter himself, although there is no concrete evidence to support this common hypothesis; see Bumke, *Mäzene*, 16f.

impressed sufficiently with his courtly romance to be entrusted by
King Conrad with one of the most ambitious poetic enterprises
of the period: the writing of the first vernacular chronicle of
universal history.

Konrad von Würzburg can be associated with a substantial
number of documented personages in yet another distinctive socio-
historical context: the medieval towns of Strassburg and Basle.[106]
With their cathedral chapters episcopal cities had always been important centres of literary production in the Middle Ages. However,
as German towns boomed as part of the rapid economic and demo-
graphic growth across Western Europe in the thirteenth century,
manifestations of a fully fledged vernacular literary culture became
apparent there as well.[107] Konrad's references to patrons in Strassburg and, above all, Basle, prove extremely illuminating in this
context. Not only did he clearly have contact with prominent ecclesiastical figures in both cities: in Strassburg, Berthold von Tiersberg
(provost from 1261; d. 1277) and Konrad von Lichtenberg (bishop
1273–99); in Basle, Liutolt von Roeteln (canon, archdeacon, provost;
d. 1316) and Dietrich am Orte (canon, precentor; attested 1255–89).
But he also found employment with members of the lay aristocracy
in Basle: most notably Peter Schaler (attested 1258–1307) who held
the office of mayor on more than one occasion, and other distinguished noblemen such as Johannes von Bermeswil (attested
1273–93?), Heinrich Iselin (attested 1265–94), and Johannes von
Arguel (attested 1277–1311). As Bumke emphasizes, the invariably
high social standing of these men and the character of the works
they commissioned—a short story; love poetry; saints' lives; courtly
epics—should disabuse us of any notion of 'town literature' as a
separate poetic category for this period.[108] Konrad was engaged by
the social and political elite of Basle to write largely within the traditional scope of courtly literature; if anything, the tastes of these
individuals tended to be conservative, the courtly epics *Partonopier
und Meliur* (composed for Peter Schaler) and the *Trojanerkrieg* (for
Dietrich am Orte) being based on French sources that were already

---

[106] Ibid., 259f., 262ff., 287ff. See also Rüdiger Brandt, *Konrad von Würzburg*, Darmstadt
1987 (EdF 249), 70–80; Ernst Schubert, 'Die deutsche Stadt um 1300', *JOWG* 5 (1988–9),
37–56.

[107] Ursula Peters, *Literatur in der Stadt: Studien zu den sozialen Voraussetzungen und kulturellen
Organisationsformen städtischer Literatur im 13. und 14. Jahrhundert*, Tübingen 1983 (Studien und
Texte zur Sozialgeschichte der Literatur 7), 61–168.

[108] Bumke, *Mäzene*, 292f.; Peters, *Literatur in der Stadt*, 1–59.

over 100 years old. The aesthetic affinity between Peter Schaler and Dietrich am Orte is indicative of a second key feature of the broader circumstances surrounding Konrad's literary career. Namely, that there is little apparent correlation between the patron's office (ecclesiastical or secular) and the texts in question. Both Dietrich am Orte and Berthold von Tiersberg instigate the composition of overtly secular works (*Trojanerkrieg, Heinrich von Kempten*), and their respective decisions seem to be rooted in a desire to participate in an essentially aristocratic form of social entertainment. Given that Konrad's patrons in Basle were all high-ranking public figures with manifold political and economic ties, in relatively close physical proximity to one another, it is quite feasible that they formed one and the same audience, unified further by their interest in maintaining and participating in an exclusive vernacular literary culture.

Social diversification aside, the thirteenth century also saw important developments in the growth of lay literacy and the production of vernacular literary manuscripts. By 1300 vernacular texts were being read privately as well as being recited publicly to an audience; and a number of these new readers may even have read German without having first learnt Latin.[109] The literate— in the first instance clergy and noblewomen—were still in the minority at secular aristocratic courts and in cities, but we can suppose that their number gradually swelled as laymen too acquired reading skills, and as systems of economy and administration became increasingly dependent on the written word.[110] The literary texts themselves offer mixed evidence of this seismic, but slow, change within secular society. A small number of poetic devices presuppose a readership; the acrostic, as used by Gottfried von Strassburg, for example,[111] falls into this category as does the famous opening of the Arthurian romance *Wigalois* (c. 1210–25) by Wirnt von Grafenberg:

> Wer hât mich guoter ûf getân?
> sî ez iemen der mich kan
> beidiu lesen und verstên,

[109] Bumke, *Höfische Kultur*, ii. 595–637.

[110] Ibid., 633–7.

[111] In other cases readerly attention is explicitly drawn to the presence of the acrostic by the poet, especially if it is unusually elaborate. In Ebernand von Erfurt's legendary epic *Heinrich und Kunigunde* (c. 1220?) the first letters of all sixty-one chapters make up the author's name and the title of the work; the reader is only informed of this in the penultimate chapter (4453–63).

der sol genâde an mir begên,
ob iht wandels an mir sî,[. . .] (1–5)

(Who is the good person who has opened me? If it is someone who is able both to read and understand me, they should have mercy on me, if I have any shortcomings [. . .])

Here the book addresses its own reader, a conceit that is only intelligible if contemporary recipients really were able to read. Yet, as Michael Curschmann (1984) observes,[112] this 'private' prologue is followed by a 'public' one reflecting the alternative scenario of a recital to an audience.[113] The device of the 'speaking text' is an indication of the growing fascination with bookishness in the vernacular, but Wirnt von Grafenberg caters for both readers and (illiterate) listeners. This blend of orality and literacy is explored most thoroughly by Dennis Green (1994) who scours German vernacular literature from 800–1300 for evidence of reception by listening and/or reading.[114] One of Green's central findings is that for many genres in the thirteenth century both modes co-existed, whereby private reading grew alongside the predominant practice of collective listening. The typical audience was effectively 'stratified', sharing literary tastes but varying quite considerably in degrees of literacy. Poets could reckon with listeners and, increasingly, readers as well with the result that often one and the same literary work functioned on at least two distinct levels.

The expansion of lay literacy was matched on the material side by notable developments in the production of German literary manuscripts. Put crudely, whereas the codices of the twelfth century were small and had a single-column format (in which the text was written continuously), in the thirteenth century they tended to be larger with two and occasionally three columns of text (with each verse set out in a new line).[115] As Nigel Palmer (1993) suggests with reference to the important collective manuscript St Gallen, Stiftsbibliothek, cod. 857, c. 1250–60, within three or four decades vernacular codicological principles had evolved sufficiently for different layouts to be chosen for different kinds of literature,

---

[112] Curschmann, 'Hören–Lesen–Sehen', 225ff.

[113] 'Mîn kunst diu was verborgen ie; | die wold ich nu offen hie, | ob ich mit mînem munde | möhte swaere stunde | den liuten senfte machen, | und von solhen sachen | daz guot ze hoeren waere. | nu wil ich iu ein maere | sagen,[. . .]' (124–32).

[114] Green, *Medieval Listening and Reading*; for the following: 203–33, 270–315.

[115] Bumke, *Höfische Kultur*, ii. 739–51.

enabling readers to recognize the nature of the text in front of them by its appearance on the page.[116] The thirteenth century also appears to have been particularly significant in terms of the amount of manuscripts that were produced as well as the numbers of texts contained therein. Notwithstanding the difficulty of interpreting such figures, it is telling that over half of the 86 or so known manuscripts of Wolfram von Eschenbach's *Parzival* can be dated to the thirteenth century.[117] Similarly, our knowledge of the courtly lyric would be immeasurably poorer without the large retrospective collections of songs that began to be assembled from around 1270. In view of these various factors it is tantalizing that so little information survives about where exactly these codices were made, and who made them. Even though all the signs are that thirteenth-century manuscripts were produced in workshops of one kind or another, we are not yet in a position to say whether this most impressive phase of codification of German literature was advanced by scriptoria specializing in vernacular works.[118]

Turning finally to the poetic activities of the authors themselves, we see that all the while developments in patronage, lay literacy, and manuscript production were taking place, Middle High German texts were being composed in ever greater numbers.[119] This proliferation of German literature encompassed innovations such as the writing of a book of secular law (Eike von Repgow's *Sachsenspiegel*, c. 1225–35), an Arthurian prose narrative (*Prosa-Lancelot*, in part before 1250), and a spiritual autobiography (Mechthild von Magdeburg's *Fließendes Licht der Gottheit*, c. 1250). New types of text

---

[116] Nigel F. Palmer, *German Literary Culture in the Twelfth and Thirteenth Centuries: An Inaugural Lecture delivered before the University of Oxford on 4 March 1993*, Oxford 1993, pp. 20f.

[117] According to Schirok, *Parzivalrezeption*, 57, forty-four *Parzival* manuscripts can be dated to the thirteenth century. His figures for two other widely transmitted works of the 'Blütezeit' also reveal a weighting towards the 1200s: *Iwein*: 14 (13C)–8 (14C)–7 (15C)–2 (16C); *Tristan*: 11 (13C)–9 (14C)–7 (15C).

[118] This question has been considered most carefully with respect to the high-profile manuscripts Codex Sangallensis 857, and Munich, BSB, Cgm 19, c. 1225–50; see Karin Schneider, *Gotische Schriften in deutscher Sprache: I. Vom späten 12. Jahrhundert bis um 1300*, 2 vols., Wiesbaden 1987, ii. 133–42, 150–4; Nigel F. Palmer, 'Der Codex Sangallensis 857: Zu den Fragen des Buchschmucks und der Datierung', *Wolfram-Studien* 12 (1992), 15–31; Thomas Klein, 'Die Parzivalhandschrift Cgm 19 und ihr Umkreis', *Wolfram-Studien* 12 (1992), 32–66.

[119] The following account is by no means exhaustive; for comprehensive expositions of this aspect of the period see Kuhn, *Minnesangs Wende*, 159–96; Heinzle, *Wandlungen und Neuansätze*, 85–184; Nigel F. Palmer, 'The High and Later Middle Ages (1100–1450)', in *The Cambridge History of German Literature*, ed. Helen Watanabe-O'Kelly, Cambridge 1997, pp. 40–91.

in couplet verse were also being introduced. Both the full gamut of shorter didactic forms (exempla or 'Bispel'; allegories; diatribes; fables; dialogues; short stories) and traditional (oral) stories about the Germanic hero Dietrich von Bern assumed written literary form for the first time in this period. As in the twelfth century German authors often still wanted their work to be associated with French literary culture,[120] but the big difference now was that their primary points of orientation lay with the German works of the 'Blütezeit'. Thus, poets of 1220–90 also set about completing earlier unfinished texts. Ulrich von Türheim (*c.* 1230–50), for example, appears to have specialized in this field, writing continuations to both Gottfried's *Tristan* and Wolfram's *Willehalm*. In fact, these German responses to German literary tradition were manifold, ranging from wholesale stylistic and linguistic revision (Der Stricker's *Karl* [1220s] displacing Pfaffe Konrad's *Rolandslied*),[121] to thematic antithesis (the ethos of reconciliation in *Kudrun* [*c.* 1250] offering an alternative to the thirst for revenge in the *Nibelungenlied?*),[122] to the parodistic treatment of a genre: Der Stricker subverting texts like *Iwein* with his own freely invented Arthurian epic *Daniel von dem Blühenden Tal* (*c.* 1220–40).[123]

As a number of the poetic activities outlined above suggest, the transition from the 'Blütezeit' (*c.* 1170–1220) to the post-classical period involved the formation of a veritable canon of vernacular literature, the core of which was made up by the works of Hartmann, Wolfram, and Gottfried.[124] This concept is openly expressed in so-called literary excursuses (panegyrical catalogues of authors), most notably in Rudolf von Ems's *Alexander* and *Willehalm von Orlens*, but also in *Diu Crône* by Heinrich von dem Türlin (*c.* 1230) and the later didactic work *Der Renner* of Hugo von Trimberg

---

[120] Palmer, 'The High and Later Middle Ages', 62.

[121] Bumke, 'Autor und Werk', 99f.

[122] Werner Hoffmann, *Kudrun: Ein Beitrag zur Deutung der nachnibelungischen Heldendichtung*, Stuttgart 1967 (Germanistische Abhandlungen 17), 274–8.

[123] Der Stricker's text gave rise to a counter-response by Der Pleier whose *Garel von dem Blühenden Tal* presents an ultra-orthodox vision of the Arthurian ideal; see also Haug, *Literaturtheorie*, 267–73.

[124] Walter Haug, 'Klassikerkataloge und Kanonisierungseffekte: Am Beispiel des mittelalterlichhochhöfischen Literaturkanons', in *Brechungen auf dem Weg zur Individualität: Kleine Schriften zur Literatur des Mittelalters*, Tübingen 1995, pp. 45–56. Further references to critical literature on this subject are amassed by Bumke, 'Autor und Werk', 97 note 45.

(*c.* 1290–1300).[125] Exactly the same notion is articulated, albeit in less elaborate form, in a multitude of other thirteenth-century texts by means of the naming and celebration of one or two 'past masters'. A good example of this practice is found in the prologue of the courtly epic *Meleranz* by Der Pleier (active *c.* 1240–70):

> Nu hoert ein frömdez maere.
> daz hât der Pleiaere
> von welschem getihtet,
> in tiutschen sin gerichtet
> mit rîmen als er beste kan.
> lebet noch her Hartman
> von Ouwe, der kunde baz
> getihten, daz lâz ich ân haz,
> und von Eschenbach her Wolfram:
> gên sîner künste bin ich lam
> die er het bî sînen tagen. (101–11)

(Now hear an extraordinary tale. Der Pleier composed it from the French, and made German sense of it, in verse, as best he could. If lord Hartmann von Aue were still alive, he could compose poetry better, I happily concede that, and lord Wolfram von Eschenbach: I am mute in the face of the artistry he had in his day.)

Such keen awareness of the authorship of the 'greats' of decades past is extremely widespread in the literature of 1220–90.[126] However, these expressions of deference are only one side of the coin. What emerges from passages like the prologue of *Meleranz* is a concurrent self-consciousness on the part of the later poets themselves. With the sense of a distinctive literary tradition in the vernacular comes an awareness of one's own position in it. Der Pleier may praise Hartmann and Wolfram up to the hilt but he names himself in his text as well.

These observations form the immediate background to this study and its investigation of the principal manifestation of authorial self-consciousness in the Middle Ages: the presentation of authorship within the literary work itself. How exactly did authorial self-naming function in the narrative literature of this period? How did poets

---

[125] These passages are conveniently assembled in an anthology: Günther Schweikle (ed.), *Dichter über Dichter in mittelhochdeutscher Literatur*, Tübingen 1970 (Deutsche Texte 12), 12–33. Famously, the first literary excursus proper in Middle High German is in a work of the 'Blütezeit', Gottfried's *Tristan* (4621–820).

[126] Schweikle, *Dichter über Dichter*, 1–4, 33–119.

describe their own authorial activities and their relationships with their patrons, and what were the concepts of authorship underpinning these descriptions? What happened to these primary passages of authorial self-presentation in the subsequent course of manuscript transmission? These are some of the main questions that will be addressed in the following chapters. Obviously, the narrative literature of 1220–90 in its entirety is too much for any single study, and so four bodies of texts have been chosen that are both representative and significant in their own right: the works of Rudolf von Ems and Konrad von Würzburg, and the genres of the later heroic epic and the secular short story. Quite apart from the fact that the working lives of Rudolf von Ems (c. 1220–55) and Konrad von Würzburg (c. 1257–87) combine to span the whole of the 'postclassical' thirteenth century, their self-consciousness as poets is unrivalled; it is in their texts, if anywhere, that we can gain an insight into the workings of authorship at the heart of the written tradition of medieval German literature. The genres of the later heroic epic and the secular short story, on the other hand, offer evidence of attitudes towards authorship on the boundary with oral traditions of storytelling. The thirteenth century was not just a time of change and experimentation in the production of vernacular manuscripts: by electing to analyse texts of such radically differing literary status it should prove possible to uncover the full range of forces that were brought to bear on the issue of authorship in this key phase of the German Middle Ages.

PART I:

Authorship at the Heart of Literary Tradition

2

RUDOLF VON EMS AND THE ART OF AUTHORIAL SELF-REFERENCE

Rudolf von Ems occupies a special position in the first half of the thirteenth century by virtue of the extent to which he instils the vernacular narrative with a Latinate sense of written literature. All of Rudolf's texts are concerned with history, even his courtly romance *Willehalm von Orlens* ends on a genealogical note anchoring the 'fictional' tale in political and historical reality, to say nothing of his life of Alexander or his chronicle of universal history. That Rudolf could work with such material betrays a clerical education, and the influence of Latin literary culture is further manifest in his subdivision of three of these texts into book-like sections.[1] Yet at the same time, like many of his contemporaries, he was very much aware of his vernacular literary heritage, and the greater part of his writings can also be read as containing literary theoretical responses to the principal texts of the 'Blütezeit'.[2] This conjunction of the Latinate and the vernacular was to prove extremely fruitful for the presentation of authorship. As Rudolf made the transition from the continuous narrative structure of his first texts, where the main body of the narrative is simply bracketed by a prologue and an epilogue, to the arrangement of his later works in 'books', each with their own prologue and epilogue, the opportunities for addressing the theme of authorship in any one narrative came to be increased greatly. Consequently, Rudolf's authorial self-reference is often truly multifaceted: incorporating acrostics, a wide range of authorial roles, and statements from a variety of perspectives. Rudolf may owe a number of these devices to his 'classical' predecessors Hartmann, Wolfram, and Gottfried, but the ways in which he combines them are his own.

---

[1] Nigel F. Palmer, 'Kapitel und Buch: Zu den Gliederungsprinzipien mittelalterlicher Bücher', *FMSt* 23 (1989), 43–88, esp. 70f.

[2] Haug, *Literaturtheorie*, 288–343.

I. DER GUOTE GÊRHART

Rudolf's first work, *Der guote Gêrhart*,[3] deals with the true nature of Christian humility: a generous but vain emperor (Otto) is brought to see the error of his ways by the eponymous hero, a merchant of Cologne, who reluctantly tells him about his own incredible acts of selflessness. Moral lessons concerning virtue, vainglory, and humility are set out in full in the prologue, and we have to wait until the epilogue for the first references to authorship. Despite the apparently conventional nature of the constructions and motifs used in this passage, the presentation of authorship here is deliberately fashioned to agree with the ethical message of the preceding tale. In this respect, the contents of the epilogue are a direct function of the broader didactic programme of the work.

The narrative proper concludes with Otto's decision to have the story of his encounter with Gerhard written down for the good of Christians everywhere. The transcription of an eye-witness report is of course an established historiographical topos, a widely documented means of authentification which is employed in other Middle High German works, such as the *Klage* (4295–313) and *Herzog Ernst* B (5994–6007), to explain the origination of the literary text.[4] Regardless of the historical validity of the details imparted by the topos in *Der guote Gêrhart*, this account of the origins of the story represents the broadest framework of reference for Rudolf's description of his own authorship:

> nû dâhte er daz ditz maere
> ein bezzerunge waere
> der kristenheit, ob man ez schribe,
> daz ez verborgen niht belibe.
> daz maere dô nâch im wart
> offenbârlîch enbart
> und mit der schrift behalten.
> diu phafheit hiez es walten
> nâch des keisers vergiht,
> daz ez uns verdurbe niht.

---

[3] The text is preserved in two manuscripts; see Asher (ed.), *Der guote Gêrhart*, pp. VIII–XI. For the chronology of Rudolf's works see Brackert, *Dichtung und Geschichte*, 11–23.

[4] Brackert, *Dichtung und Geschichte*, 203–8; Fritz Peter Knapp, 'Historische Wahrheit und poetische Lüge: Die Gattungen weltlicher Epik und ihre theoretische Rechtfertigung im Hochmittelalter', *DVjs* 54 (1980), 581–635, esp. 589–601.

dô behielt diu schrift den hort,
des maeres wârheit und wort. (6801–12)

(Now he [Otto] thought that this story would be improving for Christendom, if it were to be transcribed so that it should not remain a secret. On his instructions the story was then proclaimed publicly and kept in writing. The clergy ordered it to be safeguarded in accordance with the Emperor's edict, so that it would not be lost to us. The transcription then preserved the treasure: the truth and wording of the tale.)

The transition which the Emperor's tale makes as it first assumes written form entails a movement from the secular to the ecclesiastical sphere, the unrivalled domain of literary culture in the Middle Ages. The participation of the Church (6808) would suggest that this transcription occurred in Latin, although surprisingly, in view of the function of authorization of the passage, this is not expressly stated.[5] Under the guardianship of the clergy the aspect of the written preservation of the story overshadows the process of public, and perhaps oral, disclosure that was also instigated by Otto (6805f.). A fixed text becomes the focal point of these lines as the (sole) repository of the 'treasure' of the true and uncorrupted story, with no further mention at this stage of a wider dissemination.

The literary origins of the story form a backdrop to the following depiction of the poet's composition of the German work:

Wie ich ditz selb maer vernam
und wie ez her ze lande kam,
des vernement die wârheit.
ez hât uns ein man geseit,
der ez alsus geschriben las
daz ez gar behalten was
mit der schrift gewaerlîche.
der fuor von Ôsterrîche,
der brâht ez her in ditz lant,
als er ez geschriben vant.
der seit ez ze maere
dem werden Steinachaere,

[5] References to the ecclesiastical sphere and Latin are commonplace in such strategies of authorization: 'Von Pazowe der biscof Pilgerîn | durh liebe der neven sîn | hiez scrîben ditze maere, | wie ez ergangen waere, | in latînischen buochstaben, | daz manz für wâr solde haben' (*Klage* 4295–300); 'ist aber hie dehein man | der dise rede welle hân | vür ein lügenlîchez werc, | der kome hin ze Babenberc: | dâ vindet ers ein ende | ân alle missewende | von dem meister derz getihtet hât. | ze latîne ez noch geschriben stât' (*Herzog Ernst* B 4467–74).

herrn Ruodolf, dem genamen mîn.
der bat mich durch den willen sîn
ditz maer in tiutsch berihten,
in rehte rîme tihten.
dô begund ich ez durch in. (6815–31)

(Hear the truth of how I became acquainted with this very tale and how it came here to this land: a man told us it, who had read a version in which the story was preserved entirely and truthfully. He travelled from Austria, and he brought it here into this land as he found it in writing; he made it known to the worthy man from Steinach, Lord Rudolf, my namesake, who asked me to set out this story in German for him and to compose it in proper verse. I did it for his sake.)

Rudolf's authorship is presented as the culmination of an intriguing process of transmission which proceeds from an anonymous individual's knowledge of a written source to the commissioning of a literary work in German verse. Lines 6812–21 outline this process in truncated form before the specific roles of the mediator, patron, and poet are expounded in 6822–31. Notably, the written basis of the source (6819ff., 6824), which relates to the earlier authoritative clerical text, is coupled with an apparently oral mode of transmission (6818, 6825).[6] We can read this peculiar combination as a means of conveying the first step in another public disclosure of a story that has long since ceased to be commonly known beyond the ecclesiastical sphere. Similarly, the assertion of the vernacular in the depiction of Rudolf von Steinach's subsequent commission emphasizes that—quite in the spirit of the original imperial programme—the story may once more reach a broader audience.

It is an important part of the agenda behind the authorial self-presentation in this passage that Rudolf's patron is highlighted. In contrast to the anonymity of the first mediator of the source the patron is both named and praised (6826f.).[7] Great care is then taken

[6] Xenja von Ertzdorff, *Rudolf von Ems: Untersuchungen zum höfischen Roman im 13. Jahrhundert*, Munich 1967, pp. 160f.; Bumke, *Mäzene*, 323 note 131, 441 note 178; Dennis H. Green, 'On the Primary Reception of the Works of Rudolf von Ems', *ZfdA* 115 (1986), 151–80, esp. 177f.

[7] The anonymous mediator is identified as 'der fürst von Österrîche' in a variant for line 6822 in the later fifteenth-century manuscript B (Vienna, ÖNB, cod. 2793). However, in view of Rudolf von Steinach's social station as a ministerial of the bishop of Constance this would seem to be one of those mischievous alterations for which the scribe is well known; see John A. Asher, 'Der üble Gêrhart: Einige Bemerkungen zu den von Gabriel Sattler geschriebenen Handschriften', *PBB* (Tüb.) 94 (1972), Sonderheft 416–27.

to subordinate the poet's authorial activity to the part played by Rudolf von Steinach: the details of the nature of the composition do not stand in their own right but are described emphatically in terms of the latter's commission. Furthermore, the very identification of the author in the text is dependent on the patron as his namesake (6827). Authorial self-deprecation and glorification of the patron are commonplace in thirteenth-century medieval German narrative tradition. Yet the extent to which they are combined here, affecting even the naming of the author, is striking and points beyond the merely conventional.

The tone of self-disparagement is maintained in the next phase of the epilogue as Rudolf passes over himself to address the issue of the reception of his work, admitting that his composition will deserve some criticism (6832–48). It seems, however, that the poet is only prepared to accept constructive criticism (6849–57), and this turn in the argument draws on the idiom of the prologue:

> swaz der man durch guoten muot
> ze guote in guotem muote tuot,
> daz man es im ze guote jehe
> und niht sîn unfuoge spehe [. . .]
> an mich selben mein ich daz.
> ich spraeche, kunde ich, gerne baz. (6861–4, 6867f.)

(What a man does with good intent, to the good and in good spirit, one should credit him with, without seeking out his mistakes [. . .] I mean this with reference to myself. I would gladly speak with more skill, if I were able.)

The evocation in the epilogue of the first words of the prologue reintroduces the themes of the main narrative into the discussion, while its intertextual resonance (*Tristan* 1–8) now serves to lend the poet's self-presentation greater conviction.[8] The allusion to such a recognized vernacular literary authority as Gottfried at this point may be understood to reinforce Rudolf's implicit claim that his own humility is the most appropriate platform from which to reiterate the moral lessons of the tale:

> ein ander spruch nâch disem gât,
> den gît ouch mîn tumber rât,

---

[8] 'Swaz ein man durch guoten muot | ze guote in guotem muote tuot, | des sol man im ze guote jehen, | wan ez in guote muoz geschehen' (*Der guote Gêrhart* 1–4). For more on the references to Gottfried in Rudolf's prologue see Haug, *Literaturtheorie*, 288ff.

> daz man daz rüemen lâze sîn;[. . .]
> ich hân iu hie bewaeret
> an dirre âventiure wol
> daz niemen sich versprechen sol. (6873ff., 6880ff.)

(Another moral follows this one—this again is my simple-minded advice—
that one should forbear from boastfulness; [. . .] I have demonstrated to
you here by means of this tale that no one should harm themselves by their
own words.)

The efficacy of Rudolf's exhortations to the audience to do good
for good's sake without falling back on vainglory (6883–901) rests on
the attitude he assumes towards his own literary achievement. In
other words, the poet must be seen to be consistent. For all their
apparent topicality, the drastic belittlement of his own authorial
activity and identity in favour of the patron, and his fears concerning
an appropriately charitable reception provide the fitting poetological complement to Gerhard's exemplary acts of selflessness in the
narrative. Thus, not only do the two spheres of the narrative world
and the present storytelling situation merge towards the end of the
text in the depiction of the story's origins (6785–835), but they are
also shown to be informed with the same spirit of humility and
generosity; both prove to be functions of the didactic programme
of the work as a whole.

The subsequent invitation to the audience to pray represents a
common strategy of closure in the narratives of this period.[9] In *Der
guote Gêrhart* it preludes a further statement of authorship in a
different form:

> ouch gert der tihtaere
> der iu ditz selbe maere
> ein teil durch guotes muotes rât
> ze kurzwîl getihtet hât
> daz ir im wünschet heiles,
> ze himel werndes teiles,
> und ruochent in geniezen lân
> daz er des hât vil guoten wân,
> wirt im ein anderz kunt getân,
> daz noch mac vil wol ergân,

---

[9] 'nû wünschet al gelîche | mit vreuden zühteclîche | daz uns got in sîn rîche |
vroelîchen sende | ûz disem ellende' (6902–6). For further examples see Christian Thelen,
Das Dichtergebet in der deutschen Literatur des Mittelalters, Berlin 1989 (Arbeiten zur
Frühmittelalterforschung 18), 511–95, 620–45.

daz er dâ wil ze buoze stân,
hât er an disem missetân.
des bîtet ûf den selben wân
und lât ditz hie ein ende hân. (6907–20)

(The poet too, whose good will led him in part to compose this same tale
for your enjoyment, desires you to wish that he may enjoy salvation and a
lasting lot in heaven; deign to allow him to benefit from having good hope
of that, so that if another tale is made known to him—which may still well
happen—he will make amends with that one, if he has fallen short here.
Wait for the next story in the same hope, and let this story now come to
an end.)

The perspective from which the figure of the author has been
presented in the epilogue so far changes here as the obvious identification of the author with the first-person voice of the narrator
is undermined. The former is now referred to in the third person,
as if in a scribal superscription or colophon, although these lines
are still very much part of the literary text. Hartmann is the most
prominent exponent of this standard construction of authorial self-
presentation in Middle High German,[10] and we should note that
Rudolf's combination of the third person with the plea for the audience's intercession is reminiscent of passages such as the epilogue
of *Gregorius* (3989–99) and the prologue of *Der arme Heinrich* (18–25).[11]
However, given that the motif of intercession on the poet's behalf
is so widespread,[12] a specific intertextual reference at this point to
either of Hartmann's texts seems unlikely, and Rudolf's deployment
of the third-person perspective may instead be explained in terms
of internal literary function. As opposed to previous phases in the
epilogue the independent space or distance which the third person
typically creates is used in lines 6907–20 to raise issues relating to
the author in his own right. Hopes for spiritual reward (6911f.) and
a second literary commission (6913–19) can now be articulated as
possibilities without seeming to deviate from the programmatic tenor

---

[10] See Chapter 1 section II.

[11] 'Hartman, der sîn arbeit | an diz liet hât geleit | gote und iu ze minnen, | der gert
dar an gewinnen | daz ir im lât gevallen | ze lône von in allen | die ez hoeren oder
lesen | daz si im bittende wesen | daz im diu saelde geschehe | daz er iuch noch gesehe
| in dem himelrîche' (*Gregorius* 3989–99); 'dar umbe hât er sich genant, | daz er sîner
arbeit | die er dar an hât geleit | iht âne lôn belîbe, | und swer nâch sînem lîbe | si
hoere sagen ode lese, | daz er im bittende wese | der sêle heiles hin ze gote' (*Der arme
Heinrich* 18–25).

[12] Thelen, *Dichtergebet*, 405–576.

of humility. An awareness of earlier self-deprecation is also reflected in the poet's concession that his personal intentions were only one factor behind the production of the work ('ein teil' 6909),[13] and in the stylization of his readiness to be engaged in another literary project as an atonement for the present one ('ze buoze' 6917). Thus, this internal colophon ends the work with a stamp of authorship whose content and perspective are shaped by the poetics of what has come before. The ethical correspondence between the narrative of *Der guote Gêrhart* and the presentation of its authorship is maintained to the last.

II. *BARLAAM UND JOSAPHAT*

Rudolf's next work, the saint's life *Barlaam und Josaphat*,[14] is a story of religious instruction and conversion, and here too there is a certain correspondence between narrative content and the presentation of authorship, this time in both the prologue and the epilogue. However, a further excursus midway through the narrative draws on the altogether more secular idiom of courtly love, which seems quite at odds with the broader thematic context. In this case then, the range of techniques of authorial self-presentation at the poet's disposal is not restricted by the overtly religious ethos of the work as a whole.

The work opens with a prayer to God (1–124), a widespread exordial construction in medieval German literature which is ultimately derived from Latin traditions of Christian writing that extend back to late antiquity.[15] After the fashion of the beginning of Wolfram's *Willehalm* (1,1–2,25), Rudolf's prayer consists largely of a praise of

---

[13] Cf. also 6832f.

[14] The text is preserved in fourteen 'complete' manuscripts and over thirty fragments; five other manuscripts contain individual parables from *Barlaam und Josaphat* as independent shorter texts. For further details see Siegmund Prillwitz, *Überlieferungsstudie zum Barlaam und Josaphat des Rudolf von Ems: Eine textkritisch-stemmatologische Untersuchung*, Copenhagen 1975, pp. 16–108. Recent discoveries are listed by Klaus Klein, 'Ein "Barlaam"-Fragment in Herdringen', *ZfdA* 120 (1991), 202–9; Karin Schneider, *Die Fragmente mittelalterlicher deutscher Versdichtung der Bayerischen Staatsbibliothek München (Cgm 5249/1–79)*, Stuttgart 1996 (*ZfdA* Beiheft 1), 106f.

[15] Gerhard Strunk, *Kunst und Glaube in der lateinischen Heiligenlegende: Zu ihrem Selbstverständnis in den Prologen*, Munich 1970 (Medium aevum 12), esp. 85–104; Eckart C. Lutz, *Rhetorica divina: Mittelhochdeutsche Prologgebete und die rhetorische Kultur des Mittelalters*, Berlin 1984 (Quellen und Forschungen zur Sprach- und Kulturgeschichte der germanischen Völker NF 82 [206]), esp. 78–83; Thelen, *Dichtergebet*, 214–491.

the Godhead, focusing on the acts of Creation and Redemption.[16]
This statement of faith on the poet's part serves as the basis for a
plea for inspiration:

> durch die gnâde bite ich dich,
> daz dû geruochest hoeren mich
> und mir in mîne sinne
> des heiligen geistes minne
> ze lêre geruochest senden,[. . .]
> sît dû daz anegenge bist
> und daz ende hâst erkant,
> sô biut mir dîner helfe hant
> und wis nû mînen sinnen bî.
> in nomine dominî,
> hilf, herre got, verenden mir,
> des ich beginnen wil mit dir. (103–7, 118–24)

(I beseech You in view of this mercy that You deign to hear me and inform
my senses with the love of the Holy Spirit for my instruction [. . .]. Since
You are the Beginning and have recognized the End, so offer me the hand
of Your help and attend my mind and senses. In the Name of the Lord,
help me, Lord God, to end what I want to begin with You.)

The plea for inspiration represents a high-powered strategy of
authorization in which human authorship is shown to be informed
by and dependent on God. This is analogous to the model of authorship that was postulated for scriptural texts in the Middle Ages,
according to which the human author was viewed as an instrument
used by God like a pen. As Alastair Minnis has shown, scholars of
the thirteenth and fourteenth centuries attributed an increasingly
significant role to the human author,[17] and in this context it is
intriguing to observe how a vernacular poet of the same period
creates space for himself whilst retaining the notion of divine inspiration. At this stage of the prologue Rudolf takes the first steps toward
achieving this by lending a slightly more distinctive profile to the
topical. First, divine aid is said to be taught to him ('ze lêre' 107).
This forges an associative link with the following story which centres

---

[16] See also Haug, *Literaturtheorie*, 316–28. For further analysis of this prayer see Adrian
K. Stevens, 'Rudolf von Ems's "Barlaam und Josaphat": Aspects of its Relationship to
Christian Rhetorical Tradition, With a Consideration of its Thematic Structure', Ph.D.
thesis, University of Cambridge 1971, pp. 114–29; Lutz, *Rhetorica divina*, 243–77; Thelen,
Dichtergebet, 284–95.

[17] See Chapter 1 section I.

on the miraculous *lêre* of one blessed individual as characterized in brief in lines 111–17.[18] Second, the presentation of God's omnipotence and omniscience (118f.) recalls earlier phraseology (1–24), encapsulated in the initial invocation 'Alphâ et Ô, künec Sâbâôt' (1), in order to relate to the particular needs of the poet: the human author appeals to the Beginning and End of all existence, the supreme Author, for help in the beginning and completion of his literary work.[19]

As soon as the poet turns his attention to the audience of the work, in the second part of the prologue (125–64), he is able to emphasize his own role and explore the human aspect of the authorship of this text. Here, in a kind of parallel of the ('mixed') chain of transmission claimed for *Der guote Gêrhart*, the poet provides an account of the lineage of the story of *Barlaam und Josaphat* in terms of a process of written transmission from Greek to Latin, and from Latin to German:

> Jôhannes hiez ein herre guot,
> der truoc ze gote staeten muot:
> von Damascô was er genant,
> der diz selbe maere vant
> in kriecheschem getihte.
> ze latîne erz rihte [. . .]
> ez brâhte her in tiuschiu lant
> des ordens von Zîtels ein man,
> von dem ichz von êrste gewan:
> von Kapelle abbet Wîde. (125–30, 144–7)

(John was the name of a good lord who served God faithfully: [John] 'of Damascus' he was called, who found this very tale in the form of a Greek composition. He translated it into Latin [. . .]. It was brought here to German lands by a man of the Cistercian Order. I first gained possession of it from him: Abbot Wido of Kappel.)

This process of translation follows an archetypal movement from East to West in accordance with a concept of cultural inheritance (*translatio*) prevalent in the Middle Ages.[20] Rudolf emphasizes the

---

[18] 'ze sprechenne von einem man, | wie des lêre dir gewan | vil der heidenischen diet, | wie er von ungelouben schiet | mit dîner lêre liute, lant | und den glouben tet erkant | in dînem namen, süezer Krist' (111–17).

[19] For more on this analogy see C. Stephen Jaeger, 'Der Schöpfer der Welt und das Schöpfungswerk als Prologmotiv in der mhd. Dichtung', *ZfdA* 107 (1978), 1–18, esp. 5–17.

[20] Franz Josef Worstbrock, 'Translatio artium: Über die Herkunft und Entwicklung einer kulturhistorischen Theorie', *AKG* 47 (1965), 1–22.

religious dimension in this case by enlarging upon the pastoral motivation behind the translation from Greek by the author of his Latin source, John of Damascus, with which he himself claims a particular affinity (131–40).[21] That the mediator of the Latin source in Germany, and possibly the patron of the vernacular work, should be a Cistercian abbot adds to this impression.

The passage culminates in a more detailed disclosure concerning the German author's own motives:

> ich hân dâ her in mînen tagen
> leider dicke vil gelogen
> und die liute betrogen
> mit trügelîchen maeren:
> ze trôste uns sündaeren
> wil ich diz maere tihten,
> durch got in tiusche berihten,[. . .]
> der urhap dises maeres
> wil ich in tiuscher zungen wesen
> als ich die wârheit hân gelesen. (150–6, 162ff.)

(Unfortunately, I have often lied greatly in my life up until now and deceived people with fraudulent stories. I want to compose this tale as a comfort for us sinners, casting it in German for the sake of God [. . .]. I want to be the originator of this story in the German tongue in accordance with the truth as I have read it.)

Whereas the poet's sin was first presented in this prologue as part of the human condition, it is now formulated with specific reference to his activity as an author through the widespread topos of the renunciation of profane works.[22] The patent similarity with the prologue of *Gregorius* is less indicative of intertextual play than of the status of the role of 'author as sinner' as a poetological axiom of Christian literature.[23] The composition of *Barlaam und Josaphat* hereby assumes the significance of an act of piety, one of spiritual

---

[21] 'durch got und durch alsolhe site, | daz sich die liute bezzern mite. | des selben hân ouch ich gedâht. | mag ez werden vollebrâht, | daz mir got der sinne gan, | daz ich ez vollebringen kan, | sô weiz ich wol, diz maere gît | den liuten ze etlîcher zît | an kristenlîcher êre | vorbilde in guoter lêre' (131–40). See also Green, 'Rudolf von Ems', 170ff.

[22] For further discussion of this topos see Julius Schwietering, 'Die Demutsformel mittelhochdeutscher Dichter', in *Philologische Schriften*, edd. Friedrich Ohly/Max Wehrli, Munich 1969, pp. 140–215, esp. 203–7.

[23] Strunk, *Kunst und Glaube*, 80–4; Thelen, *Dichtergebet*, 397–404.

benefit to both audience and poet ('uns sündaeren' 154).[24] Rudolf's subsequent insistence on his own role as originator of the tale in German may seem to undermine these sentiments. However, this assertion is tantamount to a programmatic declaration of the way in which the poet may make amends in his authorial capacity by spreading knowledge of the tale (to those who cannot understand Latin).

In view of the space that Rudolf manages to create for himself in the prologue as a whole it is worth noting that in two later manuscripts this passage is accompanied by a pictorial representation of authorship.[25] What is striking about these pictures is that they appear to offer evidence of alternative concepts of authorship that compete with Rudolf's self-definition within the text. In the first of the relevant manuscripts—Los Angeles, The J. Paul Getty Museum, Ms. Ludwig XV 9, dated 1469, fol. 9^v [originally 4^v]—the picture is situated after the poet's prayer to God: a male figure kneels at an altar, holding a rosary, characterized as an author by the way his hands gesture towards an image of Christ on the cross. On the face of it, the illustration corresponds to Rudolf's authorial self-presentation in lines 1–124. However, we should be aware that as a rule the pictures in this manuscript relate to the text on the following page,[26] which might well mean that the author depicted is not Rudolf but John of Damascus, whose translation of the Greek text is described in the lines immediately following the illustration (125–32). Thus, the 'identity' of the authorial figure depends on the concept(s) of authorship of those who produced the codex. If the subject of this picture is Rudolf then it was conceived as a visual counterpart to the text of the prologue itself, in which the German poet describes his own position as a human author seeking divine aid. If, on the other hand, the figure depicted is John of Damascus, as is generally believed to be the case,[27] then Rudolf's authorship as a vernacular writer was

[24] Cf. also 157–61: 'und bite, swer diz maere lese, | daz er sich bezzernde wese | mit staete an dem glouben sîn. | und durch got gedenke mîn | vil armen sündaeres'.

[25] An expert overview of the illustrated manuscripts of this text is given in 'Barlaam und Josaphat', *KDIHM* 2 (1996), 11–20. See also Norbert H. Ott, 'Anmerkungen zur Barlaam-Ikonographie Rudolfs von Ems "Barlaam und Josaphat" in Malibu und die Bildtradition des Barlaam-Stoffs', in *Die Begegnung des Westens mit dem Osten: Kongreßakten des 4. Symposions des Mediävistenverbandes in Köln 1991 aus Anlaß des 1000. Todesjahres der Kaiserin Theophanu*, edd. Odilo Engels/Peter Schreiner, Sigmaringen 1993, pp. 365–85.

[26] 'Barlaam und Josaphat', *KDIHM* 2 (1996), 15.

[27] Anton von Euw/Joachim M. Plotzek, *Die Handschriften der Sammlung Ludwig*, 4 vols., Cologne 1979–85, vol. iv. 256, plate 188.

1. Rudolf von Ems, *Barlaam und Josaphat* (The author in prayer) (reproduced by permission of the J. Paul Getty Museum, Los Angeles)

2. Rudolf von Ems, *Barlaam und Josaphat* (The author holding a scroll) (reproduced by permission of the Biblioteka Uniwersytetu Mikołaja Kopernika, Toruń)

evidently felt to be of secondary importance in comparison with the greater authority (*auctoritas*) of the Latin source-text.

In a second manuscript—Toruń, Biblioteka Uniwersytetu Mikołaja Kopernika, Rps 40/IV, datable to 1400s, fol. 92vb—*Barlaam und Josaphat* opens with a historiated initial 'A' which features a man holding and pointing to a scroll that gives the title of the work: 'Dis ist das buch barlam.' The bearing and appearance of the figure (seated; bearded; wearing a cap and gown) are standard for an author portrait, and indicate that this is a man of wisdom and authority. Again we are faced with the problem of establishing the identity of the subject of this miniature. Is it a depiction of the German author introducing his work? Rudolf is certainly a prime candidate, but once more the broader codicological context would seem to suggest a possible, if not probable alternative. *Barlaam und Josaphat* is the second of five religious texts assembled in this manuscript, a collection that was almost certainly made for the lay brotherhood of the Order of the Teutonic Knights.[28] The other texts, including fourteenth-century verse-couplet paraphrases of the Old Testament books of Job (*Hiob*; dated 1338) and Daniel (*Daniel*; c. 1331), and an extract (*Marienlob*) from the *Passional* (c. 1280–1300), reflect the needs of this group of largely uneducated but zealous recipients, who—it must be suspected—were not interested in fine distinctions of authorial responsibility.[29] In the prologue of *Hiob* that opens the manuscript, for example, an utterly orthodox and basic explanation of biblical authorship is offered by the poet:

> Gnuc ist der bucher unde vil.
> Der zal ich hy geswigen wil
> Und wil mit Job begrifen mich,
> Durch des munt Got sitelich
> Uns hat gesprochen und gelart [. . .] (219–23)

(There are many and plenty enough of these books [of the Bible]. I shall refrain from telling you their number, and shall [instead] get to grips with Job through whose mouth God has spoken purely and taught us [. . .])

The divine Author speaks through the human author of the biblical text, in this case Job, and the role of the anonymous vernacular poet

---

[28] Ott, 'Barlaam Ikonographie', 368.

[29] For more on the literature of the Teutonic Order see Hans-Georg Richert, 'Die Literatur des Deutschen Ritterordens', in *Europäisches Spätmittelalter*, ed. Willi Erzgräber, Wiesbaden 1978 (Neues Handbuch der Literaturwissenschaft 8), 275–86.

is relatively insignificant. Consequently, the question of authorial identity relates only to the saintly individuals who lend their names to the sacred texts.[30] For readers and viewers of the manuscript this passage may well have acted as a key to the pictorial depiction of authorship that follows in both *Barlaam und Josaphat*, and the third text in the collection, *Daniel*, which also contains a historiated opening initial 'A' (fol. 187vb) with an almost identical authorial figure.[31] Given that in the prologue of *Hiob* it is the authorship of Job himself that is emphasized, it seems likely that Daniel would have subsequently been understood as the subject of the miniature in *Daniel*. Similarly, if this principle lay behind the illustration in *Barlaam und Josaphat*, then Rudolf von Ems's authorship would have been relegated in favour of the authority of his saintly protagonist, and it is Barlaam, not Rudolf, who is pictured in the manuscript.

Let us now return to the presentation of authorship within Rudolf's text itself. A number of the key themes of the prologue such as the work's prehistory and the activity of the vernacular poet are reconsidered in the epilogue. The Greek text translated by John of Damascus is now revealed to be a transcription of eye-witness reports (16022–8) composed at the behest of Josaphat's successor (16036–47). Rudolf affirms the necessity of the Latin version in view of the decline in Greek learning, before describing his relationship with the Cistercian abbot Wido von Kappel, the mediator of the (Latin) source, as one of 'counsel'.[32] Similarly, the didactic purpose of the vernacular work is portrayed at greater length here with regard to the spiritually improving nature of the tale as well as its truth (16075–104), whereby Rudolf's authorial activity is characterized by means of the role of *compilator*.[33]

---

[30] 'Got wolde offenbaren sich | In den buchern der heiligen schrift, | Der icliches besunder trift | Sinen sin, den Got uns sayt | Durch des munt gar unverdayt | Nach dem man daz buch benennit' (202–7).

[31] For a reproduction of this initial see 'Bibelerzählung', *KDIHM* 2 (1996), 224, plate 110; see also Hübner (ed.), *Daniel*, pp. VIIIf. For evidence to suggest that *Hiob* opened with such an initial as well see Karsten (ed.), *Hiob*, pp. XXIVf. The historiated initial 'A' (!) at the start of the *Marienlob* (fol. 237^r) depicts Mary with a baby Jesus, not an authorial figure; see Hans-Georg Richert, *Wege und Formen der Passionalüberlieferung*, Tübingen 1978 (Hermaea Germanistische Forschungen NF 40), 78.

[32] 'ich nam daz redelîche leben | von Zitels ze râtgeben, | ob ich ez solde tihten | und in tiusche berihten | ûf bezzerunge oder niht' (16059–63).

[33] Bonaventure's definition of the activity of the *compilator* fits well here ('Aliquis scribit aliena, addendo, sed non de suo; et iste *compilator* dicitur'); see Chapter 1 section 1.

zuo der gewaeren wârheit
hân ich anders niht geleit
wan des ich geschriben vant. (16803ff.)

(To the authentic truth I have added nothing other than material that I found in written sources.)

The devout character of this assembly of authoritative material is such, it is stressed, that no member of the audience can reject it with impunity (16105–28); the text is not about knighthood or love ('diz maere ist niht von ritterschaft, | noch von minnen' 16105f.) but is instead antagonistic to all that is worldly ('der welte widerstrît' 16110).

The epilogue enters its final phase with the poet expressing his desire to continue to honour the promise made at the conclusion of *Der guote Gêrhart*:

ich hâte mich vermezzen ê,
dô ich daz maere enbarte
von dem guoten Gêrharte,
haet ich mich dran versûmet iht,
daz lîhte tumbem man geschiht,
daz ich ze buoze wolde stân,
ob mir würde kunt getân
ein ander maere: dêst geschehen.
nû kan ich des niht verjehen,
ob ich hân iht gebezzert mich:
des weiz ich niht. noch wil ich
mit dirre buoze mich bewarn,
mîn sprechen an ein anderz sparn,
swes ich mich hie versûmet hân. (16130–43)

(Previously I dared to suggest, when I had disclosed the story of Good Gerhard, that if I had failed in it in any way—which a stupid man might easily do—that I wanted to make recompense if another tale were made known to me: that has happened. Now I cannot tell whether I have improved: I have no idea. [Thus] I wish to continue with this penance and save my storytelling for another tale to make up for my failings here.)

This is a clever ploy, for it allows Rudolf to solicit for another commission whilst maintaining a semblance of humility. These lines also represent the first major piece of evidence of Rudolf's sense of himself as an author of a body of works, which is an aspect of his self-presentation that assumes a rather more elaborate form in two

of his later texts. The idiom of self-denigration is subsequently combined with a plea for the audience to intercede on the poet's behalf
(16144–50). Significantly, however, this closing statement of shared
hope and belief is intensified by a direct address of Christ, into
which an acrostic of the author's name is embedded:

> **R**einer Krist, nû loese mich
> **V**on mînen sünden, in den ich
> **O**fte sunte wider dich.
> **D**în güete ist sô genaedeclich,
> **O**b alle zungen vlizzen sich
> **L**êren dîner verte strich,
> **F**ür wâr waer in daz zwîvellich.
> Krist, herre got, durch dînen tôt,
> in den dîn menscheit sich bôt,
> hilf uns, daz wir von schame rôt
> vor dir iht stên und uns der sôt
> der helle iht slinde in wernder nôt!
> des helf uns daz lebende brôt
> Alphâ et Ô, künec Sâbâôt. (16151–64)

(Most perfect Christ, now free me from the sins which I have often
committed against You. Your goodness is so merciful that if all tongues
were to strive to teach the extent of Your movements, truly that would be
a desperate task even for them. Christ, Lord God, for the sake of Your
death, the self-sacrifice of Your human nature, help us so that we do not
stand red with shame before You, and that the seething mire of Hell does
not engulf us in everlasting suffering. May the bread of life aid us in this,
Alpha and Omega, Lord of Sabaoth.)

With this prayer the text has come full circle. There is a symmetry
to the way the expressions of religious devotion in the prologue and
epilogue bracket the main narrative, as signalled by the repetition
of the invocation 'Alphâ et Ô, künec Sâbâôt' in the first and last
lines of the whole work. The use of two blocks of continuous
rhyme (16151–7; 16158–64) divides the concluding appeal into two
distinct seven-line prayers, concerned respectively with the salvation
of the poet as an individual and—together with the audience—
as a member of a wider religious community.[34] The inclusion of
the authorial name in the first of these prayers reflects the
poet's awareness of the text as a material object, and this actually
found codicological resonance in the form of red lettering in one

---

[34] Thelen, *Dichtergebet*, 526f.

later thirteenth-century manuscript (Munich, BSB, Cgm 5249/21, *c.* 1275–1300).[35] In terms of literary function this instance of authorial self-presentation invites the reader to regard Rudolf as the author of a book, whilst also forming part of a devotional act: the poet identifies himself (for posterity) so that reading recipients of the text know for whom they should pray. The acrostic inextricably associates the voice of the named supplicant with the prayer, emphasizing the extent to which the author is to be identified with the pious sentiments expressed.[36]

In spite of the high degree of correspondence between the religious content of this saint's life and the nature of the authorial self-presentation in its prologue and epilogue, not every treatment of the theme of authorship in the work is indebted to such a strategy. The main body of the narrative, namely, features a lengthy excursus (11735–870) in which the author plays out a quite different, more secular role.[37] The excursus in question is stylized as an impromptu authorial response to a cynical episode in the text (11622–725) in which Theodas, the magician, uses an anecdote to persuade Josaphat's father that his son will give up his Christian beliefs if he is surrounded by beautiful women:

A king has his son brought up in darkness for the first ten years of his life. On seeing the world and the royal court for the first time he demands to know the name for the beautiful women there. A mischievous courtier tells the boy that they are the devil ('daz wîp der tiuvel waere genant' 11721). The boy reports back to his father later that nothing pleased him more than the devil himself.

The poet, it appears, is unable to let this episode pass without comment, and in raising objections of his own to the content of the story material he effectively pre-empts the adverse reactions of his envisaged audience:

> Nû lât mich sunder swaere
> mit urloube ûz dem maere

---

[35] Schneider, *(Cgm 5249/1–79)*, 43f.

[36] For further discussion of acrostics in the Middle Ages see Chapter 1 section II.

[37] Von Ertzdorff, *Untersuchungen*, 214f., 322 note 45; Rüdiger Schnell, *Rudolf von Ems: Studien zur inneren Einheit seines Gesamtwerkes*, Berne 1969 (Basler Studien zur deutschen Sprache und Literatur 41), 106–11; Ulrich Wyss, 'Rudolfs von Ems "Barlaam und Josaphat" zwischen Legende und Roman', in *Probleme mittelhochdeutscher Erzählformen*, edd. Ganz/Schröder, 214–38, esp. 229f.

ein wênic kêren, des ger ich,
wan es mîn muot betwinget mich. (11735–8)

(Now give me leave to deviate from this tale for a moment, as is my desire,
for I feel compelled to do so.)

Once again the first-person perspective provides a basis for the
presentation of authorship as the tense in the passage subsequently
changes from the 'here and now' to an unspecified time in the past
(11739–820): we are told that when the poet read this section of his
source he could only think of the courtly virtues of womankind,[38]
and that after consulting his own heart (11752–807) he was even more
forthcoming in his praise of women (11809–20). The time spheres
then merge as the glorification of women continues in the present,
combined with the poet's protestations of his inability to do this
theme justice (11821–40). The excursus culminates in the reiteration
of Rudolf's willingness to defend and extol women in the hope of
some recompense from them (11841–70), all addressed directly to the
female sex at large in the second person singular ('Reiner name, nû
wizzest daz' 11841).

Authorship becomes an explicit theme in the excursus when the
poet enters into the mock dialogue with his heart:

mîn herze vrâget ich alsô:
'wes wildû von wîben mir
helfen jehen, des volge ich dir.'
mîn herze ein teil von zorne sprach:
'Ruodolf, mir ist ungemach,
ob dû von in iht anders gihst,
wan des dû dich von in versihst:[. . .]' (11752–8)

(I asked my heart in this way: 'Whatever you wish to help me say about
women, I will take your lead in it.' My heart spoke partly in anger: 'Rudolf,
I find it distressing if you say anything about them, other than that which
you yourself hope for from them [. . .]')

Digressions in the form of a dialogue between the author and a
fictional interlocutor are in fact widespread in German narratives
of the late twelfth and thirteenth centuries. Examples range from
dramatized exchanges with a member of the audience, to dialogues

---

[38] 'dô ich an disem maere las, | daz dort durch schimph gesprochen was, | [. . .] |
dô gedâhte ich dar an, | wie lebendes mannes vreuden lîp | an vreuden tiurent werdiu
wîp, | und nam in mîne sinne | die gêrten wîbes minne | wie diu mit werder güete, |
mit lobe, mit hôhgemüete | tuot êre gerndez herze vrô' (11739f., 11744–51).

with personifications such as 'Lady Minne' and 'Lady Adventure', or even the poet's mind.[39] Notwithstanding the obvious relation of a number of these passages to Latin dialogue and debate literature, in vernacular tradition this kind of construction gained a momentum of its own as a model of authorial self-presentation, serving as another means of securing the inscription of the author's name within the work itself—this time from a second-person perspective.[40]

In *Barlaam und Josaphat* the dialogue between the named author and his heart may also be read as a dramatic realization of the standard psychological motif of the 'heart's advice'.[41] Notably, this exchange draws heavily on the idiom of the love lyric. The poet is hereby cast in the role of a miserable lover, reluctant to add to his initial praise of women and to comply with his heart because of previous unhappy experiences at their hands.[42] Only when the heart argues that this is an opportune moment to earn the favour of courtly ladies, reminding the author of one lady in particular (11802f.), is the emphatic praise of women resumed (11809–70). Thus, in terms of the excursus as a whole the dialogue lends Rudolf's courtly defence of the female sex a mock profile of individuality. The values with which authorship is associated in this passage contrast sharply with those articulated in the prologue and epilogue of the work. Rudolf is evidently conscious of the disparity (11843ff., 11851ff.), as were several subsequent scribes,[43] yet this does not

[39] Audience: *Erec* 7106–11, 7493–525, 7826–33, 9169ff.; *Iwein* 7027–7; Eilhart von Oberg, *Tristrant* 7628–44; Reinbot von Durne, *Der heilige Georg* 699, 2855–900, 4781–825. 'Frau Minne': *Iwein* 2971–3024. 'Frau Aventiure': *Parzival* 433,1–434,10. Author's mind: *Wigalois* 5753–81. Author's pen: Thomasin von Zerklaere's *Der welsche Gast* (12223–351).

[40] Cf. *Erec* 7493 ('"nû swîc, lieber Hartman [. . .]"'), 9169 ('"geselle Hartman, nû sage [. . .]"'); *Iwein* 2974 ('sî sprach "sage an, Hartman [. . .]"'), 2982 ('"dune hâst niht wâr, Hartman"'), 7027 ('"Ich waene, vriunt Hartman [. . .]"'); *Wigalois* 5755 ('"sag an, Wirnt, ist daz wâr [. . .]"'); *Der heilige Georg* 699 ('"wer wîzt dirz denne, Reinbot?"'), 2857f. ('"ey, guote, sage sunder spot | von Durne lieber Reinbot [. . .]"'), 4781f. ('"ey, guote, sage sô dir got | von Durne lieber Reinbot [. . .]"'). The few authorial namings that occur in the German lyric of this period often form part of comparable dialogues, as in the songs of Walther von der Vogelweide: 'Der hof ze Wiene sprach ze mir: | "Walther, ich solte lieben dir [. . .]"' (L. 24,33f.); '"Walther, dû zürnest âne nôt [. . .]"' (L. 100,33); '"Hoerâ Walther, wie ez mir stât, | mîn trûtgeselle von der Vogelweide"' (L. 119,11f.).

[41] Further examples of dialogue between poet and heart are found in the 'Minnerede'; see Ingeborg Glier, *Artes amandi: Untersuchung zu Geschichte, Überlieferung und Typologie der deutschen Minnereden*, Munich 1971 (MTU 34), 402–6.

[42] 'Sus antwurt ich dem herzen mîn: | "ich wolte dir der lêre dîn | gerne helfen unde jehen: | waer mir von in sô wol geschehen, | daz dû getörstest jehen mir, | daz mir ofter unde ouch dir | waer geschehen baz von in, [. . .]"' (11769–75).

[43] It would appear that the excursus is not included in five of the work's 'complete' manuscripts; see Pfeiffer (ed.), *Barlaam und Josaphat*, 449.

impinge on his worldly self-presentation where the immediate narrative context demands it. The presentation of authorship in *Barlaam und Josaphat* in its entirety is revealed to be more ambivalent than first seemed likely, embracing multiplicity even if this involves a degree of contradiction.

III. *WILLEHALM VON ORLENS*

The technical diversity of Rudolf's statements of authorship is most evident in his third complete work, the romance *Willehalm von Orlens*.[44] Influenced by Hartmann, Wolfram, and Gottfried in the usage of specific features, Rudolf lends his authorship a striking profile in this text through the sheer number and variety of the devices assembled. This variety is also matched by a new insistency, for *Willehalm von Orlens* is subdivided into five book-like sections with their own prologues, which creates a regular space for the explicit formulation of the themes of the work as well as the expression of its authorship. Scholars often call these subsections 'books' although Rudolf fails to designate them as such in the actual text.[45]

Each of the five sections or books features an opening acrostic. Rudolf stamps his authorship on *Willehalm von Orlens* from the start by means of a double acrostic in the first lines of the first prologue:

> **R**ainer tugende wiser rat
> **V**on edeles herzen lere gat.
> **O**b alles lobes werdekait
> **D**en pris dú zuht allaine trait.
> **Ö**ch mûs ain man, swas er getût,
> **L**ob unde lobeliches gût
> **F**lorieren unde stâtin
> **I**n gerndes herzen râtin,

---

[44] The text is preserved in nineteen 'complete' manuscripts and twenty-nine fragments; see Eberhard Nellmann, '"Wilhelm von Orlens"-Handschriften', in *Festschrift Walter Haug und Burghart Wachinger*, edd. Johannes Janota *et al.*, 2 vols., Tübingen 1992, ii. 565–87; Schneider, *(Cgm 5249/1–79)*, 26f.

[45] See Junk (ed.), *Willehalm von Orlens*, p. XLII; Walter Lenschen, *Gliederungsmittel und ihre erzählerischen Funktionen im 'Willehalm von Orlens' des Rudolf von Ems*, Göttingen 1967 (Palaestra 250), 108–47; Brackert, *Dichtung und Geschichte*, 13–18; Christoph Gerhardt, 'Willehalm von Orlens: Studien zum Eingang und Schluß der strophischen Bearbeitung aus dem Jahre 1522', *WW* 35 (1985), 196–230, esp. 198f. These subsections were highlighted in the subsequent manuscript tradition by means of large initials and headings; see Nellmann, '"Wilhelm von Orlens"-Handschriften', Nos. 1, 3, 10.

Ob er an ime der welte pris
Hôhin wil unde werden wis.
Ạlle die getrúwe sint
Nemmet man der eren kint.
Nihtes nút getugenden kan
Einen eregernden man
So wol so reht beschaidenhait,
Dú ảlles lobes crone trait. (1–16)

(The wise advice of perfect virtue comes from the teaching of a noble heart. Decorum alone carries the prize of worthiness above all acclaim. Furthermore, whatever a man does, he should decorate and consolidate praise and laudable good in the directives of an eager heart, if he wants to increase his excellence in the eyes of the world and become wise. All who are faithful are called the children of honour. Nothing can make a man who is eager for honour virtuous so well as that true modesty which wins the crown of all praise.)

The covert invitation to readers to view RVODOLF as the author of the book accompanies a eulogy of courtly virtues ('zuht' 4; 'beschaidenhait' 15), a programmatic statement of the ethos of the following text in which not only *minne* is exemplified but every aspect of the ceremony and etiquette of courtly society is displayed. That the name of another individual (IOHANNES)—whose role is eventually specified in the epilogue—follows, may be seen to hark back to Gottfried's acrostic in the prologue to *Tristan* (GDIETERICH),[46] and suggests that Rudolf is making a bid to associate the broader circumstances of the text's production with its thematic content.

In contrast to *Barlaam und Josaphat* the exordial position of the acrostic privileges the poet's claims. The assertiveness underlying this authorial self-presentation was realized visually in at least two subsequent codices through the inclusion of an author portrait: Munich, BSB, Cgm 63, *c.* 1270–80, fol. 1ʳ; Heidelberg, UB, cod. Pal. germ. 323, *c.* 1420, fol. 3ʳ.[47] This time there seems little doubt that these pictures refer to Rudolf. Both are based on the traditional iconographic model of the author dictating to a scribe,[48] and in both the

---

[46] Burghart Wachinger, 'Zur Rezeption Gottfrieds von Straßburg im 13. Jahrhundert', in *Deutsche Literatur des späten Mittelalters: Hamburger Colloquium 1973*, edd. Wolfgang Harms/L. Peter Johnson, Berlin 1975 (Publications of the Institute of Germanic Studies University of London 22), 56–82, esp. 67f.

[47] Maria-Magdalena Hartong, *Willehalm von Orlens und seine Illustrationen*, Diss. Cologne 1938, pp. 34, 90, 97.

[48] See also Chapter I section I.

3. Rudolf von Ems, *Willehalm von Orlens* (The author dictating to a scribe) (reproduced by permission of the Bayerische Staatsbibliothek, Munich)

4. Rudolf von Ems, *Willehalm von Orlens* (The author dictating to a scribe) (reproduced by permission of the Universitätsbibliothek, Heidelberg)

wisdom and pre-eminence of the author are conveyed by his appearance (beard; cap) and physical location (under an ornate archway [Cgm 63]; on a throne [Cpg 323]). The author portrait in the Munich manuscript is famous as being the first extant example of such a picture for a German vernacular poet,[49] and it is feasible that the Heidelberg picture derives from the earlier codex. However, the Heidelberg manuscript is altogether more successful in terms of its accommodation of Rudolf's acrostic. The layout of the page is arranged in such a way that picture and text occupy equal space, whilst the transcription of the work in a single column enables the scribe to set out the lines as the author intended, to the right of the massive initial 'R'. The marking of the second letter of the first word (the 'e' of 'Reiner') is simply a function of the decorative principle of colouring the beginning of every line. That the acrostic has in fact been recognized by those involved in the production of the manuscript is indicated by the right-hand tendril of the 'R' that cordons off the author's name in lines 1–7. In Cgm 63, on the other hand, the picture overwhelms the literary text, and the chopping of the lines to the right of the 'R' disturbs and conceals the sequence of first letters as planned by the author. Thus, although both of these codices offer evidence of Rudolf's enduring status as an authoritative vernacular writer in the later Middle Ages, they feature two different types of interaction between primary and secondary (or codicological) devices for presenting authorship: the complementary relationship between picture and text in Cpg 323 contrasts sharply with the obstruction of authorial, literary strategy in Cgm 63.

The acrostic is just one aspect of the first prologue in *Willehalm von Orlens*. The enumeration of courtly virtues in lines 1–16 is followed in the rest of the passage (17–132) by the construction of a storytelling situation in which the narrator is vividly depicted as standing before an audience:

> Wis ich nu ob ieman her
> Dar uf wâr komen das er

---

[49] Frühmorgen-Voss, *Text und Illustration*, 18; Wachinger, 'Autorschaft und Überlieferung', 9. For an alternative interpretation see Erika Weigele-Ismael, *Rudolf von Ems: 'Wilhelm von Orlens'. Studien zur Ausstattung und zur Ikonographie einer illustrierten deutschen Epenhandschrift des 13. Jahrhunderts am Beispiel des Cgm 63 der Bayerischen Staatsbibliothek München*, Frankfurt a. M. 1997 (Europäische Hochschulschriften Reihe 28: Kunstgeschichte 285), 42, 157f.

Hie sâze mit spotlichen sitten,
Den wolt ich vil gerne bitten
Das er gerûchte gan hin dan:[. . .] (17–21)

(If I knew now that someone had come in order to sit here and be insulting,
I would urge him to be so good as to leave [. . .])

The issue of courtliness is now addressed with respect to the reception of the work: namely, appropriate and inappropriate audience
behaviour and the oppression suffered by the storyteller if even one
unwilling listener is present ('Als ob in druhte faste | Ain berk mit
sinem laste' 27f.). The subsequent promise of a tale of chivalry and
romance results in the reiteration of the suitability of this text for
noble recipients whatever their predilections (89–123). In terms of
the presentation of authorship, this depiction, or 'vignette',[50] of
public performance complements the earlier acrostic by encouraging
an identification of the author with the narrator through certain
first-person statements of intent:

Da von ist mines herzen rat
Das ich ârbâte mine kunst
Durch aller werder lûten gunst,
Ob ich die wol bejagen mag. (124–7)

(For this reason my heart advises me to spare no effort with my art to
capture, if I can, the favour of all worthy people.)

The poet's assurance of his willingness to exert himself emphasizes
the virtue and nobility of the audience. The euphemistic phrase
'mine kunst' (125), which may be understood to refer to the activity
of literary composition, thereby functions as a component of a
rhetorical strategy of insinuation.[51] This particular mode of authorial self-presentation continues throughout the entire text and is at
times comparable to the internal storytelling situations created
by Wolfram in *Parzival* and *Willehalm*.[52] It is especially prominent
in the openings to Books 3 and 4. In the third prologue a lengthy
self-deprecatory introduction (5595–636) is underpinned by another

---

[50] Green, 'Rudolf von Ems', 176.
[51] Franz Finster, *Zur Theorie und Technik mittelalterlicher Prologe: Eine Untersuchung zu den Alexander- und Willehalmprologen Rudolfs von Ems*, Diss. Bochum 1971, pp. 266–86. Cf. also lines 1011–15.
[52] See also Chapter I section II.

expression of the poet's desire to gain the favour of his audience.[53] The correspondence between the ethos of the work and its ideal recipients is maintained in the fourth, which also includes a burlesque of inappropriate audience behaviour (9796–852).[54] As in the first prologue, the theme of authorship is maintained throughout all of this by expressions such as 'min årebait | Mit getihte' (5601f.) and 'min getihte' (5646) and by the pledge to continue despite doubts regarding courtly society at large.[55]

Presentation of authorship from the first-person narratorial perspective is enhanced in the prologues of Books 2 and 5 by the integration of Wolfram's structure of a fictional dialogue with Lady Adventure ('Frau Aventiure').[56] In the second prologue (2143–334), which is the more substantial of the two, the dialogue is used as a framework for several other devices. The first lines draw on the distinctive opening of Wirnt von Grafenberg's *Wigalois*,[57] as Lady Adventure flatters the reader(s) of the work first ('"Wer hat mich gûter her gelesen?[. . .]"' 2143) before speaking to the author:

> '[. . .] Rŭdolf, nu sprich du mich
> Und sage der maere mere von mir,
> An den bin ich givolgic dir
> Nach der gewåren warhait
> Die dú walsh von mir sait!'—
> 'Vrŏ Aventure, sit ir das?'—
> 'Ja'—'so mohtet ir wol baz
> Sin an wiser lúte komin [. . .]' (2164–71)

('[. . .] Rudolf, give voice to me now and relate more of my stories, in which

---

[53] 'Ie doch wil ich den werden man | Prŭeven so ich beste kan, | Durch werder lúte werden gunst | Dar nach ich mit miner kunst | Dienen unde werben wil | Unz uf mines endes zil. | Wirt mir des iendert danc gesait, | So libet mir die arebait; | Das mohte doch vil wol geschehen, | Wan min getihte wirt gesehen | Und vil lihte etteswa | Gelesen da oder da | Es mir bejagt und miner kunst | Etteliche werde gunst | Der ich niht wandels wolte han' (5637–51).

[54] 'Ist aber das si des gedagent | Und von ir kurzewile sagent, | Si sprechent "ahie, wel ain win! | Wir mŭsent alle trunken sin | Die wile wir sasent da bi! | Mich rúwent ser mine dri | Die ich verlos mit toppel da!" | So si das redent, so hebent si sa | Von irn mŭtran úber al | Ain schelten, ain unmanlich schal' (9819–28).

[55] 'Nu hant si so gar begeben | Kurzewil und hŏsches leben | Das ich es ŏfte wird unvro | Und das ich gedenke also | "La varn din getihte, | Wan hat es nu ze nihte!"' (9865–70).

[56] Dialogues with 'Frau Aventiure' continued to be associated with Wolfram's authorship; see Ragotzky, *Wolfram-Rezeption*, 137ff.

[57] *Wigalois*: 'Wer hât mich guoter ûf getân?' (1). For more on this passage see Chapter 1 section III.

I will follow you according to the veritable truth as the French tells of me!'—'Lady Adventure, is that you?'—'Yes'—'Well, you might have been better off with a wiser person [. . .]')

Lady Adventure's first utterance secures a further record of the name of the author and the nature of his activity, the reworking of a French source, readdressing these fundamental aspects of authorship from an alternative, second-person perspective. The dynamics of the exchange are then shaped in such a way as to include an extensive literary excursus (2172–300), another recognizable model of authorial self-presentation, which is derived this time from Gottfried von Strassburg. Rudolf's adumbration of German narratives from Heinrich von Veldeke to Ulrich von Türheim locates the composition (and reception) of *Willehalm von Orlens* in the context of an established vernacular literary tradition.[58] Towards the end of this catalogue the interjections of 'Frau Aventiure' (2252–5, 2271–8, 2284–9, 2297–300) lend structural definition to the poet's reflections, highlighting Ulrich von Türheim, 'maister Hesse', and various 'critics' including 'min frúnt Vasolt' as members of a narrower contemporary literary circle.[59]

In like manner, the eventual capitulation to 'Frau Aventiure' in the last phase of this passage provides the basis for a discussion of how the author composed his work to commission for a named patron:

> 'Vro Aventúre, so wil ich
> Mit iu gerne arbaiten mich,
> Das ir mit gůetlichen sitten
> Gerůchent sine vrŏwen bitten
> Das si dur wibes gůte
> Im hŏhe sin gemůte
> Der er mit stătem můte,
> Mit libe und ŏch mit gůte
> Wil iemer dienen siniu zil,
> Durch den ich úch tihtin wil,[. . .]
> Das ist der werde schenke,
> Der hoh gemůte Cůnrat
> Von Winterstetten, der mich hat
> Gebetten durch den willen sin

---

[58] For isolated references to German authors in the course of the narrative cf. 4390–8 (Ulrich von Türheim), 4468–71 (Walther von der Vogelweide), 7828–36 (Wolfram).

[59] Brackert, *Dichtung und Geschichte*, 29–33. Cf. also lines 5595–605.

Das ich durch in die sinne min
Árbaite und úch tihte
In rehter rime rihte.[. . .]' (2301–10, 2318–24)

('Lady Adventure, I will gladly take great pains with you to get you to be
so courteous as to ask a mistress—in the name of womanly goodness—to
raise the spirits of the man on whose account I want to compose you. He
desires to serve her constantly with both body and kind spirit for the rest
of his days [. . .]. That is the noble cupbearer Konrad von Winterstetten
who asked me to apply my mind on his account and for his sake, to compose
and shape you in proper verse.[. . .]')

Rudolf's authorship is shown to be dependent ('Durch den' 2310,
'durch den willen sin' 2321, 'durch in' 2322) on an individual of
impeccable courtliness.[60] The patron is presented as a lover, and the
author's playful advocation of his love service creates an associative
link between courtly love and the actual circumstances of production of the text.[61] These lines would appear to reflect the atmosphere
of self-stylized gallantry in which vernacular narrative literature was
fostered at the Hohenstaufen court under the lead of Konrad von
Winterstetten,[62] for the same motif is to be found in connexion with
the latter's patronage of another work: Ulrich von Türheim's
Tristan.[63] In *Willehalm von Orlens* special interest in the subject of *minne*
is conspicuously signalled in several further digressions (4456–87,
9661–734, 11783–6), before finally being brought to bear on the
theme of authorship again in the epilogue.

The fictional dialogue between the author and 'Frau Aventiure'
is resumed in the prologue to the fifth book (12205–72). Here the
exchange is motivated by the concern of first the author and

---

[60] Cf. also 2325–31.

[61] A comparable idiom is used to describe the reception of the work in the first utter-
ance of 'Frau Aventiure': '"**W**er hat mich gûter her gelesen? | **I**st es ieman gewesen |
Lebende in solicher wise, | **L**ob er mich dez mich prise | **E**s sig man oder wip, | **H**ab
er so getrúwen lip, | **A**ne válsche sol er mich | **L**ieben, das ist frúntlich, | **M**it sûzer
sinne stúre: | [. . .]"' (2143–51).

[62] For more on the socio-historical context of this work see Chapter 1 section III.

[63] *Tristan*: 'des hât mit vlîze mich gebeten | Kuonrât der schenke von Winterstetten, |
daz ichz im ze liebe tuo. | herze und sin dâ râtent zuo, | daz ich im dran gediene sô,
| daz er mînes dienestes werde vrô | unde im genâde von ir geschehe, | der sîn herze
ze vrouwe jehe' (25–32); 'ich hân ez durh einen man getân, | der ist wol aller êren wert.
| sîn herze hôhes prîses gert: | er denket spâte unde vruo | niuwan wie er wol getuo |
und sich geliebe der werlte. | got gebiet ir, daz im gelte, | der er vil gedienet hât. | sîn
lebn an ir gnâden stât' (3662–70). See also Jan-Dirk Müller, 'Zu einigen Problemen des
Konzepts "Literarische Interessenbildung"', in *Literarische Interessenbildung*, ed. Heinzle,
365–84, esp. 366–72.

then 'Frau Aventiure' to end the lovers' suffering as soon as possible. The exhortations of the latter encompass familiar allusions to patron and audience,[64] which follow the almost obligatory naming of the poet:

> 'Rŭdolf, nu waist du wol, ich han
> Disiu mare an dich gelan
> Und han des gar bewarot dich
> Wie du solt berihten mich.' (12241–4)

('Rudolf, you know full well that I have entrusted these stories to you and have prepared you for how you should shape me.')

With this passage the author's name features in three of the five prologues, effectively punctuating the text with a record of the identity of its originator. If the first-person narratorial articulation in the third and fourth prologues is also taken into account, a strategy of authorial self-presentation becomes apparent for *Willehalm von Orlens*, which exploits the sequence of five prologues repeatedly to draw the attention of readers and listeners to the circumstances of production of the work. This strategy culminates in the epilogue (15601–89) where reflections on the mediation of the French source form a background to the final description of authorship. The second individual named in the double acrostic of the first prologue (IOHANNES) is now identified fully ('Von Ravenspurg Johannes' 15607) and revealed as the supplier of the story.[65] Similar to the depiction of Konrad von Winterstetten in the second prologue, he too is shown to be motivated in his participation in the literary enterprise by the love of a lady.[66] The figure of the German author is subsequently reintroduced:

> Von dem wart dis mảre
> Wie es geschehen wảre,

---

[64] '"[. . .] | Du tihtest mich durch ainen man | Der wol nach eren werben kan, | Durch ảllú wip dar zŭ. | Nu sage (se dir Got, daz tŭ) | Allen gŭten lúten hie | Wie es dem rainen man ergie. | [. . .]"' (12259–64).

[65] 'Diu getat des werden mannes | Wart im an walschen bŭchen kunt, | Und brahte si do sa ze stunt | Mit im her in thiusche lant, | Alse er si geschriben vant' (15608–12).

[66] 'Durch siner vrŏwen werden grŭz, | Der er wil und dienen mŭz, | Ob das bŭch iender kảme, | Daz si ez von im vernảme, | Ob si ze lange stunde | Dar an gesenftern kunde, | Das ŏch si im den sinen pin | Senfterte und den kumber sin' (15617–24). Konrad von Winterstetten's patronage is described in these terms again towards the end of the epilogue (15649–65).

Ainem knappen erkant,
Der ist Rŭdolf genant,
Ain dienest man ze Muntfort,
Der hat es braht unz an das ort,
Der ŏch das bŭch getihtet hat
Wie durch únsers schefares rat
Der gŭte Gerhart lôste
Von grossem untroste
Ain edel kumberhafte diet,
Und der das mâre beschiet
Wie diu sûze Gottes kraft
Bekerte von der haidenschaft
Den gŭten Josofaten,
Wie im das kunde raten
Barlames wiser munt:[. . .] (15625–41)

(He [Johannes von Ravensburg] made this story and what had happened
known to a squire called Rudolf, a ministerial of Montfort, who completed
it; this is the man who also composed the book about how, through the
advice of our Creator, good Gerhard released a group of distressed
noblemen from great despair; and who gave expression to the tale of how
God's sweet strength converted virtuous Josaphat from heathendom, of how
Barlaam's wise mouth issued that advice [. . .])

For the first time in the work Rudolf describes his position within
a socio-political hierarchy as a ministerial, indicating his relative
lowliness by referring to himself simultaneously as a servant or
squire. His identity is further defined through a statement of the
other literary works to his name. These elements establish a balanced
platform for the articulation of authorship in the rest of the epilogue,
as Rudolf's subordination to such aristocratic personages as
Johannes von Ravensburg and Konrad von Winterstetten is compensated for by his profile as author of an oeuvre: an emphatic model
of authorial self-presentation used elsewhere by both Chrétien de
Troyes,[67] and Wolfram von Eschenbach.[68] The idea of an authorial
corpus is intimated in the epilogue of *Barlaam und Josaphat* and also
finds expression in Rudolf's *Alexander* (see section IV below); in

[67] 'Cil qui fist d'Erec et d'Enide, | Et les comandemanz d'Ovide | Et l'art d'amors
an romans mist, | Et le mors de l'espaule fist, | Del roi Marc et d'Ysalt la blonde, | Et
de la hupe et de l'aronde | Et del rossignol la muance, | Un novel conte rancomance'
(*Cligés* 1–8).

[68] 'ich, Wolfram von Eschenbach, | swaz ich von Parzivâl gesprach, | des sîn âven-
tiure mich wîste, | etslîch man daz prîste—| ir was ouch vil, die'z smaehten | unde baz
ir rede waehten' (*Willehalm* 4,19–24).

Willehalm von Orlens the tone of self-deprecation is absent and the model openly asserts the author's literary credentials.

The description and naming of the author in the third person is unique to this passage in the text, which would again appear to function as a kind of internal literary colophon. We have already had occasion to observe this practice with reference to Hartmann and the conclusion to Rudolf's own *Der guote Gêrhart*. However, an unparalleled step is taken in *Willehalm von Orlens*, as reference to the author in the third person is hereafter made to converge explicitly with the first-person narratorial perspective (which then continues to the end of the epilogue):

> Der knappe ich bin. do mir wart kunt
> Disiu aventúre,
> Nach miner sinne stúre
> Geluste des von herzen mich
> Durch werder lúten gunst, das ich
> Mine kunst versúchte dran,
> Als ich ir von erst began. (15642–8)

(I am that squire. When I first became acquainted with these tales of adventure, taking my senses as a guide, I had the heartfelt desire to apply my art to it for the favour of worthy people, which I did from the beginning.)

The convergence of the third person and the first person at this point can be seen to be symptomatic of Rudolf's strategy of authorial self-presentation for *Willehalm von Orlens* as a whole: namely, the attempt to incorporate references to authorship in the text through a range of devices, involving a variety of complementary perspectives. This is exemplified by the four appearances of the author's name: in the form of an acrostic, in the second person as part of a fictional dialogue, and in a third-person 'colophon'. The only works of the 'Blütezeit' which bear comparison with this aspect of *Willehalm von Orlens* are *Iwein* and *Parzival* with four and three authorial namings respectively. Yet even in these texts there is less structural variety; Hartmann includes one naming in the third person (28) and three in the second person (2974, 2982, 7027), whilst Wolfram restricts himself to first-person naming (114,12; 185,7; 827,13). It is in Rudolf's multifaceted approach to the presentation of authorship in *Willehalm von Orlens*, built up over five prologues and an epilogue, that this work can be viewed as an advance on the texts of his 'classical' predecessors.

IV. *ALEXANDER*

Rudolf is thought to have worked on his fourth text, a life of
Alexander, both before and after the composition of *Willehalm von
Orlens*, but without ever completing it.[69] The text breaks off halfway
through the story after some 21,000 lines.[70] The formal subdivision
of *Alexander* surpasses that of *Willehalm von Orlens*, and clearly owes
something to the Latin source material underlying the second phase
of its composition, namely the *Historiae Alexandri Magni* of Quintus
Curtius Rufus.[71] In *Alexander* the sections are explicitly designated as
'books' and are reflected upon in the text proper, as at the end
of Book 5:

> Daz vünfte buoch hie endet sich
> und ist rehte vollekomn
> als ich die wârheit hân vernomn
> des sehsten ich mit saelden hie
> beginnen wil. nû hoeret wie! (20568–72)

(Here ends the fifth book. It is entirely complete as far as my understanding
of the truth is concerned. I now want to begin the sixth with good fortune.
Now listen how!)

The prominence of the narratorial voice in this context effectively
juxtaposes a key principle of vernacular narrative tradition—as
shaped by Hartmann, Wolfram, and Gottfried—with a concept of
textual organization derived from Latin literary culture.[72] Passages
such as these occur in four of the work's five complete books and
serve to lend them considerably greater definition as individual
units.[73] The self-consciousness exhibited in this subdivision of

---

[69] Carl von Kraus, *Text und Entstehung von Rudolfs Alexander*, Munich 1940 (Sitzungsberichte der Bayerischen Akademie der Wissenschaften. Philosophisch-historische Abteilung Jahrgang 1940:8), 46–91; Roy Wisbey, *Das Alexanderbild Rudolfs von Ems*, Berlin 1966
(Philologische Studien und Quellen 31), 109–26, esp. 112–17; Brackert, *Dichtung und
Geschichte*, 15–23.

[70] *Alexander* is preserved in two illustrated manuscripts of the fifteenth century and in
an earlier fragment containing lines 14389–588; see 'Alexander der Große', *KDIHM* 1
(1986) 102–5.

[71] Wisbey, *Alexanderbild*, 113f.

[72] Palmer, 'Kapitel und Buch', 66f., 70f.

[73] Book 2: 'daz ander buoch sich endet hie. | nû vernemet vürbaz wie | daz dritte
buoch sich hebet an | von dem edelen wîsen man!' (8009–12); Book 3: 'Hie endet sich
daz dritte buoch | von Alexanders getât. | diz buoch alhie geteilet hât | in maneg âven-
tiure sich, | wan die âventiur sint mislich | durch daz nenne ich über al | an disem
buoche solhe zal | als ir mê dan einez sî,—| dem einen wonent gnuoge bî—| und hât

Alexander is also reflected in the presentation of the text's author-ship. Whilst Rudolf draws heavily on Gottfried in this context he surpasses the authorial self-presentation in *Tristan* by exploiting the overtly Latinate structure of his own work. Each of its six extant books opens with a prologue,[74] and Rudolf uses this sequence of passages to project his authorial profile against a variety of back-grounds.

In the prologue to Book 1 (1–106) Rudolf sets out his stall much as he did in the opening of *Willehalm von Orlens*. In a first section of seven quatrains the poet introduces the thematic complex which lies at the heart of his interpretation of the life of Alexander, that is to say the relationship between good fortune (*saelde*) and merit:

> Rîchiu saelde, hôher sin
> daz ist von Gote ein grôz gewin
> den Got alsô besinnet
> daz er saeldè gewinnet. (1–4)

> Ûf hôhe kunst ist ahte niht,
> ist si sunder saelden phliht,
> sô wirt si gar vernichtet,
> ob saelde ir niht zuo phlichtet. (5–8)

(Splendid fortune; high intellect: it is a great gift from God to be blessed with such an intellect that good fortune may be won. Great ability is dis-regarded, if it is not accompanied by good fortune; likewise, it [great ability] is utterly destroyed if good fortune does not lend its support.)

These strophes set the tone for an elaborate discussion of *saelde* which applies in equal measure to human endeavour in general as well as the specific activity of poetic composition.[75] As in *Willehalm von Orlens*, the thematically dense opening lines are given an additional

---

doch niht wan einen namn | von dem werden lobesamn. | Wie er Persîam betwanc, | hebt sich des vierden anevanc' (12910–22); Book 4: 'Daz vierde buoch ist volle komn | und hât ende hie genomn. | welt ir daz vünfte, heb ich an | und spriche sô ich beste kan' (15635–9). Book 1 has no equivalent conclusion, which may be a remnant of the earlier continuous form of the narrative; see Brackert, *Dichtung und Geschichte*, 14, 17f.

[74] See also Gustav Ehrismann, *Studien über Rudolf von Ems: Beiträge zur Geschichte der Rhetorik und Ethik im Mittelalter*, Heidelberg 1919 (Sitzungsberichte der Heidelberger Akademie der Wissenschaften. Philosophisch-historische Klasse 1919:8), 3–43; Finster, *Theorie und Technik*, 117–258.

[75] The poetological function of *saelde* in this work is thoroughly investigated by Haug, *Literaturtheorie*, 299–315, esp. 303–10. See also Brackert, *Dichtung und Geschichte*, 127–40; Wilfried Schouwink, *Fortuna im Alexanderroman Rudolfs von Ems: Studien zum Verhältnis von Fortuna und Virtus bei einem Autor der späten Stauferzeit*, Göppingen 1977 (GAG 212).

dimension through the infusion of a record of the author's identity in the form of an acrostic:

> **R**íchiu saelde, hôher sin [. . .]
> **Û**f hôhe kunst ist ahte niht,[. . .]
> **O**rthabunge rehter kunst [. . .]
> **D**er kunst geleite saelde treit.[. . .]
> **O**fte ergât ouch diu geschiht [. . .]
> **L**obelich guot getihte [. . .]
> **F**lorieret saeldekunst ie kraft,[. . .] (1–25)

The fashioning of the acrostic, the only instance of authorial naming in the text as it stands, out of the first initials of the prologue's quatrains is reminiscent of Gottfried's cryptographic technique in *Tristan*.[76] However, Rudolf's formal emulation of his 'classical' predecessor does not detract from the self-assured character of this strategy of self-naming. Unlike *Tristan*, or the beginning of *Willehalm von Orlens* for that matter, it is the name of the author alone which stands at the head of *Alexander*, unqualified by a reference to anyone else.

For an alert readership this acrostic would have constituted a striking expression of authorship in the vernacular. But as we have already seen in connexion with *Willehalm von Orlens* this kind of authorial strategy did not always come to fruition in the realization of the literary text as a manuscript book, even when those involved in the production of the codex set great store by the pictorial representation of the author. One of the two principal manuscripts of Rudolf's *Alexander*—Munich, BSB, Cgm 203, *c.* 1400–50—is worth mentioning in this context. It too includes an author portrait (fol. 2ʳ), based this time on the iconographic model of the reading author, which is located immediately before the start of the text (and the acrostic). Yet as in Cgm 63 (see Illustration 3) the secondary, codicological device of the picture usurps the page. Rudolf's status as an author is communicated visually (beard; attire; book) but not verbally. The impressively decorated initial 'R' stands on its own, as the second letter of the original acrostic (U) is missing—'Ûf' being omitted from line 5 in this manuscript. It is ironic that whilst the intricate acrostic, Rudolf's innately literary device of authorial self-presentation, has been corrupted beyond recognition in Cgm 203, its fundamental significance has been translated into a visual image

---

[76] See Chapter 1 section II.

5. Rudolf von Ems, *Alexander* (The author at a lectern) (reproduced by permission of the Bayerische Staatsbibliothek, Munich)

that would have been comprehensible to the most illiterate recipient
of the work.

Again the acrostic is only one aspect of Rudolf's authorial self-
presentation in the prologue. In its lengthier non-strophic part
(29–106) the internal storytelling situation of the work comes to the
fore. Here the narrator seeks to gain his audience's attention for the
forthcoming story by outlining the stature of its hero, whilst stress-
ing the tale's authenticity and the challenges its rendering will pose
him. The authorial identity of the narrator is conveyed at this point
through several expressions that relate to the activity of literary composition. The assertion of endeavour in lines 29–40, involving some
of the programmatic phraseology of the preceding strophes,[77] is subsequently expounded in terms of the poet's authorial career.[78] This
provides a framework of reference for the first of numerous statements in *Alexander* concerning the research involved in such a project:

> durch daz hân ich gevlizzen mich
> al mîne tage sît daz ich
> tihtens ie begunde,
> wiech diu maere vunde
> wie der tugentrîche
> Alexander wunderlîche
> wunders ûf der erde hie
> mit wunderlîcher kraft begie.
> dar an hât diu wârheit mir
> ervüllet mînes herzen gir:[. . .] (67–76)

(For that reason since first starting to compose poetry I have spent all my
days searching diligently for the story of how the virtuous and miraculous
Alexander performed amazing feats here on earth with wondrous power.
In this regard the truth has satisfied my heart's desire [. . .])

The character of this instance of authorial self-presentation is
illuminated by a comparison with Gottfried's description of his investigation into the story of Tristan.[79] Whereas Gottfried is at pains to
state his intent to find the 'truest' version, Rudolf appears excited

---

[77] 'Nû was ich, als ich eht noch bin, | als gemuot daz ich den sin | ie dar ûf arbeite
| daz Got zuo geleite | geruochte vüegen mîner kunst | saelde und edeler herzen gunst.
| sol des gelücke walten | und mir den prîs behalten | ûf den ich sus garbeitet hân, |
sô wil ich ûf den süezen wân | und ûf des lônes gewin | arbeiten aber mînen sin' (29–40).

[78] Lines 29–40 already point toward this; the use of 'aber' (40) suggests that the present
work is not the poet's first.

[79] *Tristan*: 'daz ist, als ich iu sage, gewesen: | sine sprâchen in der rihte niht, | als
Thômas von Britanje giht, | der âventiure meister was | und an britûnschen buochen

by the very stories themselves ('wunderlîche' 72, 'wunders' 73, 'mit wunderlîcher kraft' 74), and these sentiments seem to have a reve-latory quality. The subject-matter of Alexander has been of lasting concern to the poet (67ff.), and the success of his research is shown to afford him 'personal' satisfaction (76). The integration of this element of subjectivity is of course a deliberate poetic strategy, which in this context fulfils the specific function of persuading the work's recipients of both the immense material basis of the story and of the poet's individual effort. Yet, as we shall see, it is also a strategy which resonates throughout the work, not least because of the absence of any references to patronage to diminish the role of the author in the literary enterprise.

The first-person voice of the narrator is the sole mode of author-ial self-presentation in the prologues that follow. It is from this perspective that the composition of the work is discussed in a series of different literary historical contexts. Similar to *Willehalm von Orlens*, the prologue of the second book of *Alexander* (3063–294) revolves around an extensive literary excursus, reminiscent once more of Gottfried's *Tristan*.[80] The poet's awareness of his own artistic defi-ciencies leads him to appeal to his betters and to reflect on art in general: contemporary poetry is deemed inferior to that of the previous generation, and a catalogue of seventeen vernacular authors follows, from Heinrich von Veldeke and the triumvirate of Hartmann, Wolfram, and Gottfried to Ulrich von Türheim.[81] Rudolf then reintroduces himself into this sketch of medieval German literary history by stating his desire to emulate other poets past and present, and reviewing his own authorial oeuvre:

> [. . .] mir'st ir lêre nôt
> daz sie mîn zwî niht werfen abe

las | aller der lanthêrren leben | und ez uns ze künde hât gegeben. | Als der von Tristande seit, | die rihte und die wârheit | begunde ich sêre suochen | in beider hande buochen | walschen und latînen | und begunde mich des pînen, | daz ich in sîner rihte | rihte dise tihte. | sus treip ich manege suoche, | unz ich an einem buoche | alle sîne jehe gelas, | wie dirre âventiure was' (148–66).

[80] In the first phase of composition of *Alexander* this passage operated as an excursus proper—within a continuous narrative—directly preceding the coming of age of the hero; thus, it may well predate the analogous prologue in *Willehalm von Orlens*; see Wisbey, *Alexanderbild*, 112–17; Brackert, *Dichtung und Geschichte*, 28–33.

[81] See also Haug, *Literaturtheorie*, 310ff.; Adrian K. Stevens, 'Zum Literaturbegriff bei Rudolf von Ems', in *Geistliche und weltliche Epik des Mittelalters in Österreich*, edd. David McLintock/Adrian Stevens/Fred Wagner, Göppingen 1987 (GAG 446. Publications of the Institute of Germanic Studies University of London 37), 19–28.

daz ich ûf gestôzen habe
dô ich daz maere beschiet
wie vil nôtiger diet
der Guote Gêrhart lôste
von grôzem untrôste,
und wie der guote Jôsaphât
sich durch Barlââmes rât
der Gotes gnâde koufte
dô er sich Gote toufte,
und wie sich von der heidenschaft
bekêrte nâch der Gotes kraft
der guote Sant Eustachîus. (3276–89)

([. . .] I am in need of their instruction, lest they discard the branch which I thrust out, when I told the story of how good Gerhard freed greatly suffering people from deep despair, how good Josaphat bought God's grace on the advice of Barlaam, when he baptized himself for God, and how good Saint Eustachius converted from heathendom by the power of God.)

Rudolf is now identified in terms of his other works, including the lost legend *Eustachius* which is not referred to in the equivalent passage of self-presentation of *Willehalm von Orlens*.[82] Altogether such a collection of stories gives the impression that the author of *Alexander* has a substantial corpus of previous compositions to his name. This oeuvre is directly tied into the literary tradition adumbrated in the preceding catalogue by the use of metaphor: similar to the depiction of Hartmann, Wolfram, and Gottfried ('driu künsterîchiu bluomenrîs' 3119), as well as Konrad Fleck ('ein zwî der kunst gestôzen hât' 3239), Rudolf's texts are described as a branch ('mîn zwî' 3277) on the tree of German literature which has grown from the poetry of Heinrich von Veldeke ('des stam hât wol gebreitet sich' 3116). The metaphor of the tree also appears to be taken from *Tristan*,[83] but the function of Rudolf's catalogue differs significantly from Gottfried's. For all its topicality the accent of humility in the poet's insistence on instruction and in the fear that his works may be rejected from this canon, is diametrically opposed to Gottfried's strategy of self-aggrandizement: Rudolf's *Alexander* is to

[82] Brackert, *Dichtung und Geschichte*, 23 note 76.
[83] Ursula Schulze, 'Literarkritische Äußerungen im Tristan Gottfrieds von Straßburg', in *Gottfried von Strassburg*, ed. Alois Wolf, Darmstadt 1973 (WdF 320), 489–517, esp. 506ff.; Schouwink, *Fortuna*, 203–10.

be understood as one text in a broader authorial corpus which itself belongs to—rather than crowns—an established tradition of literary production in the vernacular.

The prologues to Books 3 and 4 return to the theme of the German author's avid research, an aspect of Rudolf's authorship that we first encountered in the opening prologue.[84] Each of the later passages begins with a general question of poetics, brevity of expression (8013-24), and didactic function (12923-60) respectively, before the issue of the sources of the work is addressed. The third prologue gives an unspecified impression of the vastness of the material, together with the poet's determined commitment to the truth.[85] In the fourth, an assurance of the comprehensiveness of his research (12965-70) paves the way for a report detailing particular sources by the name of their writers: 'Lêô' (12972-13030), 'Curtus Rûfus' (13031-8), 'Jôsephus' (13039ff.),[86] and 'Metôdîus' (13042-50).[87] The literary activity of these men forms an impressive backdrop to the actions of our poet:

> Nâch der urkünde wârheit
> die ieglîcher von im seit,
> hân ich gesuochet lange her [. . .]
> nâch der wil ich vollevarn,
> die wârheit an der tiusche bewarn
> daz ich dar zuo spriche niht
> wan des diu âventiure giht,[. . .] (13051ff., 13059-62)

(I have long been after the truth of the written history, which each one tells of him [Alexander] [. . .]. I want to complete my task in accordance with it [the truth], to retain the truth in the German language in such a way that I do not add anything that is not borne out by the adventurous tale itself [. . .])

Rudolf may be seeking to enhance his role by emphasizing the affinity between himself and Leo ('ein meister alsô wîs' 12987). The depiction of the German poet's archival research is certainly

---

[84] For the Latin text underlying part of the fourth prologue see Walther Bulst, 'Zum *prologus* der *Natiuitas et uictoria Alexandri magni regis*: II. Die Paraphrase im "Alexander" Rudolfs von Ems', *Historische Vierteljahrschrift* 29 (1935), 253-67; Schnell, *Studien zur inneren Einheit*, 145-8.

[85] 'Dâ von mac ich niht komen abe | des ich mich an genomen habe, | daz müeze werden vollebrâht' (8063ff.). For a fundamental study of Rudolf's concept of *wârheit* see Brackert, *Dichtung und Geschichte*, 92-157.

[86] Cf. also 12884-8, 16070, 16937-43, 16965ff.

[87] Cf. also 16968-96, 17321-36.

reminiscent of Leo's brand of scholarship.[88] However, as in sections
of *Barlaam und Josaphat*, the concept of a process of linguistic and
cultural translation provides the key to the dynamics of this passage.
Following on from the transmission of the history of Alexander from
Greek to Latin,[89] the (vernacular) author and his audience are
engaged in the realization of the next phase of the movement: from
Latin to German.[90]

The third and fourth prologues both establish a broad and authoritative literary historical context for the composition of this work by
first characterizing and then accounting for the story material itself.
The extent to which Rudolf's authorial profile in *Alexander* is bound
up with this aspect is encapsulated in a few lines towards the end
of Book 4:

> Diz maere und ander wârheit
> diu von Alexander seit
> sô vil gewârhafter sage,
> liebet mir von tage ze tage
> diu maere und daz getihte
> daz ich von im gerihte. (15629–34)

(This tale, and the truth which tells so much of the veracious story of
Alexander, increases, from day to day, the pleasure I take in the stories and
the poem that I am shaping about him.)

This passage provides the audience with another glimpse of the
autonomous authorial figure that appeared in the first prologue.
That the authorial subject's pleasure in the story material and
his fashioning of it may be focused on in this way, and without
taking refuge in self-deprecation, makes for a remarkable, if brief,
instance of self-presentation in what we might call an appendix to
the main discussion of the work's sources. This discussion continues
in Book 5.[91] A review of all the rulers of the Persian world empire

---

[88] 'nâch sîner gernder suoche | vant er dô vil buoche | diu er complierte' (13009ff.);
see Schouwink, *Fortuna*, 201. For similarities with Gottfried's authorial role in the prologue
to *Tristan* (149–66) see also Brackert, *Dichtung und Geschichte*, 151–5; Haug, *Literaturtheorie*,
312–15.

[89] 'Lêô begunde suochen | an kriecheschen buochen | etelîchiu maere, | diu waeren
sô gewaere | daz er niht taete wider Gote | und wider sînem gebote, | ob er ir schrift
berihte | und in latîne tihte' (12999–13006). Cf. also 13017f., 13035.

[90] Green, 'Rudolf von Ems', 163ff.

[91] The apparent lack of a prologue here is often related to Rudolf's need to begin
with the letter 'X' ('**X**erses der künec rîche' 15639) as part of the overarching acrostic

that Alexander has just conquered (15639–745) illustrates the poet's claim (15746–66) that mastery of this conglomerate of stories is completely beyond dull minds ('den sint von im diu maere | ze lanc, ze starc, ze swaere' 15757f.). Three other German authors of histories of Alexander, the first and third of which no longer exist, are then recalled: Berthold von Herbolzheim (15772–82), Pfaffe Lamprecht (15783–8), and a certain Biterolf (15789–803). The poet's initial sense of his own inferiority is soon dispensed with as doubt is cast on their approach to the sources, and this sequence culminates in Rudolf's explicit assertion of his own authorship:

> wan ich in tiutscher zungen wil
> ein urhap dirre maere wesn:
> als ich die wârheit hân gelesn,
> vert ez, als ich hân gedâht,
> sît ich hân zesamene brâht
> allez daz diu schrift uns seit [. . .] (15804–9)

(For I want to be the originator of these stories in the German tongue. My tale unfolds as I have read the truth, as I have considered it since my collection of everything that the written word tells us [. . .])

The familiar principles of the adherence to truth and the attempt to cover all written source material are reiterated in order to lend substance to the poet's claim that his authorship of this story is preeminent in the vernacular;[92] a statement which functions not only against the background of the German tradition of lives of Alexander, but also in terms of the broader process of linguistic and cultural translation expounded in the previous prologue. This phase of the authorial self-presentation in *Alexander* may well have been inspired by Gottfried's criticism of other versions of the story of Tristan, but Rudolf does not retain Gottfried's polemical edge.[93] The tone of this passage is tempered almost immediately by the poet's

---

(RALEXA[NDER]) which is made up of the first initial of each book; see Brackert, *Dichtung und Geschichte*, 14 note 21. This acrostic is generally thought to be derived from Walter of Châtillon's *Alexandreis*.

[92] See also Green, 'Rudolf von Ems', 163f.

[93] *Tristan* 8605–19: 'Si lesent an Tristande, | daz ein swalwe ze Îrlande | von Kurnewâle kaeme, | ein frouwen hâr dâ naeme | ze ir bûwe und z'ir geniste, | (i'ne weiz, wâ sî'z dâ wiste) | und fuorte daz wider über sê. | geniste ie kein swalwe mê | mit solhem ungemache, | sô vil sô sî bûsache | bî ir in dem lande vant, | daz si über mer in fremediu lant | nâch ir bûgeraete streich? | weiz got, hie spellet sich der leich, | hie lispet daz maere'.

readiness to stand down if someone else has been as comprehensive and accurate as he has.[94]

Yet another literary backdrop to Rudolf's composition of *Alexander* is invoked in the prologue to Book 6 (20573–688), which constitutes the last passage of authorial self-presentation in the text as it stands. As in the first prologue, the sixth opens with an abstract, and formally elaborate, discussion of *saelde*, followed now by references to the vernacular authors Gottfried (20621–31) and Freidank (20632–40) as authorities on the fickleness of Fortune.[95] The question of good fortune is then readdressed in the context of the storytelling scenario within *Alexander* itself, which is reminiscent of the first prologue of *Willehalm von Orlens*.[96] The poet's awareness of the inherently precarious nature of his relationship with the audience leads him to acknowledge the spectrum of contemporary literary tastes, alluding to a number of distinct poetic traditions:

> einer hoeret gerne
> wie Dietrîch von Berne
> mit kraft in vremden landen streit,
> von Artûses hövescheit
> wil ouch einer hoeren sagn,
> einer von den liehten tagn,
> einer wil von minnen,
> einer von wîsen sinnen,
> von Gote ouch einer hoeren wil.
> den site hât ouch liute vil
> daz in ist allez sagn ein wiht,
> der in von ribaldîe niht
> seit, daz ist genuoger site. (20667–79)

(One man likes to hear about the mighty battles of Dietrich von Bern in strange lands, while another wants to hear tales of Arthur's courtliness. They either want to hear about days of great joy, or about love, or wisdom,

---

[94] 'ist abr iemen vür mich komn | und hât sich des an genomn | daz er diu maere tihte | nâch der histôrje rihte | als ich sî gelesen hân, | dem wil ich diu maere lân: | hât er verrer und baz | dan ich gesprochen—âne haz | lâze ich im diu maere, | sint sie ganz und gewaere' (15813–22).

[95] Schouwink, *Fortuna*, 189–93; Haug, *Literaturtheorie*, 308ff.

[96] *Alexander*: 'Ûf die gedinge wil ouch ich | vürbaz mit dem getihte mich | und ûf genâde arbeiten | und disiu maere breiten, | obe ein tugent rîcher lîp, | ez sî man oder wîp, | iht hoere dran daz im behage, | daz er mir gunne mîne tage | güetlîchen âne haz | saelde und êren deste baz. | [...] | er gê dâ von, swer niht sî | mit willen disen maeren bî, | und lâze sie die hoeren sagn, | den sie mit willen wol behagen!' (20641–50, 20661–4).

or about God as well. Many have the custom not to care one bit about storytelling, if someone does not tell them of pranks and japes: there are quite enough of those who are like that.)

There is little by way of disparagement in this exposition of poetic activity in the vernacular at large, which includes such recognizable genres as the heroic and Arthurian epic. Only those listeners who insist on the frivolous to the exclusion of all else attract a touch of animosity. Rudolf is simply seeking to maintain his own authorial position in a world of multiple legitimate interests, and the prologue is concluded with a further expression of this resolve.[97]

It is unfortunate that Rudolf failed to complete *Alexander*, not least because it means that the text has been left with only one naming of the author and no references to patronage, and these are precisely the features which we might have expected to encounter in the prologues and epilogues of the following books. Nevertheless, the opportunities for reflection, which the subdivision of the work provides, are exploited systematically and self-consciously throughout. Without matching the complex of perspectives of *Willehalm von Orlens*, Rudolf highlights his authorship of *Alexander* in an acrostic and through narratorial evocation of multiple literary historical contexts that range from established Middle High German narrative tradition as a whole to a chain of transmission extending back to antiquity, and from other German histories of Alexander to vernacular poetic activity at large.

V. WELTCHRONIK

Rudolf's last work, the massive but fragmentary *Weltchronik*,[98] features the same core techniques of authorial self-presentation as in

---

[97] 'den allen mac ich niht gesagn | diu maere gar diu in behagn, | beide disem, dem und deme. | swer gerne daz von mir verneme | wie Alexander gelanc, | wie er elliu rîche twanc | und waz er wunders begie, | dem wil ich ez sagen hie' (20681–8).

[98] There are over one hundred textual witnesses for the *Weltchronik*, including at least twenty-five 'complete' codices; see Ehrismann (ed.), *Weltchronik*, pp. VI–X; Hubert Herkommer, 'Der St. Galler Codex als literarhistorisches Monument', in *Rudolf von Ems, Weltchronik. Der Stricker, Karl der Große. Kommentar zu Ms 302 Vad.*, edd. Kantonsbibliothek (Vadiana) St Gallen *et al.*, Luzern 1987, pp. 127–273, esp. 127–46; Danielle Jaurant, *Rudolfs 'Weltchronik' als offene Form: Überlieferungsstruktur und Wirkungsgeschichte*, Tübingen 1995 (Bibliotheca Germanica 34), 61–269. Determining an exact number is complicated by the compilatory nature of much of the transmission of vernacular world chronicles in the fourteenth and fifteenth centuries; see Kurt Gärtner, 'Überlieferungstypen mittel-

Alexander: acrostic and first-person narratorial articulation. The extent to which the theme of authorship is treated here is also fundamentally determined by the subdivision of the text into sections with their own openings.[99] Six such sections were envisaged by the author although the fifth was never completed, and the question of authorship is primarily addressed in the resulting sequence of five prologues. The subdivision of the *Weltchronik* corresponds to the established paradigm of Christian historiography of the six ages of the world (*aetates mundi*) seen in the context of salvation history.[100] The sections are denoted as 'worlds' (*werlte*), and—with the exception of the first—include a titular acrostic of the name of the leading figure for each age (NOE 867ff.; ABRAHAM 3794–800; MOISES 8798–803; DAVID 21518–22). The religious preoccupations in this text have a decisive bearing on the presentation of its authorship which, unlike *Alexander*, encompasses a reference to patronage as well.

The first prologue (1–188), and introduction to the work as a whole, opens with a prayer to God.[101] In accordance with what has obviously become Rudolf's standard mode of self-presentation at this privileged exordial moment, the highly stylized invocation is infused with an acrostic giving the author's name:

> **R**ichter Got, herre ubir alle kraft,
> **V**ogt himilschir herschaft,
> **O**b allin kreften swebit din kraft:
> **D**es lobit dich ellú herschaft.
> **O**rthaber allir wisheit,
> **L**ob und ere si dir geseit!
> **F**rider, bevride mit wisheit
> den der dir lob und ere seit. (1–8)

(Governing God, Lord omnipotent, Ruler of the heavenly host, Your might exceeds all others. For this reason Your whole kingdom praises you. Originator of all wisdom, let Your praises and honour be proclaimed!

hochdeutscher Weltchroniken', in *Geschichtsbewußtsein in der deutschen Literatur des Mittelalters: Tübinger Colloquium 1983*, edd. Christoph Gerhardt/Nigel F. Palmer/Burghart Wachinger, Tübingen 1985 (Publications of the Institute of Germanic Studies University of London 34), 110–18.

[99] The closures to the sections are less well-defined than in *Alexander*; cf. 860–6, 3746–95, 8778–97, 21507–17.

[100] Ingrid von Tippelskirch, *Die 'Weltchronik' des Rudolf von Ems: Studien zur Geschichtsauffassung und politischen Intention*, Göppingen 1979 (GAG 267), 92–101; Herkommer, 'Monument', 146–57, 175–89.

[101] See also Lutz, *Rhetorica divina*, 289–309; Haug, *Literaturtheorie*, 327f.; Thelen, *Dichtergebet*, 426–30.

Peacemaker, lend that man the peace of wisdom who proclaims Your praises and honour.)

In the first instance the religious context of the acrostic renders a devotional function likely. As in the epilogue of *Barlaam und Josaphat*, Rudolf inextricably conflates the pious sentiments of the text with his own name in order to benefit from them 'personally', whenever they were read (out). However, the position of the acrostic aligns it with those found in *Willehalm von Orlens* and *Alexander*. The naming simultaneously operates as an authorial hallmark that is designed to become apparent as soon as the literary composition takes its place on the written page.[102]

In terms of the content of Rudolf's prologue as a whole the initial depiction of Divine omnipotence, and in particular the evocation of God's authorship of all existence,[103] forms a backdrop to the subsequent narratorial presentation of Rudolf's authorship. Having demonstrated his faith and understanding,[104] the poet appeals for inspiration to start his literary work from the Lord of all Beginning and Ending:

> so wil ich bittin dich dastu
> begiezest mine sinne nu
> mit dem brunnin dinir wisheit,
> der ursprinc allir witze treit;
> und schoffe ein anegenge mir,
> wan ih beginnen wil mit dir
> ze sprechinne und ze tihtinne,
> ze bescheidenne und ze berihtinne [. . .] (67–74)

(So I want to beg You to pour the waters of Your wisdom, which bear the origin of all intellect, onto my senses. Create a start for me! For with You I want to begin to tell and to compose, to order and to shape [. . .])

As in the prologue of *Barlaam und Josaphat* a claim of ultimate authorization is being made in these lines, whereby the poet's own authorial activity is held to be grounded in divine wisdom. The baptismal metaphor (69f.) suggests further that the human author must undergo a process of 'initiation' before he can embark on this

---

[102] Jaurant, *Überlieferungsstruktur*, 289f.

[103] 'als ez dú witzebernde kraft | dinir gotlichin meistirschaft | alrest von nihte tihte, | geschúf und gar berihte' (25–8). See also Jaeger, 'Schöpfer der Welt', 5–17.

[104] 'Got herre, sit daz nu din chunst | bi dir ie was ane begunst | und anegenge nie gewan, | und doh wol mag und machin kan | anegenge und endis zil, | alse din gebot gebietin wil' (61–6).

literary project.[105] The following outline of the work makes clear that such claims are justifiable and even appropriate, for the poet has set himself the enormous task of retelling the course of salvation history from the moment of Creation up until the present sixth age which dawned with the Incarnation (75–146). The final part of the prologue is addressed to the audience and deals with the course of profane history ('und welhe kúnege schone | trŏgin der lande krone' 161f.). Identification of the author with the narrator is encouraged here by several statements of intent that relate to literary composition: namely, the assurance of authorial endeavour and the subscription to the principles of truth and brevity.[106] Although these expressions are conventional, they introduce important elements of Rudolf's authorial profile for the text as a whole which recur again and again in the following prologues.[107]

The second (867–900),[108] third (3794–877),[109] and fourth (8798–825) prologues share a basic structural model derived from the various components of the first, in which the motifs of the author's dependence on God and subscription to the principles of truth and brevity are interwoven with 'abstracts' of the preceding and following ages of the world. The principal function of these passages is one of demarcation, of first closing and then opening consecutive sections of the work by highlighting the transition from one *werlt*

---

[105] For more on this metaphor see Lutz, *Rhetorica divina*, 296.

[106] 'Diz han ich minir willekúr | genomin ze einir ummŭze fúr | und wil ez tihtin unde sagin' (147ff.); 'des han ih mŭt und gŭtin wan, | ob mir Got der tage so vil | gan, daz ih diz alliz wil | tihtin mit warheit, doh kúrzeklike' (174–7); 'als úns mit rehte warheit | dú bŭh der warheit hant geseit, | dú mit der heiligen schrift | sint des geloubin rehtú stift: | mit dien wil ih beginnen hie | der rehten mere, hŏrent wie: | als úns dú schrift bescheidin hat, | da dú warheit geschribin stat' (181–8).

[107] Jaurant, *Überlieferungsstruktur*, 290 note 1029, 292f.

[108] 'Nu han ich hie berihtet, | Offenliche getichtet | Eine werlt, [...] | [...] | das han ich al hie geseit | kúrzeliche und ouh mit warheit: | nu wilich in dem namin Gotis | und in der lere Gotis gebotis | ein teil mit kranchin sinnin | ze saginne hie beginnin | wie Got die andirn welt began' (867ff., 877–83).

[109] 'An disin meren der ih han | Begunnen unde hergetan | Rehte in rehtir richte | An umbekreiz mit slihte, | Han ich kúrzecliche her geseit | Ane valsch die warheit | Mit kurzin wortin uz gesniten | und al die umberede virmittin, | davon dú mere lengent sich. | der chúrzze flizzich gerne mich, | das deste balder vollebraht | werdin, als ich han gedaht, | dú mere dú ich tihtin wil: | der rede wrde anders gar ze vil | ob ich, darnah ich solte, | gar vollesagin wolte | dú mere dú mit warheit | dú heiligú scrift darinne seit | [...] | zŏ welt, der urhap und der zil | han ih nu getihtet hie | kúrzeclich und doch rehte wie | Got ietwedir den urhap | von erst gedahte und ende gab: | [...] | als ih iuh harnah sol sagin | und saginde wirde, ob mir der zil | Got únsir herre gan so vil, | in des gnadin lere | ih abir fúrbas mere | der mere wil beginnen hie | ze saginne wie ez dort irgie' (3794–811, 3817–21, 3871–7).

to the next. The fourth prologue is somewhat exceptional, for here
the authorial self-presentation gains more of a momentum of its
own. The conventional assurance of the poet's fidelity to the truth
from the very start soon develops into a discussion of the necessary
consequences of failing to adhere to this principle:

> wand dú mere alse reine
> sint und alse gemeine
> gelerten wisen lúten,
> woltich iht andirz tútin
> wand des mit rehter warheit
> dú scrift der rehten warheit seit
> mit gewerem urkunde,
> so lûdich groze súnde
> uf mich und itewize vil:[. . .] (8808–16)

(For the tales are so pure and so well-known to wise scholars, that if I
wanted to expound anything other than that which the writing of the proper
truth tells with the utmost veracity and true testimony, I would be loading
great sin upon myself and much reproach [. . .])

Since the poet has obviously been dealing with the sacred material
of the Old Testament, to deviate from the truth is quite categorically to sin. Yet, just as the moral obligations involved in this work
are heightened, so the poet may reaffirm his claim to a privileged
authorial status, and this is underlined in the rest of the prologue
by two evocations of his divine inspiration (8826–35, 8850–67).[110]
This overtly religious dimension to the poet's authorship is accompanied by his awareness that scholars (8810) may easily check the
poem against his sources for falsification. The *Weltchronik* is the first
of its kind in German verse, and Rudolf uses allusions such as these
to set his work against a background of clerical (Latin) literary
culture.[111]

The fifth prologue (21518–740) also features an outline of salvation history, but with its extensive eulogy (21572–707) of King
Conrad IV, the Hohenstaufen patron of the *Weltchronik*, this prologue
represents an important new stage in the presentation of the
work's authorship. Up until this point the composition of the work
has largely been explained in terms of the divine inspiration of the

---

[110] 'nu wilih mit der lere kraft | des heiligen geistes meisterschaft | erbeiten minir sinne
kraft' (8826ff.); 'das ih alleine tihten wil | mit der wisen lere Gotis | und mit der helfe sins
gebotis, | ob sin gnade mir gúnnen wil | der sinne und ouh so langir zil' (8857–61).

[111] Gärtner, 'Überlieferungstypen', 111f. Cf. also lines 2680–8, 8831–4.

human author, but now a third agent—the royal instigator of the project—becomes apparent.[112] In the course of the highly politicized panegyric which follows,[113] the poet comes to speak of King Conrad's role as his patron at greater length:

> Min libir herre, durh den ich
> an diz bůch noch min erbeit
> mit getihte han geleit
> und ez mit Gotis helfe wil
> fúrsih tihtin uf das zil,
> ob mir Got der jare gan
> das ih im mag gedienen dran,
> Das ist der kúnig Chůnrat,
> des keisirs kint, der mir hat
> geboten und des bete mich
> gerůchte biten des das ich
> durh in dú mere tihte,[. . .]
> von gewêren dingen
> bat er mih allis bringen
> in tútsche getihte durh in,
> das sinis lonis hoch gewin
> mir kumbirs vil beneme,[. . .] (21656–67, 21685–9)

(My beloved lord, for whom I have toiled away at this book with my composition and—with God's aid—want to continue to do so, if God grants me the years to do him this service; King Conrad, that is, child of the emperor, who has commanded me and who deigned to commission me, by request, to compose the tales for his sake [. . .]. He instructed me to translate all of the true things into German verse on his account, so that the great profit of his reward would relieve me of much of my suffering [. . .])

In view of the king's social and political stature it is not surprising to find that the author is presented as utterly subordinate to his employer. The authorship of the *Weltchronik* still depends on God, but it is also shown to originate with Conrad's commission. Similarly, the ideas of veracity and the composition of a work in the vernacular are accredited to the patron whose benevolence is enhanced by the authorial self-stylization as a 'poet in material need' (21688f.).

---

[112] 'so wil ouh ih in Gotis namen, | ob allin namin dem lobesamen, | dem hohsten und dem hersten, | dem jugisten und dem ersten | der iemir wert und was ouh îe, | beginnin disú mere hie, | berihten unde tichtin, | mit tihtinne berihten | durh einin kúnig lobesamen' (21564–72).

[113] For more on the political content of these lines see Brackert, *Dichtung und Geschichte*, 83–91, 182ff., 195–8; Herkommer, 'Monument', 138ff., 263–9.

The ultimate functions of the text, the poet now reveals (21690–707), are to create an everlasting (literary) monument ('ein eweclih memorial' 21697) to the German King as well as to entertain him with suitable and improving histories.[114]

In the last phase of the prologue (21708–40) the pre-eminence of the patron is emphasized once more, as the courtly audience is exhorted to extend their heartfelt thanks to King Conrad (21730ff.); only then does the poet appeal to them to intercede on his behalf as well:

> [. . .] und das Got gúnne mir das ich
> Gote und im gerbeite mich
> mit disim getihte also
> das ich ir lonis werde vro
> an dirre welte und hernah dort. (21733–7)

([. . .] that God may allow me to apply myself so much to this composition for God and him [King Conrad], that I may enjoy their reward in this world and afterwards in the next.)

These lines set the seal on the strategy of authorial self-presentation which pervades the exposition of the political, if not propagandistic,[115] interests behind the *Weltchronik* in this fifth prologue. The poet ends on a concise reformulation of his subservience and of the terms under which he is working: namely, for the highest spiritual and temporal powers, in the hope of both worldly and heavenly reward.

All in all, Rudolf's presentation of his authorship of the *Weltchronik* corresponds in character to the overtly religious subject-matter of the Old Testament and salvation history. The poet's dependence on God is reiterated throughout the work and is repeatedly linked with topoi such as truthfulness and adherence to the sources, and this basic strategy is enhanced by extensive reference to an illustrious patron in the final relevant passage in the text as it stands. In light of the ideological weight of this project it is perhaps not surprising that issues of authorship and the broader circumstances of composition of the *Weltchronik* attract further attention in the subsequent manuscript transmission. Consequently, although Rudolf himself employs only two modes of authorial self-presentation (acrostic; first-person narratorial voice), the presentation of the authorship of the work as found in the manuscript books is on occasion rather more elaborate.

---

[114] Cf. also 21668–84. These functions are discussed in greater detail by Brackert, *Dichtung und Geschichte*, 230–4, 239–47.

The first addition to the authorial profile within the *Weltchronik* is of a textual nature. The poet of the so-called 'first continuation' of the work (33347–6338), which was transmitted as one with Rudolf's text even in the earliest manuscripts,[116] inscribes the monumental fragment with an epitaph to its author:

> Der dis bůch getihtet
> hat unze her uns verrihtet
> wol an allen orten
> an sinnen und worten,
> der starb in welschen richen.
> ich weis wer sich im glichen
> muge an solicher meisterschaft,[. . .]
> Got gebe im ze lone
> ein liehte crone in himelrich
> nu iemer eweclich.
> sin name ist iu wol bekant:
> Rŭdolf von Ense was er genant. (33479–85, 33492–6)

(The man who composed this book up to this point and arranged it well at every turn, in meaning and in style, he died in Latin lands [Italy?]. I know of no one who might compare with him such was his [poetic] mastery [. . .]. May God reward him with a bright crown in the kingdom of heaven, now, always and forever. His name is well known to you: he was called Rudolf von Ems.)

Interest in Rudolf as the author of the *Weltchronik* leads ultimately to concern for him as a Christian as the audience is entreated to pray for his soul; and only then is he named. Blended in are the notion of literary mastery and a teasing detail from the author's biography which may or may not be true.[117] This apparent fascination with the death of the author is in fact part of a broader medieval phenomenon: the important fourteenth-century manuscript known as the 'Hausbuch' of Michael de Leone, for instance, contains an analogous scribal colophon (fol. 191ᵛ) which refers to the supposed places of burial of the vernacular poets Walther von der Vogelweide and Reinmar von Zweter.[118] At least in the eyes of the

---

[115] Jaurant, *Überlieferungsstruktur*, 298–302.

[116] Brackert, *Dichtung und Geschichte*, 185f.; Gärtner, 'Überlieferungstypen', 110.

[117] Brackert, *Dichtung und Geschichte*, 12.

[118] The 'Hausbuch'—Munich, UB, 2° Cod. ms. 731, datable 1345–54—is accessible in a facsimile edn. by Horst Brunner. For further discussion of this phenomenon see Margaret T. Gibson/Nigel F. Palmer, 'Manuscripts of Alan of Lille, "Anticlaudianus" in the British Isles', *Studi Medievali*, 3ᴬ Series, 28:2 (1987), 905–1001, esp. 922.

6. Rudolf von Ems, *Weltchronik* (The author dictating to a scribe) (reproduced by permission of the Bayerische Staatsbibliothek, Munich)

7. Rudolf von Ems, *Weltchronik* (The author at a desk) (reproduced by permission of the Bayerische Staatsbibliothek, Munich)

poet and primary recipients of the 'first continuation' of the *Weltchronik*, Rudolf, by virtue of his composition of this mammoth fragment, joins the ranks of a select band of authors who were not to be forgotten but continued to arouse curiosity even after their deaths.

Other secondary responses to the question of authorship take the form of pictures.[119] A number of the illustrations that open the work, either on leaves immediately preceding the text or on the same page as Rudolf's prologue, relate to the manuscript as a literary object and prize.[120] Elsewhere, the authorship of the text itself appears to be represented visually at the outset. A particularly impressive author portrait was added to Munich, BSB, Cgm 8345, *c.* 1270/80–1300. The iconographic model here (I^r) is that of the author dictating to a scribe, whereby the similarities with the opening miniature in Cgm 63 (Illustration 3) are so striking that the picture in Cgm 8345 was most probably copied from the earlier codex.[121] In contrast with the religious content of Rudolf's prologue, that is to say the poet's self-subordination to God, the picture constitutes an image of relatively autonomous human authorship in which the emphasis is on the wisdom and the authority of the poet in his own right, as indicated by all the usual motifs: beard; cap; gown (with gold buttons!). If anything, it corresponds with the poetological, self-assertive function of the opening acrostic of the author's name, and it can also be regarded as a visual pendant to the epitaph in the 'first continuation', as a celebration of Rudolf's masterly composition of the text.[122]

---

[119] The illustrated manuscripts of the *Weltchronik* are comprehensively described in Jörn-Uwe Günther, *Die illustrierten mittelhochdeutschen Weltchronikhandschriften in Versen: Katalog der Handschriften und Einordnung der Illustrationen in die Bildüberlieferung*, Munich 1993 (tuduv-Studien: Reihe Kunstgeschichte 48).

[120] Codex Los Angeles, The J. Paul Getty Museum, Ms. 33 [88.MP.70], *c.* 1410, features miniatures of both a later owner (fol. 2^v), and the original (female) patron receiving the manuscript from a scribe or painter (fol. 3^r). The figures in the second of these pictures address each other: 'genad liebew fraw zart'—'got grüzz ew her pernhart'. See also Günther, *Weltchronikhandschriften*, 191f., 199; Jaurant, *Überlieferungsstruktur*, 163.

[121] For further discussion of this famous picture see Ehrismann (ed.), *Weltchronik*, pp. XVIIf.; Ellen J. Beer, 'Die Buchkunst der Hs. 302 der Vadiana', in *Kommentar zu Ms 302 Vad.*, edd. Kantonsbibliothek (Vadiana) St Gallen *et al.*, 61–125, esp. 90f.; Wachinger, 'Autorschaft und Überlieferung', 9; Günther, *Weltchronikhandschriften*, 269f.; Weigele-Ismael, *Cgm 63*, 16off.

[122] In another manuscript the religious aspect of the process seems to have been emphasized: Günther, *Weltchronikhandschriften*, 153f., notes that the first page of the *Weltchronik* in Fulda, Hessische LB, Ms. Aa 88, *c.* 1360, is decorated by a sixteen-line initial

A second main site of relevant pictures is at the start of the fifth section of the work, heralding the fifth prologue with its extensive praise of Rudolf's patron, King Conrad. At this crucial point of narratorial reflection the illustrators of four manuscripts chose to highlight either the imperial patronage and illustrious political background to the work, or the aspect of authorship. In Cgm 8345, for example, six Hohenstaufen emperors and kings are pictured in dialogue with one another (fol. 159ᵛ).[123] In Munich, BSB, Cgm 6406, c. 1300, fol. 134ʳ, and Stuttgart, Württembergische LB, cod. bibl. fol. 5, dated 1383, fol. 115ᵛ, on the other hand, this same passage is marked out by an author portrait. Both of these latter pictures are based on the fundamental iconographic model of the 'author at his desk', to which heightened connotations of divine inspiration are added in Cgm 6406 through the three (!) birds that encircle the writer. The miniature in the Stuttgart manuscript decorates the first initial ('D') of the first word of the prologue; the author portrait in Cgm 6406 is located between the end of the fourth 'world' (in the columns above) and the beginning of the fifth (starting on fol. 134ᵛ). In view of Rudolf's explicit authorial self-presentation in this part of the *Weltchronik*, it would seem perfectly legitimate to read these pictures as referring to him. However, we should note that there is an element of ambiguity about the identity of the authorial figures depicted here. The acrostic at the head of the fifth prologue (21518–22) gives the name of DAVID who was not only significant as a biblical king but also as an author. Thus, although these author portraits may well represent further examples of the codicological elevation of Rudolf's authorship, they can be understood to relate to the sacred literary activity of one of the most prominent human authors in the Old Testament.[124] As was the case with the two pictures in the transmission of *Barlaam und Josaphat*, the author portraits in Cgm 6406 and Stuttgart, cod. bibl. fol. 5 work in one of two ways: either enhancing or competing with the presentation of authorship in the literary text itself.

*   *   *

'R' featuring an authorial figure together with Adam, as well as a picture of a second individual (the patron?) being blessed.

[123] Günther, *Weltchronikhandschriften*, 120, refers to the existence of another picture of a king just before the fifth prologue in Colmar, Bibliothèque de la Ville, Ms. 305, dated 1459, fol. 233ʳ, and suggests that this is a depiction of King Conrad.

[124] See Günther's verdict on the picture in Cgm 6406: 'Ein Schreiber bei der Arbeit (David schreibt den Psalter?)' (*Weltchronikhandschriften*, 244).

8. Rudolf von Ems, *Weltchronik* (The author at a desk) (reproduced by permission of the Württembergische Landesbibliothek, Stuttgart)

Having concentrated almost exclusively on Rudolf's texts in themselves, it would now seem appropriate to contextualize our findings and determine Rudolf's significance for the period 1220–90 as characterized in Chapter 1. We have seen that the adoption of a new narrative structure (the subdivision into 'books') has a decisive impact on Rudolf's practice of authorial self-reference, and it is worth noting that this transition coincides with commissions from individuals at the German imperial court. The two points appear to be related. Rudolf's implementation of such a Latinate device of textual organization in his vernacular narratives may well have been a response to his new environment and a new group of recipients, many of whom are likely to have had substantial experience of books, the Hohenstaufen court having long been a centre of Latin literary patronage and production. The proliferation of acrostics in Rudolf's later works is also to be viewed against this background, in particular the development of a standard opening acrostic of the German author's name. We know of no other Middle High German poet of this period who refers to himself in this way so often and who so demonstratively lays claim to being an author of a book. With Rudolf's move to Konrad von Winterstetten's literary circle, vernacular narrative literature fully attains the status of a written literary medium. By the mid-thirteenth century, and the start of the *Weltchronik* for King Conrad, German is regarded as a suitable vehicle for the most ambitious and exalted of historiographical enterprises.

Yet it would be wrong to stress such 'Latinization' at the cost of the other central characteristic of Rudolf's work: its self-conscious positioning in vernacular literary tradition. Two of the same works of the second phase of Rudolf's career, *Willehalm von Orlens* and *Alexander*, contain the lengthiest literary excursuses of the thirteenth century, displaying the greatest possible awareness of a distinctively German vernacular literary heritage. The investment Rudolf makes in his identity, as constructed within the text, as an author of vernacular literature is further suggested by his borrowing of numerous identifiable models of self-presentation from his 'classical' predecessors. The resulting blend of the vernacular and the Latinate in works such as *Willehalm von Orlens* and *Alexander* is encapsulated by the appearance of a prominent narratorial figure at the various openings and closures of the 'books' into which these texts are subdivided. In spite of his expressions of humility Rudolf is able to develop an extraordinary technique of authorial self-reference from the conjunction of these two literary spheres. There are signs of a tendency in this direction in the early works *Der guote Gêrhart* and *Barlaam und Josaphat* with their juxtaposition of several different devices and perspectives. But it was, apparently, only under the auspices of members of the Hohenstaufen court that Rudolf had the opportunity to realize this potential.

Another aspect of Rudolf's significance both for the discussion of authorship and in terms of medieval German literary history as a whole lies in the manuscript transmission of his texts, which features an unrivalled number of author portraits in codices from the later thirteenth to the fifteenth centuries. There are a number of possible reasons for this phenomenon. First, the apparent historicity and authenticity of the story material of the narratives in question may have rendered them peculiarly suitable to this kind of pictorial distinction. Second, these images of authority may reflect Rudolf's status as an imperial poet; after all, the first pictures that 'definitely' refer to Rudolf are preserved in manuscripts of *Willehalm von Orlens* and the *Weltchronik*. The early dates of two of the author portraits (Cgm 63; Cgm 8345) and the Latinate iconographic models on which they all draw (dictation; writing; reading) might even suggest that the association between this codicological device and Rudolf's works extended back to his own lifetime and employment at the Hohenstaufen court.[125] The celebration of authorship that these pictures represent is quite remarkable in the context of vernacular narrative literary tradition. In effect, they translate the self-consciousness of the author in the text into impressive (and colourful) visual images. Part of the importance of this process from our point of view, however, is that evidently it was not a smooth one. There are the examples of practical problems of 'mise-en-page' where the picture seems to displace the text and the authorial acrostic is obstructed; and it is indicative of the co-existence of radically differing concepts of authorship in the Middle Ages that on occasion those involved in the production of the codices appear to honour the authors of Rudolf's source-texts—and not him. In these cases Rudolf's presentation of his own vernacular authorship in the text encounters opposition and the reassertion of Latinity in the manuscript book.

---

[125] See also Wachinger, 'Autorschaft und Überlieferung', 9.

3

PATRONAGE, CO-OPERATION, AND ARTISTIC SELF-ASSURANCE: ASPECTS OF AUTHORSHIP IN THE NARRATIVE WORKS OF KONRAD VON WÜRZBURG

Konrad von Würzburg is the leading German author in the second half of the thirteenth century. His massive oeuvre encompasses love and gnomic lyric poetry, as well as a eulogy of the Virgin Mary, three legends, two romances, a retelling of the story of the Trojan war, and a substantial body of shorter narratives. Much of this material bears witness to a formal expertise to rival his 'classical' predecessor of choice Gottfried von Strassburg, and Konrad himself came to be regarded as an ideal vernacular poet by later writers such as Frauenlob and Heinrich von Mügeln.[1] Even two contemporary Latin chronicles allude to Konrad's literary activity in favourable terms.[2]

The codicological representation of Konrad's authorship in the transmission of his non-narrative works perpetuates his profile as a vernacular author of the highest order. In the 'Große Heidelberger Liederhandschrift' Konrad's lyric oeuvre is introduced by both a rubric ('Meist' Chûnrat von Wúrzburg') and an author portrait (fol. 383[r]) in accordance with the programme of the codex as a whole.[3] Like a number of the pictures associated with Rudolf von Ems this illustration is based on the iconographic model of the author dictating to a scribe, and Konrad is one of only a handful of poets in this codex to be openly associated with literary production, reflecting perhaps his peculiar status as a writer of epic texts as well.[4]

---

[1] Brandt, *Konrad von Würzburg*, 213–17.

[2] 'Obiit Cuonradus de Wirciburch, in Theothonico multorum bonorum dictaminum compilator' (*Annales Colmarienses maiores a. 1277–1472*, MGH SS 17, p. 214,43f.); 'Conradus de Wirciburc vagus fecit rhitmos Theutonicos de beata Virgine preciosos' (*De rebus Alsaticis ineuntis saeculi XIII*, MGH SS 17, p. 233,38f.).

[3] For more on this manuscript see Chapter 1 section 1 above. The picture is reproduced in Walther (ed.), *Codex Manesse: Die Miniaturen*, 255.

[4] Curschmann, '*Pictura laicorum litteratura?*', 225.

Elsewhere, the interest in the last resting places of prominent authors that is displayed in the 'Hausbuch' of Michael de Leone (c. 1345–54) also extends to Konrad in the form of a scribal colophon at the end of the *Goldene Schmiede*, his mariological text:

Hie get vz die gûldin smitte. die meist' Cûnrad geborn võ wirzeb'g tíchte: vnd ist zv̂ friburg i prisgev̂ begraben. (fol. 58ᵛ)

(Here ends the *Goldene Schmiede* which master Konrad composed, who was born in Wurzburg and buried in Freiburg in Breisgau.)

Another one of Konrad's lyric works, the *Klage der Kunst*, is explicitly attributed to him in this manuscript as well:

Diz ist meister Conrades von Wirtzburg getichte von vnmiltckeit gein kûnstrîchen leuten. (fol. 253ᵛ)

(This is master Konrad von Würzburg's poem concerning stinginess towards gifted artists.)

Similarly, Konrad's later reception as one of the twelve legendary 'Meistersinger' is exemplified by the numerous references to his authorship of melodies in the 'Kolmarer Liederhandschrift' (Munich, BSB, Cgm 4997, c. 1450–75).[5]

The key term in these rubrics and superscriptions is that of *meister*, which generally signifies education (*magister*) as well as 'mastery' of an art, skill, or craft. For many recipients of Konrad's texts this 'mastery' resided in their polished style. That Konrad was aware of his own accomplishment is made explicit in the prologues and epilogues of his narratives, where reflections on the art of poetry and authorial self-presentation are commonplace.[6] In contrast to Rudolf von Ems, Konrad refers to his authorship from the narratorial first-person perspective only, but he functionalizes this single mode in two outstanding and seemingly contradictory ways. First, he places a new emphasis on patronage and the involvement of other individuals. Although allusions to patrons are a regular feature of medieval German

---

[5] For a comprehensive collection of these superscriptions see Günter Mayer, *Probleme der Sangspruchüberlieferung: Beobachtungen zur Rezeption Konrads von Würzburg im Spätmittelalter*, Diss. Munich 1974.

[6] Wolfgang Monecke, *Studien zur epischen Technik Konrads von Würzburg: Das Erzählprinzip der 'wildekeit'*, with an introduction by Ulrich Pretzel, Stuttgart 1968 (Germanistische Abhandlungen 24); Haug, *Literaturtheorie*, 344–63; Brandt, *Konrad von Würzburg*, 195–207; Hartmut Kokott, *Konrad von Würzburg: Ein Autor zwischen Auftrag und Autonomie*, Stuttgart 1989, passim.

narrative tradition (they are well represented in Rudolf's works, for example), Konrad goes to unparalleled lengths to identify—and subordinate himself to—a total of nine personages in his narrative texts.[7] Second, Konrad uses strategies of self-presentation that convey a sense of artistic self-assurance. One of his main achievements here lies in the revitalization of a form of (first-person) signature that was eschewed by Rudolf and previously employed to effect by Wolfram von Eschenbach. In oscillating between these two approaches, sometimes even within the same work, Konrad lends remarkable expression to the diverse notions of authorship of his day.

The eye-catching consistency with which Konrad addresses the theme of authorship also applies to a certain degree to his lyric and non-narrative output. Against the trend for lyric poets not to name themselves,[8] Konrad openly plays with his authorial identity in the *Minneleich* when he signs off at the end of the song:

> disen tanz hât iu gesungen
> Cuonze dâ von Wirzeburc:
> wünschent daz von sîner zungen
> niemer rîm gefliege lurc! (134–8)

(It was 'Cuonze' von Würzburg who sang this dance for you: wish that from his tongue never a rhyme flies off badly.)

Konrad's reference to himself in the third person creates an impression of humility, and this is compounded by the familiar form of 'Cuonze', which is a neat piece of self-stylization as lowly singer-cum-performer. However, this is the humility of a superior poet engaged in a game of self-mockery, and consequently the singer does not plead with the audience to overlook his inadequacies. Instead their best wishes are only requested to ensure that Konrad's poetic technique does not deteriorate. The inclusion of Konrad's name in the *Klage der Kunst* is similarly self-serving. In the penultimate strophe of this short allegorical work the poet describes how Lady Justice issues a warning to courtly society not to fail to cultivate the arts properly:

> '[. . .] Ir habet staete swaz iu sî
> von mir geteilet hiute:

---

[7] For more on the socio-historical context of Konrad's literary activity see Chapter one section III above.

[8] Wittstruck, *Der dichterische Namengebrauch*, 397–462.

> er sî iu swaere alsam ein blî,
> swer rehte kunst niht triute,
> minne und aller fröuden frî,
> im fremden hie die liute!
> bî Cuonzen der uns stât hie bî,
> die rede ich iu enbiute.' (31,1–8)

('[. . .] You can depend on what you are told by me today: whosoever does not cherish good art will be as grievous a burden to you as a lead weight. Bereft of love and of every joy, all the people here will shun him! Through "Cuonze", who is standing close to us here, I send you this message.')

In this context 'Cuonze' emphasizes Konrad's unique position as a favourite of Justice and of all the other courtly virtues assembled at her court. He will champion the rights of Art in society.[9] Finally, in Konrad's mariological show-piece, the *Goldene Schmiede*, authorial self-presentation is prominent in both the prologue and a later excursus, whereby the first-person formulations used are more typical of Konrad's technique in his narrative works:

> künn ich dich, frouwe, niht geloben
> nach volleclichen eren,
> darzuo so soltu keren
> din uzerwelte gnade,
> also daz mir Cuonrade
> von Wirzeburc daz heil geschehe,
> daz mir din güete ez übersehe
> swaz ich vermide an dinem lobe. (116–23)

(If I am not able to praise you, Lady, as befits all Your honour, apply Your exceptional mercy so that I, Konrad von Würzburg, receive the blessing that Your goodness forgives me for whatever I have failed to include in Your praise.)

The self-deprecating tone of Konrad's statements in the *Goldene Schmiede* is a function of the poet's overarching role as supplicant to the Virgin Mary.[10] Nevertheless, the extensive clusters of metaphors that make up the greater part of this work are so elaborate and sovereignly handled that in spite of all his protestations to the

---

[9] For further discussion of these texts see Edward Schröder, 'Studien zu Konrad von Würzburg IV–V', *GGN* 1917, pp. 96–129, esp. 110; Ingeborg Glier, 'Der Minneleich im späten 13. Jahrhundert', in *Werk–Typ–Situation*, edd. Glier *et al.*, 161–83, esp. 171.

[10] Cf. also 884–93: 'ob mir din helfe stiure birt, | und wil din trost mir geben rat, | so schir ich tumber CUONRAT | ab einvaltigem sinne | die rede uz der ich spinne | dir ein richez erenkleit'.

contrary, it seems that on another level Konrad has set out to impress his audience with his skill as a vernacular author.[11]

Tension between self-negation (in favour of some kind of higher authority) and artistic self-assertion is a crucial aspect of Konrad's presentation of authorship in his narrative texts as well. These will now be read in three groups that are defined on the basis of either uniformity of genre (legends) or of scale (longer/shorter narratives). Once the themes of patronage, authorial co-operation, and artistic self-assurance have been described for each text in its respective grouping, works which are generally thought to lay a 'false' claim to Konrad's authorship will be reconsidered with a view to establishing the degree to which they take account of Konrad's own strategies of authorial self-presentation.

I. THE LEGENDS

Patronage is central to the presentation of authorship in Konrad's legends (*Silvester, Alexius, Pantaleon*) although its precise significance varies from text to text.[12] As a generically unified group these works provide impressive evidence of the space that Konrad is prepared to create in order to describe his relationship with those who commission him.

The poet largely defers to his patron in *Silvester*,[13] but this does not entirely preclude the incorporation of another, self-assured authorial role that is based on independent literary theoretical reflections. In fact, it is with these reflections that the prologue opens:

> Ez bringet zweiger hande fruht
> daz man die wârheit mit genuht
> von götlichen maeren saget.

[11] Karl Bertau, 'Beobachtungen und Bemerkungen zum Ich in der "Goldenen Schmiede"', in *Philologie als Kulturwissenschaft: Studien zur Literatur und Geschichte des Mittelalters. Festschrift für Karl Stackmann zum 65. Geburtstag*, edd. Ludger Grenzmann/Hubert Herkommer/Dieter Wuttke, Göttingen 1987, pp. 179–92.

[12] See also Timothy R. Jackson, 'Konrad von Würzburg's Legends: Their Historical Context and the Poet's Approach to His Material', in *Probleme mittelhochdeutscher Erzählformen*, edd. Ganz/Schröder, 197–213, esp. 204–10; Joachim Knape, 'Geschichte bei Konrad von Würzburg?', *JOWG* 5 (1988–9), 421–30, esp. 421ff.; Thelen, *Dichtergebet*, 315f., 521f., 527f.

[13] *Silvester* is preserved in a single manuscript: Trier, StB, Ms. 1990/17, datable to the late 1200s; see Edward Schröder, 'Studien zu Konrad von Würzburg I–III', *GGN* 1912, pp. 1–47, esp. 3–13.

> ez trîbet vürder und verjaget
> den liuten swaeren urdrutz
> und gît dâ bî sô rîchen nutz
> daz man dervon gebezzert wirt.[. . .]
> des hân ich allen mînen muot
> dar ûf geleit die mîne tage
> daz ich von einem man gesage,[. . .] (1–7, 30ff.)

(Telling pious stories in all their truth bears two kinds of fruit. It drives off
and chases away people's oppressive boredom, and at the same time it is
so greatly beneficial that it has an improving effect.[. . .] For that reason, I
have put my whole mind all my days to the telling of a story about a man
[. . .])

The argument that poetry should have the twin effects of entertainment and moral improvement is conventional and represents a quin-
tessential aspect of medieval literary theory.[14] It is unusual, however,
to open a saint's life in this way. In contrast to Rudolf von Ems's
Barlaam und Josaphat, for example, the authorial profile conveyed here
by the motifs of endeavour does not draw on the idea of the poet's
'personal' religious consciousness. Konrad's compositional activity is
directly associated with literary didacticism only, and the ensuing
outline of the sanctity of the central protagonist (33–75) affirms the
programmatic potential of this specific text.

The author's endeavour is subsequently put into context in the
conclusion to the prologue which gives details of the broader circumstances of production of the work:

> sô hât ein herre mich gebeten
> daz ich entslieze die getât,
> die sîn lîp begangen hât
> um den êweclichen solt.
> von Roetenlein her Liutolt
> der hât mit sînen gnâden
> mich tumben Cuonrâden
> von Wirzeburc dar ûf gewent
> daz sich dar nâch mîn herze sent
> daz ich diz buoch verrihte
> und ez in tiusch getihte
> bringe von latîne.
> durch die bete sîne

---

[14] Joachim Suchomski, *'Delectatio' und 'utilitas': Ein Beitrag zum Verständnis mittelalterlicher
komischer Literatur*, Berne/Munich 1975 (Bibliotheca Germanica 18).

> tuon ich ez als ich beste kan.
> der selbe tugentrîche man,
> der mich hier umbe alsus erbat,
> der hât ze Basel in der stat
> ze deme tuome pfrüende.
> dar umbe daz ez stüende
> ze nutze werden liuten,
> sô hiez er mich bediuten
> diz götliche maere. (76–97)

(Thus, a lord has asked me to expound the deeds which he [Silvester] performed for eternal reward. It is Lord Liutolt von Roeteln who has, through his support, induced me, dull-witted Konrad von Würzburg, to long with my heart to compose this book and translate it into German verse from Latin. On his requests I am doing so as best I can. The same very virtuous man, who asked me to do this in this way, has a position at the cathedral in the city of Basle. He commanded me to tell this pious tale in order for it to be of benefit to worthy people.)

Konrad records his own authorship in these lines by naming himself, specifying that he is reworking a Latin source in German verse, and providing reassurances of his effort. Yet it is the emphatic presentation of the poet's subordination to his patron that determines the tone and structure of the passage. Aside from the praise of the patron for his generosity, virtue, and ecclesiastical office, Konrad invokes the external instigation of this literary enterprise at every turn (76, 81ff., 88, 91, 96). The author is identified only after the patron and is effectively characterized as the instrument of Liutolt von Roeteln's will rather than as an active agent. Even the 'longing' (84) in the poet's heart is said to have been induced within him ('dar ûf gewent' 83). In accordance with this view of the production of the text Liutolt is credited with his own didactic programme, as befitting the pastoral concerns of a high-ranking church official in Basle.[15]

The author's didactive imperative and his deference to the patron recur in the epilogue (5186–222) in a new atmosphere of religious pathos. The audience is exhorted to venerate Silvester and then to intercede on behalf of the patron, as the authorial 'independence' of the first phase of the prologue is converted here into an emphatic gesture of admonition:

[15] For further discussion of Konrad's patrons in Basle see Chapter 1 section III above.

dar umbe ich zallen stunden
wil râten stille und überlût
daz man den werden gotes trût
mit ganzen triuwen êre
und man des wünsche sêre
Liutolde dâ von Roetelein
daz im der vröuden honicsein
zuo lange müeze sîgen
und daz er künne stîgen
ze himel ûf der saelden berc,
wand er gevrumet hât diz werc
mit bete beide und mit gebote
ze prîse dem vil werden gote,
der sunder ende und âne zil
rîhsen unde leben wil. (5208–22)

(For that reason I would advise unconditionally that one honour the worthy man beloved of God utterly faithfully, and that one wish for the honey of joy long to flow towards Liutolt von Roeteln and for him to ascend to heaven on the mountain of salvation. For he has helped this work on by both prayer and command in praise of illustrious God whose rule and existence are everlasting and boundless.)

In terms of the depiction of the work's production Konrad is again self-effacing and refers solely to Liutolt's devout promotion of the process. This appeal on the patron's behalf is strengthened by a complementary pair of images that convey earthly abundance (5214f.) and heavenly reward (5216f.) respectively.[16] That the poet does not ask the audience to consider his own spiritual benefit, as we might have expected, is part of the same strategy.

The religious dimension to Konrad's authorial self-presentation in *Alexius* is greater,[17] involving a complex layering of interdependent relationships between God, the author, and the patrons of the text. The first of these, the author's dependence on God, is signalled in the opening lines:

[16] 'der vröuden honicsein' (5214) is clearly related to the biblical image of worldly abundance 'in terram quae fluit lacte et melle' (Exodus 3. 8). Cf. also Exodus 3. 17; Joshua 5. 6; Jeremiah 11. 5. The word *honicseim* also occurs in the corresponding passages of the *Altdeutsche Exodus* (518f.; 640f.).

[17] *Alexius* is preserved today in two fifteenth-century manuscripts, whilst two printed sources transmit the text of an earlier third codex; see Nigel F. Palmer, 'Eine Prosabearbeitung der Alexiuslegende Konrads von Würzburg', *ZfdA* 108 (1979), 158–80, esp. 174f.

Got, schepfer über alliu dinc,
sît daz der wîsheit ursprinc
von dir fliuzet unde gât,
sô lâ mir dîner helfe rât
zuo vliezen und die sinne sleht,
daz ich geprîse dînen kneht,[. . .]
dâ von sô lâ mir dînen
wîsen rât ze helfe komen,
sô daz sîn leben ûz genomen,
daz in latîne stât geschriben,
werde in tiusch von mir getriben
alsô bescheidenlîche nu
daz dâ von geprîset du
werden müezest unde ouch er.
sîn hôher name was dâ her
sô vremde gnuogen liuten. (1–6, 16–25)

(God, Creator of all things, since the spring of wisdom flows and courses
from You, so let the guidance of Your aid flow to me and equip me with
lucid senses, that I may praise Your servant [. . .]. For that reason let me
profit from Your wise counsel, so that [a record of] his superb life, which
is written in Latin, may be furthered by me in German with such understanding now that through this You must be praised as well as him [Alexius].
His glorious name has previously been unknown to too many people.)

Prayer for divine inspiration is an appropriate beginning for a saint's
life. Yet a number of the standard features of this construction, as
modelled, say, by Wolfram, are absent in *Alexius*. Konrad evidently
feels no need to demonstrate his faith through an introductory
hymn—line 1 ('Got, schepfer über alliu dinc') is really quite perfunctory—and topoi concerning sinfulness are dispensed with as well.
The thematic emphasis of this particular passage is on the literary
project itself and the relationship between the human author and
God that underpins it. The poet invokes divine aid in order to
authorize a programme of transmission and disclosure. The life of
this saint, it is argued, is exceptional but relatively unknown.
Konrad's translation from Latin to the vernacular ensures that it will
reach a wider (lay) audience, to the greater glory of God.

The rest of the prologue (26–56) is addressed directly to the audience, and it is in this passage, rather as in lines 1–32 of *Silvester*, that
the human author's moral imperative comes to the fore:

nu wil ich iu betiuten
unde entsliezen die getât

> die der vil saeldenrîche hât
> begangen ûf der erden,
> durch daz gebezzert werden
> müg eteswer von sîner tugent. (26–31)

(Now I want to tell and inform you of the deeds which the most blessed man performed on earth, so that someone may be improved by [the example of] his virtue.)

The programme of a broader transmission is alluded to here by the verb 'entsliezen' (27) which is especially resonant against the background of lines 16–25.[18] But for the main part, the change of addressee involves the exposition of another function of the composition. As well as the praise of God, the moral improvement of the audience is now shown to be a central authorial concern.[19]

Further light is thrown on the issue of authorship in the epilogue (1381–412). Having urged his audience to venerate Alexius,[20] the poet provides a statement on the broader circumstances of production of the work:

> von Basel zwêne bürger hânt
> sô rehte liebe mir getân
> daz ich von latîne hân
> diz maere in tiusch gerihtet.
> ez wart durch si getihtet
> gern unde willeclichen doch,
> daz man dâ bî gedenke ir noch
> und mîn vil tumben mannes.
> von Bermeswîl Jôhannes
> unde ouch Heinrich Îsenlîn,
> die zwêne vlîzic sint gesîn
> daz ich ez hân zeim ende brâht. (1388–99)

---

[18] For comparable examples of *entsliezen* in *Silvester* cf. 77, 509, 1725. See also Monecke, *Erzählprinzip*, 122–30; Timothy R. Jackson, *The Legends of Konrad von Würzburg: Form, Content, Function*, Erlangen 1983 (Erlanger Studien 45), 176–85.

[19] 'wan swer daz leben sîner jugent | durnehteclîche merket, | der mac dâ von gesterket | an guoter sache werden hie. | des saeldenrîchen leben ie | macht ander liute saeldenhaft. | er gap in edel bîschaft | und ein sô nützez bilde | daz in diu sünde wilde | wart von gotes lêre. | dâ von hab ich nu sêre | mînen muot geleit daran | daz ich gesage von einem man | der haete gar ein heilic leben, | durch daz sîn tugent müeze geben | den liuten hôhe saelikeit | den hie sîn leben wirt geseit' (32–48).

[20] 'Dâ von sô râte ich gerne deme | der sîn leben hie vernerne | und von im diz getihte lese, | daz er im undertaenic wese | mit ganzen triuwen iemer. | sîn trôst verlât si niemer | die sich ûf sîne gnâde lânt' (1381–7).

(Two citizens of Basle have been so very good to me that I have recast this
story in German from Latin. It was composed for their sakes most willingly and gladly, so that all the while people should think of them and of
me, stupid man that I am. Johannes von Bermeswil and Heinrich Iselin as
well, these two have worked hard so that I could finish it.)

Another fundamental authorial relationship is revealed as the poet
explains that he is working for two patrons.[21] The process of translation from Latin to German is therefore described now as part of
a specific commission; and the poet's euphemistic reference to his
material dependence (1389) functions as a complement to the invocation of spiritual aid in the prologue. It is also intimated that
Konrad's patrons were actively involved in the composition of the
work (1398), a detail which plays with the notion of an authorial
co-operative, raising the patrons' stock in the eyes of the audience
(who are to intercede on their behalf).

Konrad renews his prayer for the patrons in the final phase of
the epilogue, but—in contrast to the depiction of Liutolt von Roeteln
in *Silvester*—he explicitly maintains his own position as an active
agent in the production of the text by seeking to include himself in
the audience's thoughts as well:

> si müezen beide saelic wesen
> an lîbe und an der sêle dort.
> got gebe in staeter vröuden hort
> und êweclicher wunnen rât,
> und daz ich armer Kuonrât
> von Wirzeburc gelebe alsô
> daz mir diu sêle werde vrô:
> des helfe mir der süeze Krist,
> der got bî sînem vater ist
> bî sîner zeswen sîten
> ân ende zallen zîten. (1402–12)

(May they both be blessed, in body and then in soul [in heaven]. May God
give them the treasure of constant joy and guide them to eternal glori-
ousness; and may I, poor [sinful] Konrad von Würzburg, live in such a way
that my soul will rejoice. Let sweet Christ help me in this who sits at the
right-hand side of God His Father for all eternity.)

---

[21] For more on these individuals see Chapter 1 section III above.

The final set of relationships between God, the author, and the patrons of the text is marked out in this overtly religious closure in which all of the humans involved are shown, as individual Christians, to be at the mercy of God. However, whilst there is no reason to doubt the sincerity of Konrad's expressions of his religiosity (1406, 1409), they may also be seen to fulfil a poetological function. The devotional context allows the poet to name himself in his own right, and maintain a record of his authorship beyond that of the patronage of Johannes von Bermeswil and Heinrich Iselin without seeming to be inappropriately self-assertive or even vainglorious.

Notably, Konrad's authorial self-presentation varies in the subsequent manuscript transmission of *Alexius*. The relevant passages (1–56; 1381–412) were both preserved in their entireties in manuscript A (Strassburg, Johanniterbibl. A 100, datable to the 1300s [lost 1819]). However, the other two codices differ significantly.[22] In J (Innsbruck, Ferdinandeum FB 32034, dated 1425) the prologue is retained, and the epilogue finishes on the considerably earlier line 'sîn trôst verlât si niemer' (1386). Thus, although the authorial act of admonition (1381–7) remains largely intact, all details of the broader circumstances of production as well as a record of the identity of the poet are discarded (1388–412). In S (Benediktinerstift Engelberg, cod. 240, dated 1478) there is no prologue and the epilogue has been reworked: lines 1388f. now underline the impression of an authorial co-operative in Basle ('von Basel zwêne bürger hânt | Diss mer uff dûtsch geticht'), whilst verses 1396–412 are replaced by an expression of communal religiosity.[23] Such disregard for Konrad's composition of the text is indicative of another, rather less particular, attitude towards authorship in the transmission of vernacular narrative in the Middle Ages, and it highlights the perilous status of exactly those passages with which we are concerned. As we shall see, this phenomenon is a characteristic feature of the transmission of a number of Konrad's shorter narratives which include texts whose authorial profile varies from manuscript to manuscript, as well as those whose preservation in a single codex presents us with seemingly intractable problems.

---

[22] The following details are taken from the apparatus in Gereke's edn. (pp. 3, 62f.). See also Jackson, *Legends*, 375–9; Brandt, *Konrad von Würzburg*, 128.

[23] 'Das ûns got all fûre in das himelriche | Vnd wir da mit im̃ lebent ewenkliche | Dar zů helf vns gott der vatter vnd der sun | Vnd der heilig geist yemer vnd nun'.

Patronage is treated most radically in Konrad's third saint's life, *Pantaleon*,[24] where the patron would seem to be stylized as the author of the text. In accordance with a strategy that is familiar to us from both *Silvester* and *Alexius*, the prologue of *Pantaleon* (1–66) contains reflections on didacticism which come to be directly associated with the poet's own storytelling.[25] These are then underpinned by the exposition of the saint's credentials and reassurances of the spiritual rewards that Pantaleon, and his story, can offer.[26] However, as much as Konrad's didactic imperative is asserted, there are no actual references in the prologue to an authorial act of composition.

The function of this absence becomes clear in retrospect when considering the epilogue of the work (2132–58). Here the call to venerate Pantaleon is followed by a remarkable depiction of patronage:

> von Arguel Johannes,
> der Winharten tohter kint,
> geschuof daz sîniu wunder sint
> alsus getihtet schône.
> mit sîner miete lône
> brâht er si von latîne
> ze tiuscher worte schîne,
> dar umbe daz die liute
> vernaemen dran ze diute
> daz er kan trûren stoeren.
> die diz getihte hoeren,
> und swer die marter sîn verneme,
> die wünschen heiles alle deme
> der diz werc gefrumet hât.
> und wizzent daz helfe unde rât
> der reine marteraere tuot
> in allen die getriuwen muot
> ze herzen tragent wider in:
> er stoeret leides ungewin. (2140–58)

[24] The text is preserved in one fragmentary manuscript: Vienna, ÖNB, cod. 2884, *c.* 1380–90; see Woesler (ed.), *Pantaleon*, p. v.

[25] 'ein herze wirt gesterket | an reines willen krefte | von guoter bîschefte | und wirt im sünde wilde. | von guoter liute bilde | den liuten allez guot geschiht. | ûf alsô rîche zuoversiht | wil ich ein wârez maere sagen' (20–7).

[26] 'er ist ein lieht der kristenheit, | daz in des herzen sinne | den glanz der wâren minne | kan bieten unde reichen. | dâ von ich sîniu zeichen | und sîne marter wil enbarn. | daz wunder sol ze liehte varn | daz got durch sîne tugent begie. | mit rede wil ich ensliezen hie | den namen und die helfe sîn, | durch daz den liuten werde schîn | daz sîn genâde manicvalt | si müge erloesen mit gewalt | von allem ungevelle' (48–61).

(Johannes von Arguel, child of the daughter of the Winharts, created the conditions in which his [Pantaleon's] miracles could take such beautiful poetic form. By the reward of his payment he brought them to light in the German language from Latin, in order for people to understand clearly through this work that he [Pantaleon] can dispel grief. All those who hear this poem, and anyone who hears of his martyrdom, should wish for the salvation of the man who promoted this work. Know too that the pure martyr gives help and counsel to all who are true in their hearts towards him. He can dispel the misfortune of suffering.)

Konrad's self-subordination to his patron in *Silvester* is taken one step further in *Pantaleon* with the virtual abdication of his own authorial role in favour of Johannes von Arguel.[27] In lines 2142f. the latter's patronage is described as the necessary precondition for the poetic composition of the work, which is portrayed as an indeterminate anonymous process. The patron himself is stylized as the German author in 2144ff. where the phrase *von latîne bringen* is used to denote his material agency in the translation of the text.[28] The suggestion that the instigator of the literary enterprise should receive the credit due to its author as well is a great honour,[29] and it is in this context that the absence both of Konrad's name and of any reference to his act of composition in the prologue is to be seen. Similarly, the concluding appeal for the audience's intercession is solely on behalf of Johannes von Arguel.

The suppression of the figure of the author in this passage is striking, but a final assessment of its significance is complicated by several factors. First, there is a distinct possibility that the text as preserved in its single manuscript is incomplete. The last six pages of the codex have been cut out and lines 2088–158 of *Pantaleon* fill the final folio of the manuscript as it stands (162ᵛ). Thus, the epilogue may have continued on the following—missing—pages.[30] Second, the last lines of the extant text might be corrupt anyway. Line 2153 certainly provides some evidence of later interpolation: the manuscript reading of 'der diz werc geschriben uñ gefrúmet hat' seems to reflect an attempt by the scribe either to include himself in the thoughts of the audience or to shore up the authorial role of the patron (Johannes von Arguel being the subject of both

---

[27] For more on the historical background see Chapter I section III above.

[28] Konrad employs this phrase to describe his own authorial activity in *Silvester* (85ff.).

[29] Konrad's portrayal of Johannes von Arguel is read differently by Thelen, *Dichtergebet*, 521f.

[30] Woesler (ed.), *Pantaleon*, 73.

'geschriben' and 'gefrúmet'). Furthermore, scholars have long suspected that line 2154 originally contained the poet's first name (*Kuonrât*).[31] The text therefore does not allow us to make a definitive statement regarding the epilogue which might have included references to Konrad in his own right that were subsequently reworked or lost. What remains is the poet's radical strategy of self-effacement and deference towards his patron in lines 2140–9.

References to patronage are an integral part of Konrad's presentation of authorship in his legends. This does not necessarily exclude elements that convey a degree of artistic self-assurance, such as the literary theoretical reflections in *Silvester* and the plea for divine inspiration and independent authorial naming in *Alexius*. However, in *Silvester* and *Pantaleon* there is a distinct tendency for the German author to minimize or even relinquish his own role. Such a strategy reflects a view of intellectual property that largely discounts the claims that the poet himself may stake, and which ensures in this overtly religious context that Liutolt von Roeteln and Johannes von Arguel garner every possible blessing.[32]

II. THE LONGER NARRATIVES

Konrad privileges the alternative aspect of artistic self-assurance in his longer secular narratives (*Engelhard, Partonopier und Meliur, Trojanerkrieg*). He employs his authorial signature more assertively in these texts, for example, and his most extensive literary theoretical reflections are found here as well. That is not to say that reference—and deference—to patronage fails to occur in any of these works, as the prologue of *Partonopier und Meliur* illustrates. It should also be noted that in contrast to *Engelhard*, whose main narrative body (6,000 lines) is bracketed by a prologue and an epilogue, both *Partonopier und Meliur* (21,000 lines) and the *Trojanerkrieg* (40,000 lines) are incomplete. In spite of their length the presentation of authorship in these two texts is largely restricted to a single opening prologue. The implications

---

[31] Karl Lachmann, 'Berichtigungen und zusätze zum sechsten bande', *ZfdA* 6 (1848), 580; Franz Pfeiffer, 'Über Konrad von Würzburg', *Germania* 12 (1867), 1–48, esp. 25f.; Jackson, 'Konrad von Würzburg's Legends', 205f. For opposition to this idea see Bartsch (ed.), *Partonopier und Meliur*, Vienna 1871, p. XI.

[32] See also de Boor, *Die deutsche Literatur im späten Mittelalter*, 43.

of these circumstances will be taken into account with particular reference to the *Trojanerkrieg*.[33]

In *Engelhard* Konrad presents us with an unequivocal profile of didactic authorship.[34] The prologue (1–216) opens with a poetically refined plea for the revival of *triuwe* ('constancy'), a virtue which the poet perceives to have almost completely disappeared (1–88 [strophic]; 89–139).[35] The poet intends to rectify this situation (140–207) by strengthening the resolve of those capable of *triuwe* with an exemplary tale, a statement that culminates in an avowal of authorship:

> von Wirzeburc ich Kuonrât
> hân si ze saelden für geleit
> den liuten von der kristenheit
> in tiuscher worte schîne.
> ich hân si von latîne
> in rîme alsô gerihtet
> und ûf den wân getihtet
> daz sich nâch mînes herzen ger
> dâ bî gebezzer etewer. (208–16)

(I, Konrad von Würzburg, have presented it [the adventure] in the form of the German language to the people of Christendom for their ultimate benefit. I have reworked it in verse from Latin and composed it in the hope that somebody may be improved by it, as my heart desires.)

This passage secures a record of the identity of the author in a particularly self-assured way. As in *Silvester* and *Alexius* the naming of the author occurs in the first person, but here it remains unqualified either by self-deprecatory epithets, or references to a patron as the instigator of the project.[36] The result is an assertive model of

---

[33] See also Christoph Cormeau, 'Überlegungen zum Verhältnis von Ästhetik und Rezeption', *JOWG* 5 (1988–9), 95–107, esp. 103ff.; Elisabeth Lienert, *Geschichte und Erzählen: Studien zu Konrads von Würzburg 'Trojanerkrieg'*, Wiesbaden 1996 (Wissensliteratur im Mittelalter 22), 251–61.

[34] The text is preserved in a sixteenth-century print of which there are seven known copies; see Steinhoff (ed.), *Der 'Engelhard' Konrads von Würzburg*, 3.

[35] 'swaz guot gewinnet, daz ist wert. | dâ von der valsch nû brichet für | und wirt gedrungen ûz der tür | frou Triuwe an manegen enden. | bî der liute wenden | wirbet si genôte | nâch dem wibelbrôte | und stât vil hungermaelec. | si dunket unliutsaelec | beide frouwen unde man. | herberge si gewinnen kan | niender an den gazzen. | man wil si leider hazzen | und treit ir lützel iemen gunst' (126–39).

[36] For the hypothesis that lines referring to patronage were cut from this prologue before the text came to print see Helmut de Boor, 'Die Chronologie der Werke Konrads von Würzburg, insbesondere die Stellung des Turniers von Nantes', *PBB* (Tüb.) 89 (1967), 210–69, esp. 254.

self-identification which clearly harks back to Wolfram's practice of authorial signature.[37] In accordance with the thrust of the preceding part of the prologue the description of the poet's activity is then conflated with two final expressions of didactic intent with reference to both the collective (210) and the individual (216). Taken together these several elements create an irrevocable association, before the start of the narrative proper, between Konrad's authorship and a programme of (moral) improvement.

The prologue of *Engelhard* finds a pendant in the epilogue (6474–504). Here too, consideration of the desired effect of the story and the qualities of *triuwe* leads up to a piece of forthright self-presentation:

> von Wirzeburc ich Kuonrât
> hân ez von latîne
> ze tiuscher worte schîne
> geleitet und gerihtet
> und ûf den trôst getihtet
> daz ein herze wol gemuot
> dar an ein saelic bilde guot
> ze lûterlicher triuwe neme [. . .] (6492–9)

(I, Konrad von Würzburg, have brought and shaped it [the story] from Latin to its form in the German language and have composed it in the hope that a well-disposed heart may take from it a shining example of pure constancy [. . .])

There are a number of obvious parallels between this passage and lines 208–16. The presentation of the authorship of the work rests once more on assertive first-person naming together with an outline of the nature of the composition and its overtly didactic function. The absence of any reference to patronage again enables Konrad to construct an image of himself as an author who is motivated solely by moral concerns. That no 'new' dimensions are added to the authorial profile in the epilogue is symptomatic of a strategy of repetition and reiteration. Konrad stamps his authorship on the text through practically identical statements at both the opening and conclusion of the tale.

---

[37] 'ich bin Wolfram von Eschenbach' (*Parzival* 114,12); 'mir Wolfram von Eschenbach' (*Parzival* 185,7); 'ich Wolfram von Eschenbach' (*Parzival* 827,13); 'ich, Wolfram von Eschenbach' (*Willehalm* 4,19).

In the prologue of *Partonopier und Meliur* Konrad combines two seemingly contradictory ideas of authorship within one passage.[38] Whilst the independence of the poet is maintained in an initial sequence of theoretical reflections (1–149), the composition of the work itself is subsequently described in terms of patronage and authorial co-operation (150–225). A keynote of the first part of the prologue is struck through the image of the nightingale:

> in holze und in geriuten
> diu nahtigale singet,
> ir sanc vil ofte erklinget,
> dâ niemen hoeret sînen klanc;
> si lât dar umbe niht ir sanc
> daz man sîn dâ sô lützel gert:
> si hât in selber alsô wert
> und alsô liep tag unde naht
> daz si durch wünneclichen braht
> ir lîbe grôzen schaden tuot:
> wan der dunket si sô guot
> und alsô rehte minneclich
> daz si ze tôde singet sich. (122–34)

(In forest and field the nightingale sings. Very often its song rings out where nobody can hear its melody. It does not stop singing just because it is so unwanted there. It treasures its own song and holds it so dear, day and night, that it does itself great physical harm through this marvellous noise: it considers its own song so fine and so very lovely that it sings itself to death.)

The independence of the nightingale is offered as an example to gifted poets who so often remain unappreciated in a world of mediocre talents or 'larks' ('lerchen' 78, 80).[39] As the opening makes clear, vernacular poetry fulfils important social functions,[40] but it also has an intrinsic value that cannot be negated by undiscerning

---

[38] The text is preserved in one fifteenth-century manuscript and two earlier fragments; see appendix by Rainer Gruenter in *Partonopier und Meliur*, ed. Bartsch, 339–74, esp. 339–51. For further analysis of the prologue see Haug, *Literaturtheorie*, 351–63; Susanne Rikl, *Erzählen im Kontext von Affekt und Ratio: Studien zu Konrads von Würzburg 'Partonopier und Meliûr'*, Frankfurt a. M. 1996 (Mikrokosmos 46), 207–26.

[39] See also Sabine Obermaier, *Von Nachtigallen und Handwerkern: 'Dichtung über Dichtung' in Minnesang und Sangspruchdichtung*, Tübingen 1995 (Hermaea Germanistische Forschungen NF 75), 218 note 232; Rikl, *Affekt und Ratio*, 216ff.

[40] 'Ez ist ein gar vil nütze dinc, | daz ein bescheiden jungelinc | getihte gerne hoere | und er niemen stoere, | der singen unde reden kan. | dâ lît vil hôhes nutzes an | und ist ouch guot für ürdrutz' (1–7).

audiences. The shocking detail of the nightingale's death conveys the existential relationship between singer and song. If he has no one to perform to, the human poet should not betray his own being by refraining from entertaining himself with his *kunst* (135, 137, 140, 148).

The predominant tone of lines 1–149 is one of artistic self-assurance, and Konrad is openly dismissive towards those he regards as bad poets.[41] However, he treats the idea of his own artistic 'autonomy' cautiously:

> haet ich bescheidenlichen sin,
> der nütze und edel waere,
> ungerne ich sîn enbaere [. . .] (116ff.)

(If I had an understanding mind that was useful and noble, I would be unwilling to go without it [. . .])

The tenor of humility becomes still more apparent when Konrad addresses his concrete situation in the second part of the prologue. It is gradually revealed that he himself enjoys a receptive courtly audience whose qualities, it seems, are embodied in one individual, the patron:

> ich weiz ir einen, wizze Krist,
> sô tugentlichen gartet
> daz sîn gemüete wartet
> ûf guot getihte gerne.
> der saelden leitesterne
> der wîset in ûf êren rât.
> der selbe diz gefüeget hât
> daz ich in tiutsch getihte
> diz buoch von wälsche rihte
> und ez ze rîme leite.[. . .]
> den ich hie meine, daz ist der
> Schaler, mîn her Pêter.
> der tugende strâze gêter
> und ist ûf êren pfat getreten.
> er hât ze Basel mich gebeten
> daz ich diz werc volende.
> mit sîner gebenden hende
> hât er dar ûf gewîset mich

---

[41] 'ez tihtet unde schrîbet | rede unde sanc vil manic man, | der alsô vil ze rehte kan | gesingen und gesprechen, | als ich mit blîje brechen | kan durch einen quâderflins' (88–93).

daz mîn tumbez herze sich
vil kumbers an genomen hât.
von Wirzeburc ich Kuonrât
erfülle gerne sînen muot. (168–77, 182–93)

(I know one of them, may Christ know it, to be of such a virtuous nature
that he gladly looks out for good poetry. The guiding star of good fortune
leads him toward a wealth of honour. This same man caused me to make
a German composition out of this French book and to set it in rhyme.
[. . .] The man I am referring to is my Lord Peter Schaler. He travels the
road of virtue and has taken the path of honour. He asked me in Basle to
carry this work out to its conclusion. With his giving hand he has so directed
me that I, simple soul, have accepted great trials. I, Konrad von Würzburg,
fulfil his wishes gladly.)

The extensive homage to the patron, Peter Schaler, provides the
initial context for the explicit presentation of Konrad's authorship
of *Partonopier und Meliur*.[42] Accordingly, whilst these lines record
Konrad as the author of the German text, he is subordinated to
Peter Schaler at every turn. The authorial activity of composition
that is referred to on various occasions throughout this passage
(175ff., 187, 191) is repeatedly shown to be instigated by the patron
('gefüeget' 174, 'gebeten' 186, 'gewîset' 189); and the poet employs
self-deprecation to downgrade his own role still further. Even the
characteristic first-person naming of the author ('von Wirzeburc ich
Kuonrât' 192) forms part of an expression of subservience ('erfülle
gerne sînen muot' 193).[43]

Peter Schaler's involvement is subsequently shown to extend to
the choice of the story material.[44] This last detail paves the way for
another fundamental qualification of Konrad's authorial profile:

ouch hât mich Heinrîch Marschant
ûf diz werc gestiuret wol.
ob ez volendet werden sol,
des hilfet er mir sêre.
sîn rât mir süeze lêre

[42] For more on Peter Schaler as a historical personage see Chapter one section III
above.

[43] The patron may also be seen to be glorified here in terms of the central motifs of
the story of the Magi (Matthew 2. 1–11): anticipation (170f.); guiding star (173); journeying
(184f.); generosity (188).

[44] 'diz maere dûhte in alsô guot | und des tugent alsô breit, | von dem dis âventiure
seit, | daz er durch sînen reinen sin | mich hât gelêret, daz ich bin | ûf diz buoch mit
vlîze komen. | ich hân des werkes an genomen | mich durch sîne milte hant' (194–201).

zuo wîset unde biutet.
daz buoch er schône diutet
von wälhisch mir in tiutschiu wort.
er hât der zweier sprâche hort
gelernet als ein wîser man.
franzeis ich niht vernemen kan,
daz tiutschet mir sîn künstic munt.
dâ bî sô tuot mir helfe kunt
Arnolt der Fuhs spât unde fruo,
wande er flîzet sich dar zuo
daz für sich gê diz werc von mir.
mit willecliches herzen gir
wont er mir dicke und ofte bî,
durch daz ich sô betrehtic sî,
daz ich der âventiure gar
als ordenlichen mite var
daz si mit lobe neme ein zil. (202–23)

(Heinrich Merschant too has guided me well with this work. He helps me greatly towards its eventual completion. His counsel provides and offers me sweet instruction. He translates the book beautifully for me from French into German. He has learnt the sum of both languages like a wise man. I do not understand French; his skilful tongue turns it into German for me. At the same time Arnolt Fuchs lends me his aid at all hours, for he strives that this work should issue forth from me. Out of the desire of his willing heart he frequently spends time with me in order that I take enough thought in following all of the tale of adventure properly, so that it reaches a laudable conclusion.)

Konrad presents himself here as working in a kind of authorial co-operative with two other named individuals who fulfil the roles of translator and general 'collaborator' respectively.[45] Regardless of the extent to which these details reflect the real process of composition, the poet is clearly seeking to emphasize the contribution of these men at the cost of his own. The flattering depiction of Heinrich Merschant, Konrad's surprising admission of his ignorance of French (212),[46] and the ambiguity surrounding the exact activity of Arnolt Fuchs all combine to suggest that the function of this passage

[45] Rikl, *Affekt und Ratio*, 219–26. For medieval co-authorship see Bumke, 'Autor und Werk', 87–95. Heinrich Merschant and Arnolt Fuchs belong to the upper social stratum in Basle as described in Chapter 1 section III above; see also Bumke, *Mäzene*, 287ff.

[46] These lines are treated with scepticism by Monecke, '*wildekeit*', 27ff. Elsewhere in the work Konrad refers only to his literacy in German and Latin: 'wande er was der schoenste knabe, | von dem ich noch gelesen habe | in tiutsche und in latîne' (289ff.).

is, first and foremost, a representational one. The sketch of these particular stages in the production of the work is a highly self-conscious statement of the interest of these individuals in the pursuit of courtly literature.

The profile of Konrad's authorship that emerges in the second part of the prologue is one of a poet who is not only deeply indebted to his patron, but who is also a member of an authorial co-opera-tive. This may explain Konrad's earlier reluctance to associate himself too directly with the image of the solitary nightingale and the hypothesis of artistic 'autonomy'. However, the literary theoret-ical exposition of lines 1–149 is not as diametrically opposed to what follows as it at first appears. Artistic self-sufficiency is deemed desir-able only if the proper environment is not given. Konrad's circumstances turn out to be ideal in this respect: he has an appre-ciative audience that includes an enthusiastic patron and prominent 'co-authors'. In effect, by upholding the intrinsic value and exclu-sive status of vernacular poetry in the first part of the prologue, Konrad is probably articulating the values and presuppositions of those others who come to be associated with this literary enterprise.

The *Trojanerkrieg* contains Konrad's most ambitious prologue (1–324).[47] Here he repeatedly addresses his role as an author, with special reference to the enormity of the task in hand, whilst acknow-ledging a degree of dependency on both his patron and God. As in *Partonopier und Meliur*, the first part of the prologue culminates in an image of the nightingale. It is indicative of the new level of atten-tion paid to Konrad's authorial activity that this time the image expresses his defiance in the face of the defective courtly culture of the day:

> dur waz verbaere ich die vernunst,
> diu dicke und ofte fröuwet mich?
> ob nieman lepte mêr, denn ich,

---

[47] There are thirty-four known textual witnesses for the *Trojanerkrieg*, but only six 'complete' manuscripts and ten fragments; two excerpts of the text are transmitted as 'Minnereden', a further sixteen in the context of 'Weltchroniken'; see Elisabeth Lienert, 'Die Überlieferung von Konrads von Würzburg "Trojanerkrieg"', in *Die deutsche Trojaliteratur des Mittelalters und der Frühen Neuzeit: Materialien und Untersuchungen*, ed. Horst Brunner, Wiesbaden 1990 (Wissensliteratur im Mittelalter 3), 325–406; Hartmut Beckers, 'Brüsseler Bruchstücke aus Konrads "Trojanerkrieg"', *ZfdA* 124 (1995), 319–27. For further analysis of the prologue see Elisabeth Lienert, 'Der Trojanische Krieg in Basel: Interesse an Geschichte und Autonomie des Erzählens bei Konrad von Würzburg', in *Literarische Interessenbildung*, ed. Heinzle, 266–79, esp. 266ff.; *Geschichte und Erzählen*, 17–29.

doch seite ich unde sünge,
dur daz mir selben clünge
mîn rede und mîner stimme schal.
ich taete alsam diu nahtegal,
diu mit ir sanges dône
ir selben dicke schône
die lange stunde kürzet.[. . .]
seht, alsô wil ich unde sol
dur daz niht lâzen mînen list,
daz ir sô rehte wênic ist,
die mîn getihte wol vernemen.
mîn kunst mir selben sol gezemen:
wan mir ist sanfte gnuoc dâ mite. (186–95, 206–11)

(Why should I refrain from using the ability which entertains me most frequently? If no one were alive other than myself, I would still tell stories and sing in order that my speech and the sound of my voice would ring out to myself. I would do as the nightingale does, that often shortens the long hour for itself beautifully with the sound of its song.[. . .] You see, I too do not want to and must not abandon my skill, just because there are so very few people who receive my poetry well. My art must suit me, myself: for I am comfortable enough with it.)

Such artistic self-consciousness is anticipated and explained in the course of the reflections on the value of poetry that open the prologue (1–139). All social and ethical functions are entirely taken for granted in this sequence. Emphasis is placed instead on the poet's bewilderment at contemporary disregard for master poets ('meister') even though they are few and far between,[48] and on an exposition of the unparalleled nature of the activity of poetic composition: the art ('kunst' 74) of poetry can be taught by God only; poets require solely God-given tools ('daz si bedürfen nihtes mêr | wan zungen unde sinnes' 134f.).[49] Thus, it would appear that as a poet Konrad is morally bound to practice his art, if not in and for society, then for himself.

In further contrast to *Partonopier und Meliur*, the subsequent discussion of the composition of the *Trojanerkrieg* itself (212–324) maintains

---

[48] 'man siht der meister wênic leben, | die singen oder sprechen wol; | dâ von mich wunder nemen sol, | daz beide rîche und arme sint | an êren worden alsô blint, | daz si die wîsen ringe wegent, | die wol gebluomter rede pflegent, | diu schoene ist unde waehe' (6–13).

[49] Konrad treats these themes in his gnomic lyric as well; cf. 32,166–93; 32,301–15. See Obermaier, *Von Nachtigallen und Handwerkern*, 218–27.

the tone of artistic self-assurance. In the first of three phases, the poet describes the dimensions of the work he has undertaken and what these mean for him:

> dâ von ich mînen alten site
> ungerne wil vermîden:
> ich muoz eht aber lîden
> den kumber, des ich hân gewent.
> mîn sin der spannet unde dent
> dar ûf mit hôhem flîze,
> daz ich vil tage verslîze
> ob einem tiefen buoche,
> dar inne ich boden suoche,
> den ich doch vinden kûme.
> z'eim endelôsen pflûme,
> dar inne ein berc versünke wol,
> gelîchen man diz maere sol,[. . .]
> mîn lop daz würde krenker,
> ob ich des hie begünde,
> daz ich mit rede niht künde
> z'eim ende wol gerihten.
> ich wil ein maere tihten,
> daz allen maeren ist ein her. (212–24, 230–5)

(For that reason I should be most unwilling to relinquish my old habit. I must suffer once more the trials which I have become accustomed to. My mind expands and stretches with all diligence so that I may spend many days over a voluminous book, the depths of which I plumb, but with scant success. This story should be compared to a fathomless river in which a mountain could be sunk [. . .]. My reputation would be diminished if I started this work in such a way that I could not bring it to an end properly with my speech. I want to compose a tale to end all tales.)

Konrad's claim of familiarity with the pain of poetic composition plays on the notion that he is a poet with an authorial career, and provides a framework for the following description of the story material.[50] It is odd that Konrad does not list his other works at this point. But this may relate to the emphasis he places elsewhere on the aspects of patronage and co-operation. In other words, Konrad does just enough to suggest that he is a poet of stature without reclaiming texts such as the legends as his own intellectual property.

---

[50] For further examples of Konrad's use of *kumber* in this sense cf. *Partonopier und Meliur* 191; *Trojanerkrieg* 11365, 19686.

The scale of this particular composition immediately assumes super-
lative proportions, conveyed by the various images of the strain upon
the poet's mind (216f.) and the depths of the material (222).[51] The
enormity of the task is such that it is presented as a defining moment
in the author's career: the bold statement of the poet's ambitious
programme (234f.) is coupled with an awareness of the consequences, should he fail to complete it (230).[52]

Only after the special relationship between author and story
material has been established are other factors admitted. In lines
244–65 Konrad qualifies the image of his authorship by introducing
details of his dependency on patron and God, although it is worth
noting that even in this passage he does not lose sight of his own
role:

> daz ich ez hebe mit willen an,
> dar ûf hât wol gestiuret mich
> der werde singer Dietrich
> von Basel an dem Orte,
> der als ein êren borte
> mit zühten ist gesteinet;
> vor schanden ist gereinet
> sîn herze alsam ein lûter golt.
> dur sîner miltekeite solt,
> den ich hân dicke enpfangen,
> ist von mir an gevangen
> vil snelleclîche ein ursuoch,
> der zieren künne wol diz buoch
> mit rede in allen enden.
> geruochet helfe senden
> ein meister aller künste mir,
> sô kêre ich mînes herzen gir
> mit flîze ûf einen prologum,
> der nütze werde und alsô frum,
> daz er den liuten künne geben,

---

[51] 'als in daz wilde tobende mer | vil manic wazzer diuzet, | sus rinnet unde fliuzet
| vil maere in diz getihte grôz. | ez hât von rede sô wîten vlôz, | daz man ez kûme
ergründen | mit herzen und mit münden | biz ûf des endes boden kan' (236–43). For
more on the complex of 'water'/'sea' imagery see Lienert, *Geschichte und Erzählen*, 20f.
Several later passages underline the impression of the sheer mass of material as well:
11350–79; 12908–21; 36490–3.

[52] See also Christoph Cormeau, 'Quellenkompendium oder Erzählkonzept? Eine
Skizze zu Konrads von Würzburg "Trojanerkrieg"', in *Befund und Deutung: Zum Verhältnis
von Empirie und Interpretation in Sprach- und Literaturwissenschaft. (Hans Fromm zum 26. Mai 1979
von seinen Schülern)*, edd. Klaus Grubmüller et al., Tübingen 1979, pp. 303–19, esp. 303f.

ein bilde ûf tugentrîchez leben
und ûf bescheidenlîche tât. (244–65)

(That I commence this work willingly is the result of the guidance of the
noble cantor of Basle, Dietrich am Orte, who, like a girdle of honour, is
jewelled with courtliness. His heart is free of wrongdoings, as flawless as
pure gold. Through his generous payment, which I have received often, I
have started an 'exposition' most boldly that could adorn this book with its
speech in every way. If the Master of every art deigns to send me help,
then I will diligently turn my heart's desire towards a 'prehistory' that will
be, I hope, useful and so decent that it may provide people with an image
of virtuous living and suitable behaviour.)

Konrad praises his patron in no uncertain terms, and the comparison of Dietrich am Orte's nobility and virtue with an expensive
courtly garment and gold lends resonance to the assertion of his
generosity.[53] Nevertheless, Dietrich's involvement is restricted to this
provision of material aid; he does not encroach on the poet's domain
of literary activity. The patron may create the ideal conditions for
the composition of an 'exposition' ('ursuoch' 255) to the main body
of the work,[54] but Konrad is keen to stress that this composition is
his (254). The following invocation of divine aid operates in much
the same fashion. In accordance with the concept of poetry outlined
earlier in the prologue, the pre-eminence of God's artistry (259) is
acknowledged before the focus returns to the poet's execution of the
'exposition' ('prologum' 261) albeit from a different angle. Whereas
the stylistic brilliance of the prehistory is highlighted in the context
of Dietrich am Orte's patronage, now its exemplary value is
affirmed.

Konrad's self-presentation remains bound up with the description
of the story material in the final phase of the prologue. This is epit-
omized by the strategy of self-naming that occurs here, in which the
author identifies himself in tandem with the first disclosure regarding
the subject matter of the work:

von Wirzeburc ich Cuonrât
von welsche in tiutsch getihte

---

[53] For more on Dietrich am Orte's position in Basle see Chapter I section III above.

[54] The terms 'ursuoch' (255) and 'prologum' (261) are taken to refer to the expansive
prehistory in the work (325–23639), which Konrad clearly demarcates by means of an
excursus in lines 23640–752. See Monecke, 'wildekeit', 107f.; Lienert, Geschichte und Erzählen,
21.

mit rîmen gerne rihte
daz alte buoch von Troye. (266–9)

(I, Konrad von Würzburg, gladly render the old book of Troy, from French into German rhymed verse.)

The author's dependence on others is not entirely forgotten in the lines that follow. Divine aid is invoked on two further occasions in conjunction with sketches of the fundamental themes of the text: fighting (280–95) and love (308–24). However, for the most part— and in keeping with his assertive self-naming—the poet discusses his compositional activity in its own right. Playing on a stock metaphorical field for the description of stylistic mastery, he contends that by virtue of his rendering, the 'old book of Troy' will flourish once again ('schôn als ein vrischiu gloye | sol ez hie wider blüejen' 270f.);[55] and we are left in no doubt as to his good will or his ability to harmonize the many strands of this story.[56] Finally, the wider cultural background to the text is taken into account:

> Dâres, ein ritter ûz erwelt,
> der selbe vil vor Troye streit,
> swaz der in kriechisch hât geseit
> von dirre küniclichen stift,
> daz wart mit endelicher schrift
> ze welsche und in latîne brâht.
> dâ wider hân ich des gedâht,
> daz ich ez welle breiten
> und mit getihte leiten
> von welsche und von latîne:
> ze tiuscher worte schîne
> wirt ez von mir verwandelt. (296–307)

(What Dares, a superb knight who himself fought many battles in front of Troy, said in Greek concerning this royal city was translated exhaustively in writing into French and Latin. Against this background, I thought I would spread word of it and transfer it with poetic composition from the French and the Latin: I have transformed it into the German language.)

This reference to the origins of the material, shown to lie with Dares' authoritative eye-witness account, establishes the grand historical

---

[55] See also Bruno Boesch, *Die Kunstanschauung in der mittelhochdeutschen Dichtung von der Blütezeit bis zum Meistergesang*, Berlin/Leipzig 1936, pp. 198–205.
[56] 'beginnet sich des müejen | mîn herze in ganzen triuwen, | daz ich ez welle erniuwen | mit worten lûter unde glanz, | ich büeze im sîner brüche schranz:| den kan ich wol gelîmen | z'ein ander hie mit rîmen, | daz er niht fürbaz spaltet' (272–9).

framework within which Konrad's own activity is to be regarded.[57] His translation of the story into German represents the latest stage in a process of exhaustive written transmission extending back to the Greek. It seems reasonable to view this process in terms of a cultural *translatio* from East to West, analogous to the chain of acts of translation described by Rudolf in *Barlaam und Josaphat*. We should note, however, that Konrad deviates from a strictly linear sequence of the three preceding stations (Greek–Latin–French) to create a rather different effect. Latin and French are not presented in their proper chronological order as consecutive stages but as sources of equal standing ('ze welsche und in latîne' 301; 'von welsche und von latîne' 305) as if to emphasize the amount of material from which Konrad composes his work.

This prologue offers prime evidence of Konrad's self-assured perception of himself as a vernacular poet and is undoubtedly the centrepiece of the presentation of authorship in the *Trojanerkrieg*. Yet for all its assertiveness, it is detrimentally affected by the sheer size of the text, being overwhelmed by the 40,000 lines that follow.[58] Those few later excursuses which are relevant to the question of authorship (11350–79; 12908–21; 13080–97; 19684–707) occur irregularly and contain no further authorial namings.[59] For a work of such large dimensions the selection of this format (and not the subdivision into book-like sections, for example) had potentially severe consequences in respect of the course of manuscript transmission. If the preservation of a record of authorial identity depended on a single passage, especially the opening of the text, it could be eradicated only too easily by subsequent scribes. This is illustrated well by the actual transmission of the *Trojanerkrieg* which is almost totally

[57] Cf. also 13080–7: 'ich tuon des wâre maere kunt, | als ich an der hystôrje las. | Dâres, der in dem strîte was, | swaz der geseit in kriechisch hât | von dirre strîteclichen tât, | daz wirt mit tiuschen worten | von mir in allen orten | entslozzen und betiutet'.

[58] The same kind of observation could also be made for *Partonopier und Meliur*, where the prologue's opening statement of authorship remains isolated in a fragment of some 20,000 lines.

[59] The excursuses in lines 11350–79 and 12908–21 reiterate the poet's preoccupation with the size of his task: 'ich hân mit rede grôze nôt | mir selber ûz gesundert, | ob mîn noch waeren hundert, | wir haeten kumbers gnuoc dâ mite, | daz wir nâch lobelichem site | diz werc zeim ende braehten' (11362–7); 'diz buoch sô rederîche | wirt von kampfes bîle, | daz ich niht hân der wîle, | daz ich gezel besunder | daz jaemerlîche wunder, | daz an Troiaeren dâ geschach' (12916–21). In lines 13080–97 the poet deals with the historical validity of the story and in 19684–707 his inability to describe Helen of Troy's beauty.

anonymous.[60] Only two of six complete manuscripts include the prologue, and in at least three of the others the text begins with verse 325.[61] Such a singular lack of interest in Konrad's authorship can be explained in terms of a later preoccupation with the story material itself, the *Trojanerkrieg* being the most widely-received vehicle of the history of Troy in German for the next three centuries. Nowhere is this more apparent than in the continuation of Konrad's text (40425–9861) that follows it seamlessly in every complete manuscript. In stark contrast to the epitaph to Rudolf in the 'first continuation' of the *Weltchronik*, the continuator of the *Trojanerkrieg* depicts the rest of the events of the war without displaying the slightest awareness of Konrad's authorship.[62]

In terms of Konrad's three longer secular narratives as a group, the prologue of the *Trojanerkrieg* represents the most articulate expression of artistic self-assurance. Here Konrad's authorship is characterized as a career-defining struggle with a monumental literary project. The theoretical reflections on the primacy of the art of poetry and Konrad's readiness to identify himself with the independence of the nightingale are anticipated in the prologue of *Partonopier und Meliur*, but in the latter they are held in check by an extensive depiction of patronage and authorial co-operation. In the *Trojanerkrieg* such restrictions are minimal: Konrad's reliance on his patron and God are acknowledged as significant factors, but only after a special relationship has been established between the author and the story material. In *Engelhard* details relating to the composition of the work are rather more perfunctory. Their emphatic formulation at both the beginning and end of the text allows Konrad to stamp his authorship on the work, another strategy that conveys a distinct sense of authorial self-assurance.

III. THE SHORTER NARRATIVES

The problem of textual instability that arose in connexion with the legends *Alexius* and *Pantaleon* is most prominent in the context of Konrad's five shorter narratives (*Turnier von Nantes*, *Schwanritter*, *Der*

---

[60] Lienert, 'Überlieferung', 389f., 402.

[61] A further fragment contains lines 243–324 of the prologue; see Beckers, 'Brüsseler Bruchstücke', 326.

[62] For more on the continuation see Lienert, *Geschichte und Erzählen*, 332–50.

Welt Lohn, Heinrich von Kempten, Herzmaere). Short stories, both religious and secular ('Mären'), were typically transmitted in large collections with other shorter forms such as the 'Rede' and 'Bispel' and were subject to a significant degree of reworking at the hands of scribes and later performers.[63] Nevertheless, within the course of just such a process of fluctuating transmission it is possible to make out passages of authorial self-presentation for almost all of Konrad's shorter works. The references to authorship here tend to be concise and assertive in tone, with a great deal of emphasis on the authorial signature. The following analyses have been arranged to form a scale from one apparent extreme (*Turnier von Nantes*) to another (*Herzmaere*) and will include brief accounts of manuscript variants and codicological evidence where appropriate.

The *Turnier von Nantes* is exceptional in that it does not have a prologue or an epilogue and contains no authorial self-presentation.[64] We may view this work as more than a negative example, however, as it provides specific evidence of the 'creative' scribal activity which often affects the openings and closures of these shorter narratives. The text as preserved in its single codex, the 'Hausbuch' of Michael de Leone, actually ends with the following ten lines:

> Diz ist der werde turnei.
> Nu sprechent alle heya hei
> Das er sus ein ende hat.
> Wie wol er hie geschriben stat
> Von des meisters handen.
> Man fünde in allen landen
> Keinen schriber so gůt.
> Got gebe uns frâude und hohen mût.
> Swer tugent hat der ist wol geborn,
> Ane tugent ist adel gar verlorn. (1157–66)

(This is the splendid tournament. Now everyone cry 'Hurray!' since it ends in this fashion. How beautifully it is written here by the master's hand. You

---

[63] Arend Mihm, *Überlieferung und Verbreitung der Märendichtung im Spätmittelalter*, Heidelberg 1967; Hanns Fischer, *Studien zur deutschen Märendichtung*, Tübingen 1968, 2nd revised edn. by Johannes Janota, 1983, pp. 18ff., 256–61, 274ff.; Ziegeler, 'Wiener Codex 2705'; Sarah Westphal-Wihl, *Textual Poetics of German Manuscripts 1300–1500*, Columbia, SC 1993. For a detailed and enlightening case-study see Christoph Gerhardt, 'Überlegungen zur Überlieferung von Konrads von Würzburg "Der Welt Lohn"', *PBB* (Tüb.) 94 (1972), 379–97.

[64] The text is preserved in one manuscript: Munich, UB, 2° Cod. ms. 731 ('Hausbuch' of Michael de Leone), datable 1345–54, fol. 59ʳ–68ʳ; see also the facsimile edn. by Horst Brunner.

couldn't find another scribe as good in all the lands. May God give us joy and high spirits. Whosoever has virtue is noble born; without virtue, nobility is utterly worthless.)

Although (anonymous) third-person self-presentation is quite feasible, the style and content of these lines would seem to preclude the possibility of Konrad's having composed them himself. Thus, this passage is generally disregarded as the handiwork of a scribe.[65] It is tempting to read lines 1160–3 as a secondary reference to Konrad's literary activity, accustomed as we are to finding the title of *meister* being conferred upon him in the rubrics of lyric manuscripts. Yet it is scarcely credible that the author's name should not be included here, and in the context of the later designation of 'schriber' (1163), verse 1160 ('Wie wol er hie geschriben stat') is more likely to refer to scribal excellence than the poet's stylistic mastery. The absence of an explicit closure in the final lines of the work proper (1–1156), which again is unusual for Konrad's narrative oeuvre, might even suggest that these 'Schreiberverse' represent more than an addition to Konrad's text. Perhaps the original epilogue of the *Turnier von Nantes* was supplanted by this passage in the course of manuscript transmission.[66] In any case, for the reader of this codex in the mid-fourteenth century, these lines were no longer recognizable as a 'foreign' body. Far from being set off, they are presented—in black ink—as part of the literary text itself, and are followed by an *explicit* ('Hie get vz der turnei von Nantheyz') which is written in red. Such circumstances sound a useful warning note regarding the instability of exactly those passages that interest us.

In spite of similarly precarious transmission the *Schwanritter* retains Konrad's presentation of authorship as a distinct element in its conclusion.[67] The epilogue (1328–58), which is largely concerned with the credibility of the marvellous story (1328–51), culminates in a statement of the identity of the author:

---

[65] The *Turnier von Nantes* is invariably described as a text of 1156 lines, and this passage has not been discussed in any detail since the observations of Bartsch (ed.), *Partonopier und Meliur*, Vienna 1871, p. XI; and Schröder, 'Studien IV–V', 118. In Schröder's edn. this passage is consigned to the apparatus (p. 75).

[66] This is asserted by Schröder, 'Studien IV–V', 118. See also Stefan Weidenkopf, 'Poesie und Recht: Über die Einheit des Diskurses von Konrads von Würzburg "Schwanritter"', in *Kontakte und Perspektiven*, ed. Cormeau, 296–337, esp. 335ff.

[67] The text is preserved in one manuscript: Frankfurt a. M., StB und UB, Ms. germ. 4° 2, *c.* 1350–1400; see Schröder (ed.), *Kleinere Dichtungen*, ii. pp. VI–VIII; Brandt, *Konrad von Würzburg*, 100.

Dis âventiure wilde
hiemite ein zil genomen hât:
von Wirzeburc ich Cuonrât
wil ir zehant ein ende geben.
got lâze uns hie sô wol geleben
daz wir besitzen iemer dort
der êwiclichen fröuden hort. (1352–8)

(With that, this extraordinary tale has run its course. I, Konrad von Würzburg, want to finish it immediately. May God permit us to live so well on earth that we may own the treasure of eternal joy in heaven forever.)

As we have already seen, Konrad names himself towards the end of both *Alexius* and *Engelhard* but, in contrast to these passages, in the epilogue of the *Schwanritter* the poet dispenses with discussion of his literary activity and programmatic intent. Instead, the author is identified in conjunction with his declaration to end the work, a device that allows Konrad to stamp his authorship on the text succinctly and at virtually the last moment; only an expression of shared religiosity follows it here (1356ff.).

The possibility that the missing first 140 lines of the *Schwanritter* may also have addressed the theme of authorship, makes it difficult to assess the significance of this passage for the text as a whole. However, lines 1352–8 would seem to feature a particularly distinctive model of authorial self-presentation: authorial naming as a strategy of closure.[68] The choice of this model might even be said to be genre-determined, for it occurs with regularity in shorter literary forms such as the secular short story ('Märe'). Other examples from Konrad's lifetime include the works of Herrand von Wildonie (*c.* 1230–78/82),[69] and *Helmbrecht* by Werner der Gärtner (*c.* 1280),[70] and this practice anticipates the famous trademark signatures of the later writers Heinrich der Teichner (active *c.* 1330–75), Heinrich Kaufringer (active *c.* 1390–1450), and Hans Rosenplüt (*c.* 1400–70).[71] Konrad's retention of a first-person form ('von

---

[68] See also Iwand, *Schlüsse*, 138–44; Sayce, 'Prolog, Epilog', 65f.

[69] 'Swaz noch getriuwer konen sî, | die tuo got alles leides frî. | den allen sol ich sîn bekant | von Wildonie Herrant' (*Die treue Gattin* 273–6); 'der iuch der âventiure mant, | der ist von Wildonie Herrant' (*Der betrogene Gatte* 363f.); 'des ger ich armer Herrant | von Wildonie genant' (*Der nackte Kaiser* 667f.); 'den rât iu râtet Herrant | von Wildonie genant' (*Die Katze* 301f.).

[70] 'Swer iu ditze maere lese, | bitet daz im got genaedec wese | und dem tihtaere, | Wernher dem Gartenaere' (1931–4).

[71] See also Fischer, *Märendichtung*, 142; Eberhart Lämmert, *Reimsprecherkunst im Spätmittelalter: Eine Untersuchung der Teichnerreden*, Stuttgart 1970, pp. 17–20.

Wirzeburc ich Cuonrât' 1354) ensures that in spite of the concision of this model the tone of artistic self-assurance is not lost.

There can be no doubt regarding the principal site of authorial self-presentation in Konrad's *Der Welt Lohn*.[72] Whilst the opening of the text does not contain any narratorial self-reference to speak of,[73] first-person naming of the author occurs in the epilogue:

> Nu merkent alle die nu sint
> dirre wilden werlte kint
> diz endehafte maere:
> daz ist alsô gewaere
> daz man ez gerne hoeren sol.
> der werlte lôn ist jâmers vol,
> daz muget ir alle hân vernomen.
> ich bin sîn an ein ende komen:
> swer an ir dienste funden wirt,
> daz in diu fröude gar verbirt
> die got mit ganzer staetekeit
> den ûzerwelten hât bereit.
> Von Wirzeburc ich Cuonrât
> gibe iu allen disen rât,
> daz ir die werlt lâzet varn,
> welt ir die sêle bewarn. (259–74)

(Now all those who are children of this terrible world should take heed of this tale as it nears its end. It is so true that one should gladly listen to it. The reward of the world is full of suffering, that is what you all have heard here. I have found this out: whoever is discovered in the service of the world forgoes the joy that God has prepared with utter constancy for the chosen. I, Konrad von Würzburg, give all of you this advice: you should abandon the world if you want to save your soul.)

The authorial signature in *Der Welt Lohn* (271), located as it is at the end of the work, has the same intrinsic poetological significance as its counterpart in the *Schwanritter*. However, it is spoken with the authority of moral censure. Konrad's naming simultaneously marks out the last phase in the adumbration of the lesson of the tale, in which the essential meaning of lines 259–70 is extracted and refor-mulated in a final verse couplet: the addressees of the work stand in danger of losing their very souls (273f.). This admonition is offered

---

[72] The text is preserved in nine manuscripts; see Bleck (ed.), *Der Welt Lohn*, 1–91.

[73] 'Ir werlte minnaere, | vernement disiu maere, | wie einem ritter gelanc | der nâch der werlte lône ranc | beidiu spâte unde fruo' (1–5).

in the form of authorial advice ('rât' 272).[74] In effect, the vernacular author refers to himself here as the guarantor and authority for the validity of the moral sentiments expressed.

However effective this may be as a strategy, the location of the naming in *Der Welt Lohn* rendered it vulnerable to loss and change in the course of transmission, and this is highlighted by the different versions of the epilogue in the manuscripts.[75] Whereas the earliest textual witnesses (Munich, BSB, Cgm 16, dated 1284; Berlin, SBB-PK, mgf 737, *c.* 1300) both contain lines 271–4, two distinctive kinds of reworking are on show in the other relevant manuscripts. In five codices the epilogue consists only of lines 259–70. That is to say, the authorial function has been eradicated, whereby the recapitulation of the tale's moral (*moralisatio*) loses its final, decisive component and the text is preserved as anonymous.[76] In yet another (Karlsruhe, Badische LB, cod. Donaueschingen 104, *c.* 1430–3), the authorial function is retained although the force of the passage as a whole is weakened. First-person naming—now in a less than elegant form— is still coupled with the aspect of authorial advice ('dar vmb gib ich Conrat | Von Würtzburg uch disen rat') but the poetically refined encapsulation of the moral in verses 273f. has been replaced with an unwieldy sermon of some twenty lines.[77] Konrad's authorship of *Der Welt Lohn* is revealed to be an elusive quantity in the main body of the transmission of the work in spite of its original closing strategy. As far as many readers of the later collections were concerned, this text was not to be attributed to Konrad at all.

Contours of a basic structural format in Konrad's shorter texts

---

[74] For the motif of authorial advice in the epilogues of shorter secular narratives see Karl-Heinz Schirmer, *Stil- und Motivuntersuchungen zur mittelhochdeutschen Versnovelle*, Tübingen 1969 (Hermaea Germanistische Forschungen NF 26), 103 note 136. For a further instance of this motif elsewhere in Konrad's work cf. *Silvester* 5208–11.

[75] For much of the following see also Gerhardt, 'Überlieferung'.

[76] The five manuscripts in question are: Heidelberg, UB, cod. Pal. germ. 341, *c.* 1300–25; Cologny-Genève, Bibliotheca Bodmeriana, Cod. Bodmer 72, *c.* 1300–25; Vienna, ÖNB, cod. 2677, *c.* 1300–50; Gotha, Forschungsbibl., Chart. A 216, *c.* 1400; Karlsruhe, Badische LB, cod. Karlsruhe 408, *c.* 1430–5.

[77] The text of this manuscript is quoted from Bleck (ed.), *Der Welt Lohn*, 48: 'Die diz gerichten [sic] hörent lesen | Daz si der welt vigent wesen | Vnd got den werden mine [sic] | Mit hertzñ vñ mit sinne | So mag die sel dort genesen | Vnd dester baß än sünde wesen | Wan an der welt lit anders nit | Dañ ain bösi zuv'sicht | Vñ wirt v'loren die arbait | Ze jungst daz si uch gesait | Vnd so gar vergessen | Wer mit jr ist bessessen | Der gefachet swachñ lon | Dez müß er doch ze himel schon | Sin ewikait besitzen | Dez schowent gar mit witzen | Daz ir fügent uwer arbait | Ze recht' stätt' ewikeit | Vnd lant die welt v'derbñ | So mügent jr gotz huld erwerbñ'.

emerge at the latest with our reading of *Heinrich von Kempten* which again includes an epilogue (744–70) but not a prologue.[78] Just as in *Der Welt Lohn*, Konrad privileges the ending of the work by addressing the theme of his authorship at this point only. Nevertheless, the epilogue of *Heinrich von Kempten* differs significantly in terms of its content. The poet expounds the chivalric ethos of the preceding tale in the form of a *moralisatio*,[79] yet this is not brought to bear upon the references to authorship which follow. These are shaped instead by the new factor of patronage:

> Hie sol diz maere ein ende geben
> und dirre kurzen rede werc,
> daz ich dur den von Tiersberc
> in rîme hân gerihtet
> unde in tiutsch getihtet
> von latîne, als er mich bat:
> ze Strâzburc in der guoten stat,
> da er inne zuo dem tuome
> ist prôbest unde ein bluome
> dâ schînet maneger êren.
> Got welle im saelde mêren,
> wand er sô vil der tugende hât.
> von Wirzeburc ich Cuonrât
> muoz im iemer heiles biten.
> er hât der êren strît gestriten
> mit gerne gebender hende.
> hie hât daz buoch ein ende. (754–70)

(Here this story should come to an end; this work of short speech that I, at the behest of that man of Tiersberg, have shaped in rhyme and composed in German from the Latin, as he asked me in the good city of Strassburg, where he is provost of the cathedral and resplendent with the highest honours. May God increase his good fortune for he is greatly virtuous. I, Konrad von Würzburg, shall always plead for his salvation. He has fought the battle of honour with a gladly generous hand. Here the book is at an end.)

The emphasis in the passage is on the figure of the patron, who is named almost immediately (756), identified further with the

---

[78] The text is preserved in six complete manuscripts and one fragment; see facsimile edn. by André Schnyder, 7–17.

[79] Dar umbe ein ieslich ritter sol | gerne sîn des muotes quec, | werf alle zageheit enwec | und üebe sînes lîbes kraft. | wan manheit unde ritterschaft | diu zwei diu tiurent sêre: | si bringent lob und êre | noch einem iegelichen man | der si wol gehalten kan | unde in beiden mag geleben' (744–53).

description of his ecclesiastical office (760ff.), and praised as honourable (762f.), virtuous (765), and generous (768f.). A record of
Konrad's authorship of the text is secured through an outline of his
compositional activity (757ff.) and first-person authorial naming
(766). However, in similar fashion to the prologues of *Silvester* and
Partonopier und Meliur, such authorial self-presentation is subordinated
here to the depiction of an external instigator of the literary enterprise. This strategy is most apparent in the final verses (764–70)
where the identity of the German poet is revealed as he reiterates
his concern for Berthold von Tiersberg's spiritual welfare. The
author is not named in the immediate context of his own achievement, but later as if to lend weight to the intercession on his patron's
behalf.[80]

The presentation of Konrad's authorship is a feature of *Heinrich
von Kempten* in all of its manuscripts, although again not without
some variation.[81] In one of the complete codices (Heidelberg, UB,
cod. Pal. germ. 395, datable to the 1300s) the epilogue is cut drastically, lines 755–70 being replaced by a mere four verses:

> Svnd' alle missetat
> von wirzeburch ich conrat
> kan da von niht me v'iehen
> Got laze vns allen wol geschen (H fol. 98ʳ)

(I, Konrad von Würzburg, can say no more about it [the tale] without
misdeed. May God take care of us all.)

The details of the circumstances of production of the text (patronage; process of composition) are dispensed with now in the interests
of a new, emphatic closure: a refunctionalization of the author's
signature which recalls the wording of Konrad's own ending of the
Schwanritter (1352–8). Elsewhere, lines 764–70 are also preserved as a
fragment (Library of the Institute of Germanic Studies, London, 5
(a), *c.* 1380) in which the naming of the author is recast in the third
person: 'Von Wurtzburg meist' Cûnrat | der mûs ime iem' heiles
bittē' (L). The substitution of the term *meister* for the first-person
pronoun underlines the status of the work by augmenting the aspect
of the poet's authority, and this procedure clearly draws on Konrad's
title as found in the rubrics of lyric collections as well as in another

---

[80] For more on Berthold von Tiersberg see Chapter 1 section III above.
[81] In what follows, the various versions of the text are quoted from Schnyder's facsimile
edn.

manuscript of *Heinrich von Kempten* itself (Vienna, ÖNB, cod. 10100^a,
c. 1645: 'Die Redt haizt Chaiser Oto vnd hat geticht maister
Chunrad von Wirczpurckh' [W fol. 17^v]).[82] That there is no equivalent to the eradication of the authorial function of *Der Welt Lohn* in
the transmission of *Heinrich von Kempten* indicates that the fluctuating
transmission of these shorter texts is not necessarily hostile to the
literary presentation of authorship.

The final text to be analysed in this section, the *Herzmaere*, goes
beyond the structural format of *Der Welt Lohn* and *Heinrich von Kempten*
with a relatively extensive framework of narratorial reflection,
involving both a prologue (1–28) and an epilogue (530–88).[83] The
prologue establishes a self-assured role for the poet from the beginning as well as locating the work in a broader literary context:

> Ich prüeve in mîme sinne
> daz lûterlîchiu minne
> der werlte ist worden wilde.
> dar umbe sô sulen bilde
> ritter unde frouwen
> an disem maere schouwen,
> wand ez von ganzer liebe seit.
> des bringet uns gewisheit
> von Strâzburc meister Gotfrit:
> swer ûf der wâren minne trit
> wil eben setzen sînen fuoz,
> daz er benamen hoeren muoz
> sagen unde singen
> von herzeclichen dingen,[. . .]
> dar umbe wil ich flîzec wesen
> daz ich diz schoene maere
> mit rede alsô bewaere
> daz man dar ane kiesen müge
> ein bilde daz der minne tüge,
> diu lûter unde reine
> sol sîn vor allem meine. (1–14, 22–8)

(I recognize in my mind that pure love has become foreign to the world.
Thus, knights and ladies should take this tale as an example, for it tells of
perfect love. Master Gottfried von Strassburg proves to us that whoever

---

[82] Fischer, *Märendichtung*, 143 note 15.
[83] The text is preserved in twelve manuscripts; see Grubmüller (ed.), *Novellistik*, 1120ff.
Two further manuscripts list the *Herzmaere* in a table of contents; see Schröder (ed.),
Kleinere Dichtungen, i. p. XIX.

desires to set foot on the path of true love must surely hear sing and tell of the affairs of the heart [. . .]. For this reason I want to be diligent, so that I may so form this beautiful tale with [my] speech that it might be taken as an example befitting love, which should be pure and free of all deception.)

The presentation of the authorial activity of composition in the prologue is largely restricted to an assurance of effort (22) and is subsumed under the all-important, didactic aspect of the work.[84] The poet's aims regarding form (23f.), therefore, appear as part and parcel of a concern for the effectiveness of the story as an exemplum. Similarly, the text opens with a forthright expression of the poet's moral imperative; and the intention to set in motion the improvement of a seemingly loveless courtly society with a tale of true love represents a didactic programme analogous to that of *Engelhard* and its exemplary depiction of the virtue of *triuwe*. Konrad's stated purpose is lent further significance in the *Herzmaere* through the explicit reference to Gottfried von Strassburg as an authority ('meister' 9) underpinning the validity of such an enterprise (10–14). Gottfried's *Tristan* exerts a considerable influence on the style and thematic content of the text,[85] and this special relationship may be seen to be signalled by the naming. Elsewhere Konrad alludes to Gottfried by name only in the *Goldene Schmiede*.[86] Gottfried is also evoked as the archetypal vernacular author of a love story, and Konrad hereby lays claim to an association of his *Herzmœre* with the literary tradition of courtly romance in German as headed by Gottfried's own work.

Much of the epilogue (530–79) consists of a contrast between the lady of the tale's readiness to die for her love and the faithlessness

[84] For further analysis of this passage see Ursula Schulze, 'Konrads von Würzburg novellistische Gestaltungskunst im "Herzmaere"', in *Mediaevalia litteraria: Festschrift für Helmut de Boor zum 80. Geburtstag*, edd. Ursula Hennig/Herbert Kolb, Munich 1971, pp. 451–84, esp. 462f.; Christa Ortmann/Hedda Ragotzky, 'Zur Funktion exemplarischer *triuwe*-Beweise in Minne-Mären: "Die treue Gattin" Herrands Wildonie, "Das Herzmaere" Konrads von Würzburg und die "Frauentreue"', in *Kleinere Erzählformen im Mittelalter: Paderborner Colloquium 1987*, edd. Klaus Grubmüller/L. Peter Johnson/Hans-Hugo Steinhoff, Paderborn 1988, pp. 89–109, esp. 94–9.

[85] Wachinger, 'Zur Rezeption Gottfrieds', 71–6.

[86] In the *Goldene Schmiede* the naming functions as part of a strategy of authorial self-deprecation: 'ich sitze ouch niht uf grüenem cle | von süezer rede touwes naz, | da wirdeclichen ufe saz, | von Strazburc meister Gotfrit, | der als ein waeher houbetsmit | guldin getihte worhte. | der haete an alle vorhte, | dich gerüemet, frouwe, baz, | dann ich, vil reinez tugentvaz, | iemer künne dich getuon' (94–103).

of lovers in contemporary society. Konrad draws on Gottfried's 'Minnebußpredigt' (*Tristan* 12187–361) to portray just how cheap love has become.[87] Only when this situation is reversed, the poet asserts, will lovers be prepared to suffer for one another again (566–79). The theme of authorship comes to the fore as part of a sequence of closure, and this section of the epilogue is in itself comparable with the endings of Konrad's other shorter narratives:

> Niht anders kan ich iu verjehen,
> von Wirzeburc ich Cuonrât.
> swer alsô reine sinne hât
> daz er daz beste gerne tuot,
> der sol diz maere in sînen muot
> dar umbe setzen gerne,
> daz er dâ bî gelerne
> die minne lûterlichen tragen.
> kein edel herze sol verzagen! (580–8)

(I, Konrad von Würzburg, can tell you nothing different: whoever is so pure in mind that he does the best thing gladly, he should take this tale to heart in order that he may learn through it to bear love faultlessly. A noble heart should not be afraid [to do so]!)

Konrad's first-person naming in this passage serves to impose a record of his authorship on the *Herzmaere* in its last lines, a self-assertive practice which we have already observed for the *Schwanritter*, *Der Welt Lohn*, and *Heinrich von Kempten*. In terms of this epilogue as a whole, the naming also signals a change in the focus of the poet's reflections from the status of *minne* in society (536–79) to the didactic import of this specific text. In stark contrast to the earlier critical tone, a rhetorical strategy of flattery is now employed to ensure that as many of the audience as possible pay attention to the final reiteration of the tale's exemplary quality (586f.). The concluding line of the critical text operates as part of this strategy as well. However, in light of the special relationship that the *Herzmaere* enjoys with

---

[87] 'frou Minne gît bî disen tagen | in selten alsô guoten kouf. | wîlen dô sie niender slouf | ze tugentlôser diete | umb alsô swache miete, | dô dûhte ir süezekeit sô guot | daz durch si manic edel muot | biz ûf den tôt versêret wart. | nu hât verkêret sich ir art | und ist sô cranc ir orden, | daz sie wol veile ist worden | den argen umbe ein cleinez guot. | dar umbe lützel iemen tuot | durch si nû dem lîbe wê' (552–65). Gottfried's influence on this passage was first noted by Helmut de Boor, *Die deutsche Literatur im späten Mittelalter*, 38f. Cf. also *Engelhard* 126–39.

Gottfried's *Tristan*, the incorporation of the phrase 'edel herze' in this verse would seem to fulfil an additional function: allowing Konrad to maintain an affinity between this work and that of his authoritative 'classical' predecessor.[88]

The *Herzmaere* is another prime example of a shorter narrative whose transmission involves a high degree of variance. The text as preserved in its complete manuscripts ranges in size from 484 to 602 lines, and in this case, as with *Der Welt Lohn*, such fluctuation has a significant impact on the presentation of authorship in the work.[89] In six of eight relevant manuscripts the text is curtailed, lines 533–88 being supplanted by ten new verses which curse the lady's husband and fail to include the naming of the author.[90] Although one of these codices (Heidelberg, cod. Pal. germ. 341) retains Konrad's name in the prologue instead of Gottfried's ('Von wierzburch meister Conrat') knowledge of the authorship of the work was consequently impaired, as evinced by the *titulus* in an important early manuscript (Strassburg, Johanniterbibl. A 94, *c.* 1330–50 [destroyed 1870]): 'dise mere mahte meister gotfrit von strazburg und seit von der minnen'.[91] Two further manuscripts contain the epilogue in full, whereby in one (Munich, BSB, Cgm 714, *c.* 1455–8) the final section of lines 580–8 is reworked: the authorial signature occurs here in the third person ('von Wirzeburc der Cuonrât' 581); verses 582–8 are substituted by an apparent interpolation from the conclusion of Rudolf's *Willehalm von Orlens*,[92] which represents a playful elaboration of the

[88]   See de Boor, *Die deutsche Literatur im späten Mittelalter*, 38f. The only manuscript which preserves this last section of the epilogue contains two further lines: 'Da mit hat disz red ain end | Das got die valschen hertzen schend.' Their inclusion in the critical text—as advocated by Schulze, 'Gestaltungskunst', 474ff.—would certainly reduce the structural prominence of line 588, but would hardly undermine the significance of the allusion entirely; see also Wachinger, 'Zur Rezeption Gottfrieds', 72.

[89]   Fischer, *Märendichtung*, 141; Brandt, *Konrad von Würzburg*, 105f.; Grubmüller (ed.), *Novellistik*, 1122f. Much of the following can also be extrapolated from the apparatus in Schröder's edn.

[90]   'Hie hât diz maere ein ende. | der rîche got in schende | daz er der spîse ie gewuoc, | diu sô jämerlîche truoc | sô gar getriuwem wîbe | daz leben von ir lîbe. | daz muoz mich riuwen iemer, | und ich vergizze niemer | sîner törperheite, | daz erz ir ie geseite.'

[91]   Schröder (ed.), *Kleinere Dichtungen*, i. p. XIX. Schröder also notes that the table of contents of a much later manuscript (Vienna, ÖNB, cod. 10100ᵃ, *c.* 1645) lists the *Herzmaere* under the title of 'Der Ritter mit dem Herczen Meister Gotfrid von Strasburg' (fol. 31ʳ). See also von der Hagen (ed.), GA i. 549.

[92]   *Herzmaere* N 582–8: 'Disz ain zil genumen hat | Welch mein freunt meins freunds rat | Erzaygen on missethat | Und mich nicht enpfilcht yrrlat | Das ist ain freuntlich rat | Der leg an mich der trewen wat | Wer mein freunt sei der geb mir guten rat.' These verses would seem to be borrowed from the nine-line passage of monorhyme with

last syllable of Konrad's name: *rât*.[93] It is to be noted that the single transmitter of what is generally regarded as the 'authentic' ending of the *Herzmaere* (Karlsruhe, Badische LB, cod. Donaueschingen 104) is dated to *c.* 1430–3. Evidently, the character of this process of transmission is such that the earliest codices are not always the most reliable carriers of (thirteenth-century) authorial self-presentation.

The presentation of authorship is a regular component of Konrad's shorter narratives, although it is one which was liable to be reworked and even eradicated in the course of their highly variable manuscript transmission. On the whole, Konrad uses assertive strategies to identify himself as the author: he repeatedly employs a self-assured first-person form of signature and only defers to a patron once. The location of these references towards the end of the respective epilogues suggests a tendency to address the theme of authorship as part of a strategy of closure, as exemplified by the *Schwanritter*. However, this does not preclude the possibility of its inclusion in a more expansive thematic framework such as the evocation of a broader literary tradition in the *Herzmaere*.

IV. THE 'FALSELY' ASCRIBED WORKS

Detailed analysis of Konrad's authorial self-presentation may usefully be brought to bear upon a number of texts that are generally thought to lay spurious claims to his authorship (*Ave Maria, Der Mönch als Liebesbote* A, *Frau Metze, Die halbe Birne* A). The false attribution of authorship in medieval German literature is a phenomenon which is well documented for Wolfram von Eschenbach,[94] and it would also appear to be a feature of Konrad's reception as an author of praise of the Virgin Mary and of shorter narratives.[95] Setting the issue of authenticity to one side, the literary form of the authorial namings in these four works will now be assessed against the background of Konrad's own established practices. Is there any

---

which *Willehalm von Orlens* ends: 'Swas min frúnt mir fruindes rat | Ir zaiget ån missetat, | Ob mir der rat ze staten stat | Unde mich niht under wegen lat, | Der lait an mich der trúwen wat | Und tût mir wol, swie ez ergat. | Dis ist ain vriuntlich getat. | Nu helfe úns der erbermde sat! | Dis mære alhie an ende hat' (15681–9).

[93] Westphal-Wihl, *Textual Poetics*, 174f.
[94] See Chapter 4 section II below.
[95] Fischer, *Märendichtung*, 144, 164, 197; Gerhardt, 'Überlieferung', 382–5; Brandt, *Konrad von Würzburg*, 217–20.

perceptible relationship between the presentation of authorship in
these texts and equivalent passages in Konrad's canonical works?

Konrad's authorship of the *Goldene Schmiede*, the most widely transmitted of any of his works,[96] provides an obvious point of reference
within the vernacular tradition of mariological writing for the authorial namings in the *Ave Maria*, composed *c.* 1300.[97] The first of
the two namings in this text, which runs to forty 16-line strophes,
occurs near the outset of the panegyric:

> Ave Marîa! muoter aller gnade,
> hilf, daz mir Chuonrade
> mueze heil geschehen   hie vor minem ende. (2,1ff.)

(Ave Maria! Mother of all mercy help me, Konrad, to be blessed here
before my end.)

The exordial position of this authorial identification enables it to
act as a signal for the quality of the ensuing work. In terms of its
form the use of the first person for the authorial agent is typical
for Konrad, whilst the rhyme of 'gnade'/'Chuonrade' (2,1f.) and
the wording of the plea itself (2,2f.) are particularly reminiscent
of the prologue of the *Goldene Schmiede* (118–23). The deployment of
the author's first name only is paralleled in the later excursus there
as well (*Goldene Schmiede* 888–93).[98] The second authorial reference
operates rather differently, giving Konrad's name in full as part of
a later exchange between the supplicant and Mary concerning her
suffering at Christ's crucifixion:

> '[. . .] Von Würzeburk Chuonrat, daz ist dir gar unkunt,
> wes ich krankez wib mich da getroste.[. . .]' (17,11f.)

('[. . .] Von Würzburg Konrad, you are ignorant of what I, poor woman,
comforted myself with there.[. . .]')

Such second-person address and naming of the author is not to be
found in the *Goldene Schmiede* or anywhere else in Konrad's oeuvre

---

[96] Thirty-seven manuscripts of the *Goldene Schmiede* are known to have existed; see Karl
Bertau, 'Die "Goldene Schmiede" zwischen Rittern und Reuerinnen', in *Hof und Kloster*,
edd. Palmer/Schiewer, 113–40, esp. 131.

[97] *Ave Maria* is preserved in two manuscripts; see Peter Appelhans, *Untersuchungen zur
spätmittelalterlichen Mariendichtung: Die rhythmischen mittelhochdeutschen Mariengrüße*, Heidelberg
1970, p. 29. The earlier of the two (Heidelberg, UB, cod. Pal. germ. 350, part H) is datable
to the second quarter of the fourteenth century; see Cormeau (ed.), *Walther von der
Vogelweide*, p. XXIX.

[98] These passages are quoted in full in the introduction to this chapter.

for that matter,[99] although it was an established poetic device in the vernacular as our discussion of Rudolf von Ems has shown. In the *Ave Maria* it serves to confirm the authorship of the work through the mouth, as it were, of an unquestionable authority, and this additional strategy of authorization evidently overrides the desire for stylistic compatibility with Konrad's authorial self-presentation in the *Goldene Schmiede*.

The three other texts in question belong to the tradition of the secular short story ('Märe'). In *Der Mönch als Liebesbote* A, probably composed *c.* 1400, the attribution of the text to Konrad is one of several disparate ways in which the authorship of the work is addressed.[100] The prologue, for example, includes a singular narratorial statement on the length of time needed to compose the work,[101] whilst a third-person naming of the author is located in the epilogue:

> Seß ich pey meinn gesellen,
> ich nem kößt und wein
> und ain schönß freulein
> für aller hande missetat.
> der uns das geticht hat,
> den will ich euch allen tun bekant:
> Cunrat von Wirzpurk ist er genant. (340–6)

(If I were sitting with my friends I would prefer food and wine and a pretty girl to any other vice. I want to make known to you all the man who composed the story for us: Konrad von Würzburg is his name.)

This summoning up of a bawdy social gathering relates to a number of openings and closures in the 'Märe',[102] but it is utterly foreign to Konrad's customary style of self-presentation. Similarly, while such explicit severing of the association between the first-person voice of

---

[99] The *Klage der Kunst* includes the most comparable construction, where Lady Justice mentions the author by name in her last utterance; see the introduction to this chapter.

[100] The text is preserved in one manuscript: Munich, BSB, Cgm 714, datable 1455–8; see Grubmüller (ed.), *Novellistik*, 1196.

[101] 'Ein obenteur ward mir gesait. | ein herre, der auß wallen rait, | der mir die warhait hat verjehen, | wa oder wenn das sei geschehen; | der sagt mirs auch also, als ichs euch sag. | ich hab mich geflissen vier tag | in also guter andacht, | e ichs hab zu reimen pracht. | künt es iemants getichten pas, | des wer ich fro, tet er das, | und künt sein wol gelachen | mit frölichen sachen. | es tichtet mancher schwere, | dem rat ich, das er lere | bei weiln nach schimpflichem sit, | da tempft man die sorg mit. | ich kan euch nit gesagen pas' (1–17).

[102] Fischer, *Märendichtung*, 261–74.

the narrator and the authorial agent (344ff.) is not uncommon elsewhere, it is scarcely paralleled in Konrad's works. Even on the single occasion when he names himself in the third person (*Minneleich*: 'disen tanz hât iu gesungen | Cuonze dâ von Wirzeburc'),[103] care is taken to avoid the kind of clash with a first-person pronoun that occurs in *Der Mönch als Liebesbote* A ('der uns das geticht hat' 344). The impression is difficult to dispel that the reference to Konrad in this epilogue was tacked on to secure the authority of the text and without concern for Konrad's characteristic approach to self-naming.[104]

The attribution of the later fourteenth-century *Frau Metze* to Konrad von Würzburg occurs in four of the work's five manuscripts which all date to the fifteenth and sixteenth centuries.[105] As in *Der Mönch als Liebesbote* A the authorial naming is again situated towards the end of the text (422f.):

> Von wirtzburg uō chůrat
> Hat diß red gemachet vnd gesait. (m³ [s⁶, m¹])

([Von] Konrad von Würzburg composed and told this tale.)

> Von würtzburg maister conratt
> Hat die red gemachet vnd gesait. (n²)

(Master Konrad von Würzburg composed and told this tale.)

The third-person perspective adopted in these passages—especially in conjunction with the title of 'maister'—is similar to the reworkings and variants we have already noted for Konrad's signature in certain manuscripts of *Der Welt Lohn*, *Heinrich von Kempten*, and the *Herzmaere*. Scholars generally privilege the reference to the author as preserved in the earliest codex l ('Ditz maere der arme Kuonrat | hat getihtet und geseit' [422f.]), supposing the real poet of *Frau Metze* to have been another individual called 'Der arme Konrad', whom subsequent scribes misidentified due to the setting of the story in Würzburg.[106] We are in a position to note that the two versions

---

[103] For more on the *Minneleich* see the introduction to this chapter.

[104] Fischer, *Märendichtung*, 144 note 16, 164 note 97.

[105] Manuscripts: l = Karlsruhe, Badische LB, cod. Donaueschingen 104, *c.* 1430–3; m³ = Munich, BSB, Cgm 379, *c.* 1454; s⁶ = Salzburg, Bibl. des Stiftes St. Peter, Cod. b IV 3, *c.* 1500; m¹ = Munich, BSB, Cgm 270, dated 1464; n² = Nuremberg, Germanisches Nationalmuseum, Hs. Merkel 2° 966 ('Hs. des Valentin Holl'), datable 1524–6. The passages quoted are taken from the apparatus of the critical edn. (NGA i. p. 82).

[106] Fischer, *Märendichtung*, 134, 164 note 98, 197; Gerhardt, 'Überlieferung', 385.

of the signature quoted above are analogous to those that emerge in the secondary stages of transmission of Konrad's canonical shorter narratives. Although their poetic form is unauthentic, they seem at least to derive from the literary tradition of Konrad's works.

The most striking treatment of the presentation of Konrad's authorship is contained in *Die halbe Birne* A, composed in the later thirteenth or early fourteenth century.[107] In accordance with the structural format of *Der Welt Lohn* and *Heinrich von Kempten* the text has no prologue but an epilogue (487–515) which includes the motif of authorial advice (again as in *Der Welt Lohn*).[108] In four of five complete manuscripts the author is named as part of the work's closure:

> von Wirzeburc ich Kuonrât
> kan iu anders niht verjehen.
> got lâze uns allen wol beschehen! (ed. Wolff, 512ff.)

(I, Konrad von Würzburg, can tell you nothing different. May God take care of us all!)

This signature, in the earliest attested version of the text (Strassburg, Johanniterbibl. A 94, *c.* 1330–50 [destroyed 1870]), is almost identical to the authorial naming in the *Herzmaere*: 'Niht anders kan ich iu verjehen, | von Wirzeburc ich Cuonrât'. Furthermore, not even the common variant of 'von Wirzburc maister Kuonrat' of the three other codices can detract from the essential similarity of these final lines to the abbreviated epilogue of *Heinrich von Kempten* in Heidelberg, cod. Pal. germ. 395.[109] This passage would therefore seem to be a definite factor in the course of the transmission of Konrad's canonical works, although the exact nature of its relationship to the relevant lines in the *Herzmaere* and *Heinrich von Kempten* must remain

---

[107] The text is preserved in seven manuscripts; see Grubmüller (ed.), *Novellistik*, 1083. Unless otherwise indicated both the passages quoted and the line-numbering are taken from Grubmüller's edn.

[108] 'Dar umbe wil ich râten | allen guoten wîben, | daz si die zühte trîben, | die reinen wîben wol gezemen, | und ein saelic bilde nemen | an der küniginne, | wie sie betrouc diu minne, | dô si den list eröugete, | dâ mite si erzöugete | ir manne die grôze leckerheit. | des wart ir ungemüete breit: | er was ir iemer mê gehaz. | ein saelic man der merke daz, | wie der ritter Arnolt | aller sîner tugende solt | von ir unminniclîch verlôr, | ob er niht worden waere ein tôr, | daz er geschendet waere. | ein hübescher minnaere | der flîze sich der dinge, | daz im niht misselinge, | daz ist mîn bete und mîn rât' (487–508).

[109] *Heinrich von Kempten* H 755–8: 'Svnd' alle missetat | von wirzeburch ich conrat | kan da von niht me v'iehen | Got laze vns allen wol geschen.' See also Wolff (ed.), *Diu halbe Bir*, pp. 188f.

open. To all intents and purposes the archetypal first-person naming in the earliest known manuscript of *Die halbe Birne* A is an 'authentic' ending to a shorter narrative by Konrad von Würzburg.

The respective attributions to Konrad in these four works achieve their functions of enhancement and authorization with varying degrees of sophistication. On the 'lowest' level, Konrad is named in *Der Mönch als Liebesbote* A without any awareness of his own style of self-presentation, whilst in *Frau Metze* the third-person forms of reference used are commensurate with variants occurring in the transmission of Konrad's canonical shorter works. Only the signatures featured in the *Ave Maria* and *Die halbe Birne* A take demonstrable account of 'authentic' literary forms and structures. *Die halbe Birne* A in particular provides evidence of an early recognition of Konrad's customary approach to authorial self- presentation in the generic context of the shorter narrative.

In taking stock of what we have observed in Konrad von Würzburg's works it becomes clear that practices of authorial self-presentation did not develop in a linear and straightforward way in the course of the thirteenth century, not even at the heart of literary tradition. In chronological terms Konrad's activity as a poet follows on almost seamlessly from Rudolf von Ems's, and together these authors represent the two most important points on the axis of 'post-classical' narrative literature, yet Konrad's presentation of authorship bears little or no relation to Rudolf's. It is tempting to reason that this is due primarily to the distinctive socio-cultural environment in which Konrad spent much of his career: the cities of Strassburg and, above all, Basle. The striking uniformity of Konrad's technique of self-reference—strict adherence to a first-person perspective; location of self-naming only at the beginning and end of a work, regardless of its length—is commensurate, we might speculate, with the image of Konrad as a poet variously employed by one and the same literary circle (in Basle): that is to say, working for patrons who knew him, as well as each other, and thus quite possibly what other members of their group had commissioned him to do. There is certainly something about Konrad's method of self-identification that smacks of the routine. The relatively constant accompaniment of references to patronage, and the extent to which Konrad is willing to abdicate his own authorial role in favour of his patrons, add to this impression of consummate professionalism.

But this alone represents a reductive interpretation of the evidence. The underlying tension between Konrad's subordination to his patrons on the one hand and his highly developed artistic self-consciousness on the other is worked out differently in each text. Where there are no references to the broader circumstances of a work's composition Konrad's presentation of authorship, and in particular his custom of using his authorial signature as a device of closure, is extremely assertive. The position he assumes in respect of the preceding tradition of vernacular literature in German is illuminating in this context as well. As we have seen, Konrad only mentions one 'great' vernacular author of the past—Gottfried von Strassburg—whom he praises highly but without actually taking advantage of any of the latter's characteristic devices of self-presentation. The very selectiveness of this approach suggests that irrespective of his acknowledgements of Gottfried's superiority, Konrad has in fact chosen a predecessor worthy of himself. The distance in time between Konrad and the 'Blütezeit' has brought with it a crucial change of perspective. As a narrative poet in the second half of the thirteenth century Konrad achieves a degree of detachment towards Middle High German literary tradition that would have been inconceivable in Rudolf von Ems's day.

Similarly, Konrad's failure to employ a wider range of devices and constructions of authorial self-presentation reflects a new lack of concern for the secondary stages of reception of the works he composes. Against the background of the growth of lay literacy in the course of the thirteenth century, and after Rudolf von Ems's works, we might perhaps have expected Konrad too to cater for a later readership, but not once does he attempt to secure a record of his identity in the form of an acrostic. Equally, he does not pre-empt the reality of secondary public recitals by (occasionally) naming himself in the third person, and thereby allowing for a differentiation between a later reciter and himself, the author of the text. He is, it appears, interested only in his own reading of the text to his primary recipients, and in maintaining a trademark style of first-person naming. Thus, in a curious way, the presentation of authorship in Konrad's works demonstrates just how far German literature has come over the seventy years or so of the 'post-classical' period. Whilst Konrad leaves little doubt as to his material dependence on patronage, he attains a new level of conceptual independence of both preceding narrative tradition and posterity.

PART II:

Authorship on the Boundary
with Orality

4

THE AUTHOR DISPLACED, THE AUTHOR RESTORED: THE CASE OF THE LATER HEROIC EPIC

So far we have been concerned with the works of two self-conscious littérateurs. Before we go on to examine an altogether different category of narrative literature, it may be as well to remind ourselves that literacy and orality were relative and not absolute values in this period.[1] Orality could play a role in both the composition and reception of written literature: the author might only have an oral account to use as his source; the composition of the text would then in many cases have involved dictation to a scribe (as widely depicted in author portraits); finally, public (oral) recital was still the main mode of reception of vernacular texts in the thirteenth century. By situating Rudolf von Ems and Konrad von Würzburg at the 'heart of literary tradition' we are not denying them any of these aspects of orality in principle, but rather characterizing them on the basis of the overtly literary and textual background to their works which are in the main reworkings of Latin and French source-texts. Conversely, whilst the narratives that are the subject of the second part of this book are self-evidently literary, they stand in no such well-worn textual tracks, representing instead the first literary manifestations of traditionally oral story materials. The question is: what happens to the presentation of authorship in texts that are situated in this way on the boundary with orality?

The prime example of this alternative category of narrative is the genre of the heroic epic which treats material that has its origins in the fourth and fifth centuries and that was subsequently transmitted orally as 'saga' (in both prosaic and poetic sung form) throughout the Middle Ages.[2] As far as we can tell, this mass of material represented a secular counterpart to Latin historiography,

---

[1] Green, *Medieval Listening and Reading*, 147ff.; Ursula Schaefer, 'Zum Problem der Mündlichkeit', in *Modernes Mittelalter*, ed. Heinzle, 357–75.

[2] Alois Wolf, 'Die Verschriftlichung von europäischen Heldensagen als mittelalterliches Kulturproblem', in *Heldensage und Heldendichtung im Germanischen*, ed. Heinrich Beck, Berlin/New York, NY 1988 (Ergänzungsbände zum Reallexikon der Germanischen

and—reviled by the clerical establishment—it was fostered by leading aristocrats as a source of genealogical knowledge and a means of political legitimation.[3] Notwithstanding the Old High German *Hildebrandslied* (of which a written copy was made in the early ninth century) and the tenth-century *Waltharius* (in Vergilian hexameters), an enduring process of literarization only set in at the end of the twelfth century with the composition of the *Nibelungenlied*, and most if not all of the numerous tales that revolve around Dietrich von Bern assumed literary form in the course of the thirteenth century. The crucial feature of this process is that the oral tradition continued alongside the new literary one, which explains why apparently archaic motifs still surface in the fifteenth century quite independently of earlier literary texts.[4] This is in fact an area within medieval German literature in which the semi-oral or semi-literate nature of thirteenth-century lay society is particularly tangible. Only now are scholars starting to explore in detail the poet-ological and literary theoretical implications of this situation and the epic literature it produced, Jan-Dirk Müller's investigation (1998) of the narrative strategies of the *Nibelungenlied* being a case in point.[5] It remains to be seen just what traces of authorship can be detected in these works.

As is well known, the single greatest indicator of an alternative attitude towards authorship in the heroic epic is the widespread anonymity of the poets involved. It would appear that even in their literary form heroic tales were regarded as cultural common prop-erty rooted in an oral tradition of storytelling in which individualistic claims of authorial achievement were out of place.[6] Such anonymity finds 'classic' poetic expression in the first strophe of the *Nibelungenlied* in manuscripts A and C:

Altertumskunde 2), 305–28; Michael Curschmann, 'Zur Wechselwirkung von Literatur und Sage: Das "Buch von Kriemhild" und Dietrich von Bern', *PBB* 111 (1989), 380–410, esp. 383f.

[3] Bumke, *Mäzene*, 42ff.

[4] Heinzle, *Nibelungenlied*, 38–42.

[5] Jan-Dirk Müller, *Spielregeln für den Untergang: Die Welt des Nibelungenliedes*, Tübingen 1998. See also Walter Haug, 'Mündlichkeit, Schriftlichkeit und Fiktionalität', in *Modernes Mittelalter*, ed. Heinzle, 376–97.

[6] Otto Höfler, 'Die Anonymität des Nibelungenliedes', in *Zur germanisch-deutschen Heldensage: Sechzehn Aufsätze zum neuen Forschungsstand*, ed. Karl Hauck, Bad Homburg 1961 (WdF 14), 330–92; Georges Zink, 'Pourquoi la *Chanson des Nibelungen* est-elle anonyme?', *EG* 10 (1955), 247–56; Werner Hoffmann, *Mittelhochdeutsche Heldendichtung*, Berlin 1974 (Grundlagen der Germanistik 14), 11–17; Joachim Heinzle, *Mittelhochdeutsche Dietrichepik:*

Uns ist in alten maeren wunders vil geseit
von helden lobebaeren, von grôzer arebeit,
von fröuden, hôchgezîten, von weinen und von klagen,
von küener recken strîten muget ir nu wunder hoeren sagen.

(We have been told many amazing things in old tales concerning praise-worthy heroes and great suffering; of joys, festivities and crying and lamenting, of the fighting of courageous warriors you can now hear wonders told.)

Here the binding nature of the story of the Nibelungen is shown to reside in a continuous process of time-honoured storytelling that extends down to the present. The role of the poet as author is disregarded within this continuum, a poetic strategy which echoes the formulaic opening of the *Hildebrandslied*: 'Ik gihorta ðat seggen' ('I heard it told that [. . .]').[7] This paradigm is transformed in later heroic epics to the extent that they almost invariably seek out an association with established literary tradition.[8] Within this new poetological frame of reference the failure to feature an author leads to a certain disharmony in many of these works, whilst several others do come to include explicit statements of authorship. The most important precedent for these developments is found in the short text that follows the *Nibelungenlied* in all of its complete manuscripts: the *Klage* (*c.* 1200).[9] Here—in direct and programmatic opposition to the *Nibelungenlied*—several obscure references to a process of composition anchor the story of the Nibelungen in a written tradition that is ultimately shown to be based on a Latin transcription of eye-witness accounts.[10] Elsewhere authorship and Germanic heroic

Untersuchungen zur Tradierungsweise, Überlieferungskritik und Gattungsgeschichte später Heldendichtung, Munich 1978 (MTU 62), 92–6.

[7] Michael Curschmann, 'Dichter *alter maere*: Zur Prologstrophe des "Nibelungenliedes" im Spannungsfeld von mündlicher Erzähltradition und laikaler Schriftkultur', in *Grundlagen des Verstehens mittelalterlicher Literatur: Literarische Texte und ihr historischer Erkenntniswert*, edd. Gerhard Hahn/Hedda Ragotzky, Stuttgart 1992 (Kröners Studienbibliothek 663), 55–71; Volker Mertens, 'Konstruktion und Dekonstruktion heldenepischen Erzählens: "Nibelungenlied"–"Klage"–"Titurel"', *PBB* 118 (1996), 358–78, esp. 360–6; Müller, *Spielregeln*, 99f., 103ff.

[8] Green, *Medieval Listening and Reading*, 162.

[9] Curschmann, '"Nibelungenlied" und "Nibelungenklage": Über Mündlichkeit und Schriftlichkeit im Prozeß der Episierung', in *Kontakte und Perspektiven*, ed. Cormeau, 85–119; Joachim Bumke, *Die vier Fassungen der 'Nibelungenklage': Untersuchungen zur Überlieferungsgeschichte und Textkritik der höfischen Epik im 13. Jahrhundert*, Berlin/New York, NY 1996 (Quellen und Forschungen zur Literatur- und Kulturgeschichte 8 [242]), 460–8; Müller, *Spielregeln*, 59–68.

[10] 'Ditze alte maere | bat ein tihtaere | an ein buoch schrîben' (17ff.); 'der rede meister hiez daz | tihten an dem maere' (44f.); 'Diz hiez man allez schrîben' (295). These passing

material are previously only coupled in *Waltharius*, where it is an unmistakable sign of the assimilation of the tale into Latin literary culture that the author is identified twice alone in an initial dedication.[11]

Our discussion of the later heroic epic will draw on seventeen works that are widely held to have been composed in the course of the thirteenth century.[12] Although they vary considerably in metrical form and thematic character their repeated transmission in collections (so-called 'Heldenbücher') underlines their status as representatives of an identifiable genre:

Alpharts Tod	*Ortnit**
Biterolf und Dietleib	*Rabenschlacht*
Dietrich und Fasold	*Rosengarten**
Dietrich und Wenezlan	*Sigenot**
Dietrichs Flucht	*Virginal**
*Eckenlied**	*Walther und Hildegund*
Goldemar	*Wolfdietrich**
Kudrun	*Wunderer**
*Laurin**	

The eight works marked with an asterisk are preserved in two or more versions, the result of a relatively 'free' process of transmission in which texts were not just copied out but were also reworked.[13] This process is another sign of the proximity of these works to a vibrant oral tradition, and betrays a lack of concern for individual authorship and for the text as intellectual property. On occasion, however, this freedom actually facilitated the presentation of authorship, allowing later poets and scribes to readdress or insert the theme of authorship in the text at any stage of its transmission. Such 'openness' in the literary transmission of the heroic epic is prob-

references are then elucidated in the epilogue: 'Von Pazowe der biscof Pilgerîn | durh liebe der neven sîn | hiez scrîben ditze maere, | wie ez ergangen waere, | in latînischen buochstaben, | [. . .] | daz maere prieven dô began | sîn schrîber, meister Kuonrât. | getihtet man ez sît hât | dicke in tiuscher zungen. | [. . .]' (4295–9, 4314–17).

[11] 'Praesul sancte dei, nunc accipe munera servi, | Quae tibi decrevit de larga promere cura | Peccator fragilis Geraldus nomine vilis, | [. . .] | Sis felix sanctus per tempora plura sacerdos, | Sit tibi mente tua Geraldus carus adelphus' (9ff., 21f.). Authorship is also a theme at the close of the text, where the poet draws attention to his blunted pen (1452) and compares himself to a chirping cricket (1453ff.).

[12] Joachim Heinzle, *Einführung in die mittelhochdeutsche Dietrichepik*, Berlin/New York, NY 1999, esp. 29–36.

[13] See also Heinzle, *Mittelhochdeutsche Dietrichepik*, esp. 56–96; Bumke, *Überlieferungsgeschichte und Textkritik*, 1–88.

lematic for not only does it give rise to uncertainties regarding the dating of the material but it renders precise enumeration impracticable. A single work, such as the *Eckenlied*, may include the presentation of authorship in one version and not in another, and may, thus, prove to be relevant to a discussion of both the 'restoration' and 'displacement' of the author. In view of these difficulties this chapter consists of synchronic analyses that concentrate on literary form and function and presuppose that all of the passages analysed are relevant to a discussion of this genre in the period 1220–90. Unnecessarily complicated statistical calculation is dispensed with; it will simply be noted whether the two principal groups of readings draw on a majority or minority of texts. Only three works in the corpus do not include any relevant material, and all of these are extremely fragmentary: *Dietrich und Fasold*, *Dietrich und Wenezlan*, and *Walther und Hildegund*. The remaining fourteen will be read with reference to two key phenomena: the displacement of the figure of the author in passages in which the literary status of the work is openly acknowledged; and the occasional restoration of the author through allusions to authorial agency, whether named or anonymous. These analyses ought to bring to light models of authorship that lend a sense of perspective to the achievements of contemporary poets such as Rudolf von Ems and Konrad von Würzburg.

I. THE AUTHOR DISPLACED

References to authorship are conspicuously absent in the overwhelming majority of the heroic epics in our corpus. Although these works lay claim to an association with literary tradition, both the theme of authorship and the figure of the author remain negative quantities. Most of these texts are presented as products of literary activity but the authors themselves are expelled from any references to this process. The devices used to establish such an expressly literary framework range from allusions to the written background of the story to relatively extensive exordial passages on the textual nature of the work itself. As we shall see, the more detailed the statement, the more apparent the displacement of the author becomes.

In its most primitive form the evocation of literary tradition is achieved through an appeal to indeterminate written sources, as in

Kudrun: 'Ez was ein michel wunder, als uns diu buoch kunt tuont' 505,1 ('It was a great miracle, as the books make known to us').[14] The allusion to the literary background of the tale serves as a rudimentary means of authorization and remains unspecific. We have no idea whether or not the 'books' are Latin or vernacular, and the relationship between the epic and its written sources goes unexplored.[15] A similarly vague reference fulfils an exordial function in the *Eckenlied*:[16]

> swer das fur aine luge hat,
> der frag es wise lute,
> won es wol gesriben stat,
> als ich uch hie betute. (1,7–10)

(Whoever regards that as a lie should ask wise people about it; for truly it can be found written down, as I can now tell you.)

Here the authoritative effect of the mention of a written source is compounded by the deference of the narrator towards certain unnamed wise people. These would seem to be learned men (and women?) in general, individuals capable of reading but not participants in the process of composition of the work.[17]

Claim to an association with literary tradition is taken one step further with the designation of the work itself as a written text. This may occur as a strategy of closure, as in *Virginal*: 'nu hât daz buoch ein ende' 1097,10 ('Now the book is at an end');[18] or it may be repeated several times within one work, as in the *Rosengarten*: 'tuot uns daz buoch bekant' 319,1 ('as the book informs us'); 'tuot uns diz buoch bekant' (447,3; 612,3); 'alsô nimet daz buoch ein ende' 633,4 ('thus the book is at an end').[19] These references to 'the book' still

---

[14] *Kudrun* is preserved in a single manuscript: Vienna, ÖNB, cod. Ser n. 2663 ('Ambraser Heldenbuch'), datable 1504–15; see Stackmann (ed.), *Kudrun*, pp. LXXXVIIIff.

[15] For further comparable material see Uwe Pörksen, *Der Erzähler im mittelhochdeutschen Epos: Formen seines Hervortretens bei Lamprecht, Konrad, Hartmann, in Wolframs Willehalm und in den 'Spielmannsepen'*, Berlin 1971 (Philologische Studien und Quellen 58), 61–75.

[16] The *Eckenlied* is preserved, in at least three versions, in seven manuscripts and twelve prints; see Heinzle, *Einführung*, 109–13. The passage quoted is from version E₂.

[17] Matthias Meyer, *Die Verfügbarkeit der Fiktion: Interpretationen und poetologische Untersuchungen zum Artusroman und zur aventiurehaften Dietrichepik des 13. Jahrhunderts*, Heidelberg 1994 (*GRM*-Beiheft 12), 190.

[18] *Virginal* is preserved, in at least three versions, in thirteen manuscripts; see Heinzle, *Einführung*, 135f. The verse quoted is from version V₁₀.

[19] The *Rosengarten* is preserved, in at least five versions (A, DP, F, C, and a Lower German fragment), in twenty-one manuscripts and six prints; see Heinzle, *Einführung*, 169–73. The

function as a simple device of authorization, but at the same time their repetition serves to impress the literary status of the epic on the audience's consciousness. The formulaic character of the phrasing does not altogether preclude intriguing variation, as displayed in another work, *Sigenot*: 'Ez liegen denn die buochstaben' 37,11 ('Unless the letters are lying'); 'Und daz es in dem buoche | Nieman kan volsagen' 118,12f. ('And [such] that no one can describe it all in the book'), 'Als uns daz buoch verkündet hie | Daz es uns nit enliege' 199,5f. ('As the book declares at this point; hope that it does not lie!').[20] The isolation of the feature of the very letters demonstrates a relish for the literary, which leaves the question of who composed the text all the more pressing.

The voice of the narrator is present in the epics mentioned so far.[21] Nevertheless, identification of this narrator with the authorial agent is openly discouraged in many of the references to 'the book'. This is achieved through the passive role that the narrator often adopts within these formulaic lines. It is 'the book' that informs and tells, the plural first-person pronoun *uns* suggesting a community of reception of narrator and audience for the 'active' text. References of this kind are to be found in the *Rabenschlacht*,[22] in which 'the book' even assumes a slightly human profile: 'wie mir daz buoch hât geseit' 339,4 ('As the book told me'); 'wie uns daz buoch las' 447,2 ('As the book read to us'); 'uns welle daz buoch liegen' 752,3 ('Unless the book means to lie to us'). Such anthropomorphism appears distantly related to the personifications of text and story that occur in the tradition of the courtly romance (Wirnt von Grafenberg's *Wigalois*; Rudolf's *Willehalm von Orlens*),[23] and represents a curious function of the displacement of the authorial figure through the presentation of the literary composition.

lines quoted are from version D. Cf. also *Rosengarten* A 382,4; *Rosengarten* C 808, 818, 874, 1650.

[20] *Sigenot* is preserved, in two versions (*Der ältere Sigenot*; *Der jüngere Sigenot*), in eight manuscripts and twenty-one prints; see Heinzle, *Einführung*, 127–31. The lines quoted are from *Der jüngere Sigenot*.

[21] A storytelling scene is evoked in the last strophe of *Virginal* V_{10}: 'Nu hânt ir daz ende vernomen: | heizent ein mit wîne komen, | daz er uns allen schenke. | wir sullen hôhes muotes wesen, | sît die herren sint genesen' (1097,1–5). Only the fragmentary *Dietrich und Fasold* contains no narratorial self-reference to speak of, whilst the narrator is most prominent in *Dietrichs Flucht*, the *Rabenschlacht*, and *Biterolf und Dietleib*.

[22] The *Rabenschlacht* is preserved in four complete manuscripts and one fragment; see Heinzle, *Einführung*, 58–63. For further allusions to 'the book' in this text cf. 112,4; 154,4; 196,4; 396,4; 617,4; 677,2.

[23] See Chapter 1 section III and Chapter 2 section III above.

In several other works we are told more about the respective literary object, which renders the absence of the agent of the process of composition quite striking. In *Alpharts Tod* 'the book' is expressly defined as a German one:[24]

> Heime alsô von Berne   mit der boteschaft schiet,
> als uns saget diz diutsche buoch   und ist ein altez liet. (45,1f.)

(So Heime left Bern with the message, as this German book tells us: it is an old song.)

This direct evocation of literary activity in German reflects, for one moment, a new degree of poetic self-consciousness in the heroic epic.[25] However, individual participants are still overlooked, and the authority for the enterprise continues to reside in the age of the native heroic material (45,2).[26] Elsewhere, in the *Wunderer*,[27] the text is denoted as a poetic composition—'nûn hat ein end das gdichte' 215,1 ('now the poem is at an end')—but there are no signs of a *tihtaere*.[28] Even the concluding depiction of the contemporary transcription of the events studiously avoids any reference to those who actually composed the text and put pen to parchment:

> Nit lenger woltens bleiben   die künig vñ fürsten gůt.
> dz wunder ließents schreiben   vñ hielten das in hůt. (212,1f.)

(They did not want to stay any longer, the good kings and princes; they had the amazing adventure written up and kept it in their custody.)

Although the kings' determination to ensure the preservation of this initial work is reminiscent of the emperor's actions in the epilogue

---

[24] *Alpharts Tod* is preserved as a fragment of a manuscript from the last third of the fifteenth century: Berlin, SBB-PK, mgf 856; see Heinzle, *Einführung*, 83f.

[25] Other references to 'the book' in *Alpharts Tod* do not retain this element: '(ir mugent ez hoeren gerne,   als wir ez vernomen hân) | Wie ez an dem buoche   hie stêt geschriben' (55,4f.); 'nû hât diz buoch ein ende   und heizet ALPHARTES.TÔT.' (467,4).

[26] The term *liet* is not uncommon in these heroic epics: in *Alpharts Tod* (55,3), *Eckenlied* E₂ (179,7), and *Der jüngere Sigenot* (205,13), for example, it is used to refer to the stories in their entireties. For the full range of terms that occur see Klaus Düwel, *Werkbezeichnungen der mittelhochdeutschen Erzählliteratur (1050-1250)*, Göttingen 1983 (Palaestra 277), 167-90.

[27] The *Wunderer* is preserved, in at least two versions (strophic; in verse couplets), in two manuscripts and three prints; see Heinzle, *Einführung*, 188f. The lines quoted are from the strophic version (w₂) which is accessible in a facsimile edn. by Georges Zink.

[28] Cf. also the closure to one of the versions of *Wolfdietrich* [D] as found in Vienna, ÖNB, cod. 15478 ('Wiener Piaristenhandschrift' or 'Lienhart Scheubel's "Heldenbuch"'), *c.* 1480-90: 'Hie hat ein end diß tichte   Wolffditereich genant: | Der lidlein sein zwey tausent   vir hundert mer bekant | Und auch neün lidlein mere,   die hie geschriben sint. | Maria, bit mit trewen   fur uns dein libes kint!' (2131).

of *Der guote Gêrhart*,[29] there is no parallel in this passage to Rudolf's elucidation of the relationship between his composition and its prehistory. It is precisely this relationship, and hence the authorship of the 'gdiechte' that is suppressed in the *Wunderer*.

The strategy of sketching the prehistory of a work assumes spectacular form in the last and most important texts to be analysed in this group, *Ortnit* and *Wolfdietrich*, where presentation of the epic as a literary object is used as the basis for a prologue. *Ortnit* contains the more concise of the two comparable passages:[30]

> Ez wart ein buoch funden   ze Suders in der stat,
> daz het geschrift wunder,   dar an lac manic blat.
> die heiden durch ir erge   die heten daz begraben.
> nu sul wir von dem buoche   guote kurzwîle haben.
>
> Swer in freuden welle   und in kurzwîle wesen,
> der lâze im von dem buoche   singen unde lesen [. . .] (1,1–2,2)

(A book was found in the city of 'Suders', which had a wondrous amount of writing in it and consisted of many leaves. The heathens had buried it in their spite. Now we can take great pleasure from the book. Whoever wants to be joyful and entertained should have someone sing and read from the book [. . .])

The sphere of literary culture is immediately evoked here by means of the claim of the discovery of a book,[31] a widespread motif which served to authenticate both religious and profane works throughout antiquity and the Middle Ages.[32] In *Ortnit* the form of

---

[29] See Chapter 2 section I above.

[30] *Ortnit* is preserved in ten manuscripts and six prints, whilst two further codices are known to have been destroyed; see Edward R. Haymes [facs. ed.], *Ortnit und Wolfdietrich: Abbildungen zur handschriftlichen Überlieferung spätmittelalterlicher Heldenepik*, Göppingen 1984 (Litterae 86), 5–13. At least six versions (AW, Ka, a, e, y, z) may be distinguished for this work, although the degree of variance between them is not always very great; see Wolfgang Dinkelacker, *Ortnit-Studien: Vergleichende Interpretation der Fassungen*, Berlin 1972 (Philologische Studien und Quellen 67), 62–111. The passage quoted is from *Ortnit* AW.

[31] See also Arthur Amelung (ed.), DHB iv. 239 with reference to Wilhelm Wattenbach, *Das Schriftwesen im Mittelalter*, 3rd revised edn. Leipzig 1896, repr. Graz 1958, pp. 411–14; Christian Schmid-Cadalbert, *Der 'Ortnit' AW als Brautwerbungsdichtung: Ein Beitrag zum Verständnis mittelhochdeutscher Schemaliteratur*, Berne 1985 (Bibliotheca Germanica 28), 10f.

[32] Cf. II Kings 22. 8–11. For extensive references to this motif in medieval saints' lives see Friedrich Wilhelm, 'Antike und mittelalterl. Studien zur literaturgeschichte: I. Ueber fabulistische quellenangaben', *PBB* 33 (1908), 286–339, esp. 303–25; Wolfgang Speyer, *Bücherfunde in der Glaubenswerbung der Antike: Mit einem Ausblick auf Mittelalter und Neuzeit*, Göttingen 1970 (Hypomnemata 24), esp. 99ff. Prominent secular examples include the Pseudo-Ovidian *De vetula* (introitus 1–7), the spurious eye-witness account of the Trojan war by a certain Dictys Cretensis (2,17–3,1), and Gervase of Tilbury's *Otia imperialia* (3, 112).

the motif is relatively simplistic. The intimations of the size of the book, for example, fall well short of the delight in physical detail that is often taken in Latin saints' lives.[33] Nevertheless, this rudimentary prehistory lends the current telling of the story a vital historical dimension. The heathens' wicked burial of the book relates specifically to the events of the narrative, Ortnit's conflict with the heathen king Machorel and his bridal expedition to the latter's capital city of *Suders* in Syria, and represents a spiteful attempt to hide the truth about Machorel's shameful defeat and treachery. Thus, the unearthing of the book in the very same city ('Suders' 1,1) creates a link between the events as they occurred and their transcription, and the current reception of the story is at the same time characterized as an act of defiance in the face of heathen 'erge'.

It is curious that nothing is said about the book's transmission from the Middle East to Germany, which would have provided another opportunity to underpin the literary pedigree of this epic. The function of this reticence may lie in the poet's wish to avoid any depiction of individual, authorial activity. The book is presented by default as a finished literary product whose authorship is shrouded in mystery, whilst the narrator clearly aligns himself with his audience as a recipient of the text (1,4). In this context, the appeal to the audience's sense of religious identity and their animosity towards heathendom can be seen as a way of masking the glaring omissions in the account of the prehistory of the book.

A considerably longer passage of the same kind occurs in *Wolfdietrich*,[34] as the prologue to version D:[35]

---

[33] Cf. Heriger, *Translatio sci. Landoaldi Sociorumque*, MGH SS 15:2, p. 603,34–7 (covered in wax); Hinkmar, *Vita ss. Sancti et Antonii epp. Meldensium*, AASS Oct. 5, p. 587 §8 (barely visible ink); Thomas Walsingham's *Gesta abbatum monasterii Sancti Albani*, vol. i. p. 26 (illumination; silk; oak binding-boards).

[34] *Wolfdietrich* is preserved, in at least four versions (A, B, C, D), in twelve manuscripts and six prints, whilst four further codices have either been destroyed or are missing; see Haymes [facs. ed.], *Ortnit und Wolfdietrich*, 5–13; Gisela Kornrumpf, 'Strophik im Zeitalter der Prosa: Deutsche Heldendichtung im ausgehenden Mittelalter', in *Literatur und Laienbildung im Spätmittelalter und in der Reformationszeit: Symposion Wolfenbüttel 1981*, edd. Ludger Grenzmann/Karl Stackmann, Stuttgart 1984 (Germanistische Symposien Berichtsbände 5), 316–40, esp. 335.

[35] *Wolfdietrich* D is the most widely transmitted of all the versions, preserved in six manuscripts (and six prints) dating from the early fifteenth century onwards. Due to this relatively late transmission the question of whether the prologue of *Ortnit* pre-dates that of *Wolfdietrich* D must be left open; however, it is unlikely that the two are not connected, given the consistent transmission of the two epics together. For references to 'the book' in the other versions of *Wolfdietrich* cf. *Wolfdietrich* B 3,2; 111,2; 213,3; *Wolfdietrich* C 10,1.

Hie mügend ir gerne hören singen und sagen
von kluger aventur, so müsent ir getagen.
Ez warde ein buch funden daz sage ich uch fur war
zu Tagemunt in dem kloster da lag ez manig jar.

Sit ward ez gesendet uf in Peyern lant,
dem bischoff von Eichstett ward daz buch bekant.
Er kurzet im darabe die wile wol sibenzehen jar:
do fand er afenture, daz sag ich uch fur war.

Also den fursten verdrosz, daz buch er uberlas.
Manig seltzen wunder daran geschriben was.
Er kurzete sine wile unze er sin ende nam.
Darnach über zehen jare do fand ez sin cappellan.

Also er daz buch uberlas, an den arm er es genam,
er trug ez in das closter fur die frowen wolgetan
da zu sant Waltburg zu Eichsteten stat.
Merkent von dem guten buchel, wie ez sich zerspreitet hat.

Die äptisse was schöne also uns daz ist gesaget,
sie sach daz buch gerne, wenn ez ir wol behaget.
Sie satzte für sich zwen meister, die lertenz durch ihr hüpscheit:
daz sie daran funden geschriben daz brachten sie in die cristenheit.

Nahen und ferre furen sie in die lant,
sie sungen und seiten, davon ward ez bekant,
die seltzen aventure wolten sie nit verdagen.
Erst mugent ir gerne hören von einem kunige rich sagen. (1,1–6,4)

(I hereby call you to hear sing and tell of entertaining adventure, so you must be quiet. A book was found—what I am telling you is true—in the monastery at Tagemunt. It lay there for many a year [1]. Thereafter, it was sent up into Bavaria and the Bishop of Eichstätt became acquainted with the book. For seventeen years he enjoyed it, in it he found adventure, I assure you of the truth of this [2]. Whenever the prince grew bored he read the book through. Many a strange marvel was written in it. He enjoyed it until he died. Ten years afterwards his chaplain found it [3]. When he had read the book through, he took it under his arm and carried it into the convent before the charming ladies of St Walburg in Eichstätt. Take note how the good book was circulated [4]. The abbess was charming, so we are told. She liked to look at the book as it pleased her greatly. She sat two men of learning before her, and they promoted its dissemination out of courtliness: they brought what they found written in it to the people of Christendom [5]. They travelled near and far in the lands. They sang and told [the story] with the result that it became well known. They did not want to keep silent about the marvellous adventure. Now I call you to hear tell about a rich king [6].)

This prologue represents the most extensive depiction of the origination of a story to occur in the heroic epic after the epilogue of the *Klage*, with which it shares several key features.[36] The motif of the 'discovery of the book' is deployed here as the first station in a chain of transmission that brings the story to the attention of the Christian populace at large. An accumulation of topographical and chronological references lends the whole a sense of authenticity, and although identification of 'Tagemunt' is problematic,[37] the construction of a particular historical framework of high-ranking figures and institutions is unmistakable: Eichstätt was the most important ecclesiastical town in its diocese and the Benedictine abbey of St Walburg, together with the cathedral, were its centres. It is not unfeasible that these lines constitute a veiled reference to the patrons of the vernacular work.[38]

However, even if the events depicted preserve a core of historical reality, this does not diminish their significance in terms of the poetic thrust of the passage. The integration of (apparently) historical personages and places in the chain of transmission serves as a basic means of authorization, and each of the individual stations contributes to the further characterization of this process. The discovery of the 'original' book in a monastery certainly elevates the literary pedigree of the story, as does the enduring personal interest of the bishop, although there is an innate tension between the heroic material and this social and cultural environment, which is signalled by a period of neglect both at the outset (1,4) and after the bishop's death (3,4).[39] The transmission of the work is subsequently given new momentum by the chaplain and especially the abbess who, in stark contrast to the bishop's self-serving possession of the book, ensures that the story emerges from narrow circles of ecclesiastical reception into the broader public arena.[40]

[36] Curschmann, 'Mündlichkeit und Schriftlichkeit', 111; Müller, *Spielregeln*, 65ff.

[37] Oskar Jänicke (ed.), DHB iv. 323, suggests Admont in Styria. This proposal is often reiterated, although it is by no means certain that the poet had a real monastery in mind.

[38] Bumke, *Mäzene*, 257f.

[39] The element of neglect is reinforced in the greatly abbreviated version of the prologue in Vienna, ÖNB, cod. 15478: 'Das lag in einem closter   verschlossen manig jar' (1,4); the text in this manuscript is sometimes referred to as *Wolfdietrich* y.

[40] This process of transmission runs parallel to that described in the epilogue of the *Klage*, which also involves a high ecclesiastical figure (bishop Pilgrim) and moves from an exclusively clerical sphere to the secular world at large (4316–19).

The various, almost anecdotal points of detail in this passage may be regarded as satisfying the audience's interest in the work as an object of curiosity in itself; an interest which we also find reflected in the prologues and epilogues of earlier courtly epics, such as Ulrich von Zatzikhoven's *Lanzelet*,[41] and most (in)famously the *Eneasroman* by Heinrich von Veldeke, in which an account is given of the theft of the poet's unfinished manuscript and its completion nine years later.[42] In terms of *Wolfdietrich* D as a whole the prologue functions as the keystone of the work's claim to an association with literary tradition, and the main narrative body supports this remarkable opening through a host of formulaic references to the story as a 'book'.[43] There is no corresponding epilogue to provide a fitting conclusion to this strategy, although the metaphorical description of the monks involved in Wolfdietrich's last battle (2113–242) may be read as a deliberate evocation of the very cultural sphere from which the book itself will later emerge:[44]

> Die griffel sie faste triben   die edel brüder gut,
> die dinte, domit sie schriben,   daz was daz rote blut (2193,1f.)

(The styluses they drove forcefully, the good noble brothers; the ink with which they wrote was red blood.)

The link between the work and this sphere is further emphasized from the second of the six editions of the printed 'Heldenbuch' onwards (Augsburg, Johann Schönsperger, dated 1491) by a woodcut set above the prologue, depicting bishop, chaplain, and nuns in one and the same scene.[45] What is notable from our perspective is the way in which the visual representation of the prologue identifies the key figures in the process of transmission without worrying too much about the specific details of their interaction. (Just who is passing

---

[41] *Lanzelet*: 'wan als ein welschez buoch seit, | daz uns von êrst wart erkant, | dô der künec von Engellant | wart gevangen, als got wolde, | von dem herzogen Liupolde, | und er in hôhe schatzte. | der gevangen künec im satzte | ze gîseln edel herren, | [. . .] | Hûc von Morville | hiez der selben gîsel ein, | in des gewalt uns vor erschein | daz welsche buoch von Lanzelete' (9324–31, 9338–41).

[42] Cf. 352,19–354,1. See also Bernd Bastert, '*Dô si der lantgrâve nam*: Zur "Klever Hochzeit" und der Genese des Eneas-Romans', *ZfdA* 123 (1994), 253–73.

[43] Cf. 9,2; 34,2; 66,2; 74,2; 96,1; 129,4; 143,2; 150,2; 440,4; 446,4; 448,2; 673,2; 735,2; 835,4; 895,2; 963,2; 965,2; 1025,2; 1039,2; 1162,2; 1287,4; 1389,3; 1646,1; 1768,3; 1876,3; 2036,2; 2242,2.

[44] Cf. also 2141,4; 2147,4f.; 2201,3ff. For a reading of these lines which stresses the parodic see Müller, *Spielregeln*, 196f.

[45] Norbert H. Ott, 'Die Heldenbuch-Holzschnitte und die Ikonographie des heldenepischen Stoffkreises', in *Heldenbuch*, ed. Heinzle, ii. 245–96, esp. 268ff., 294f.

9. *Wolfdietrich* (The transmission of the book) (reproduced by permission of the Bayerische Staatsbibliothek, Munich)

the book to whom here?) To those who made this picture it was evidently the ecclesiastical dimension that mattered.

The relative wealth of detail in the prologue renders the displacement of the theme of authorship all the more apparent. The treatment of the issue of language is most enlightening as well, for although the strictly ecclesiastical environment of the 'original' book suggests that it is written in Latin, this is never explicitly stated.[46] Such an omission is surprising,[47] but it is functional in that it allows the poet to obfuscate the exact nature of the activity of the two 'meister' (5,3) commissioned by the abbess. Instead, the focus is on the broadcasting of the story in the world at large, and verbs such as *lêren* (5,3) and *bringen* (5,4) do not betray whether or not the work is first translated into the vernacular and retained in written form.[48]

---

[46] Kornrumpf, 'Strophik im Zeitalter der Prosa', 330f.

[47] Latin was the unrivalled medium of literary culture in the Middle Ages and vernacular poets often alluded to a Latin source (real or invented) to elevate their own works. Cf. Pfaffe Konrad's *Rolandslied* 9082; *Herzog Ernst* B 4466–76; *Klage* 4299; Konrad von Würzburg's *Heinrich von Kempten* 759; *Herzog Ernst* D 2051. See also Dieter Kartschoke, '*in die latine bedwungin*: Kommunikationsprobleme im Mittelalter und die Übersetzung der "Chanson de Roland" durch den Pfaffen Konrad', *PBB* 111 (1989), 196–209.

[48] In the first edition of the printed 'Heldenbuch' (Strassburg, Johann Prüss, *c.* 1483) this ambiguity is dispelled: 'Zwen meister bev in bleiben | die bat sie fil gereit | das sie das bůch abschreiben | zů tůtsch der cristenheit' (fol. 45ʳ); this text is accessible in a

The activity of the 'meister' is further defined through the alliterative phrase 'sungen und seiten' (6,2) which was previously used to characterize the internal storytelling scenario (1,1).[49] Significantly, this association represents the only link between the story's prehistory and the performance of the work in the present. The narrator hereby encourages the audience to view themselves as part of the broader process of transmission described without specifying the extent of his own authorial role.[50]

The lack of presentation of authorship in the greater part of our corpus may be regarded as a generic function which reflects the status of the story material as cultural common property. However, when these works simultaneously lay claim to an association with literary tradition the fundamental paradigm of their anonymity is no longer straightforward, and the theme of authorship becomes conspicuous by its absence. As soon as the epics themselves begin to be described as products of a literary process of composition, be it as a *buoch* or a *getihte*, the failure to depict the authorial agent as well gives rise to a certain disharmony. This process of displacement is most striking in passages with a relative wealth of detail, such as the prologues of *Ortnit* and *Wolfdietrich* D, but it is also anticipated in the brief references that are featured in a considerable number of the other works.

II. THE AUTHOR RESTORED

Displacement is not the only phenomenon relating to authorship in the later medieval German heroic epic. A few texts in our corpus

facsimile edn. by Joachim Heinzle. Elsewhere, in codex Strassburg, Seminarbibl. kl. 4 ('Diebolt von Hanouwe's "Heldenbuch"'), *c.* 1460–90 [destroyed 1870], the role of the 'meister' is understood musically: 'Die fundent disen don darzů sú brohtten ez in die kristenheitt' (5,4); the text is given here as found in Holtzmann (ed.), *Wolfdietrich*, pp. XVIIf.

[49] This phrase is used in all types of literature to denote poetic activity in general; see Julius Schwietering, 'Singen und Sagen', in *Philologische Schriften*, edd. Ohly/Wehrli, 7–58, esp. 19–40; Heinzle, *Mittelhochdeutsche Dietrichepik*, 72ff.

[50] The tradition of anonymity was evidently so strong that even where 'authorial' activity is exactly quantified the agent remains unnamed, as the last strophe of *Wolfdietrich* Ka demonstrates, the drastically abbreviated version of *Wolfdietrich* A: 'Wolfdietrich in altem dichte | Hat sibenn hundert lied | Manck vnnütz wort vernichte | Oft gmelt man als aus schid | Dreẅ hundert drei vnd dreissigk | Lied hat er hie behent | Das man auf einem sitzen dick | Müg hörn anfanck vnd ent' (334).

emulate the narratives at the heart of established literary tradition by including the presentation of authorship, effectively 'restoring' the figure of the author to this genre. The constructions that occur here range from obscure third-person reference to forthright authorial naming, whereby the latter falls into two categories: naming as an element of a poetological strategy that relates to the respective work as a whole; and fleeting reference to a named author as a means of authorization. In what follows, the various structures of presentation of authorship in the heroic epics will be analysed both on their own merits and with a view to ascertaining whether or not they bear any discernible relation to their generic context.

Authorship is addressed three times in *Biterolf und Dietleib*.[51] The first, and principal, reference belongs to the prologue in which the internal storytelling scenario is depicted at some length,[52] before it transpires that the narrator is not claiming to be the author of the ensuing work itself. Indeed, the narrator's knowledge of the background of the hero appears limited:

> Von sînen alten mâgen
> darf mich nieman frâgen:
> wie die schuofen ir leben,
> des kan ich iu niht ende geben.
> der dise rede tihte,
> der liez uns unberihte,
> und ist doch übele beliben.
> haete er iht dâ von geschriben,
> daz lieze wir iuch unverdeit:
> uns hât des nieman niht geseit. (19–28)

(Nobody should ask me about his [Biterolf's] forebears. I cannot give you an adequate account as to how they lived their lives. He who composed this text did not inform us [of this], and it is bad that it has been left like

---

[51] As is the case with *Kudrun*, *Biterolf und Dietleib* is only preserved in Vienna, cod. Ser. n. 2663 ('Ambraser Heldenbuch').

[52] 'Ob uns hie ieman wese bî | sô vertiurtes muotes frî, | den des kunde gezemen | daz er möhte vernemen | ditze fremde maere, | (daz ist sô redebaere | daz ez wol von rehte | ritter unde knehte, | dar zuo wîp unde man | wol für guot mügen hân), | den sage ich endelîche | von einem künege rîche, | wie der waere genant | ode wâ er boute sîniu lant, | sîne bürge unde stete. | nu ruochet hoeren mîne bete | daz ir swîget dar zuo, | daz ich iu daz kunt getuo' (1–18). The narrator features prominently throughout the work in a large number of formulaic asides and several extensive excursuses that have no bearing on the issue of authorship; cf. 490–502 (customs of love and marriage), 4046–66 (Etzel's generosity), 6622–34 (Bavarian loutishness!), 13380–98 (Etzel as a worthy heathen).

this. Had he written anything about it, we would not withhold it from you: no one has told us anything concerning this matter.)

The author of the text is referred to here as guarantor for what the narrator knows and can relate, the implication being that the narrator will not add anything to the author's work.[53] On one level, this represents a logical progression from the references to 'the book' that we have observed elsewhere, the authority of the written text being embodied now in a distant authorial figure. Accordingly, the two further allusions to authorship that crop up are cursory and appear analogous to subsequent formulaic evocations of literary tradition in general:[54]

> der ditze maere an schreip,
> der wolde es niht vergezzen. (2006f.)

(He who wrote on this story, he had no intention of omitting it.)

> der ditze maere êrste schreip,
> dem muoze ez wesen wol bekant. (10664f.)

(He who first wrote this story; it would surely be known to him.)

On another level, the acknowledgement within the text itself that an individual was involved in the process of composition breaks new ground, whereby the combination of the third-person perspective and anonymity ensures that such presentation of authorship remains intriguing. Third-person reference to authorship is not substandard in itself, as our readings of Rudolf's *Der guote Gêrhart* and *Willehalm von Orlens* have shown. However, in neither of these texts is the identity of the author in doubt, the choice of the third person being a function of a distinctive literary strategy in which the author plays through many different approaches. In *Biterolf und Dietleib* the absolute anonymity of the author, together with the juxtaposition of the first-person voice of the narrator and third person of the author (24), is much more akin to the final lines of the *Klage* where the narrator also seeks to justify his ignorance concerning Etzel's fate by deferring to a *tihtaere*.[55] The failure to identify the author may thus be regarded as a

---

[53] Cf. also 1968–79, 13439ff.

[54] 'an einem buoche hôrte ich sagen' (125); 'Daz buoch hoeren wir sagen' (179); 'daz buoch hât uns gesaget daz' (198); 'als uns daz buoch hât geseit' (1390); 'an einem buoche hôrte ich lesen' (1674); 'daz buoch hât uns verholn daz' (1964).

[55] *Klage*: 'uns seit der tihtaere, | der uns tihte ditze maere, | ez enwaer von im sus niht beliben, | er het iz gerne gescriben, | daz man wiste diu maere' (4349–53).

concession to the ethos of the genre as a whole. The poet of *Biterolf und Dietleib* makes quite clear, through the voice of the narrator, that this is a literary work with an author, but he stops short of transgressing the traditional anonymity of this kind of story.

Two other works contain ambitious poetological strategies in which the naming of the author plays a crucial role. In the extremely fragmentary *Goldemar*,[56] the relevant lines form an integral part of the prologue:

> Wir hân von helden vil vernomen,
> die ze grôzen strîten sint bekomen
> bî hern Dietrîches zîten.
> si begiengen degenheit genuoc,
> dô einer ie den andern sluoc.
> sî wolten niender rîten,
> sin waern ze strîten wol bereit,
> ir schilte, ir helmen veste.
> mänic kumber dô erleit.
> man sprach, er taete dez beste,
> der mänigen âne schulde ersluoc.
> dâ von ir lop geprîset wart,
> sô man die tôten von in truoc.
>
> Nu merkt, ir herren, daz ist reht:
> von Kemenâten Albreht
> der tihte ditze maere,
> wie daz der Berner vil guot
> nie gwan gên vrouwen hôhen muot.
> wan seit uns daz er waere
> gên vrouwen niht ein hovelîch man
> (sîn muot stuont im ze strîte),
> unz er ein vrouwen wol getân
> gesach bî einen zîten:
> diu was ein hôchgeloptiu meit,
> diu den Berner dô betwanc,
> als uns diu âventiure seit. (1,1–2,13)

(We have heard many tales of heroes who participated in great battles in the days of Lord Dietrich. They committed acts of heroism enough whenever one killed another. They did not want to ride anywhere unless they were fully prepared for combat with their strong shields and helmets. Many

---

[56] Just over nine strophes of *Goldemar* are preserved in a single manuscript: Nuremberg, Germanisches Nationalmuseum, Hs. 80, *c.* 1350; see Heinzle, *Einführung*, 104.

endured suffering there [in combat]. They claimed to have performed best when they slaughtered many a man without good reason. Their reputation was enhanced by this, even as the dead were being carried away from them [1]. Now pay attention, you lords, for it is right [to do so]. Albrecht von Kemenaten has composed this tale of how the noble hero of Bern had never won high spirits on account of ladies. For he tells us that he [Dietrich] was not a courtly man towards ladies (his mind was always on fighting), until he saw a beautiful lady one day: she was a highly praised maid, who conquered the hero of Bern then, as the adventure tells us [2].)

As far as we can tell, these two exordial strophes provide a key to the thematic content of *Goldemar*.[57] The first characterizes heroic story material in general as being solely concerned with bloody combat. The opening line functions as a generic marker, whereby the association of storyteller and audience and the hint of a plurality of tales are reminiscent of traditional introductions in the manner of the first verse of the *Nibelungenlied* [A, C] ('Uns ist in alten maeren wunders vil geseit').[58] The programmatic edge to this depiction becomes increasingly evident, and by the end of the strophe the tone of criticism is unmistakable (1,11). The final reference to physical conflict (1,13) evokes a scene of carnage similar to the aftermath of the cataclysmic battle between the Burgundians and Huns as related in the *Nibelungenlied* and *Klage*.

The suggestion of criticism is confirmed in the second strophe where the story of Dietrich's first love is promised, a change of theme which reconciles the heroic world with the interests of courtly romance. In this context, the presentation of authorship in lines 2,1ff. operates as a counterpart to the formulaic opening of 1,1. It signals that the following tale is different and to be associated with other kinds of narrative which commonly have a named author, such as the courtly epic.[59] The literary resonance of the passage is underlined by the third-person form of the naming, which appears to be modelled on Hartmann von Aue's basic practice of authorial signature.[60] Such emulation underpins the validity of the enterprise in hand, and furnishes the audience with an appropriate literary

[57] Heinzle, *Mittelhochdeutsche Dietrichepik*, 241f.

[58] Cf. also the opening of the much earlier *Annolied* (*c.* 1077–81): 'Wir hôrten ie dikke singen | von alten dingen: | wî snelle helide vuhten, | wî si veste burge brêchen, | wî sich liebin vuiniscefte schieden, | wî rîche kunige al zegiengen. | nû ist cît, daz wir dencken, | wî wir selve sulin enden' (1–8).

[59] Heinzle, *Mittelhochdeutsche Dietrichepik*, 40–3, 94f.

[60] See Chapter 1 section II above.

frame of reference for the treatment of the theme of love. In this way the presentation of authorship in *Goldemar*, as it stands, is loaded with significance and goes some way to approaching the complexity of the authorial self-references in the works of Rudolf von Ems and Konrad von Würzburg.[61]

The naming of the author is also a prominent feature of *Dietrichs Flucht*,[62] where it relates specifically to a strategy of narratorial self-presentation that spans the whole work. Apart from a host of formulaic utterances, including references to 'the book',[63] two extensive excursuses (187–246; 7949–8022) take particular interest in comparing an ideal past (as depicted in the story) with the sorry state of contemporary society in order to establish a level of political commentary in both the initial and final phases of the narrative.[64] This commentary is surprisingly vitriolic and seems to reflect a strong feeling of animosity among the members of the (primary) audience towards their overlords, the territorial princes.[65] In the first excursus, for example, the princes are repeatedly denigrated as the narrator constructs an analogy between their failure to appreciate the tales of virtuous heroes of old and their refusal to fulfil basic feudal obligations to those in their service.[66] The recital and reception of heroic stories are imbued with political significance in this passage, culminating in the assertion of the princes' cultural

---

[61] Evidence of the impact that Albrecht von Kemenaten had on medieval German narrative tradition may be found in Rudolf's two literary catalogues where an author of the same name is mentioned: 'von Kemenât her Albreht | des kunst gert wîter schouwe' (*Alexander* 2352f.); '"[. . .] | Öch hetti úch mit wishait | Her Albreht bas denne ich gesait, | Von Keminat der wise man, | Der maisterliche tihten kan. | [. . .]"' (*Willehalm von Orlens* 2243–6).

[62] *Dietrichs Flucht* is preserved in four 'complete' manuscripts and one fragment; see Heinzle, *Einführung*, 58–63.

[63] Cf. 280, 1924, 2022, 2028, 2270, 2308, 2392, 2683, 3537, 3686, 6210, 6324f., 6631, 6644, 8231, 8243, 8346, 8930, 9266, 9308, 10103, 10129.

[64] See also Michael Curschmann, 'Zu Struktur und Thematik des Buchs von Bern', *PBB* (Tüb.) 98 (1976), 357–83, esp. 379; Jan-Dirk Müller, 'Heroische Vorwelt, feudaladeliges Krisenbewußtsein und das Ende der Heldenepik: Zur Funktion des "Buchs von Bern"', in *Adelsherrschaft und Literatur*, ed. Horst Wenzel, Berne 1980 (Beiträge zur Älteren Deutschen Literaturgeschichte 6), 209–57, esp. 209–14.

[65] For more on the historical background see the conclusion to this chapter.

[66] 'si enruochent waz die alten | tugent haben hehalten, | si tuont niwan den niuwen site. | dâ lâze wirs beliben mite. | sît ich in niht gesagen kan | waz die alten haben getân, | lâz wir ir den tiuvel walten | unde sagen von den alten. | [. . .] | waz hilft mich nû mîn lêren | daz die vürsten nû niht tuont? | ez stêt nû niht als ez dô stuont, | sît des sites ist verphlegen, | daz man beginnet hin legen | die alten tugent unde zuht. | des komen die vürsten an die suht, | dâ von si werden nimer erlôst! | ir herrn, ir habt nû kleinen trôst, | grâven, vrîen, dienestman, | sît man iu niht dienstes lônen kan. | swie

betrayal: 'si hânt der alten maere verphlegen' (244). The same notion of injustice informs the second excursus where general reflections (7949–80) on the deplorable social phenomenon of forced service lead to a vivid portrayal of the audience's plight:

> ir werdet nimmer âne sorgen:
> sô kumt ein bote hînt ode morgen
> 'wol ûf unde sît bereit,
> ir vart ze hove wol gecleit,
> daz gebiut iu mîn herre.'
> so vertiefet ir iuch verre,
> ir setzet riute unde velt,
> ir verkoufet iuwern huobegelt.
> sus swendet ir iuwer guot.
> sô ir iu schaden dann getuot,
> sô komt ein ander bote gerant,
> der gebiut iu alzehant
> 'lât die hovevart under wegen:
> ez ist ein hervart gewegen,
> dâ vart hin mit gesellen vil.'
> man stecket iu ûf solhiu zil,
> dâ von ir alle verderbet
> und armuot erwerbet. (7981–98)

(You are never without worries. For example, a messenger comes today or tomorrow [saying]: 'Get up and make ready, you are to go to the court in fine style, as my lord commands you.' So you plunge yourselves further [into debt], you pledge cleared land and fields, and you spend the tax from your land. You waste your money in this way. While you are ruining yourself, another messenger comes running and tells you right away: 'Forget the trip to the court. A campaign of war has been decided upon, repair there with a large force.' You are toyed with in a way which will impoverish you all.)

The narrator enlarges upon earlier comments by emphasizing the materially ruinous consequences of the faulty relations between the princes and their vassals. The audience's predicament is encapsulated in the presentation of the two fundamental duties of vassalage, the visit to the court of the lord (*hovevart*) and military service

gerne ich iuch nû mahte vrî, | sô stênt die vürsten iu niht bî' (217–24, 230–42). The severity of the criticism allows us to view *Dietrichs Flucht* together with several other Austrian works of the period with express interest in political and social problems; see Heinzle, *Wandlungen und Neuansätze*, 49–59. For 'Zeitklagen' in other heroic epics cf. *Rabenschlacht* 96,1–101,6; *Biterolf und Dietleib* 4046–66.

(*hervart*),[67] as dependent on the passing fancy of the prince. It is also notable that the commentary is cast in the form of a dramatic scene in which the direct speech of the messengers may well have lent itself to mimicry in the reality of public performance. This is a poetically ambitious device, singular in our corpus of heroic epics, which finds its closest parallel elsewhere in medieval German narrative tradition in Rudolf's *Willehalm von Orlens*.[68]

The political discussion is privileged in another way for it is precisely at this moment that a naming occurs:

> Dise wernde swaere
> hât Heinrîch der Vogelaere
> gesprochen und getihtet. (7999ff.)

(Heinrich der Vogler has uttered and composed [the description of] this lasting plight.)

The combination of the third-person perspective and the apparent restriction of the claim of authorship to the excursus itself has led some to doubt the authenticity of the signature, preferring to read these lines as a deliberate attribution of the harsh critique to a third party.[69] However, as we have seen, the use of the third person is not unusual for authorial self-reference,[70] and there is no awkward juxtaposition with a first-person pronoun here to discourage identification with the narratorial voice.[71] This authorial naming may there-

---

[67] Hans K. Schulze, *Grundstrukturen der Verfassung im Mittelalter*, 2 vols., Stuttgart 1985–6 (Kohlhammer Urban-Taschenbücher 371–2), vol. i. 59, 76f.

[68] *Willehalm von Orlens*: 'Vil liht sizzet ainer da | Der sprichet "seht, dis ist an not, | Si sint vor hundert jaren tot | Von den man disiú mâre sait; | Es ist ain notlich arebait, | Suld wir alle hie gedagen | Und ainer fúr úns alle sagen."—| "Fernement, gût, an wenic hie!"—| "Knappe, sag disen rittern wie,| Wie wart dem man der rop genomen?"' (9804–13).

[69] For further details see Curschmann, 'Struktur und Thematik', 379f. Whether this 'Heinrîch der Vogelaere' is an allusion to the German King Henry I, documented in annals as *Heinricus, cognomento Auceps*, as suggested by Höfler, 'Anonymität', 364–75, must be left open here.

[70] Previously cited examples include Hartmann von Aue and Rudolf von Ems, but equally one could refer to the longer narratives of Der Stricker: *Daniel von dem Blühenden Tal*: 'hie wil der Strickaere | mit worten ziehen sîn kunst' (16f.); *Karl*: 'nu hât ez der Strickaere | erniuwet durch der werden gunst' (116f.).

[71] The excursus actually continues in the same vein for another twenty lines: 'ir sît vil unberihtet, | ir grâven vrîen dienestman. | ich sihe wol daz man iu niht gan | guotes noch der êren. | man wil iu verkêren | iuwer reht alle tage.| ez ist wâr daz ich iu sage. | man setzet die geste | ûf iuwer erbeveste | und müezet ir dar zuo sehen. | swaz iu des immer mac geschehen, | dar umb türret ir niht sprechen wort | od ir sît alle mort' (8002–14).

fore be regarded as a bold gesture, with the poet revealing his own identity in order to lend his political commentary more weight. In the broader context of the generic anonymity of the heroic epic, the self-naming has an inherent poetological significance as well, although strictly speaking the poet only seeks the status of an individual author with reference to what he can properly claim as his own achievement: the excursus.[72]

Dietrichs Flucht contains two other instances of the presentation of authorship which do not seem to form part of the same strategy as the naming in lines 7999ff. The first of these is located at an earlier point in the work, in the course of the genealogical account of Dietrich's forefathers (1–2530):

> der uns daz maere zesamne slôz,
> der tuot uns an dem buoche kunt,
> daz weder ê noch bî der stunt
> nie hôchzît sô schoene wart. (1840–3)

(He who assembled this tale informs us with regard to the book that there had never been such beautiful celebrations, either previously or at that time.)

This reference functions almost as a mirror image of the opening passage in *Biterolf und Dietleib*. Here the allusion to an unnamed authorial figure represents a means of authorization for what the narrator can relate. The choice of the verb 'zesamne slôz' (1840) is unusual, but it may well have been determined by the rhyme of the preceding line ('nie dehein hôchzît alsô grôz' 1839). In the second case, several hundred lines later, the more conventional verb *tihten* is employed as the narrator fleetingly assumes the role of author:

> nû wil ich iu tihten
> und der maere slehte berihten:[. . .] (2453f.)

(Now I want to compose for you and order the stories clearly [. . .])

Overall, such variation in perspective in *Dietrichs Flucht* does not seem calculated in the way that it is in Rudolf von Ems's works, for example. The progression from the third person to the first may indicate the poet's increased willingness to shoulder (authorial)

---

[72] For the suggestion that the author of the excursus is not the poet of the main body of the text see Müller, *Spielregeln*, 179.

responsibility for the text. However, this willingness is short-lived as first-person authorial self-presentation is not forthcoming thereafter.[73] Thus, whilst these references provide additional evidence of engagement with the theme of authorship in the text they remain disparate, and stand isolated from the authorial naming that is located some 6,000 verses later. The stuttering presentation of authorship in *Dietrichs Flucht* is a pertinent reminder of the difficulties facing poets who tried to infuse traditionally oral story material with 'foreign' poetological values.

The traditional anonymity of the heroic epic is momentarily dispelled in specific versions of three other works (*Eckenlied* E₁, *Laurin* D, *Wolfdietrich* D) although the authorial namings that occur here fall into a different category and may be compared to the spurious attributions of texts to Konrad von Würzburg that we observed in the last chapter. At some stage during the transmission of each of the works in question the name of a prominent individual becomes attached to the text, thereby supplying it with a new authorial function. It remains to be seen just which literary structures are used in this process.

The authorial naming that arises in the literary tradition of the *Eckenlied* is a conspicuous feature of the single strophe preserved in the famous 'Codex Buranus' (Munich, BSB, Clm 4660, *c.* 1230):[74]

> Uns seit von Lutringen Helferich,
> wie zwene rechen lobelich
> zesaemine bechomen:
> her Ekke unde ouch her Dieterich.
> si waren beide vraislich,
> davon si schaden namen.
> als vinster was der tan,
> da si anander funden.
> her Dietrich rait mit mannes chrafft
> den walt also unchunden.
> her Eke der chom dar gegan;
> er lie da heime rosse vil,
> daz was niht wolgetan. (1–13)

---

[73] The next instance of *tihten* in this sense is as part of the third-person naming of Heinrich der Vogler (800of.).

[74] The vernacular strophe follows three others in Latin as part of song 203 in the manuscript, and represents the earliest textual witness for the *Eckenlied*: E₁. For further detailed discussion of this passage see Heinzle, *Mittelhochdeutsche Dietrichepik*, 157–62.

(Helferich von Lutringen tells us of how two praiseworthy heroes encountered each other: Lord Ecke and also Lord Dietrich. They were both fearsome, which cost them dearly. The forest was completely dark when they met each other. Lord Dietrich rode valiantly through the unknown wood. Lord Ecke came along on foot; he left many horses at home, which was not seemly.)

The naming of 'von Lutringen Helferich' takes up a prominent position in the strophe (which may well represent the opening of an abbreviated version) authorizing the 'abstract' of the story that follows. The choice of this individual for author lies in Helferich's identity as a personage of the heroic world of Dietrich von Bern and, more specifically, as a character in the *Eckenlied*.[75] The tale is thus presented as an eye-witness report, another historiographical topos of considerable standing.[76] In this context line 1 can also be read as a reference to a source,[77] but the *uns seit* formula is an established component of explicit allusions to authorship as well, as we have already seen in this chapter (*Klage* 4349; *Biterolf und Dietleib* 28; *Goldemar* 2,6) and as may be demonstrated with reference to texts as generically diverse as the *Strassburger Alexander* ('iz tihte der paffe Lamprecht | unde saget uns ze mere' 4f.) and Der Stricker's *Pfaffe Amis* ('Nu saget uns der Stricker' 39). Furthermore, the significance of the identification itself is not to be underestimated. As soon as he is named, the guarantor of the authenticity of the tale assumes an individual, authorial status.

The revelation of authorial identity in certain versions of *Laurin* and *Wolfdietrich* differs in that it plays on the standing of two recognized vernacular poets of the thirteenth century: Heinrich von Ofterdingen and Wolfram von Eschenbach respectively. It was evidently thought that these heroic epics would benefit from an association with famous authors, but the choices were not arbitrary.

---

[75] Ecke encounters Helferich shortly before he catches up with Dietrich: *Eckenlied* [E₂] 55,5–68,13. Helferich von Lutringen is also an important protagonist in *Virginal*, and is mentioned once in *Dietrichs Flucht* (5156).

[76] It is difficult to overestimate the significance of this motif; further examples range from the Gospels themselves (Luke 1. 1–4) to the most influential rendering in the Middle Ages of the story of Charlemagne and Roland, the *Historia Karoli Magni et Rotholandi*, a text which purports to be Turpin's own record of the events (prologue 3–11); for the latter see also Curschmann, 'Hören–Lesen–Sehen', 227f.

[77] This aspect predominates in the version of the strophe as contained in the prints (e₁–e₁₁): 'Wir finden hie geschriben stan, | wie das zwen unverzagte man | [. . .]' (63,1f.).

In each case there is a discernible internal logic. In *Laurin* D the naming of Heinrich von Ofterdingen occurs in the epilogue:[78]

> Nu hât diz buoch ein ende.
> got uns sîne helfe sende,
> daz wir ze allen stunden
> in gnâden werden vunden,
> sô mac uns wol gelingen.
> Heinrîch von Ofterdingen
> dis âventiure gesungen hât,
> daz si sô meisterlîche stât.
> des wâren ime die vürsten holt:
> si gâben im silber unde golt,
> pfenninge unde rîche wât.
> hie diz buoch ein ende hât
> von den ûzerwelten degen.
> got gebe uns allen sînen segen! (2817–30)

(Now this book is at an end. May God send us his aid so that we may be found at all times in [His] grace and thus may fare well. Heinrich von Ofterdingen sang this song of adventure, [and that is why] it is crafted in such masterly fashion. The princes were well disposed towards him for this: they gave him silver and gold, money and rich clothing. Here this book, which concerns the best heroes, is at an end. May God bless us all!)

In a relatively elaborate closure references to the end of 'the book' and expressions of shared religiosity bracket a note on the authorship of the work. Its impressive prehistory in lines 2822–7 draws on knowledge of Heinrich von Ofterdingen's participation in a legendary singing contest at the court of Hermann von Thüringen, as portrayed in the *Fürstenlob* (c. 1200–10), one of a number of poems that go under the title of the *Wartburgkrieg*.[79] Notably, the dwarf-king Laurin and his brother figure in another of the texts in this complex, *Zabulons Buch*, which suggests that Heinrich von Ofterdingen's suitability as an author for the heroic epic *Laurin* is based on a specific association within literary tradition.[80] In terms of its function the

---

[78] *Laurin* is preserved, in at least five versions, in eighteen manuscripts and eleven prints; see Heinzle, *Einführung*, 145–54. *Laurin* D represents the 'jüngere Vulgat-Version' of Heinzle's scheme.

[79] *Fürstenlob*: 'Daz êrste singen hie nu tuot | Heinrich von Ofterdingen in des edeln vürsten dôn | von Düringen lant; der teilte uns ie sîn guot | und wir im Gotes lôn' (1,1–4).

[80] Heinzle, *Mittelhochdeutsche Dietrichepik*, 47f.

claim that Heinrich entertained princes with this very tale of adventure affirms the quality of the poem, whose form, we are assured, is 'masterly' (2824). The current storytelling situation is hereby provided with an extremely complimentary background in which the details of the princes' generosity (2826f.) also serve as a covert suggestion for the audience to emulate them in the here and now.

The naming of Wolfram in *Wolfdietrich* D does not occupy a structurally privileged position within the text but falls in the main body of the narrative in the course of Wolfdietrich's crusading expedition to the Holy Land (890–1059):

> Man sach do nider risen   an der selben stunt
> manig werk von isen;   daz ist vil wol kunt
> Mir Wolfram dem werden   meister von Eschelbach[81]
> waz von dem werden Kriechen   des tages do geschach. (969)

(Much iron armour could be seen falling down at that same time. I, Wolfram, the worthy master of Eschenbach, know only too well what deeds the worthy Greek performed on that day.)

The narrative context of Christian–heathen conflict suggests that Wolfram's authorship of *Willehalm* was a decisive factor in the naming in this strophe. The first-person form is modelled on Wolfram's standard technique of authorial self-identification (*Willehalm*: 'ich, Wolfram von Eschenbach' 4,19), although the incorporation of the title of 'meister' clearly reflects Wolfram's status in the later Middle Ages, in express contradiction of his own strategies of self-presentation and initial reputation as the wisest of (uneducated) laymen: 'leien munt nie baz gesprach' (*Wigalois* 6346). In fact this naming is an example of a broader phenomenon, for fictional attributions to Wolfram feature in several other later thirteenth-century texts such

---

[81] A variant for line 969,3 has been taken here, as recorded in the apparatus of Holtzmann's edition for the earliest manuscript of *Wolfdietrich* D: Heidelberg, UB, cod. Pal. germ. 373, datable 1413–17; for the dating of this codex see Hans-Joachim Koppitz, *Studien zur Tradierung der weltlichen mittelhochdeutschen Epik im 15. und beginnenden 16. Jahrhundert*, Munich 1980, p. 114 note 49. Holtzmann's own decision not to follow this manuscript (one of his three 'Leithandschriften') at this point seems to be an attempt to downplay the authorial fiction constructed in the strophe. In the main text of the edition verse 969,3 reads 'Wolfram dem werden   meister von Eschelbach', even although the first-person perspective is retained in four of the five other extant manuscripts: 'Daz sag ich Wolfram der werde   meister von Eschelbach'. In *Wolfdietrich* y, the redaction of *Wolfdietrich* D that is contained in codex Vienna, ÖNB, cod. 15478, Wolfram is named in the third person: 'Sin stritten und sin fechten   hat uns gemachet kunt | Der hoch gelobte maister Wolffram von Eschenbach' (910,2f.).

as the *Jüngerer Titurel* and the *Göttweiger Trojanerkrieg*.[82] In comparison with these texts, however, the Wolfram-role in *Wolfdietrich* D is extremely limited, and it is not sustained throughout the text. Thus, although the naming represents an affirmative response to the issue of authorship, it remains an isolated one which has little bearing on the strategy of displacement that we have already observed for the prologue of the work.

This concludes our study of the phenomenon of the restoration of the author which is a feature of only a minority of the texts in the corpus. In terms of the constructions and models used, it is noticeable that there is a distinct preference for the third-person perspective (*Biterolf und Dietleib* 23; *Goldemar* 2,2f.; *Dietrichs Flucht* 7999ff.; *Eckenlied* E₁ 1; *Laurin* D 2822f.). The avoidance of the immediacy of the first person ensures that a certain distance is placed between the work in the here and now and its supposed author, and it is no coincidence that such passages are often interpreted as references to a source. Third-person allusion to authorship is by no means substandard. However, the repeated deployment of the distance that it engenders may also be seen as a concession to the characteristic anonymity of the genre as a whole.

Analysis of the later heroic epic enables us to catch sight of another side to medieval German narrative literature in the period 1220–90. Clearly, this large body of material features responses to the issue of authorship that we do not encounter in the texts of Rudolf von Ems and Konrad von Würzburg. The disparate character of these responses, and the relative paucity of explicit presentation of authorship seem symptomatic of a new narrative type struggling to come to terms with its own literary nature. Whether there is any correspondence between this aspect of the genre and its broader socio-cultural context is very difficult, if not impossible, to ascertain, given the absence of unambiguous internal references to patronage. The political agenda of the narrator in *Dietrichs Flucht* has led some scholars to locate the composition and transmission of this work (and the *Rabenschlacht*) among the ranks of the minor landed nobility in Austria in the second half of the thirteenth century, who were staunchly opposed to encroaching ducal authority.[83] If this is true,

---

[82] Ragotzky, *Wolfram-Rezeption*, 137–49.

[83] Heinzle, *Wandlungen und Neuansätze*, 49–54; Müller, 'Heroische Vorwelt', 214–18; Fritz Peter Knapp, *Die Literatur des Früh- und Hochmittelalters in den Bistümern Passau, Salzburg, Brixen*

then *Dietrichs Flucht* is a product of the process of social diversification in the patronage of vernacular literature that Bumke observes
for this period.[84] Green categorically states that none of the heroic
epics feature any internal evidence of a reception by reading as well
as listening,[85] and such an absence may be a further indication that
this genre was fostered at smaller secular courts with only tenuous
links to the world of letters. However, we should tread carefully here.
Even a relatively minor secular court could enjoy a close relationship
with a monastery; conversely, even the most highly educated in
medieval society could take an interest in heroic tales, as the 'literary' predilections of bishop Gunther of Bamberg (d. 1065) famously
demonstrate.[86] In respect of heroic epic literature there is a strong
case for situating the composition of the *Nibelungenlied* at the court of
bishop Wolfger von Erla of Passau (1191–1204);[87] whilst for the later
period the same kind of association is maintained in the enigmatic
prologue of *Wolfdietrich* D. The fact that the later heroic epics did not
include acrostics of the author's name, say, does not mean that they
could not also have been composed and recited at larger courts with
greater numbers of literate men and women sitting in the audience.

Throughout this chapter it has been stressed that a strong oral
tradition continued to exert influence on written heroic literature.
But there are signs that the poets of these texts were conscious of
vernacular literary tradition as well, and this again has significant
implications for our understanding of the presentation or non-
presentation of authorship in these works. In the first instance, there
appears to have been an element of 'intertextual' reference within
the genre of the heroic epic itself. *Kudrun* is not the only epic to
counter the *Nibelungenlied* in some way, for example. Version A of the
Rosengarten represents a savage criticism of Kriemhild,[88] and both
Dietrichs Flucht and the *Rabenschlacht* can be read as attempts to re-
habilitate the figure of Dietrich von Bern.[89] Furthermore, in *Biterolf*

und Trient von den Anfängen bis zum Jahre 1273, Graz 1994 (Geschichte der Literatur in Österreich von den Anfängen bis zur Gegenwart 1), 321–6.

[84] See Chapter 1 section III above.

[85] Green, *Medieval Listening and Reading*, 208, 231.

[86] Bishop Gunther is reputed to have preferred tales about Etzel and the Amelungen
(Dietrich von Bern's relatives and heroes) to the writings of the Church Fathers; see
Bumke, *Mäzene*, 42, 256.

[87] Heinzle, *Nibelungenlied*, 47–52.

[88] Heinzle, *Mittelhochdeutsche Dietrichepik*, 244–63.

[89] Elisabeth Lienert, 'Dietrich contra Nibelungen: Zur Intertextualität der historischen
Dietrichepik', *PBB* 121 (1999), 23–46.

und Dietleib, we have what has been described as the heroic equivalent of Heinrich von dem Türlin's *Diu Crône*, constituting a veritable compendium of motifs, characters, and structures from the genre as a whole.[90] The degree of sophistication that we are willing to accord such 'intertextuality' will determine the degree to which we regard the treatment of the issue of authorship in these works as deliberate and reasoned, rather than naive or instinctive. Secondly, if we accept that as the heroic tales assumed literary form they effectively entered into competition with the courtly romance,[91] it seems likely that the poetological focal point of this ongoing process of interaction would have been authorship. The naming of Albrecht von Kemenaten in *Goldemar* is the most famous example of a deliberate act of affiliation with the principle of authorial self-consciousness of the courtly romance, but by the same token anonymity and the displacement of the author could be viewed as poetologically loaded strategies, representing perhaps an assertion of collective identity. That in some texts an authorial figure is referred to but not named, or several apparently contradictory strategies occur, is an indication that poets of heroic epics were not always able to reconcile the presuppositions underpinning the story material with those of their new (literary) medium.

[90] Heinzle, *Wandlungen und Neuansätze*, 125.
[91] Id., *Mittelhochdeutsche Dietrichepik*, 233–44, 263–8.

5

EXPANSIVE AND CURSORY PRESENTATION OF AUTHORSHIP IN THE SECULAR SHORT STORY

The short story or 'Märe' is another kind of narrative poetry which appears inextricably linked to an oral tradition of storytelling but whose increasing popularity characterizes the German literary scene of the period 1220–90. We have already observed the presentation of authorship in several 'Mären' in the context of Konrad von Würzburg's oeuvre, where the poetic strategies involved range from the expansive (*Herzmaere*) to the cursory (*Schwanritter*). This chapter will explore just how far the short story as a genre relates to such self-conscious authorial practices, and whether or not there is any affinity to be discerned between these texts and the heroic epic.

The status of the 'Märe' as an identifiable genre has been the subject of some controversy.[1] Hanns Fischer's (1968) famous definition and cataloguing of the 'Märe', of which he finds over two hundred, have been severely criticized but they remain fundamental to all work in this area, especially after their reappraisal by Hans-Joachim Ziegeler (1985).[2] Whilst recognizing the problematic nature of several of the criteria on which it is based, such as the presupposition of a polarity between religious and secular texts, this study too makes use of Fischer's catalogue, which has the pragmatic value of enabling us to differentiate 'Mären' from the mass of other shorter literary forms with which they are predominantly transmitted.[3]

---

[1] Joachim Heinzle, 'Altes und Neues zum Märenbegriff', *ZfdA* 117 (1988), 277–96.

[2] Hanns Fischer, *Studien zur deutschen Märendichtung*, Tübingen 1968, 2nd revised edn. by Johannes Janota, 1983; Hans-Joachim Ziegeler, *Erzählen im Spätmittelalter: Mären im Kontext von Minnereden, Bispeln und Romanen*, Munich 1985 (MTU 87), esp. 29–34. Fischer's definition of the 'Märe' is as follows: '[. . .] eine in paarweise gereimten Viertaktern versifizierte, selbständige und eigenzweckliche Erzählung mittleren (d.h. durch die Verszahlen 150 und 2000 ungefähr umgrenzten) Umfangs, deren Gegenstand fiktive, diesseitig-profane und unter weltlichem Aspekt betrachtete, mit ausschließlich (oder vorwiegend) menschlichem Personal vorgestellte Vorgänge sind' (63); an English translation is given in Palmer, 'The High and Later Middle Ages', 79.

[3] See also Mihm, *Überlieferung*, esp. 105–16.

Having accepted Fischer's catalogue as a way of fencing in our primary material we are faced with another problem: the dating of the individual texts. The 'Märe' established itself as a new type of literary narrative in the course of the thirteenth century,[4] but it is clear that a high proportion of the works in Fischer's list was composed after 1300. Furthermore, although in every case a hypothesis for a date may be given, the criteria employed vary so greatly that they fail to provide a basis for a single principle of distinction. Under these circumstances it seems best to allow our choice of 'Mären' to be dictated by the manuscripts. Thus, all those 'Mären' found in manuscripts that can be dated to the first third of the fourteenth century or earlier shall be regarded here as relevant to our investigation. This approach excludes a number of 'Mären' which are considered to be of the thirteenth century but are preserved in later manuscripts,[5] and probably includes several from the beginning of the fourteenth century. However, it will ensure that this discussion rests on short stories which have an early material basis.

On reconsidering Fischer's data we find that there are eleven such manuscripts, some extremely large, some merely fragments, containing a total of fifty-two 'Mären':

I. MANUSCRIPTS[6]

E^2 = Erfurt, Domarchiv, Fragment 5, c. 1325–50

F = Freiberg i. S., Bibliothek des Gymnasiums Albertinum, no signature

---

[4] For discussion of Latin and French precursors see Jürgen Beyer, *Schwank und Moral: Untersuchungen zum altfranzösischen Fabliau und verwandten Formen*, Heidelberg 1969 (Studia Romanica 16), 9–93'; Peter Dronke, 'The Rise of the Medieval Fabliau: Latin and Vernacular Evidence', *RF* 85 (1973), 275–97; Ingrid Strasser, *Vornovellistisches Erzählen: Mittelhochdeutsche Mären bis zur Mitte des 14. Jahrhunderts und altfranzösische Fabliaux*, Vienna 1989 (Philologica Germanica 10).

[5] In particular: *Alexander und Anteloie*; *Beringer*; *Dulceflorie*; *Die böse Frau*; *Die demütige Frau*; Herrand von Wildonie's *Der betrogene Gatte* and *Die treue Gattin*; *Moriz von Craûn*; Heinrich Rafold's *Der Nußberg*; *Der Ritter im Hemde*; *Der Ritter mit den Nüssen*; Rüdeger von Munre's *Studentenabenteuer* B; *Schampiflor*; *Das Schneekind* B; *Der Schreiber*; *Der Schüler zu Paris* (versions A, B, C); *Studentenabenteuer* A; Werner der Gärtner's *Helmbrecht*. Eight of these texts unambiguously address the theme of authorship and these will be referred to in passing in the course of the chapter.

[6] The dating of the manuscripts is based on the following critical literature: Mihm, *Überlieferung*, 129–44 [E^2; F; P; S; Schloß Schönstein]; Karin Schneider, 'Cod. Bodmer 72', in René Wetzel, *Deutsche Handschriften des Mittelalters in der Bodmeriana* [. . .], Cologny-Genève

H = Heidelberg, UB, cod. Pal. germ. 341, *c.* 1300–25

K = Cologny-Genève, Bibliotheca Bodmeriana, Cod. Bodmer 72 [previously Kálocsa, Erzbischöfliche Bibliothek, Ms. 1], *c.* 1300–25

P = Paris, Bibliothèque Nationale, Ms. allemand 334, *c.* 1320

S = Strassburg, Johanniterbibl. A 94, *c.* 1330–50 [destroyed 1870]

S¹ = Nuremberg, Germanisches Nationalmuseum, Hs. 42 531, *c.* 1330–50

W = Vienna, ÖNB, cod. 2705, *c.* 1250–75

W¹ = Vienna, ÖNB, cod. 2779, *c.* 1300–25

Munich, BSB, Cgm 5249/29b, *c.* 1325–50

Schloß Schönstein bei Wissen a. d. Sieg, Fürstl. Hatzfeldt-Wildenburgsches Archiv, Nos. 7693 and 8866, *c.* 1280–1300

II. TEXTS[7]

[F3] *Das Almosen:* H; K

[F5] Jacob Appet, *Der Ritter unter dem Zuber:** S

[F6] *Aristoteles und Phyllis:* Cgm 5249/29b; S

[F7] *Das Auge:* S

[F11] *Der hohle Baum* A: H; K

[F20] *Die halbe Decke* A: H; K

[F24] Dietrich von der Glezze, *Der Gürtel:** H; K

[F37] *Frauenlist:* H; K

[F38] *Frauentreue:* H; K

[F39] *Das Frauenturnier:* F; H; K

[F41] Der Freudenleere, *Der Wiener Meerfahrt:** H; K

[F43] *Das Gänslein:* H; K

[F50] *Das Häslein:** S

[F53] *Die Heidin* A [I]: W¹

[F54] *Die Heidin* B [IV]: H; K

1994 (Bibliotheca Bodmeriana: Kataloge 7), 81–129, esp. 81 [H; K]; Reinhard Bleck, 'Eine Kleinsammlung mittelhochdeutscher Reimpaardichtungen (Nürnberg, Germanisches Nationalmuseum, Hs 42 531)', *ZfdA* 116 (1987), 283–96, esp. 290 [S¹]; Schneider, *Gotische Schriften,* ii 177f. [W]; Ziegeler, *Erzählen im Spätmittelalter,* 335 [W¹]; Hellmut Rosenfeld, 'Aristoteles und Phillis: Eine neu aufgefundene Benediktbeurer Fassung um 1200', *ZfdPh* 89 (1970), 321–36, esp. 324 [Cgm 5249/29b].

[7] Fischer's numbering is included here in square brackets. The two texts in H which he registers as 'inhaltlich unbestimmbare Bruchstücke' F150a and F150b are not included. An authorial name in brackets indicates that the attribution is uncertain or occurs only in later manuscripts.

[F62] *Der Herrgottschnitzer.* H

[F64] Johannes von Freiberg, *Das Rädlein:* * H

[F68] *Das Kerbelkraut:* S

[F70] *Kobold und Eisbär.* H

[F73] Konrad von Würzburg

[a] *Heinrich von Kempten:* * H; K

[b] *Herzmaere:* * Schloß Schönstein; H; S

[F74] Pseudo-Konrad von Würzburg, *Die halbe Birne* A:* S; S¹

[F75] *Das Kreuz:* S¹

[F79] *Der Liebhaber im Bade:* W

[F85] *Bestraftes Mißtrauen:* * H

[F101] *Der Reiher:* * H; K

[F106] Rüdeger der Hinkhofer, *Der Schlegel:* * H; K

[F113] *Das Schneekind* A: W

[F121] Sibote, *Frauenerziehung:* * H; K

[F125] *Der Sperber.* H; K; S

[F127] Der Stricker[8]

[a] *Der nackte Bote:* W; H; K

[b] *Edelmann und Pferdehändler.* H

[c] *Der begrabene Ehemann:* W; H; K

[d] *Ehescheidungsgespräch:* W; H; K

[e] *Der durstige Einsiedel:* H

[f] *Das heiße Eisen:*[9] W; H; K

[g] *Die eingemauerte Frau:* W

[h] *Das erzwungene Gelübde:* W; H; K

[i] *Der Gevatterin Rat:* W; H; K

[k] *Der kluge Knecht:* W; H

[l] *Der arme und der reiche König:* W; H; K

[m] *Die Martinsnacht:* W; H; K

[n] *Der junge Ratgeber:* W; H; K

[o] *Der nackte Ritter:* W; H; K

[p] *Die drei Wünsche:* W; H; K

[q] *Der unbelehrbare Zecher.* W; H

[F130] *Des Teufels Ächtung:* H; K

[F133] [Volrat,] *Die alte Mutter:* * H; E²

[F135] Der Vriolsheimer, *Der Hasenbraten:* * H; K

---

[8] Der Stricker does not 'sign' any of these texts, but they are widely held to be his work; *Der nackte Ritter* is attributed to Der Stricker in a scribal superscription in K.

[9] A further thirteenth-century fragment of *Das heiße Eisen*—Trento, Bibliotheca Communale [now lost]—is registered by Fischer, *Märendichtung*, 291, 410.

[F136] *Wandelart:* P
[F142] *Der dankbare Wiedergänger:* H
[F149] [Der Zwingäuer,] *Des Mönches Not:* H; K

Most of the 'Mären' in this group are anonymous, and thirty-seven of the fifty-two include no presentation of authorship. In some cases this may be the by-product of a process of transmission in which passages functionalizing authorship were excised.[10] Nevertheless, the large proportion suggests that as with the heroic epic the tendency towards authorial self-effacement in the 'Märe' is anchored in the poetological principles of the genre. A substantial core of this body of thirty-seven texts is made up by the sixteen attributed to Der Stricker, who played a pre-eminent role in the establishment of the 'Märe' as a literary form.[11] In Der Stricker's short stories the profile of the narrator is kept to a minimum, being largely restricted to the formulaic stylization of a public performance within the text itself,[12] and the colouring of a number of the moralistic closures.[13] Fourteen other 'Mären' are as minimalist as those of Der Stricker,[14] whilst eight incorporate more extensive passages of narratorial self-presentation.[15]

A clue to the absence of the presentation of authorship in so many of the texts may lie in the explicit references to the sphere of orality that they contain.[16] Only three of the fifty-two 'Mären' mention a written source, and these are all associated with Konrad von Würzburg.[17] In the vivid depiction of oral storytelling that

[10] See also Jean Rychner, *Contribution à l'étude des fabliaux: variantes, remaniements, dégradations: I. Observations*, Neuchâtel/Geneva 1960 (Université de Neuchâtel: Recueil de travaux publiés par la Faculté des Lettres 28), 134f.

[11] Fischer, *Märendichtung*, 145f.

[12] *Der nackte Bote* 46; *Der begrabene Ehemann* 171; *Der durstige Einsiedel* 228, 354; *Der Gevatterin Rat* 199; *Der kluge Knecht* 1.

[13] *Die Martinsnacht* 199–214; *Der kluge Knecht* 308–38; *Der nackte Ritter* 91–100; *Die drei Wünsche* 197–228.

[14] *Das Almosen; Aristoteles und Phyllis; Das Auge; Der hohle Baum* A; *Die halbe Decke* A; *Das Frauenturnier; Das Gänslein; Der Herrgottschnitzer; Das Kerbelkraut; Das Kreuz; Der Liebhaber im Bade; Das Schneekind* A; *Des Teufels Ächtung; Wandelart.*

[15] *Frauenlist; Frauentreue; Die Heidin* A; *Die Heidin* B; *Kobold und Eisbär; Der Sperber; Der dankbare Wiedergänger; Des Mönches Not.*

[16] *Aristoteles und Phyllis:* 'als ich hôrte sagen' (34); *Das Auge:* 'Man seite mir ein maere' (1); *Das Frauenturnier:* 'Ich hôrte sagen' (1); *Das Gänslein:* 'Ich hôrt sagen ein mer' (1); *Der Herrgottschnitzer:* 'als man mir jach' (4); *Kobold und Eisbär:* 'hôrt ich sagen' (298); *Der nackte Bote:* 'sô man seit' (1); *Des Teufels Ächtung:* 'als man saget' (7).

[17] *Heinrich von Kempten* 99, 387, 390, 533, 758f.; *Die halbe Birne* A 2; *Frauentreue* 10. *Frauentreue* is the only one of these not to include an explicit statement of authorship, although it is clearly modelled on Konrad's *Herzmaere*.

occurs in the prologue of *Der Sperber*,[18] for example, the poet negates his own authorial role as part of the advancement of a chain of oral transmission:

> Als mir ein maere ist geseit
> gar vür eine wârheit,
> niht vür ein lüge noch vür ein spel
> (ez ist hübesch unde snel)—
> ich sage ez iu, man seite mirz,
> alz ir'z gelernet, sô saget irz. (1–6)

(Just as I have been told a story as something completely true, not as a lie or fabulation—it is courtly and entertaining—so I'm telling you it, [as] I was told it; when you have got to know it, so you too [can] tell it.)

What is striking about this passage is that no distinction is made between the poet's reception of the tale, his own telling of it and the audience's future ability to do the same,[19] even though the principal function of the passage is to convince the audience of the truth of the tale. In a time when poets of extended vernacular narratives were at pains to detail the written origins of their stories, as well as the names of those involved in the transmission and composition of the text, it appears that in this generic context word of mouth could be a sufficient guarantee and the identity of individual participants was often deemed irrelevant.

Nevertheless, fourteen of the fifty-two 'Mären', marked by an asterisk in the above list, feature the presentation of authorship, and the strategies that occur in these works vary considerably in their complexity, revealing a tendency towards either expansiveness or cursoriness. In what follows attention will also be paid to the claims to an association with orality that are made in both categories. The chapter will end with a review of the role played by authorship in the first few collective manuscripts of shorter verse-couplet texts in order to ascertain whether the presentation of authorship is a distinguishing characteristic of this genre.

---

[18] *Der Sperber* is preserved in eleven manuscripts; see Grubmüller (ed.), *Novellistik*, 1210ff.
[19] First observed by von der Hagen (ed.), GA ii. p. v.

I. EXPANSIVE STRATEGIES

Seven works in the corpus feature strategies of presentation that share the expansiveness of the prologues, excursuses, and epilogues of extended narrative. These include Konrad's deference to his patron in *Heinrich von Kempten*, the evocation of a broader literary backdrop in the *Herzmaere*, and the deployment of the motif of the author's moral advice in *Die halbe Birne* A (as discussed above in Chapter 3). An analysis of the four other short stories that belong to this category will demonstrate that such expansiveness is not restricted to texts associated with Konrad von Würzburg but is an aspect of the literary potential of the 'Märe'.

This is most obviously the case with *Der Gürtel* by Dietrich von der Glezze, a tale of cross-dressing and (in)fidelity, whose main narrative body is bracketed by a prologue and an epilogue that are both shaped by the device of the 'speaking text'.[20] This highly self-conscious artifice finds its most celebrated usage in medieval German at the beginning of Wirnt von Grafenberg's Arthurian romance *Wigalois*,[21] and it also occurs in thirteenth-century religious and didactic texts as well as in works associated with the traditions of the 'Minnerede' and love-letter.[22] The epilogue of *Der Gürtel* is particularly relevant:

> Von der Glezze Ditrich
> hat mit sinen sinnen mich
> hubschen luten getihtet,
> ertrahtet unde berihtet
> so er beste kunde. (827–31)

(Dietrich von der Glezze used his intellect to compose me for courtly people; he devised and shaped [me] as best he could.)

The theme of authorship is introduced through the identification of the author and the reference to his act of composition. Authorial

---

[20] The text is also preserved in a fifteenth-century codex (Heidelberg, UB, cod. Pal. germ. 4, *c.* 1458–79) but here it includes neither prologue nor epilogue; see Meyer (ed.), *Der Borte*, 29f. For evidence of a later fourteenth-century fragment (containing lines 44–86) see Hans Gröchenig, 'Ein Fragment einer mittelalterlichen Maerenhandschrift aus der UB Klagenfurt. Ein neu aufgefundenes Fragment zur Heidin "B" und zu Dietrich von Glesse: Der Gürtel', *Buchkunde* 1 (1984), 3–10.

[21] See Chapter 1 section III above.

[22] These texts are listed and discussed by Scholz, *Hören und Lesen*, 125–35. Scribes utilized this device as well; see Wattenbach, *Schriftwesen*, 502ff., 525–30.

naming is paradigmatic for the influence of established literary tradition on the 'Märe' and, aside from *Heinrich von Kempten*, the *Herzmaere*,
and *Die halbe Birne* A, occurs in six further texts in our corpus.[23] As
previous chapters have illustrated, naming in the third person is
conventional, although in this case it is simply a function of the
construction of the 'speaking text'. We get an idea of the literariness of this strategy if we note that essentially the same model of
authorial naming is used, in acrostic form, in the courtly epics *Diu
Crône* (HEINRIKH VON DEM TVRLIN HAT MIKH GETIHTET
[182–216]) and *Arabel* (MEISTER VLRICH VON DEM TVRLIN HAT
MIH GEMACHET DEM EDELN CVNICH VON BEHEIM [7f.]).

The act of composition is denoted by a cluster of three verbs that
do not divulge anything about the poet's sources and is coloured by
an intimation of affected humility. This is expressed further in the
lines that follow:

> nu und zu aller stunde
> niman trage keinen haz—
> wan er enkunde sin niht baz—
> durch daz getihte wider in.
> in vrowendinst stunt i sin sin,
> zu allen ziten was er bereit,
> zu sprechen von der reinikeit,
> di an schonen vrowen liget. (832–9)

(Now and for evermore let no one bear any ill will—for he could not have
done it any better—towards him on account of the poem. His intent was
always to serve ladies; he was prepared at all times to tell of the purity
which is characteristic of beautiful ladies.)

The 'speaking text' operates in the role of advocate for the author
with the standard admission of limited ability compensated by great
effort.[24] The rhetorical ploy also includes a defence on the basis of
his 'courtliness' (836–9), and these verses allow us to view authorship in *Der Gürtel* in terms of the thematic complex of 'the poet's
attitudes towards women' which is widely found in the courtly epic,[25]

---

[23] Fischer, *Märendichtung*, 141ff.; Johnson, 'Blütezeit', 240–3.

[24] Cf. also Freidank's *Bescheidenheit*: 'Ich bin genant BESCHEIDENHEIT, | diu aller
tugende krône treit. | mich hât berihtet FRÎDANC; | ein teil von sinnen die sint kranc'
(1,1–4).

[25] Courtly love and service: *Parzival* 114,8–18; 337,27–30; 292,5–293,4; 293,14ff.; *Tristan*
58–70, 119–22, 12191–5, 17104–42; *Diu Crône* 231f., 246ff., 10402–56, 29990–30000; Ulrich
von Türheim's *Tristan* 3658–61; *Barlaam und Josaphat* 11735–870; *Willehalm von Orlens* 4003–9.
Sexual desire: *Willehalm* 100,2–8.

and in a number of the 'Mären' as well.[26] The notion of the author's gallantry in *Der Gürtel* forms part of a programme for stylizing the communicative situation as a whole. The characterization of the audience as 'courtly',[27] both earlier in the epilogue ('hubschen luten' 829) and in the prologue,[28] is now complemented by an equivalent designation on the side of the production of the work.

The return to the story's themes of love and fidelity in the next phase of the epilogue betrays a didactic edge that is reminiscent of Konrad's *Herzmaere*.[29] Here the critique of contemporary disregard for love (840–7) and the eulogy of the joys of courtly love (848–68) are followed by an appeal to one specific section of the audience:

> ir man, ich wil uch leren:
> vrowen sult ir eren
> und sult in undertenic sin,
> wande ire roten mundelin
> und ir wizzen wengelin
> di bringent uch von grozzer pin.
> alle reinen vrewelin
> di muzzen immer selic sin,
> des wunschet in daz herze min
> nu steticlichen ane pin. (869–78)

(You men, I want to instruct you: you should honour ladies and be ruled by them, for their lovely ['little'] red mouths and white cheeks [can] relieve you of anguish. May all pure and lovely ['little'] ladies be forever blessed; that is what my heart now wishes them constantly and without pain.)

These lines offer a model for the ideal courtly attitude towards women, and the sentiment is highlighted by its co-ordination with eight lines of monorhyme (871–8).[30] At the same time, it has become unclear whether the fiction of the 'speaking text' is still

---

[26] Courtly love and service: *Frauentreue* [in manuscripts H and K] 391–420; *Die Heidin* A 1128ff., 1161–72. Sexual desire: *Frauenlist* 543–8; *Das Rädlein* by Johannes von Freiberg, 125ff., 364ff.; *Der Sperber* [in manuscript S], 59f.

[27] For discussion of the term *hövesch/hubisch* ('courtly') see Bumke, *Höfische Kultur*, i. 78–82.

[28] 'Ich bin der Borte genant, | hubschen luten sol ich sin bekant, | den argen sol ich vremde sin, | si sullen immer liden pin | durch ir missewende | unz an ir bitter ende. | man sol mich hubschen luten lesen, | di sullen mit mir vrolich wesen | durch ir tugent manicfalt, | wan niman siner tugent engalt' (1–10). For comparable passages in the courtly epic cf. Ulrich von Zatzikhoven's *Lanzelet* 14ff.; Wirnt von Grafenberg's *Wigalois* 135–44; Der Stricker's *Daniel von dem Blühenden Tal* 18–22.

[29] See also Ortmann/Ragotzky, '*triuwe*-Beweise in Minne-Mären'.

[30] Bunching of rhyme occurs throughout the text: ('Zehnreim') 417–26; ('Vierreim') 65–8, 171–4, 193–6, 345–8, 427–30, 513–16, 541–4, 671–4, 725–8, 853–6.

being maintained. The allusion to 'daz herze min' (877) is discon-
certing and would seem to indicate a return to the more conventional first-person perspective of the human narrator.[31] Nevertheless,
the provision of instruction by the 'speaking text' is entirely in line
with the way in which this device is used elsewhere, as in one of the
precursors of the 'Minnerede', *Der Minne Freigedank*: 'Swer volget
miner lere | Der hat sin from vnd ere' (3f.).[32] Thus, it is not incon-
ceivable that a single narratorial voice is being employed throughout
the epilogue of *Der Gürtel*. The blessing of 'alle reinen vrewelin' (875)
by the text personified would add to the character of the ethos
surrounding this 'Märe' and, as a poetically ambitious construction,
would implicitly claim a higher literary status for the work.

The epilogue concludes with a further exposition of the circumstances of composition, once more from the perspective of the
'speaking text':

> Wilhelm, der vrowen kneht,
> gevlizzen an der tugende reht,
> der schuf, daz ich getihtet wart.
> kein tugent wart ni von im gespart.
> sin vater saz zu Widena,
> gewaldic voget was er da. (879–84)

(Wilhelm, servant of ladies, untiring in the order of virtue, he enabled me
to be composed. He was never stinting in virtue. His father resided in
Weidenau [in Bohemia]; he was a powerful governor there.)

The presentation of patronage is a common feature of the courtly
epic but rare in the 'Mären', occurring elsewhere in our corpus only
in Konrad's *Heinrich von Kempten* and *Der Wiener Meerfahrt* by Der
Freudenleere (see below).[33] This inevitably reflects differences in the
circumstances surrounding the process of composition of the short
story. However, just as some authors of courtly epics did not include
references to patronage in their works, most notably Hartmann von
Aue and Der Stricker, so it is unlikely that these three short stories
are the only ones to have been commissioned by a patron. It is
possible that where such references are actually included they are
imbued with an additional poetological significance. In *Der Gürtel*
this significance assumes definite contours. As in the epilogue of

---

[31] Cf. 20, 40, 64f., 71f., 79, 128, 148, 343, 465, 491, 558, 596, 658.

[32] Cf. also *Der Magezoge*: 'swer minne zuht und ere | der volge miner lere' (3f.).

[33] For more on the historical background to these lines see the conclusion to this
chapter.

Heinrich von Kempten the patron is described through a series of attributes. 'Wilhelm' is identified as a member of courtly society (879), then portrayed in terms of his virtue (880; 882), his capacity as a patron (881), and genealogically (883f.). The first epithet, 'der vrowen kneht' (879), is analogous to the presentation of patronage in Rudolf's *Willehalm von Orlens* as well as in Ulrich von Türheim's *Tristan* where the respective commissions are termed as instances of 'Minnedienst'. In *Der Gürtel* such characterization of the patron is in tune with the earlier stylization of author, audience, and text personified, which emphasizes the cultural values against which the composition and reception of the work are to be seen.[34]

The last verses of *Der Gürtel* refer to another external figure, whose identification has been central to critical discussion of the actual process of composition behind the text as it stands in manuscripts H and K:

> der Borte hat ein ende.
> Punzingeren sende,
> libe vrowe, dinen trost,
> so wirt er von sorgen erlost. (885–8)

(The 'Belt' is at an end. Dear lady, send your encouragement of love to *Punzinger*, and he will be saved from his sorrows.)

On the one hand, the variance in the transmission of prologue and epilogue, together with their own peculiar rhymes, have led several scholars to understand the suffering lover *Punzinger* to be a second author, responsible for setting Dietrich von der Glezze's story between the two statements of the 'speaking text'.[35] The value of this theory, however, is seriously undermined by its failure to explain why the later poet should then present Dietrich's authorship using affected humility.[36] Alternatively, these verses have been read as a scribal addition. Formulaic conclusions which refer to women are a common type of scribal signature, although where such passages do not include explicit pointers to the activity of the scribe their attribution to the poet of the respective work cannot be discounted.[37]

---

[34] First noted by von der Hagen (ed.), GA i. p. CL.

[35] Meyer (ed.), *Der Borte*, 63, 68–72; Fischer, *Märendichtung*, 199.

[36] Schwietering, 'Demutsformel', 182.

[37] *Der Wiener Meerfahrt*: 'Daz mere ist vz an dirre stvnt | Ich kvste gerne eînen roten mvnt' (705f.); *Die Martinsnacht* in codex k (Karlsruhe, Badische LB, cod. Karlsruhe 408, *c.* 1430–5): 'Der dîz bůch hat geschrieben | D' ist an schôn fraûwen blieben'; *Die einge-*

For our purposes it suffices to observe that the conclusion to the epilogue of *Der Gürtel* is thematically consistent with the whole. Whether taken as an instance of scribal addition, or as a second informal reference to patron, author (Dietrich), or any other member of the audience, the allusion to *Punzinger* and his lovesickness firmly relocates the text in the sphere of the courtly culture of *minne*. In this context, the construction of the 'speaking text' may be seen to function in the role of messenger,[38] an established strategy in the traditions of the 'Minnerede' and love-letter.[39]

The presentation of authorship in the prologue of Sibote's *Frauenerziehung*, concerning a knight's taming of his shrewish wife and mother-in-law, plays on a different type of relationship between the sexes: marriage.[40] In this passage the poet offers what would appear to be a parodic variation on the authorial role of 'adviser' that is familiar to us from Konrad's *Der Welt Lohn*, and *Die halbe Birne* A. The naming of the author occurs in this context:

> swelh man ein übel wip hat,
> der sol merken disen rat.
> ob ich die warheit sprechen sol,
> so bedarf ich selbe rates wol;
> wan ich die min betwungen han,
> si ist mir also undertan:
> sprich ich 'swarz', si sprichet 'wiz';
> daran keret si ir vliz
> und tuot daz sere wider gote!
> Ditz maere tihte Sibote. (7–16)

(Any man who has a shrewish wife should heed this advice. To tell the truth, I could benefit from some advice myself; for I have [so] asserted control over my wife, [that] she obeys me in the following way: if I say 'black', she says 'white'; she is most arduous in this and does so very much against [the will of] God! Sibote composed this tale.)

The poet debunks his own authority by presenting himself as the archetypal henpecked husband. The emphasis on his apparent need

mauerte Frau in codex w (Vienna, ÖNB, cod. 2885, dated 1393): 'Hie ist daz mer auz gezalt | Got mach vns m' gutñ weibñ alt'; the scribal additions to Der Stricker's texts are taken from the apparatus in Fischer's edn.

[38] This has often been understood as pointing toward the existence of a dedicatory exemplar in the manuscript tradition of the text; see Meyer (ed.), *Der Borte*, 68–72.

[39] Cf. *Der heimliche Bote* 1–16.

[40] *Frauenerziehung* is preserved, in several versions, in seven manuscripts; see Hans-Joachim Ziegeler, 'Sibote', ²VL 8 (1992), cols. 1134–38, esp. cols. 1134f.

of advice rather than that of the men in the audience represents a rhetorical strategy which defuses the situation, allowing the poet to introduce the story's theme without causing offence.[41] The ironic effect is heightened in the earliest manuscripts H and K through the authorial naming, whereby the integration of an element of external reality exaggerates the poet's self-mockery. Thus, the poet creates an atmosphere, at his own expense, in which he may confidently address the potentially more hostile section of the audience, the *vrouwen*, in the second half of the passage (17–30).[42]

The third-person form of the naming (16) may seem like a foreign body in the midst of the first-person narratorial articulation, but as we have seen on numerous occasions, interchange of perspectives is not uncommon in such passages.[43] One could compare this aspect of Sibote's prologue with sections from texts as diverse as Rudolf's *Willehalm von Orlens* (15601–89) and *Dietrichs Flucht* (7949–8022), for example. On the other hand, the location of the naming at the opening of the text is extremely assertive (even Konrad does not use this ploy in his shorter narratives), and is in keeping with the self-assured and good-humoured tone of the passage as a whole.[44] The expansiveness of the authorial self-presentation in Sibote's *Frauenerziehung* resides in the playful integration of apparently autobiographical detail in the text: the author has a wife! This strategy is diametrically opposed to the authorial self-effacement in Der Stricker's 'Mären', and represents in miniature Wolfram's celebrated technique of narratorial self-presentation in *Parzival* and *Willehalm*.[45]

[41] Schirmer, *Stil- und Motivuntersuchungen*, 71ff.

[42] 'hie enmein ich keine vrouwen mite. | mich dunket guot ir aller site, | wan daz ich si mit zühten mane: | ir enkeiniu zücke sich daz ane | daz si sich selb iht melde | als die knehte uf dem velde' (17–22).

[43] Some poets are clearly more interested in uniformity of perspective than others. In *Studentenabenteuer* B by Rüdeger von Munre authorial self-reference in both prologue and epilogue is largely conducted in the third person: 'Von gemelîchen dingen | sagen unde singen, | Swer daz gerne vernimet, | daz der jugent wol an zimet, | Swen in diu wîle dunket lank, | der sage Ruedigêre dank, | Ob er sîn gelachet, | wan er hât gemachet | Vremdîu âventiure, | der vröude ze stiure, | Diu nû der werlde mak gezemen; | ouch wil er ze lône nemen, | Daz ir ez merket rehte' (1–13); 'Ruediger von Munre | An disen rât iuch kêret' (1428f.).

[44] The epilogue, whose length varies from manuscript to manuscript, seems to lack this humour: 'Des rat ich allen vrouwen daz | daz si ir manne warten baz | danne disiu vrouwe taete. | nu merket dise raete! | ich rate ez iu allen. | daz sol iu wol gevallen' (821–6).

[45] Wolfram too refers to a wife: 'ich braehte ungerne nu mîn wîp | in alsô grôz gemenge: | ich vorht unkunt gedrenge. | etslîcher hin zir spraeche, | daz in ir minne

Concern over the audience's response is also at the forefront of the prologue of *Das Häslein*, a tale of (female) sexual naivety, which includes the presentation of authorship without actually naming the author.[46] Although anonymity may be indicative of an oral tradition of storytelling it does not necessarily preclude an interest in authorship, for attention may still be drawn to the act of composition itself. In *Das Häslein* anonymity is not accompanied by narratorial self-effacement, and the work opens with a prologue whose tenor is largely shaped by an unnamed authorial persona:

> Tribe ich die zît vergebene hin,
> sît ich von gotes genâden bin
> genemmet in der mâzen,
> man solte mich verwâzen. (1–4)

(If I spent the time in vain, since by the grace of God I am renowned to such a degree,[47] I should be cursed.)

The use of the topos of 'the dangers of idleness' in lines 1 and 4 affirms the quality of the tale to follow.[48] At the same time the poet appears to claim a certain status for himself in 2f., although the exact meaning of these verses is disputed: 'genemmet' (3) has been taken variously to mean 'chosen [by God's grace]'[49] and '[I am] called',[50] *nemmen* being a common form of *nennen* ('to name/call'). The latter meaning is preferred by those who see a cryptographic concealment of the author's name in lines 2f., which translates as 'Since I am called something like "by the grace of God"'; possible names include *Gozold*, *Gottschalk*, *Gotfried*. This issue is unlikely to be resolved. All we can say is that if these verses constitute a crypto-

staeche | und im die freude blante: | op si die nôt erwante, | daz dienter vor unde nâch. | mir waere ê mit ir dannen gâch' (*Parzival* 216,28–217,6). For more on Wolfram's narrators see Chapter 1 section II above.

[46] The text was preserved only in codex S which was destroyed in 1870; see also Fischer, *Märendichtung*, 344f.; Grubmüller (ed.), *Novellistik*, 1221. For further discussion of the prologue see Hedda Ragotzky, '"Der Sperber" und "Das Häslein": Zum Gattungsbewußtsein im Märe Ende des 13., Anfang des 14. Jahrhunderts', *PBB* 120 (1998), 36–52, esp. 49ff.

[47] For further examples of *nemmen/nennen* meaning 'to acclaim' cf. Walther von der Vogelweide L. 45,17f.; Thomasin von Zerklaere's *Der welsche Gast* 5985–90.

[48] For more on this topos see Curtius, *Europäische Literatur*, 96f.; Haug, *Literaturtheorie*, 85, 87.

[49] Niewöhner (ed.), *Sperber*, 70; Schirmer, *Stil- und Motivuntersuchungen*, 64.

[50] Helmut de Boor, 'Zum Häslein V. 1–4', *PBB* (Tüb.) 87 (1965), 200–3; Fischer, *Märendichtung*, 194f.; Grubmüller (ed.), *Novellistik*, 1223.

gram of the author's name, then it is utterly exceptional for the 'Märe' as a genre, and offers further evidence of a sophisticated response to the question of authorship in this text.

We can make out an additional dimension to lines 1–4 in any case, on the grounds that the first verse is a deliberate borrowing of a line from the prologue of Gottfried's *Tristan*: 'Trîb ich die zît vergebene hin' (41).[51] In the narrower context of the assertion of fame in 2f. such a quotation reads as a means of evoking Gottfried's authorship itself, an element of role-play which is mockingly subverted three verses later by the concession that the poet may still merit the audience's curses. It is notable that the single manuscript (S) preserving *Das Häslein* also contained the other Gottfridian 'Mären' Konrad's *Herzmaere* and *Aristoteles und Phyllis*,[52] and this codex most probably emanated from the south-west of Germany where the reception of Gottfried was especially intensive in the thirteenth century.[53] In this context it seems likely that the opening line of *Das Häslein* represents an 'intertextual' reference to *Tristan*. After all, the exact correspondence between *Das Häslein* 1 and *Tristan* 41 is incontrovertible. As we shall see, the evocation of Gottfried's authorship represents the first in a series of allusions, motifs, and metaphors which inform the prologue and serve to display the work's ties to established literary tradition.

The provocative tone of the opening is maintained in the poet's subsequent statement of intent:

> ich wil durch kurze wîle,
> den nîdaeren ze bîle,
> ein âbentmaerlîn welzen,
> unt tiutschlîchen velzen
> dise rîmes ende. (5–9)

(I want for the sake of entertainment, [standing] at bay towards ill-wishers, to roll [off] a short evening's tale and fit together the ends of the rhyme in the German manner.)

---

[51] See also von der Hagen (ed.), GA ii. 5, 653; Niewöhner (ed.), *Sperber*, 70; de Boor, 'Zum Häslein', 200; Fischer, *Märendichtung*, 227 note 23; Alan Deighton, 'Studies in the Reception of the Works of Gottfried von Straßburg in Germany during the Middle Ages', D.Phil. thesis, University of Oxford 1979, pp. 352ff.

[52] Wachinger, 'Zur Rezeption Gottfrieds', esp. 71–82; Deighton, 'Gottfried von Straßburg', 327–65.

[53] Thomas Klein, 'Ermittlung, Darstellung und Deutung von Verbreitungstypen in der Handschriftenüberlieferung mittelhochdeutscher Epik', in *Deutsche Handschriften 1100–1400*, edd. Honemann/Palmer, 110–67, esp. 124ff., 160–7; Westphal-Wihl, *Textual Poetics*, 108–15.

A convivial scene of storytelling is intimated by the designation of the tale as an 'âbentmaerlîn' (7),[54] and the inclusion of the motif of 'entertainment' ('kurze wîle' 5) common in the 'Mären'.[55] The idea of a partly hostile reception is lent humorous overtones by the idiomatic expression of the poet's defensive attitude, which draws on hunting terminology for a quarry's last stand ('ze bîle' 6).[56] The self-alignment with a hunted animal not only deprecates potentially antagonistic recipients (*nîdaere*),[57] but also introduces by association the activity of the hunt, a central theme of the story to come.[58]

Portrayal of the communicative situation is combined in these verses with a depiction of the authorial activity of composition. As opposed to the third-person constructions in *Der Gürtel* and *Frauenerziehung*, the convergence of the (first-person) narratorial voice with the authorial agent lends this presentation of authorship a sense of immediacy. Significantly, *Das Häslein* is one of only two 'Mären' in our corpus which specifically address the issue of language in this context, the other being the reference to Latin (!) in Konrad's *Heinrich von Kempten*.[59] Although a process of translation can only be inferred from these lines, such a reference to language is evocative of the presentation of authorship in the courtly epic.[60] The construction in *Das Häslein* is phrased in a typically enigmatic way by virtue of the unusual adverbial form 'tiutschlîchen' (8).

---

[54] For further examples see Fischer, *Märendichtung*, 269–73.

[55] *Die Heidin* B 156; *Kobold und Eisbär* 1–4; *Der Herrgottschnitzer* 2; *Des Mönches Not* 1ff. See Fischer, *Märendichtung*, 104–9. This motif is found in the courtly epic as well; cf. *Daniel von dem Blühenden Tal* 12; *Diu Crône* 229.

[56] David Dalby, *Lexicon of the Mediaeval German Hunt: A Lexicon of Middle High German terms (1050–1500), associated with the Chase, Hunting with Bows, Falconry, Trapping and Fowling*, Berlin 1965, pp. 21f.

[57] See also Schwietering, 'Demutsformel', 165, with reference to Jerome's expression 'latrantes canes' (PL 28, 604). For a further vernacular example cf. Bruder Hermann's *Iolande*: 'sô wil ich mîne beste kunst | dar lîen eine wîle: | den nîdêren ze vile' (22ff.).

[58] Stephen L. Wailes, 'The Hunt of the Hare in "Das Häslein"', *Seminar* 5 (1969), 92–101.

[59] The epilogue of *Moriz von Craûn* also thematizes language: 'Nû lâzen dise rede varn. | tiuschiu zunge diu ist arn: | swer dar inne wil tihten, | sal die rîme rihten; | sô muoz er wort spalten | oder zwei zesamene valten. | daz taete ich gerne, künde ich daz, | meisterlîcher unde baz' (1777–84). Elsewhere in our corpus ambiguous verbs and phrases are used; cf. *Der Gürtel* 829f. (*tihten, ertrahten, berihten*); *Der Wiener Meerfahrt* 46 (*machen*); *Das Rädlein* 3 (*würken*), 5 (*tihten*); *Herzmaere* 22 (*flîzec*), 24 (*mit rede bewaeren*); *Bestraftes Mißtrauen* 7 (*mit rimen*); *Der Reiher* 27 (*tihten*); *Frauenerziehung* 16 (*tihten*); *Die alte Mutter* 1f. (*tihten, vüegen, berihten*); *Der Hasenbraten* by Der Vriolsheimer 130 (*machen*).

[60] Pfaffe Konrad, *Rolandslied* 9080–3; Veldeke, *Eneasroman*, 352,20–8; Ulrich von Zatzikhoven, *Lanzelet* 9341–6; Herbort von Fritslar, *Liet von Troye* 47–70; Der Stricker, *Daniel von dem Blühenden Tal* 7–11; Heinrich von dem Türlin, *Diu Crône* 220f.

The ideas of the author's compositional activity and a potentially hostile reception are combined for a second time in the following lines, in the entirely different register of affected humility:

> und waer ich sô behende,
> daz ich sô reine worhte,
> daz ich mir niht envorhte
> der lôsen nîdaere schimpf,
> die dô zehant ungelimpf
> ûf ander liute hânt getân,
> und niht êren mac an in stân,[. . .] (10–16)

(If only I had the dexterity to produce work of such perfection, that I should not fear the derision of deceitful ill-wishers who have immediately cast disgrace on other people and yet have no honourable qualities themselves [. . .])

The distinct change in tone reflects the adoption of an alternative strategy. The concept of 'ill-wishers' is expounded, yet the hunting metaphor is dispensed with and the former defensive but provocative posturing gives way to timid self-denigration. The poet hereby avoids alienating his audience,[61] the same kind of rhetorical ploy as lies behind the recommendation of the poet by the 'speaking text' in *Der Gürtel* and the apparent disclosures concerning the poet's own unhappy marriage in *Frauenerziehung*. Once more, the topos of 'the fear of ill-wishers' is scarcely paralleled in our corpus of 'Mären', revealing a greater affinity with passages in the courtly epic.[62]

The theme of reception remains a concern until the end of the prologue:

> [. . .] nu wolt ich hân der edeln gunst.
> und gît vrou Venus mir vernunst,
> sô sprenge ich ûf ir zuoversiht,
> die man nâch minnen ringen siht. (17–20)

([. . .] now I would like to have the favour of the noble, and if Lady Venus endows me with understanding, then I will set off at a charge, trusting in the support of those who are seen striving after love.)

---

[61] Schirmer, *Stil- und Motivuntersuchungen*, 64f.

[62] The topos is identifiable to a limited extent in *Die Heidin* B 153–62, and the expression *die argen* in the prologue of *Der Gürtel* (3) may also be understood in this context. Cf. *Lanzelet* 18ff.; *Wigalois* 8–15, 94–121; Der Stricker, *Karl* 1–29; *Der guote Gêrhart* 6854–7; *Willehalm von Orlens* 17–36.

The poet turns from ill-wishers to his ideal recipients, the noble members of the audience, whose 'gunst' (17) and 'zuoversiht' (19) contrast dramatically with the derision of the *nîdaere*.[63] The noble are also defined in terms of their attitude towards love, and this is complemented on a poetological level by the remarkable 'plea for inspiration' to Venus, a unique construction in our corpus of 'Mären'. In a manner akin to the presentation of Dietrich von der Glezze's authorship of *Der Gürtel*, the function of this appeal is to associate irrevocably both composition and reception of the work with the notion of love.

In spite of its (apparent) anonymity *Das Häslein* features an enigmatic, resonant prologue which focuses throughout on poetic production and reception. In the case of the authorial activity of composition both the hint of translation into German and the plea for inspiration are combined with loaded expressions. The stylization in verse 19 of the commencement of the actual story as 'to set off at a charge [on a horse]' (*sprengen*) is an idiom derived from the sphere of chivalric activity,[64] similar to the earlier play on hunting (6). Thus, authorial self-presentation simultaneously functions here as an inventive means of predicting significant elements of the narrative to come.

The final text in this group is *Der Wiener Meerfahrt* by Der Freudenleere, a burlesque tale illustrating the hazards of excessive drinking.[65] Here authorship is presented in the context of the broader circumstances of the work's production as part of a lengthy prologue (1–83). Notably, the metrical form of this 'Märe' as a whole invites us to read it against the background of established literary tradition, its composition in paragraphs ending in triplets ('Dreireim') matching the courtly epics *Wigalois*, *Diu Crône*, and Ulrich von dem Türlin's *Arabel*. The denunciation of the widespread materialism of contemporary society with which the work begins, immediately establishes the critical edge to the tale.[66] The 'Zeitklage'

---

[63] Schirmer, *Stil- und Motivuntersuchungen*, 61 note 14; Fischer, *Märendichtung*, 223ff.; Haug, *Literaturtheorie*, 210. Cf. also Konrad's *Herzmaere* 4–7; *Die halbe Birne* A 487–512; *Der Gürtel* 2, 7, 829; *Kobold und Eisbär* 1f.; *Der Reiher* 23ff.; *Der dankbare Wiedergänger* 1–24.

[64] Cf. *Eneasroman* 233,28–32; *Parzival* 602,4ff.; *Trojanerkrieg* 25493f.; *Wolfdietrich* D 1045,1.

[65] The text is preserved only in H and K; see also Fischer, *Märendichtung*, 340f.

[66] 'Die werlt stvnt etswenne so | Daz die levte waren vro | In tvgentlichem mvte | Vnde kerten ze gute | Allez daz sie kvnden. | Swaz si do begvnden | Daz was gerne tvgentlich. | Nv hat die werlt verkeret sich | Allez sin nach gvte, | In wunnenclichem mvte | Vindet man ir kleine' (1–11).

also fulfils a function in terms of the subsequent description of the production of the work, providing a foil for the virtues of the patron:

> Mir hat ein warhafter mvnt
> Ein rede gemachet kvnt
> Die mag wol heizen wunderlich,
> Also hat verrichtet mich
> Von Dewen bvrgrave herman
> Der nie schanden mal gewan
> An schentlicher missetat. (28–34)

(An honest mouth has acquainted me with a tale which may truly be called amazing. Burgrave Hermann von Derwin has informed me in this way, who never acquired the mark of disgrace with an abhorrent deed.)

As opposed to the analogous passages in *Heinrich von Kempten* and *Der Gürtel*, where the act of patronage is explicitly denoted by the verbs *bitten* and *schaffen* respectively, Hermann von Derwin is described rather more ambiguously as guarantor for the veracity of the following 'amazing' tale.[67] Hermann von Derwin's high social status and virtue evidently underline the quality of his word.[68] However, both the structure and the context of these lines suggest that Hermann is also to be understood as the patron. Stylization of a high-ranking personage as an oral source represents a variation on the distinct model of the patron as procurer of a literary source-text, and is not unprecedented elsewhere in medieval German narrative tradition as we know from the epilogue of Rudolf's *Der guote Gêrhart*.[69] Furthermore, the deployment of a 'Zeitklage' as a foil for the praises of the patron is a strategy which can be found in the courtly epic as well, as in Konrad's *Partonopier und Meliur* and Ulrich von Etzenbach's *Alexander* (14691–720).

There is an additional sense of pathos about the contrast between the virtuous patron and the world at large in *Der Wiener Meerfahrt*, for apparently Hermann von Derwin was dead by the time of the composition of the passage:

---

[67] Fischer, *Märendichtung*, 222; Bumke, *Mäzene*, 26f. Cf. also *Der betrogene Gatte* by Herrand von Wildonie: 'Hêr Uolrîch von Liehtenstein, | der ie in ritters êren schein, | sagte mir ditz maere' (17ff.).

[68] For more on the historical background to these lines see the conclusion to this chapter.

[69] Cf. also *Wigalois* 11686–90; *Mai und Beaflor* 3,10–19. For more on this point see Bumke, *Mäzene*, 323 note 131.

Daz im der sele werde rat,
Des sol man im von schvlden biten.
Er was ein man von gvten siten
Gezogen vnde getriwe gar
Was der herre daz ist war
Gegen vremden vnd gegen vrvnden
Des mach in got vrî von svnden
Dort an der sele vrî
Dvrch siner hohsten namen drî.
Der saget mir ditz mere; (35–44)

(It is only right that we should plead that his soul be saved. He lived a virtuous life; the lord was utterly courteous and sincere towards strangers and friends, that is the truth; for this reason may God, who is free of sin, release his soul from sins in the name of His highest Trinity. He [Hermann] told me this story.)

It is not uncommon for poets to address the death of prominent individuals who were known or belonged to the immediate circle of a work's audience. Literary texts appear to have been an appropriate forum for the expression of collective grief. In most cases these were the patrons of the respective poets, the most famous instance being Wolfram's praise of Hermann von Thüringen in *Willehalm* (417,22–6). Elsewhere, in works such as *Wigalois* (8061–93) and Ulrich von Türheim's *Rennewart* (25756–89), veritable 'Totenklagen' are featured.[70] Lamentation is not explicit in *Der Wiener Meerfahrt*, and emphasis is placed instead on the need to pray for intercession on Hermann von Derwin's behalf, the sincerity of which we have no reason to doubt.

The nature of the prayer in these lines should not deflect our attention from its poetic functions. The exposition of Hermann von Derwin's virtues at the heart of this section of the prologue substantiates the claim of authority for the tale. The detail of Hermann's honourable behaviour towards 'vremden' and 'vrunden' builds on earlier praise (33f.), and it is against this background that the poet reiterates the patron's role as the source of the story (44). Significantly, the death of the patron and prayer for his soul also function as a framework of reference for the naming of the author:

---

[70] Cf. also Rudolf's *Willehalm von Orlens*: 'Alse man nu bi disen tagen | Den edeln Ótingåre claget, | Der sólichen pris hat bejaget | [. . .] | Nu helfe im Got durch sinen tot | Unde lóse in dort us aller not!' (2084ff., 2093f.). See Bumke, *Mäzene*, 165, 174, 251f., 268.

Daz hat der vrevdenlere
Gemachet als iz dort geschach,
Als man im zv wienen iach,
Von gvter levte worte
Do er daz mere horte. (45–9)

('One-bereft-of-joy' has composed it [just] as it happened there, as he was told in Vienna when he heard the story on the word of good people.)

While referring to his own authorial activity (*machen* 46) for the first time in the prologue, the poet insists on his grief by calling himself 'der vrevdenlere'. The use here of the definite article relates this form of pseudonym to the 'speaking names' of other poets of the period such as *der Strickaere* and *der Pleiaere*. However, whereas the latter play metaphorically on the activity of poetic composition itself, the meaning of the pseudonym in *Der Wiener Meerfahrt* appears so inextricably linked to its immediate context that despite records of analogous names for travelling entertainers it must remain open whether 'der vrevdenlere' actually represents an artist's name proper or relates rather to the situation of a poet bereft of his patron.[71]

Such a strategy of authorial self-definition increases the status of the patron and highlights the kinds of representational interest which lie behind the composition of medieval literature as well as the (professional) poet's dependence on patronage. Indeed, the potentially disastrous consequences of the death of the patron for a poet may lead us to speculate whether the direct incorporation of sorrow in the presentation of the authorship of *Der Wiener Meerfahrt* also served as a rhetorical means for (re)securing a benevolent reception.[72] The description of authorship in 45–9 ties in with the other fundamental theme of the preceding lines as well: the establishment of authority for the tale. The poet lays claim to a second oral source when he tells us that he also heard the story in Vienna, the very place where it happened. The value of this account is enhanced by the assurance of the nobility of those whose word he relies on, the term *guote liute* encompassing both status and virtue as embodied earlier by Hermann von Derwin.[73] Thus, a double movement in the description of source can be observed over the course of verses

---

[71] Fischer, *Märendichtung*, 193, 215 note 320.

[72] An indirect appeal for generosity is also made towards the end of the epilogue (682–92).

[73] *guote liute* is often used to address an audience; cf. *Der Reiher* 5ff.; *Daniel von dem Blühenden Tal* 1f.; *Rennewart* 10264f., 10284.

28–49, from a specific individual to an unidentified plurality. The relationship between these two elements is not explored in the prologue, but they combine to form an accumulative structure of authorization that we might regard as the oral equivalent to Gottfried's exposition of his written sources over and above Thomas in *Tristan* (149–66). The variation in perspective between the earlier references (28f.; 44) in the first person and the later one (46–9) in the third is similar to the abrupt switch in the prologue of Sibote's *Frauenerziehung*. The introduction of the third person accords with one conventional dictate of authorial self-naming, although the resulting installation of two complementary perspectives in the passage may also be seen to underpin its assertion of authority. The specification of the scene of the tale signals a change of focus and tone in the prologue. The second half (50–83) is no longer occupied with poetological considerations but with an ironic praise of Vienna, which elucidates the critical perspective of the opening 'Zeitklage' (1–27) and introduces themes and metaphors integral to the ensuing story. Presentation of authorship does not occur again in the text and is evidently restricted in function to the introduction of the 'Märe' in terms of its representational interests and veracity.

The conjunction of authorship and patronage in *Der Wiener Meerfahrt* allows us to view this 'Märe' together with *Heinrich von Kempten* and *Der Gürtel*, as well as Konrad's *Herzmaere*, *Die halbe Birne* A, *Frauenerziehung*, and *Das Häslein*. All of these texts include expansive strategies of authorial self-presentation which sustain readings against the background of established vernacular literary tradition, whether it be in their usage of particular motifs or in their emulation of the discussions of literary production and reception common to the courtly epic. Notably, this practice does not altogether preclude other fundamental poetological interests, as betokened by the anonymity of *Das Häslein* and the emphasis on orality in *Der Wiener Meerfahrt*. These latter aspects will assume greater prominence in the next part of this chapter.

II. CURSORY STRATEGIES

Seven other 'Mären' address the issue of authorship more cursorily. In *Der Hasenbraten* by Der Vriolsheimer,[74] for instance, a typical

---

[74] The text is preserved only in H and K; see Fischer, *Märendichtung*, 420.

medieval short story concerning the deceitfulness of women and the stupidity of men, the presentation of authorship is restricted to the last two lines:

> Ditz ungelogen maere
> macht uns der Vriolsheimaere. (129f.)

('One-from-Friolzheim' composes this true story for us.)

The closure to the text could not be more succinct. Enclosed as a syntactic unit within a single rhyming couplet, the reference to Der Vriolsheimer's authorship is formally similar to the scribal super-scriptions which are found in manuscripts H and K in conjunction with Der Stricker: 'Ditz ist von dem wolfe ein mer | Daz leret vns der stricker' (H 161/K 169); 'Ditz ist von einem Esel ein mere | Daz leret vns der strickere' (H 190/K 196).[75] This specific combination of third person (singular) and first person plural is a common structure for describing the reception of an authority,[76] which might explain why it also often underlies the naming of the author of a text, as we have already seen in connexion with the opening verse of the *Eckenlied* [E₁].[77] Certainly, in *Der Hasenbraten* the twin aspects of authority and authorship are inextricably linked, whereby the statement of Der Vriolsheimer's authorship effectively strengthens the claim of the story's veracity in the first half of the same couplet ('ungelogen' 129).

As we have observed throughout, authorial (self-)identification towards the end of a text is not uncommon in the narrative poetry of the period. The precise location of the author's name in the last line of *Der Hasenbraten* relates to a concise yet forceful closure that occurs in shorter literary forms from the later thirteenth century onwards, as has already been discussed in the context of Konrad's *Schwanritter* with reference to other 'Mären' such as Herrand von

---

[75] Other analogous superscriptions in H and K are: H191/K197; K179, 180, 181, 189, 191, 193, 198, 199, 200. These *tituli* are taken from Karl Bartsch, *Die altdeutschen Handschriften der Universitäts-Bibliothek in Heidelberg*, Heidelberg 1887 (Katalog der Handschriften der Universitäts-Bibliothek in Heidelberg 1), 82–93; Schneider, 'Cod. Bodmer 72', 84–128. For further discussion of this aspect of scribal practice see Chapter 1 section 1 above.

[76] Cf. the descriptions of the authority of Scripture: 'als uns diu schrift hât geseit' (*Der arme Heinrich* 90); 'als uns diu schrift urkünde gît' (*Barlaam und Josaphat* 166). Source references can also be structured in this way; cf. *Heinrich von Kempten*: 'uns seit von im diu wâre schrift' (390); *Herzmaere*: 'als uns daz maere giht' (354).

[77] For a collection of similar examples from the fabliau see Per Nykrog, *Les Fabliaux: Etude d'histoire littéraire et de stylistique médiévale*, revised edn. Geneva 1973 (Publications romanes et françaises 123), 28–35.

Wildonie's *Der betrogene Gatte* and *Die treue Gattin*, and Werner der Gärtner's *Helmbrecht*. This kind of closure also occurs in *Des Mönches Not* as preserved in the later manuscripts B (Berlin, SBB-PK, mgq 663, *c.* 1350) and l (Karlsruhe, Badische LB, cod. Donaueschingen 104, *c.* 1430–3):

> hie endet sich diz maere,
> daz machete der Zwickowaere [. . .] (539f.)

(Here ends this tale; Der Zwingäuer [Der Zwickauer?] composed it [. . .])

The impact of this type of ending is enhanced in *Der Hasenbraten* by the poet's previous suppression of any representation of his own presence in the narrative, an otherwise strict realization of the trend of narratorial self-effacement and anonymity in the 'Märe'. The final inclusion of the name of the author is entirely unexpected and, thus, quite arresting. The highly concentrated structure introduces Der Vriolsheimer's authorship in an unequivocal, proprietorial manner at the expense of all other detail regarding the circumstances of composition.

Succinct presentation of authorship is also a component of the conclusion to *Der Ritter unter dem Zuber* by Jacob Appet,[78] another tale about female duplicity:

> Disiu maere ist war und niht gelogen.
> wip kunnen groze kündikeit,
> als Jacob Appet da hat geseit.
> der habe, der hüete deste baz!
> verliust er iht, waz schat im daz? (392–6)

(This tale is true and not a lie. Women are capable of great craftiness, as Jacob Appet has said here. Whoever owns [something] should take all the more care of it! If [however] he should lose it, what harm does it do him?)

The combination of an assertion of truth with the author's 'signature' suggests that notions of authority are being played on once more here, although in contrast to *Der Hasenbraten* this encompasses the element of a disparaging moral commonplace. The presentation of authorship has been adapted accordingly. Instead of expressly designating the activity of composition (as with 'macht' in

---

[78] *Der Ritter unter dem Zuber* is transmitted in four manuscripts: s [destroyed 1870]; b[5] (Bremen, Staatsbibl., Ms. b 42 b, *c.* 1400–50); m[5] (Munich, BSB, Cgm 713, *c.* 1462–82); and n[1] (Nuremberg, Germanisches Nationalmuseum, Hs. 5339a, datable 1471–3). See Fischer, *Märendichtung*, 308; Grubmüller (ed.), *Novellistik*, 1202f.

Der Hasenbraten 130), Jacob Appet's authorship is stylized as an act of moral pronouncement, a model which is employed elsewhere in the 'Mären' to refer to the proverbial wisdom of Freidank: 'alsô sprach her Vrîdanc: | der vroun gemüete daz ist kranc' (*Das Rädlein* 291f.); 'die vrouwen sint ir muotes kranc, | als uns saget der Vridanc' (*Bestraftes Mißtrauen* 299f.). Evidence that Jacob Appet actually came to represent an authority on the duplicity of women can be found in the later thirteenth-century courtly epic *Reinfried von Braunschweig*, whose poet defers to Appet on the subject of women in the course of an extensive 'Zeitklage': 'die sache kan iuch Jacob Apt | vil baz bescheiden denne ich tuon' (15222f.).

Although s is the only manuscript which includes the reference to Jacob Appet's authorship for *Der Ritter unter dem Zuber*, the authoritative aspect of line 394 is retained in the subsequent transmission of the text: n^1 substitutes one authorial name for another ('So hat gedicht Gregorius awer'); b^5 expounds the inherent authority of the preceding commonplace in terms of its reception ('Das ist vns dicke vorgeseit'); and m^5 uses the name 'Iacob' to denote a specific source ('Also hat mir Iacob ye vnd ye geseit').[79] Whilst the change in n^1 may reflect a characteristic tendency of this manuscript,[80] the variants of b^5 and m^5 are derived from the common prologue to the work itself:

> Ez ist uns dicke wol geseit,
> waz liste und grozer kündikeit
> künnen sumelichiu wip,
> damite si vil dicke ir lip
> vor ir mannen vristent,
> die si dicke überlistent
> und machent si zuo toren gar.
> Hiebi nemet einer maere war,
> wie ein aventiur beschach
> einem ritter den ich sach,
> der mirz mit sinem munde
> seite zuo einer stunde. (1–12)

(We have often been told about the cunning and craftiness of which some women are capable and with which they often save their skins from their

---

[79] All details are taken from the apparatus of the edition (NGA i. 169).

[80] Fischer, *Märendichtung*, 191. Cf. also the authorial attribution for *Der Pfaffe mit der Schnur* A in n^1: 'Wann sie [women] künnen mit behendikeit ligen | Vnd von dem mannen machen ein schaur. | Also schreibt meister hanns awer' (507ff.).

husbands, whom they often outwit and make complete fools of. Now listen to a tale of an adventure which happened to a knight, whom I once saw and who told me it in his own words.)

The respective strategies of line 394 in b⁵ and m⁵ are combined here to form a bipartite introduction to the tale. First, a sense of community is established between the narrator and the audience on the basis of the universal validity of the story's theme (1–7). This is achieved by a variation on the structure of received authority in a manner akin to the opening of the *Nibelungenlied* [A/C], which allows the poet to avoid designating an individual authorial agent. Second, the truth of the following tale is then upheld with reference to a specific oral source and the word of an impressive guarantor: the knight who was directly involved in the action himself.[81] In these lines (8–12) the narratorial voice converges with the authorial agent—the immediacy of the oral source precludes any other authorial involvement—although this does not include an explicit description of authorship itself.

The prologue of *Der Ritter unter dem Zuber* is significant not least because its structure recurs in two further 'Mären' as a framework for an outright description of authorship. This is unambiguously exhibited in *Das Rädlein* by Johannes von Freiberg:[82]

> Jôhannes von Vrîberc,
> der mangez wunderlîche werc
> ûf der erden würken kan,
> der wil aber heben an
> und uns ein büechel tihten
> von seltsaenen geschihten.
> ez ist wâr, daz ez geschach,
> wan der ez hôrt unde sach,
> der sagt mirz vür die wârheit. (1–9)

(Johannes von Freiberg, who is able to perform many an amazing deed in this world, wants to start [a tale] again and compose a little book for us concerning wondrous events. It is true that it happened, for a man who witnessed it told me it as the truth.)

---

[81] Cf. also *Der dankbare Wiedergänger*: 'Ouch hort ich einen Ritter iehen | wie einem herren si geschehen' (11f.). Such guarantees are not uncommon in the 'Märe' and further examples from texts in our corpus will be featured below; see also Knapp, 'Historische Wahrheit', 608; Fischer, *Märendichtung*, 222, 250ff.; Green, *Medieval Listening and Reading*, 110.

[82] *Das Rädlein* is preserved in three manuscripts; see Grubmüller (ed.), *Novellistik*, 1228.

This passage shares key features of the prologue of *Der Ritter unter dem Zuber*: it is bipartite in form (1–6; 7ff.), threaded with a first-person perspective shifting from the plural (5) to the singular (9), and its second section portrays an impressive channel of oral transmission. The content of the first section, however, is entirely different. In contrast to the thematic exposition and authorial self-effacement in *Der Ritter unter dem Zuber*, *Das Rädlein* opens directly with an authorial figure. The third-person presentation of the author recalls the structure of authorization that we have already encountered in *Der Hasenbraten*, and a further element of authority is derived here from the suggestion of a wider poetic oeuvre ('aber' 4).[83] The privileged location of the author's name in the very first line of the text, analogous to Rudolf's acrostics, perhaps, represents the antithesis of the closing signatures of Der Vriolsheimer and Jacob Appet and functions as an emphatic means of promoting the quality of the story to come.[84]

The prologue of *Das Rädlein*, like that of *Der Wiener Meerfahrt*, demonstrates that an evocation of the oral background to a story does not necessarily preclude open and affirmative statements of authorship. But this was far from self-explanatory, and the conjunction of orality and authorship also gives rise to a number of passages in our corpus which seem curiously indeterminate. One such passage is the prologue of *Die alte Mutter* as transmitted in H,[85] which is based on the same bipartite structural model as the previous two texts:

> Mit rede ist uns getihtet,
> gevueget unde berihtet
> Ein gemelichez maere,
> man seit, daz ez wâr waere,
> Daz ez be wîlen hie vor geschach,
> des mir ein wârhaft ritter jach,
> In der stat ze Nuerenberk,
> dâ dikke willeklîchiu werk
> Geworht hânt die Swâbe
> mit herlîcher gâbe. (1–10)

[83] For examples of this motif in the fabliau see Fischer, *Märendichtung*, 139ff.

[84] This strategy occurs elsewhere in *Der Nußberg* by Heinrich Rafold: 'Heinrich Rafolt getihtet hât, | dem die sinne keinen rât | Ze sîner lêre nie gegap, | er engelêrte nie buochstap, | Wan im ist unbekant, | waz zer schrift ist gewant, | Er enkan si niht bewîsen: | ûz stâle und ûz îsen | Gewinnet er sîn nerunge. | in hât sîn herze betwungen, | Ze sprechen,[. . .]' (1–11).

[85] A fragment from the end of this 'Märe' is preserved in another early manuscript: E². The text is also transmitted in w and i (Innsbruck, Ferdinandeum FB 32001, dated 1456); see Fischer, *Märendichtung*, 419f.

(An entertaining story has been eloquently composed, shaped, and ordered for us. It is said that it is true, that it took place some time ago, as a truthful knight told me, in the city of Nuremberg where often the Swabians have performed deeds of goodwill with a display of generosity.)

Once again the first part (1ff.) of the prologue deals with authorship, and the second (4–10) with the issues of the story's truth and background of orality. Matters are complicated, however, by the remarkably awkward form of the first lines in which the act of poetic composition is underlined through a cluster of three verbs,[86] as well as the phrase 'mit rede' ('eloquently' 1),[87] whilst the authorial agent is passed over. One approach to this problem is to take the later manuscript transmission of *Die alte Mutter* into account, for the text as preserved in w (and i) offers an alternative opening to the prologue:

> Volrât hât getihtet,
> gefüeget unde gerihtet
> ein gemellîchez maere. (ed. Haupt, 1ff.)

('One-full-of-advice' has composed, shaped, and formed an entertaining tale.)

The appearance in the first verse of an authorial name—albeit an opaque 'speaking' one—draws the presentation of the authorship of the text distinctly closer to that of *Das Rädlein*. Indeed, the 'easy' reading that these verses now make may encourage us to suppose that H contains a redaction of *Die alte Mutter* in which the 'original' authorial signature has been reworked.[88] However, this question must remain open, for although the texts of *Die alte Mutter* in H and wi are related, it seems that the difference in their overall length (424 and 244 lines respectively) holds no immediate clues, 'expansion' and 'abbreviation' both being common in the course of the transmission and reception of such texts.[89] Given that the naming of the author is unlikely to have been suppressed on a scribal level

---

[86] Compositional activity tends to be denoted by a single verb in the 'Mären': *Der Wiener Meerfahrt* 46; *Herzmaere* 24; *Der Reiher* 27; *Frauenerziehung* 16; *Der Hasenbraten* 130. Two verbs are used in *Das Rädlein* (3, 5) and *Heinrich von Kempten* (757ff.), whilst *Der Gürtel* is the only other one with three: *tihten, ertrahten, berihten* (829f.).

[87] Cf. also *Herzmaere*: 'dar umbe wil ich flîzec wesen | daz ich diz schoene maere | mit rede alsô bewaere' (22ff.).

[88] Hedda Ragotzky, 'Volrat', ²VL 10 (1998), cols. 509ff.

[89] Konrad von Würzburg's *Herzmaere* is a prime example of this; see Chapter 3 section III above.

in H,[90] we must therefore accept either that no other 'better' text was to hand for transcription in H, as was perhaps the case for *Des Mönches Not*, or that the text in wi is a later version and 'Volrat' the redactor.

Regardless of the issue of the status of codices w and i, the form of lines 1ff. in *Die alte Mutter* H can be explained in terms of poetic function in context and not simply as symptomatic of a process of textual 'deterioration' in the course of transmission. The use of the passive positions the work squarely between two sets of poetological values. Its delineation of the act of composition is kept in an almost abstract realm of the third person in order to promote the standing of the literary text, without transgressing the general rule of anonymity in the genre as a whole.[91] We should also note that such description of authorial activity 'once removed' is not unparalleled in our corpus. The prologue of *Der Reiher*,[92] which is couched in the metaphor of public performance, concludes with the following verses:

> Welt ir mir nu stille dagen,
> so wold ich iu vil gerne sagen
> ein hovelichez maere
> daz ein behendigaere
> getihtet hat von einem man,
> der vienc den reiger mit dem han. (23–8)

(If you were to quieten down for me now, I would gladly tell you a courtly story which a man of dexterity has composed concerning a man who caught a heron with a cock.)

The adjectival noun ('behendigaere' 26) which is used to designate the authorial agent is reminiscent of the 'speaking' names *der Strickaere* and *der Pleiaere*. Yet, its conjunction with the indefinite article prohibits us from according it an equivalent status and discourages any identification with the narratorial 'I'.[93] In analogous fashion to

---

[90] As opposed to the complete absence of authorial identification in manuscript W, H contains a total of sixteen texts with named authors, as well as ten attributions of authorship to Der Stricker in *tituli*. For more on authorship in the early collective manuscripts W, H, K, and S see the next part of this chapter.

[91] There is a hint of this in another text in our corpus, *Frauenlist*: 'Der selbe stolze schuolaer, | von dem getihtet ist daz maer' (61f.).

[92] The text is preserved only in H and K; see Karl-Heinz Schirmer, '"Der Reiher"', [2]VL 7 (1989), cols. 1141f.

[93] Fischer does not include 'ein behendigaere' in his catalogue of known poets of 'Mären'.

the prologue of the heroic epic *Biterolf und Dietleib*, the indetermin-ate presentation of authorship in this passage functions as a sign of literariness; the reference to, and praise of,[94] the unnamed author in the third person substantiates the preceding claim of the story's 'courtliness' (*hovelich* 25) whilst also taking into account a poetic tradi-tion of authorial self-effacement.

In *Der Ritter unter dem Zuber*, *Das Rädlein*, and *Die alte Mutter* sketches of a non-literary channel of transmission are contained within a specific type of bipartite prologue in order to lay claim to an asso-ciation with orality. For *Die alte Mutter* such a strategy also involves a reshaping of the presentation of authorship on a structural level, and a further comparable example of this phenomenon may be found in *Der Reiher*. The combined discussion of authorship and orality, it thus emerges, is a key feature of a number of our texts, and this would also seem to apply, albeit in a more limited sense, to the two last 'Mären' to be analysed here. The prologue of the first of these, *Bestraftes Mißtrauen*,[95] features an unnamed authorial agent in the first person:

> Seltsaener dinge vil geschiht,
> als man hoeret unde siht
> tegelich besunder.
> der selben vremeden wunder
> ich einz ze sagen willen han
> von einem richen werden man
> mit rimen, so ich beste kan,
> und heb also zem ersten an:[. . .] (1–8)

(Many marvellous things happen, as one hears and sees everyday. I wish to tell [a story] about one of these strange wonders—concerning a rich noble man—in rhyme, to the best of my ability, and [shall] start first of all like this [. . .])

The authorial activity of poetic composition is brought to the audi-ence's attention here by means of the reference to the formal aspect of rhyme ('mit rimen' 7),[96] and the fourfold rhyme in verses 5–8 draws further attention to this self-presentation. However, the main substance of the passage lies in its elaboration of the type of story

---

[94] The adjective *behende* signifies 'skilful' in general but is also employed specifically to describe poetic activity, as in the prologue of *Das Häslein* (10). Cf. also Gottfried's *Tristan* 4713, 8142.

[95] The text is preserved only in H; see Fischer, *Märendichtung*, 374f.

[96] Cf. also *Das Häslein* 8f.; *Heinrich von Kempten* 756f.

to be told (1–5). The prologue opens with the topos of 'I bring things never heard before', as employed in other 'Mären' in our corpus,[97] yet this motif is combined with the claim that such remarkable events are witnessed daily. We can account for the apparent contradiction in these lines by recognizing that their function is twofold; as well as asserting the story's veracity they represent the attempt to elucidate the nature of the story material. The essence of the 'Märe' is declared as being drawn from the present living world and thus, by implication, as non-textual and oral.

Finally, the opening lines of the prologue of *Der Schlegel* by Rüdeger der Hinkhofer share the structure of the beginning of *Bestraftes Mißtrauen*.[98] Here too the topos of 'I bring things never heard before' is one element of the broader characterization of the story material as stemming from a continuum of an apparently non-textual human experience:

> Man hoeret, derz vernemen wil,
> wunderlîcher dinge vil,
> diu nu ergênt und sint geschehen,
> der ich iu eines wil verjehen,
> Rüedegêr der Hünchovaere,[. . .] (1–5)

(Whoever wishes to can hear about many amazing things which happen now and which have happened, one of which I, Rüdeger der Hinkhofer, would like to tell you [. . .])

The first-person form of the naming of the author in this passage contrasts with the employment of the third person in *Der Hasenbraten*, *Der Ritter unter dem Zuber*, and *Das Rädlein* (not to mention *Der Gürtel*, *Frauenerziehung*, and *Der Wiener Meerfahrt*). This is of course a model of naming with a distinguished literary pedigree in the thirteenth century, from Wolfram von Eschenbach to Konrad von Würzburg, and the only analogues in our corpus of 'Mären' occur in texts associated with the latter (*Heinrich von Kempten*; *Die halbe Birne* A). The presentation of authorship in *Der Schlegel* may be confined to its initial lines, but it would appear to be informed with a (relatively) highly developed sense of artistic self-assurance that eschews the 'distance' and safety that a third-person perspective might

---

[97] *Das Frauenturnier* 1ff.; *Der Wiener Meerfahrt* 30, 85; *Das Kerbelkraut* 10; *Des Mönches Not* 4–8. For more on this topos see Curtius, *Europäische Literatur*, 85f.; Schirmer, *Stil- und Motivuntersuchungen*, 67–70; Fischer, *Märendichtung*, 263.

[98] *Der Schlegel* is transmitted in five manuscripts; see Grubmüller (ed.), *Novellistik*, 1070.

provide.[99] In fact the central aspects of the prologue of *Der Schlegel* allow it to be viewed together with texts from both of the principal parts of this chapter. This is perhaps typical of the way in which relationships, affinities and differences, between the relevant 'Mären' shift as various points are taken into account, advising against too strict a classification of the texts with regard to the issue of authorship. Nevertheless, our arrangement of the material in two groups reflects two alternative approaches to the presentation of authorship as it occurs in the 'Märe'. For this second group of texts we can observe how passages which address the theme of authorship cursorily tend to play on notions of authority and often stress an association with orality.

III. MANUSCRIPT CONTEXTS

So far we have been dealing with passages from individual 'Mären'. The 'Märe', however, is characteristically transmitted in large collections of shorter texts in couplet verse which often belie its identification as an independent genre. The aim of this section is to cross-check the significance ascribed to the presentation of authorship in the preceding analyses by assessing the 'function' of authorship in each of the earliest four manuscripts of 'Mären' in their entireties: W, H, K, and S. For reasons of space it will not be possible to provide more than an overview of the relevant data here. The following descriptions of the manuscripts are brief, and passages from specific texts will be discussed in only a few cases.

W (Vienna, ÖNB, cod. 2705, *c.* 1250–75) is the earliest extant collection and is central to the transmission of Der Stricker's oeuvre.[100] The 271 texts in W include sixteen 'Mären'—all but two by Der Stricker—amidst 'Reden' and 'Bispel' of both secular and religious orientation. Only three texts in the entire manuscript feature authorship as a theme and these do not belong to our corpus: W156 *Die Buße des Sünders*, W165 *Die Klage*, and W169 *Von zwei Blinden*.

---

[99] Fischer, *Märendichtung*, 256 note 31.

[100] Ute Schwab, *Die bisher unveröffentlichten geistlichen Bispelreden des Strickers: Überlieferung—Arrogate—Exegetischer und literarhistorischer Kommentar*, Göttingen 1959, pp. 15–41; Hermann Menhardt, *Verzeichnis der altdeutschen literarischen Handschriften der Österreichischen National-bibliothek*, 3 vols., Berlin 1960–1 (Deutsche Akademie der Wissenschaften zu Berlin. Veröffentlichungen des Instituts für deutsche Sprache und Literatur 13), i. 142–204; Ziegeler, 'Wiener Codex 2705'.

On a scribal level there are no attributions of authorship in the superscriptions either, and two texts which elsewhere contain references to the author, do not in W: W73 *Frauenehre* by Der Stricker; W151 *Weiberzauber* by Walther von Griven.[101] Over half of the texts in W may well be the work of a single author (Der Stricker), however, those involved in the production of this manuscript were evidently not interested in preserving and recording details that relate to authorship. Literary and sub-literary traditions aside, this may reflect a programme particular to W itself (was it obvious to the primary recipients who the author was?), and is all the more striking in comparison to the transmission of poems by Der Stricker in H and K.

H (Heidelberg, UB, cod. Pal. germ. 341, *c.* 1300–25) and K (Cologny-Genève, Bibliotheca Bodmeriana, Cod. Bodmer 72, *c.* 1300–25) are generally regarded as the most representative and colourful collections of thirteenth-century shorter texts in couplet verse.[102] They contain many of the texts of W as well as a significant body of mariological material, overtly religious narrative, and a large quota of 'Mären'; 40 of the 213 [222] texts in H,[103] and 29 of the 202 in K are categorized by Fischer as 'Mären'.[104] Fourteen texts outside of our corpus in H—thirteen in K—feature the presentation of authorship: H1/K1 Konrad von Würzburg's *Goldene Schmiede*, H4a/K4 *Mariengrüße*, H5/K6 *Unser Frauen Klage*, H33/K39 *Frauentrost* by Siegfried der Dörfer, H34/K40 *Der Heller der armen Frau*, H42/K12 *Der Mönch Felix*, H55/K56 *Pfaffe Amis* by Der Stricker, H60/K57 *Reinhart Fuchs*, H104/K109 *Die Buße des Sünders*, H115/K118 *Weiberzauber* by Walther von Griven, H125/K128 *Die Klage*, H133/K141 *Der arme Heinrich* by Hartmann von Aue, H159/K167 *Frauenehre* by Der Stricker, and H213 *Die Ritterfahrt des Johann von Michelsberg* by Heinrich von Freiberg. In addition, H includes ten scribal superscriptions attributing texts to Der Stricker, a number which

---

[101] Ziegeler, 'Wiener Codex 2705', 476.

[102] H and K are so closely related (K contains only one text which is not in H) that for our purposes they can be described together. See Schneider, 'Cod. Bodmer 72', 81–129; Christoph Fasbender, '*hochvart* im "Armen Heinrich", im "Pfaffen Amis" und im "Reinhart Fuchs"': Versuch über redaktionelle Tendenzen im Cpg 341', *ZfdA* 128 (1999), 394–408.

[103] The numbering of the texts (1–213) is based on the table devised by Rosenhagen (ed.), *Kleinere mittelhochdeutsche Erzählungen*, pp. XXXV–XLI. There are probably more like 222 individual texts in the codex.

[104] The index of K records that it originally contained two further texts: [K203] Konrad von Würzburg's *Herzmaere*; [K204] Heinrich von Freiberg's *Die Ritterfahrt des Johann von Michelsberg*.

increases to eighteen in K;[105] and 'Mären' by Der Stricker are grouped together (H134–9/K142–7; H180–6/K190–2). Together with the relevant 'Mären',[106] all of these features combine to reflect a consistent interest in authorship throughout H and K, with perhaps a higher degree of concentration in the opening mariological works (H1–34/K1–40) and the closing sequence of narratives in H (200–13).

S (Strassburg, Johanniterbibl. A 94, *c.* 1330–50 [destroyed 1870]) is a much shorter manuscript.[107] It represents one of the oldest and most varied collections of 'Minnereden' and offers a different symbiosis in the transmission of the 'Märe' from W, H, and K. Eight of its twenty-eight texts belong to our corpus, and four of these include presentation of authorship.[108] Five texts outside of our corpus also feature statements relating to authorship: S15 *Die sechs Farben* [I]; S18 *Der arme Heinrich* by Hartmann von Aue; S20 *Vom mangelnden Hausrat*; S24 *Sekte der Minner*; S28 Rudolf von Ems's *Barlaam und Josaphat* (fragm. 1–2666). Furthermore, as we have already seen, one (mistaken) attribution of authorship occurs in a *titulus* in S, Gottfried von Strassburg being misconstrued as the author of S2 Konrad von Würzburg's *Herzmaere*. Therefore, although all the authors of the 'Minnereden' in this collection are anonymous, authorship represents a distinctive, if not major, feature of the manuscript as a whole.

W, H, K, and S provide us with a mixed picture of the significance of authorship in the broader context of the transmission of the 'Märe'. While explicit references (either literary or scribal) to authors are conspicuous by their absence in W, an interest in authorship is a tangible feature of H, K, and S. There is a suggestion that the religious works of prominent authors are used strategically for opening (H1/K1 Konrad von Würzburg's *Goldene Schmiede*, H2/K2 *Leich* [by Walther von der Vogelweide], H3/K3 *Leich* [by Reinmar von Zweter]) and closure (S28 Rudolf von Ems's *Barlaam und Josaphat*), for example, and large numbers of texts by Der Stricker

[105] Ziegeler, 'Wiener Codex 2705', 497f.

[106] H38/K41 *Der Wiener Meerfahrt*; H45/K46 *Der Reiher*; H47/K48 *Der Schlegel*; H128/K131 *Der Gürtel*; H131/K134 *Heinrich von Kempten*; H200/K201 *Frauenerziehung*; H202 *Herzmaere*; H204 *Bestraftes Mißtrauen*; H205 *Das Rädlein*; H208 *Die alte Mutter*; H211/K138 *Der Hasenbraten*.

[107] Glier, *Artes amandi*, 98–116, esp. 98f.; Eckhard Grunewald, 'Zur Handschrift A 94 der ehem. Straßburger Johanniterbibliothek', *ZfdA* 110 (1981), 96–105; Westphal-Wihl, *Textual Poetics*, 108–15.

[108] S2 *Herzmaere*; S3 *Der Ritter unter dem Zuber*; S25 *Die halbe Birne* A; S26 *Das Häslein*.

are collected in W, H, and K. However, it is by no means the case
that texts featuring the presentation of authorship are regularly
assembled together. One valuable observation that we can make is
that the 'Märe' is not the only type of shorter text in couplet verse
to functionalize authorship. Nineteen other texts in W, H, K, and S
include passages of authorial self-presentation, and it remains to be
seen just how these passages are employed.

For a start, non-narrative texts feature statements of authorship
in these manuscripts as well. Two mariological works of praise and
worship, the *Goldene Schmiede* (H1/K1) and the *Mariengrüße* (H4a/K4),
open with a thematically appropriate model of authorial self-presentation: the prayer for inspiration.[109] This model has already been
discussed in Chapters 2 and 3 above, and it suffices to note that, as
opposed to the anonymity and emphatic self-stylization of the author
as a sinner in the *Mariengrüße*,[110] Konrad dwells on his artistic defi-
ciencies, incorporating an evocation of vernacular literary tradition
and his stock first-person signature.[111]

In three 'Reden', *Die Klage* (W165/H125/K128),[112] *Vom mangelnden
Hausrat* (S20), and Der Stricker's *Frauenehre* (H159/K167),[113] authorship is addressed rather differently. These works include passages
which reflect less on the composition of the respective text itself than
establish that the (first-person) discourse is specifically that of a poet.
At the beginning of *Die Klage*, for example, the impressive sequence
of lamentations is based on an initial definition of the narratorial
subject:[114]

---

[109] *Goldene Schmiede* 1–138; *Mariengrüße* 1–68; cf. also the 'Zwischenprolog' in the *Goldene Schmiede* 858–93.

[110] *Mariengrüße*: 'ich bin ein sündic Almân | und krae dîn lop alsam ein han | der sich des tages wil enstân. | mîn sin ist kûme alsam ein gran | der in der aschen ist bestân | dâ gar ein rîchez fiur entbran. | doch ist dîn güete alsô getân | daz si dem sünder heiles gan. | nu entslah mir, vrouwe, mînen ban | unt swaz ich sünden ie gewan, | nâch der ich in der jugent wân, | dô ich mich bezzers niht versan, | und in der werlde vlüete ran' (36–48).

[111] *Goldene Schmiede*: 'ich sitze ouch niht uf grüenem cle | von süezer rede touwes naz, | da wirdeclichen ufe saz | von Strazburc meister Gotfrit, | der als ein waeher houbetsmit | guldin getihte worhte. | der haete, an alle vorhte, | dich gerüemet, frouwe, baz, | dann ich, vil reinez tugentvaz, | iemer künne dich getuon' (94–103). For more on Konrad's authorial self-presentation in this text see the introduction of Chapter 3 above.

[112] This text is commonly attributed to Der Stricker.

[113] W73 only preserves lines 429–510 and 569–88 of *Frauenehre* and these contain no data of note for this study.

[114] *Die Klage*: 'ich wil chlagen und chlagen | und chlagen den noch furbaz. | min chlage fullet manich faz. | min chlage wirt so manich valt, | daz iu noch nie wart gezalt

Swaz ich unz her getihtet han,
daz was durch churzwile getan.
des enmac nu leider niht geschehen:
ich han ein ander dinc gesehen;
da ist lutzel churzwile bi. (1–5)

(That which I have composed until now was done for entertainment. Unfortunately, this may not happen now: I have observed another state of affairs which has little to do with entertainment.)

The characteristic narrator of the 'Rede' in general is qualified by the reference to previous compositional activity,[115] presentation of authorship which evidently influenced the formulation of the subsequent scribal *tituli* in H ('Dise dinch claget zv mere | Des bvches tichtere') and K ('Hie claget der tichtere | Mancher hande swere').[116] This strategy is employed in *Vom mangelnden Hausrat* as well,[117] and receives its most extensive and sophisticated treatment in Der Stricker's *Frauenehre* which features a dialogue between the author and his heart and the naming of the author by the audience.[118] In yet another 'Rede' *Die sechs Farben* (S15) the narrator is confirmed as the author through a reference to his patron as the (oral) source of his material.[119]

The theme of authorship also plays a significant role in *Die Buße*

| so manic chlaeglich dinc. | min chlage ist ein ursprinc, | dar uz manic chlage fliuzet | und so grozlich begiuzet, | daz min chlage wirt erchant | noch verrer denne in osterlant' (34–44).

[115] For more on the 'Ich-Erzähler' with particular reference to the 'Minnerede' see Glier, *Artes amandi*, 394–9; Ziegeler, *Erzählen im Spätmittelalter*, 51–74.

[116] These *tituli* have also been read as clues to the existence of an earlier 'book' of poems by Der Stricker which was wholly incorporated in subsequent manuscripts such as H (and K); see Mihm, *Überlieferung*, 57f.

[117] *Vom mangelnden Hausrat*: 'Min gesang u. min getihte | Ist worden gar zuo nihte | Hie vor het ich die sinne | Uf liebe u. auf minne | Getruwelich bekeret | Hushalten hat mich geleret | Daz ich die minne muos begeben | Ich han mich uf ein ander leben | Gestellet das ist sicher war' (1–9).

[118] *Frauenehre*: 'Min herze hat mit mir gestriten, | ich wolte tihten han vermiten. | do vragete ez mich: "durch welche not?" | [. . .] | ist ieman der vor nide | ditz maere unsanfte lide, | der durch des hazzes süeze | also gedenken müeze: | "ditz ist ein schoenez maere, | daz ouch nu der Strickaere | die vrouwen wil bekennen. | ern solde si niht nennen | an sinen maeren, waere er wis. | sin leben unde vrouwen pris, | die sint ein ander unbekant. | ein pfärt unde alt gewant, | die stüenden baz in sinem lobe"' (1ff., 133–45).

[119] *Die sechs Farben*: 'Dz seite mir der schanden fri | Der w'de Grave Wernher | Von Honberg der mit richer zer | Der welte gunst so behielt | So dz er nach gar hohen eren wielt | Er waz ein tolde ritterschaft | Der seite mir der varwen kraft | Den fraget ich der mere | Wie es umbe alle varwen were | Der nante mir sú alle | Frowe ob úch das gevalle | Ich sage úch als er seite mir' (20–31).

des Sünders (W156/H104/K109),[120] a text which combines narrative
and 'Rede' (lines 1–108 and 113–406 respectively) in a manner often
associated with the 'Bispel'.[121] Reference to authorship operates here
as an axis around which the work's bipartite structure revolves:

> der uns ditz maer geschriben hat,
> der git uns selbe den rat,
> daz wir niht hohferte pflegen,
> swenne wir suchen gotes segen. (109–12)

(He who wrote this story advises us himself not to be presumptuous when
we seek God's blessing.)

In stark contrast to the narratorial self-effacement of lines 1–108,
the narrator expressly aligns himself with the audience at the structural turning-point of the text, referring to the author in the third
person, on whose (received) authority the subsequent elucidation of
the story's moral (113–406) is based. This function of authorization
is familiar to us from a number of 'Mären' such as *Der Hasenbraten*
and *Der Ritter unter dem Zuber* but was apparently of widespread
currency.[122] It occurs elsewhere in our manuscripts in the first lines
of the 'Bispel' *Von zwei Blinden* (W169),[123] as a closure for the secular
'Rede' *Weiberzauber* (H115/K118) by Walther von Griven,[124] in garbled
form in the parodic *Sekte der Minner* (S24),[125] and as part of the
prologue of the extended narrative *Pfaffe Amis* (H55/K56) by Der
Stricker: 'Nu saget uns der Stricker' (39).

---

[120] This text is also commonly attributed to Der Stricker; see Karl-Ernst Geith/Elke
Ukena-Best/Hans-Joachim Ziegeler, 'Der Stricker', ²VL 9 (1995), cols. 417–49, esp. cols.
430f. In H and K *Die Buße des Sünders* is considerably shorter than in W, closing at verse
180 in Moelleken's edition.

[121] Fischer, *Märendichtung*, 59 note 134; Ziegeler, *Erzählen im Spätmittelalter*, 101–10.

[122] Two of our manuscripts also preserve the extended narrative *Reinhart Fuchs*
(H60/K57) whose epilogue serves as a reminder that a third-person perspective is not
necessarily solely determined by internal poetic function, but may indeed describe the
authorship of another individual: 'Hie endet ditz mere. | daz hat der glichsenere | Er
Heinrich getichtet | vnd lie die rime vngerichtet. | Die richte sider ein ander man, |
der ovch ein teil getichtes kan, | Vnd hat daz ovch also getan, | daz er daz mere hat
verlan | Gantz rechte, als iz ovch was e. | an svmeliche rime sprach er me, | Danne er
dran were gesprochen. | Ovch hat er abgebrochen | Ein teil, do der worte was ze vil.
| swer im nv des lonen wil, | Der bite im got geben, | die wile er lebe, ein vrolich leben
| Vnd daz er im die sele sende, | do sie vrevde habe an ende' (2251–68).

[123] *Von zwei Blinden*: 'Vernemt ein warez maere: | hie chundet der tihtaere | ein
wunnechlichez bispel' (1ff.).

[124] *Weiberzauber*: 'Walther von Griven raet in daz: | der wîser sî der râte in baz' (43f.).
W151 does not preserve this last couplet.

[125] *Sekte der Minner*: 'Ich bredie unde lere | An froeiden michel ere | Von einre nuwen
secta | Die heisset vides recta | [. . .] | Er lebet ane sunde | Der hieher an wil gestan

Pfaffe Amis and *Reinhart Fuchs* aside, a number of other narrative works in H, K, and S include references to authorship. These predominantly religious texts invariably functionalize models of authorship which might be regarded as thematically appropriate, such as the prayer for inspiration in *Der Mönch Felix* (H42/K12),[126] or the pious motivation to translate a Latin book into German in *Unser Frauen Klage* (H5/K6).[127] In both *Der arme Heinrich* (H133/K141/S18) by Hartmann von Aue and Rudolf von Ems's *Barlaam und Josaphat* (S28) this 'spiritual' aspect is further combined with an interest in lay literary activity and the broader circumstances of composition respectively.[128] Authorship encompasses another theme in Siegfried der Dörfer's *Frauentrost* (H33/K39) by virtue of the author's epithet, 'the Villager',[129] which apparently relates to a programmatic digression earlier in the text.[130]

'Spiritual' overtones are entirely absent in the presentation of authorship of the 'religious' narrative *Der Heller der armen Frau* (H34/K40). The prologue of this text consists of an alternative strategy of authorial self-deprecation in which reference is made to the courtly culture of 'Minnesang':[131]

| Der sol ouch vil gewis han | Der minnere krone | Die git ime zelone | Sin gewaltiger bot | Das ist sin erste gebot | Daz er heisset schriben' (1–4, 8–15).

[126] *Der Mönch Felix*: 'Aller meide gimme, | sueziu wort und[e] stimme | Geruoche mir, Vrouwe, ze geben, | daz ich eines münches leben | Mueze alsô beschrîben, | daz ich âne sünde belîbe. | Ich meine dich, Marîe' (1–7).

[127] *Unser Frauen Klage*: 'Ich saz aleine an einem tage | unt gedâhte an die grôzen clage, | an die quâle unt an daz leit | unt an die swaeren bitterkeit, | die Marîen herze enphienc, | dô got an den criuze hienc. | ich nam vür mich ir herzen pîn: | der wart mir volleclîchen schîn | an einem büechelîne. | dâ vant ich in latîne, | waz diu reine maget sprach | [. . .] | dô kam zehant in mînen muot, | daz ich diu wort, diu ich dâ vant, | in tiutsche wolde tuon erkant' (83–93, 100ff.).

[128] *Der arme Heinrich*: 'Ein ritter sô gelêret was | daz er an den buochen las | swaz er dar an geschriben vant: | der was Hartman genant, | dienstman was er zOuwe | [. . .] | dar umbe hât er sich genant, | daz er sîner arbeit | die er dar an hât geleit | iht âne lôn belîbe, | und swer nâch sînem lîbe | si hoere sagen ode lese, | daz er im bittende wese | der sêle heiles hin ze gote' (1–5, 18–25). For the prologue of *Barlaam und Josaphat* see Chapter 2 section II above.

[129] *Frauentrost*: 'Got durch sîne guete | allez ungemuete | Entwende[n] von den allen, | der lîp sî hie bevallen | Mit keiner hande swaere! | des bitet der Sîfrit Dorfaere, | diz buochelîn[e]s tihtaere' (633–9).

[130] *Frauentrost*: 'Nû hoeret aber vürbaz: | ein ritter etswenne saz | In einem dorfe durch gemach, | des im vil wol dâ geschach, | Er was des guotes rîche. | nû wizzet waerlîche, | Wer in den dörfern wonen sol, | und ist sîn dorf dô râtes vol, | Er lebet alsô sanfte dâ, | als in den steten anders wâ' (17–26).

[131] *Der Heller der armen Frau*: 'Konde ich ein mere getichten, | mit guter rede berihten | daz ez gar lobebere | unde gut zu horen were, | unde daz ez wol mohte bestan, | und daz mich ein wiser man | dar umbe nicht solde strafen: | ich wil der sinne wafen | dar uf vil gerne slifen' (1–9).

kund ich als der von Nifen
den vrowen singen sûzen sanch,
dez sagten si mir billich danch.
nu kan ich leider harte kleine:
min kunst die sol doch sin gemeine
den vrowen und den gerten,
di hohen pris merten. (10–16)

(If only I could sing as sweet a song to ladies as [Gottfried] von Neifen, it would be right for them to thank me. Now, unfortunately I am not able to [do so] at all: my art, however, shall be known to the ladies and those recipients of honour who have increased [the] great acclaim [of the court].)

The allusion in verse 10 to an exemplary 'Minnesänger' of the thirteenth century, Gottfried von Neifen (attested 1234–55), as well as the courtly characterization of the audience (15f.), evokes the aristocratic sphere of secular literary activity. These are associations which we might more reasonably expect to encounter in the chivalric 'Preisgedicht' *Die Ritterfahrt des Johann von Michelsberg* (H213) by Heinrich von Freiberg, whose presentation of authorship is also shaped by affected humility.[132] However, in *Der Heller der armen Frau* they have a rhetorical function, signalling the poet's acceptance of lay aristocratic culture in anticipation of a story which discusses the often imperfect (religious) devotion of the most privileged members of secular society.

This briefest of accounts of the presentation of authorship in these two works brings our review of W, H, K, and S to a close. With the exception of W, these manuscripts reveal a consistent level of interest in authorship, which is made up to a considerable extent by the fourteen relevant 'Mären'. However, it has become clear that on occasion other kinds of shorter text functionalize authorship as well. The diversity of these texts is reflected in the range of models of presentation they employ, yet a large number are comparable with those found in our 'Mären', including basic constructs of authorial naming, the description of compositional activity, and the register of affected humility. More notably, these other shorter texts feature both the evocation of courtly literary tradition (as in *Goldene Schmiede*, *Frauenehre*, and *Der Heller der armen Frau*) and the elicitation of

---

[132] *Die Ritterfahrt des Johann von Michelsberg*: 'Ob ich Heinrîch von Frîberc | sîne ritterlîche tât, | die der helt begangen hât, | mit worten nû volsage nicht | und mîn getichte gar enwicht | gein des hêrren wirden sî, | iedoch enwirt mîn herze vrî | des willen zu deheiner stunt, | ich entuo mit worten kunt | mêr sîner ritterlîchen tât' (312–21); cf. also 11–51, 158–61.

authority from authorship (as in *Die Buße des Sünders*, *Von zwei Blinden*, *Weiberzauber*, *Sekte der Minner*, and *Pfaffe Amis*). On the basis of this evidence it would seem that in terms of the presentation of authorship the main difference between the 'Märe' and other shorter forms of verse-couplet poetry lies not so much in themes and techniques but the (relative) frequency with which it occurs: 'Märe' (14); 'Reden' (6); 'Bispel' (2); eulogies of Mary (2).[133] Established courtly literature and the need for authority are clearly widely shared concerns, but out of all of the short literary forms that find their way onto parchment during the thirteenth century it was apparently in the 'Märe' that poets felt best able to reflect on and respond to them.

When it comes to assessing the significance of the 'Märe' for the period 1220–90 we find that it shares several key features with the heroic epic, but also that it differs from the latter in a number of other important ways. As Bumke shows, the little we know about the historical background to the composition of 'Mären' also lends weight to the notion that literature began to be commissioned in increasingly diverse socio-political contexts.[134] Two of the three texts in question offer evidence of patronage among the minor nobility of Bohemia: *Der Gürtel* namely was composed for a certain Wilhelm von Weidenau (died before 1296) whose father was appointed to the advocateship of Weidenau by Duke Henry IV of Breslau; whilst *Der Wiener Meerfahrt* can be linked to burgrave Hermann von Derwin (attested 1267), a member of a noble family from Meissen.[135] Again it is notable that Green can find no internal clues to suggest that 'Mären' were composed for anything other than public recital;[136] there are for example no authorial acrostics in this genre, but as we saw with the heroic epic to relate the literary presentation of authorship to external factors such as the social and presumed educational status of the primary recipients is a precarious endeavour. After all, Konrad von Würzburg's composition of *Heinrich von Kempten* for the provost of the cathedral chapter in Strassburg (Berthold von Tiersberg) shows that it was perfectly feasible for 'Mären' to be received in a highly educated ecclesiastical environment as well. The

---

[133] Der Stricker's *Pfaffe Amis* and *Reinhart Fuchs* have not been included in these calculations as they cannot rightly be described as belonging to the supergeneric grouping of shorter verse-couplet poetry.

[134] Bumke, *Mäzene*, 263, 279.

[135] Fischer, *Märendichtung*, 192ff.

[136] Green, *Medieval Listening and Reading*, 231.

signs are that interest in the 'Märe' spanned several socio-cultural strata in the thirteenth century, and this was maintained throughout the later Middle Ages not least by virtue of the prolific 'city-authors' Heinrich Kaufringer, Hans Rosenplüt, and Hans Folz.[137]

The question of just what position the 'Märe' assumes *vis-à-vis* established literary tradition may be answered in part with reference to Hanns Fischer, whose typological and thematic discussion of the genre indicates that whilst the majority of 'Mären' offer a comic alternative of their own ('schwankhaftes Märe') to other narrative types of the day, a smaller number of 'courtly/gallant' tales seek to participate in ongoing and traditional discussions of *minne* and knighthood.[138] Fischer is also able to show how 'Mären' contain allusions to recognized poetic subject matters such as the Trojan war, Arthur and his knights, and above all Dietrich von Bern and the Nibelungen.[139] From our point of view it is instructive to observe that this practice does not extend to the naming of other authors of narrative literature. In our corpus of 'Mären' there is only one example: the reference to Gottfried von Strassburg in Konrad von Würzburg's *Herzmaere*. The concomitant of this apparent lack of interest in the authorship of others is the anonymity of the majority of our 'Mären' which we have read as the poetological function of an association with oral storytelling tradition. Add to this the distinctively high degree of textual instability of many 'Mären', and the (relative) ease with which these 'Mären' might have been memorized for the purposes of oral transmission and public delivery,[140] and it would seem entirely justifiable to align this genre with the heroic epic. Nevertheless, our corpus of texts also includes a small but significant group that address the theme of their own authorship; and we have seen how the strategies in these works range in complexity from curiously indeterminate references to a process of authorial composition, representing a compromise between the principle of authorial self-consciousness of the new literary form and the traditional anonymity of the oral story material itself, to prologues that approximate the openings of extended courtly narratives. In view of these latter cases the secular short story appears

---

[137] Fischer, *Märendichtung*, 244f.
[138] Ibid., 93–137.
[139] Ibid., 227–31.
[140] Schröder (ed.), *Konrad von Würzburg: Kleinere Dichtungen*, i. pp. IXf.; Green, *Medieval Listening and Reading*, 110.

one step closer to being fully assimilated into literary culture than the heroic epic. We might say then that in terms of German narrative literature in our period, the genre of the 'Märe' occupies an intermediate position between the works of such writers as Rudolf von Ems and Konrad von Würzburg, on the one hand, and the heroic epic on the other.

6

CONCLUSION:
THE MEDIEVAL AUTHOR
IN THE TEXT

We began with the observation that Michel Foucault's analysis of
the author as a variable function has led to the re-evaluation of
authorship for a number of historical periods. We shall now end by
considering several of the particulars of Foucault's argument and
measuring our own findings against them. Structuring our conclusion in this way has two distinct advantages. First, it will enable us
to take a step back from the primary material with which we have
been concerned. The centrepiece of Foucault's essay is his four-point
characterization of the author-function in Western literary culture.
By exploring the extent to which these points are relevant to German
narrative literature of the thirteenth century (1220–90), it should
prove possible to view the workings of medieval authorship from a
fresh perspective. Second, in view of the fact that authorship
continues to preoccupy scholars from across the board of European
literary studies, it seems desirable to find a readily compatible form
of presentation to describe what we have found. For better or for
worse, the issues that Foucault highlights still represent the best frame
of reference for any future objective comparison of data relating to
authorship in different times and cultures.

Foucault's first point concerns what he regards as an intrinsic association between the author-function and the drive to appropriate the
text; a process that took a decisive step forward in the eighteenth
century with the regulation of authorial rights and textual owner-
ship. We need hardly mention that we have been dealing with a
pre-print culture in which the circumstances of production, reception, and transmission of literature are drastically different. Yet the
close relationship between authorship and appropriation is not
without analogues in our period either, for in the 'Blütezeit' and
throughout the thirteenth century the attribution of authorship went
hand in hand with the literary activity of translation. Reworkings
of Latin and French source-texts by Rudolf von Ems and Konrad

von Würzburg, like Hartmann von Aue's translations of Chrétien de Troyes before them, were in fact acts of linguistic and cultural appropriation. The poetic activities on which these romances, saints' lives, and works of historiography were based (translation from a language unknown to the audience; shaping material to suit interests and knowledge of new recipients; setting the text in elegant German verse) were perceived to be individual achievements and hence worthy of attribution to a named author. In other words, texts such as these were felt to merit endowment with an 'author-function'. Foucault himself suggests that the aspect of appropriation was most evident in earlier periods in penal contexts, when authorial responsibility was postulated for transgressive texts. The only parallel to this that we can lay claim to is found in the heroic epic *Dietrichs Flucht*, in which a passage of stinging social and political criticism is unambiguously attributed to a named author, flouting a generic rule of anonymity.

The contrast between the named authorship of the courtly romance, for example, and the anonymity of the heroic epic leads us to Foucault's second point: that the application of the author-function is not universal or constant but reflects essential differences between texts and their respective modes of existence, transmission, and their status within society; moreover, that the kinds of texts in receipt of the author-function vary from period to period and are subject to modification within any one period. Such variability is exemplified by the (German) Middle Ages, and the thirteenth century in particular, with the establishment of a vernacular literary culture that is characterized by the interplay of diverse forces (orality, literacy, the vernacular, Latin) with their concomitant value systems. Not only did these factors have a bearing on the form that an authorial attribution might take (the choice between first-person naming or an acrostic, for instance), but also on whether the author-function was appropriate at all. There is clearly a categorical difference between the signed Middle High German versions of French courtly romance or Latin hagiography, and the anonymous written adaptations of traditionally oral heroic tales that formed part of an indigenous and time-honoured cultural heritage. In the latter, concepts of individual authorial responsibility were largely out of place. However, that the author-function was on occasion also lent to this type of narrative reflects the intermittent attempt to assimilate fully this genre into established literary tradition in the course of the later Middle Ages. A similar process of assimilation may also be seen to take hold of the secular short story, but with considerably more success.

A further historical reason for the fluctuating endowment of the author-function in the Middle Ages lies in the nature of the written transmission of the texts. In the overwhelming majority of cases the author's literary work is preserved in the form of a transcription by another hand. The actions of those involved in the production of manuscripts (scribes, illustrators) could often directly impinge on the text's initial author-function, either by eradicating it (as in a number of manuscripts of Konrad von Würzburg's shorter works) or by adding a new and not necessarily complementary one (as in the transmission of Rudolf von Ems's *Barlaam und Josaphat* and *Weltchronik*). In short, medieval manuscripts can be a rich source of information about the issue of authorship because they often play host to different author-functions in respect of one and the same text, and even on the same page.

The third characteristic of the author-function as identified by Foucault is that it is a construct, the result of a series of operations on the part of the recipient of the text; texts are not spontaneously attributed to authors, there are always specific reasons for any such link. This point would appear to hold good for all periods including the Middle Ages. As far as our primary material is concerned the most obvious examples are the spurious attributions to Konrad von Würzburg, and in the context of the heroic epic to the mythical Heinrich von Ofterdingen and Wolfram von Eschenbach. In most if not all of these examples the initial requirement of finding an authoritative authorial figure is further qualified by the nature and content of the text in question. Authority is so often the key issue in the 'construction' of medieval authorship. We need only recall the variety of contexts in which the term *meister* has cropped up. Just as Rudolf von Ems compiles whole lists of *meister* in two of his works, so his own literary technique comes to be described as *meisterlîch* after his death by the continuator of the *Weltchronik*. Similarly, the title of *meister* is a constant element in later scribal references to Konrad von Würzburg's authorship of both texts and melodies. In some of the narratives that we have encountered even the author's name, which we would otherwise regard as being of primary importance, seems secondary in relation to notions of authority, mastery, and excellence. Thus, anonymous figures can still function as *meister* in the process of authorial composition that is re-constructed for the story of the Nibelungen in the *Klage*, and in the account of the prehistory of the book in the prologue of *Wolfdietrich* [D]. Finally, in the outstanding pictorial definitions of authorship that appear in certain codices of Rudolf von Ems's works it is as if the poet's authority is being built up before our eyes, motif upon iconographic motif.

If Foucault's third point deals with the construction of authorship outside of the text in the minds of recipients, then the fourth and final issue that he highlights is the signs within the text that refer to the author. These he describes as the grammatical coordinates (pronouns, adverbs of time and place, verb forms) of an 'I' whose relationship with the author varies throughout the text, effectively engendering a plurality of authorial selves. This aspect of the 'author-function' corresponds exactly with the central theme of the present study, and we are clearly in a position to confirm the existence of comparable material for medieval German narrative literature. There are of course altogether different material reasons for the occurrence of such signs in medieval texts (authorial awareness of recital by another; lack of prescribed space within narrative manuscripts to record authorial identity), nevertheless the range of techniques of self-reference and the strategies underpinning these techniques are striking. The two most important narrative poets of 1220–90 appear to adopt diametrically opposed positions in respect of this issue: the plurality of the authorial self reaches its apotheosis in Middle High German in Rudolf's *Willehalm von Orlens*, whilst Konrad von Würzburg strives for a uniform authorial first-person perspective. On the boundary with orality traces of the author-function in the texts of the heroic epic and the short story are considerably fewer, drastic authorial self-effacement being a concomitant of anonymity in many, but not all, cases. Aside from the straightforward exceptions in these genres in which the author-function is invoked under the influence of established literary practices, we have also had occasion to observe texts with curious internal dissonances (references to literary processes of composition that pass over the authorial agent involved; retaining an authorial figure whilst suppressing the latter's identity). These most enigmatic of author-functions are indicative of new types of narrative text in the thirteenth century that are struggling to come to terms with their own literary nature.

It remains to be seen whether this projection of our findings against a point-for-point breakdown of Foucault's 'author-function' will facilitate comparisons between our period and others in respect of the issue of authorship. One thing that it does make clear, however, is the vigorous character of medieval German literary culture, in which first the poets themselves and then the scribes (and illustrators) after them continually re-evaluated authorship, that is to say: the relationship between the author and the text, and the profile of the author in the text.

BIBLIOGRAPHY

PRIMARY LITERATURE (I):
FACSIMILES, DIPLOMATIC TRANSCRIPTIONS

Die Große Heidelberger 'Manessische' Liederhandschrift, ed. Ulrich Müller, with an introduction by Wilfried Werner, Göppingen 1971 (Litterae 1)
Codex Manesse: Die Miniaturen der Großen Heidelberger Liederhandschrift, ed. Ingo F. Walther, Frankfurt a. M. 1988
Das Hausbuch des Michael de Leone (Würzburger Liederhandschrift) der Universitäts-bibliothek München (2° Cod. ms. 731), ed. Horst Brunner, Göppingen 1983 (Litterae 100)
Heldenbuch: Nach dem ältesten Druck in Abbildung, ed. Joachim Heinzle, 2 vols., Göppingen 1981/1987 (Litterae 75:1–2)
Die kleine Heidelberger Liederhandschrift in Nachbildung, ed. Carl von Kraus, Stuttgart 1932
Ein schöne Historia von Engelhart auss Burgunt: Der 'Engelhard' Konrads von Würz-burg in Abbildung des Frankfurter Drucks von 1573. Mit einer bibliographischen Notiz zu Kilian Han, ed. Hans-Hugo Steinhoff, Göppingen 1987 (Litterae 107)
Konrad von Würzburg, Kaiser Otto und Heinrich von Kempten. Abbildung der gesamten Überlieferung und Materialien zur Stoffgeschichte, ed. André Schnyder, Göppingen 1989 (Litterae 109)
Konrad von Würzburg: 'Der Welt Lohn'. In Abbildung der gesamten Überlieferung, synoptische Edition, Untersuchungen, ed. Reinhard Bleck, Göppingen 1991 (Litterae 112)
Ortnit und Wolfdietrich: Abbildungen zur handschriftlichen Überlieferung spätmittelal-terlicher Heldenepik, [ed.] Edward R. Haymes, Göppingen 1984 (Litterae 86)
Wolfram von Eschenbach: Willehalm. Die Bruchstücke der 'Großen Bilderhandschrift': Bayerische Staatsbibliothek München Cgm 193,III; Germanisches Nationalmuseum Nürnberg, Graphische Sammlung Hz 1104–1105 Kapsel 1607, ed. Ulrich Montag, Stuttgart 1985
Le Wunderer: Fac-Similé de l'édition de 1503, ed. Georges Zink, Paris 1949 (Bibliothèque de philologie germanique 14)

PRIMARY LITERATURE (II): EDITIONS

Alpharts Tod. In DHB ii. 1–54
Die altdeutsche Exodus, ed. Edgar Papp, Munich 1968 (Medium aevum 16)
[Volrat.] *Die alte Mutter*. In GA i. 89–100 (cit.)
'Von der alten Mutter', ed. Moriz Haupt, *ZfdA* 6 (1848), 497–503

Das Annolied, ed. Eberhard Nellmann, 3rd revised edn. Stuttgart 1986 (Reclam Universal-Bibliothek 1416)

Appet, Jacob. *Der Ritter unter dem Zuber*. In *Novellistik*, ed. Grubmüller, 544–65

Aristoteles und Phyllis. In *Novellistik*, ed. Grubmüller, 492–523

Das Auge. In NGA i. 244–50

Ave Maria. In HMS iii. 337–44

Bestraftes Mißtrauen. In NGA i. 185–91

Biterolf und Dietleib. In DHB i. 1–197

Doctoris Seraphici S. Bonaventurae [. . .] *Opera omnia* [. . .], 10 vols., Quaracchi 1882–1902

Chrétien de Troyes. *Le Chevalier de la Charrete*, ed. Mario Roques, Paris 1958 (Les Romans de Chrétien de Troyes édités d'après la copie de Guiot [Bibl. nat. fr. 794]: 3)

Le Chevalier au Lion (Yvain), ed. Mario Roques, Paris 1960 (Les Romans de Chrétien de Troyes édités d'après la copie de Guiot [Bibl. nat. fr. 794]: 4)

Cligés, ed. Alexandre Micha, Paris 1957 (Les Romans de Chrétien de Troyes édités d'après la copie de Guiot [Bibl. nat. fr. 794]: 2)

Le Conte du Graal (Perceval), ed. Félix Lecoy, 2 vols., Paris 1972/1975 (Les Romans de Chrétien de Troyes édités d'après la copie de Guiot [Bibl. nat. fr. 794]: 5/6)

Erec et Enide, ed. Mario Roques, Paris 1952 (Les Romans de Chrétien de Troyes édités d'après la copie de Guiot [Bibl. nat. fr. 794]: 1)

Conrad of Hirsau. In *Accessus ad auctores; Bernard d'Utrecht; Conrad d'Hirsau, Dialogus super auctores*, ed. Robert B. C. Huygens, revised edn. Leiden 1970

Die poetische Bearbeitung des Buches Daniel aus der Stuttgarter Handschrift, ed. Arthur Hübner, Berlin 1911 (DTM 19. Dichtungen des Deutschen Ordens 3)

[*Der dankbare Wiedergänger* =] *Die Rittertreue*, ed. Marlis Meier-Branecke, Hamburg 1969 (Hamburger philologische Studien 10)

Dictys Cretensis Ephemerídos belli Troiani libri a Lucio Septimo ex Graeco in Latinum sermonem translati; accedunt papyri Dictys Graeci in Aegypto inventae, ed. Werner Eisenhut, 2nd revised edn. Leipzig 1973

[*Der Gürtel* =] *Der Borte des Dietrich von der Glezze*, ed. Otto R. Meyer, Heidelberg 1915 (Germanistische Arbeiten 3)

Dietrichs Flucht. In DHB ii. 55–215

Heinrich und Kunegunde von Ebernand von Erfurt, ed. Reinhold Bechstein, Quedlinburg/Leipzig 1860 (BNL 39)

Das Eckenlied: Sämtliche Fassungen, ed. Francis B. Brévart, 3 vols., Tübingen 1999 (ATB 111)

Eilhart von Oberge, ed. Franz Lichtenstein, Strassburg 1877 (Quellen und Forschungen zur Sprach- und Culturgeschichte der germanischen Völker 19), repr. Hildesheim/New York, NY 1973

[Der arme Konrad.] *Frau Metze*. In NGA i. 70–83

Frauenlist. In NGA i. 87–95

Frauentreue. In *Novellistik,* ed. Grubmüller, 470–91

Frauenturnier. In GA i. 371–82

[Freidank.] *Fridankes Bescheidenheit,* ed. Heinrich E. Bezzenberger, Halle 1872

Der Freudenleere. *Der Wiener Meerfahrt,* ed. Richard Newald, Heidelberg 1930 (Germanische Bibliothek 2:30)

Fürstenlob. In *Der Wartburgkrieg,* ed. Simrock, 1–49

Das Gänslein. In *Novellistik,* ed. Grubmüller, 648–65

Des Gervasius von Tilbury Otia Imperialia, ed. Felix Liebrecht, Hanover 1856

Goldemar. In DHB v. 201–4

Gottfried von Strassburg: Tristan, ed. Reinhold Bechstein, revised edn. by Peter F. Ganz, Wiesbaden 1978 (Deutsche Klassiker des Mittelalters NF 4)

Grubmüller, Klaus (ed.), *Novellistik des Mittelalters: Märendichtung,* Frankfurt a. M. 1996 (Bibliothek deutscher Klassiker 138. Bibliothek des Mittelalters 23)

von der Hagen, Friedrich H. (ed.), *Minnesinger: Deutsche Liederdichter des zwölften, dreizehnten und vierzehnten Jahrhunderts* [. . .], 4 vols., Leipzig 1838, repr. 1963

—*Gesammtabenteuer: Hundert altdeutsche Erzählungen* [. . .], 3 vols., Stuttgart/ Tübingen 1850, repr. Darmstadt 1961

Die halbe Birne A. In *Novellistik,* ed. Grubmüller, 178–207 (cit.)

Diu halbe Bir: Ein Schwank Konrads von Würzburg, ed. Georg Arnold Wolff, Erlangen 1893

Hartmann von Aue: Der arme Heinrich, ed. Hermann Paul, 16th revised edn. by Kurt Gärtner, Tübingen 1996 (ATB 3)

Erec von Hartmann von Aue, ed. Albert Leitzmann, 6th revised edn. by Christoph Cormeau/Kurt Gärtner, Tübingen 1985 (ATB 39)

Gregorius von Hartmann von Aue, ed. Hermann Paul, 14th revised edn. by Burghart Wachinger, Tübingen 1992 (ATB 2)

Hartmann von Aue: Iwein, edd. Georg F. Benecke/Karl Lachmann/Ludwig Wolff, 3rd revised edn., with translation and notes by Thomas Cramer, Berlin/New York, NY 1981

Hartmann von Aue: Die Klage. Das (zweite) Büchlein aus dem Ambraser Heldenbuch, ed. Herta Zutt, Berlin 1968

Die vier Redaktionen der Heidin, ed. Ludwig Pfannmüller, Berlin 1911 (Palaestra 108), repr. New York, NY 1966

Die Heidin B. In *Novellistik,* ed. Grubmüller, 364–469 (cit.)

[*Der heimliche Bote* =] 'Die sogenannten "Ratschläge für liebende"', ed. Ottokar Fischer, *ZfdA* 48 (1906), 421–5

Heinrich von Freiberg mit einleitungen über stil, sprache, metrik, quellen und die persönlichkeit des dichters, ed. Alois Bernt, Halle 1906

Die Gedichte Heinrichs des Teichners, ed. Heinrich Niewöhner, 3 vols., Berlin 1953–6 (DTM 44/46/48)

Diu Crône von Heinrich von dem Türlîn, ed. Gottlob H. F. Scholl, Stuttgart 1852 (StLV 27), repr. Amsterdam 1966

Heinrich von Veldeke: Eneasroman, ed. Hans Fromm, with an essay by Dorothea and Peter Diemer, Frankfurt a. M. 1992 (Bibliothek deutscher Klassiker 77. Bibliothek des Mittelalters 4)

Der Heller der armen Frau. In *Kleine mittelhochdeutsche Erzählungen*, ed. Rosenhagen, 19f.

Herbort's von Fritslâr liet von Troye, ed. Karl Frommann, Quedlinburg/Leipzig 1837 (BNL 5), repr. Amsterdam 1966

Bruder Hermanns Leben der Gräfin Iolande von Vianden, ed. John Meier, Breslau 1889 (Germanistische Abhandlungen 7)

Herrand von Wildonie: Vier Erzählungen, ed. Hanns Fischer, 2nd revised edn. by Paul Sappler, Tübingen 1969 (ATB 51)

Der Herrgottschnitzer. In NGA i. 229–33

Herzog Ernst: Ein mittelalterliches Abenteuerbuch. In der mittelhochdeutschen Fassung B nach der Ausgabe von Karl Bartsch mit den Bruchstücken der Fassung A, ed. Bernhard Sowinski, revised edn. Stuttgart 1979 (Reclam Universal-Bibliothek 8352)

Herzog Ernst D (wahrscheinlich von Ulrich von Etzenbach), ed. Hans-Friedrich Rosenfeld, Tübingen 1991 (ATB 104)

Hildebrandslied. In *Althochdeutsches Lesebuch*, ed. Wilhelm Braune, 16th revised edn. by Ernst A. Ebbinghaus, Tübingen 1979

Die mitteldeutsche poetische Paraphrase des Buches Hiob, ed. T. E. Karsten, Berlin 1910 (DTM 21. Dichtungen des Deutschen Ordens 4)

Historia Karoli Magni et Rotholandi ou Chronique du Pseudo-Turpin, ed. Cyril Meredith-Jones, Paris 1936

Jänicke, Oskar, *et al.* (eds.), *Deutsches Heldenbuch*, 5 vols., Berlin 1866–73, repr. Berlin/Zurich (from ii. Dublin/Zurich) 1963–8

Johannes von Freiberg. *Das Rädlein*. In *Novellistik*, ed. Grubmüller, 618–47

Heinrich Kaufringer: Werke, ed. Paul Sappler, Tübingen 1972

Das Kerbelkraut. In NGA i. 96–9

Diu Klage. Mit Lesarten sämmtlicher Handschriften, ed. Karl Bartsch, Leipzig 1875, repr. Darmstadt 1964

[*Kobold und Eisbär* =] *Schrätel und Wasserbär*. In *Novellistik*, ed. Grubmüller, 698–717

Das Rolandslied des Pfaffen Konrad, ed. Carl Wesle, 3rd revised edn. by Peter Wapnewski, Tübingen 1985 (ATB 69)

Kleinere Dichtungen Konrads von Würzburg, ed. Edward Schröder, 3 vols., Berlin 1924–6

Konrad von Würzburg: Die Legenden [I–III], ed. Paul Gereke, 3 vols., Halle 1925–7 (ATB 19–21)

Alexius. In *Legenden II*, ed. Gereke

Konrad von Würzburg: Engelhard, ed. Paul Gereke, 3rd revised edn. by Ingo Reiffenstein, Tübingen 1982 (ATB 17)

Die Goldene Schmiede des Konrads von Würzburg, ed. Edward Schröder, Göttingen 1926, repr. 1969

Heinrich von Kempten. In *Kleinere Dichtungen*, ed. Schröder, i. 41–68

Herzmaere. In *Kleinere Dichtungen*, ed. Schröder, i. 12–40

Die Klage der Kunst. In *Kleinere Dichtungen*, ed. Schröder, iii. 1–8

Minneleich. In *Kleinere Dichtungen*, ed. Schröder, iii. 15–19

Pantaleon von Konrad von Würzburg, ed. Paul Gereke, 2nd edn. by Winfried Woesler, Tübingen 1974 (ATB 21)

Konrads von Würzburg Partonopier und Meliur, Turnei von Nantheiz, Sant Nicolaus, Lieder und Sprüche, ed. Karl Bartsch, Vienna 1871, repr., with an appendix by Rainer Gruenter, Berlin 1970

Der Schwanritter. In *Kleinere Dichtungen*, ed. Schröder, ii. 1–39

Silvester. In *Legenden I*, ed. Gereke

Der trojanische Krieg von Konrad von Würzburg, ed. Adelbert von Keller, Stuttgart 1858 (StLV 44), repr. Amsterdam 1965

Das Turnier von Nantes. In *Kleinere Dichtungen*, ed. Schröder, ii. 40–73

Der Welt Lohn. In *Kleinere Dichtungen*, ed. Schröder, i. 1–11

Kudrun, ed. Karl Bartsch, 5th revised edn. by Karl Stackmann, Wiesbaden 1980

Lachmann, Karl/Haupt, Moriz (eds.), *Des Minnesangs Frühling. I: Texte*, 38th revised edn. by Hugo Moser/Helmut Tervooren, Stuttgart 1988

Laurin A; *Laurin* D. In *Laurin und der kleine Rosengarten*, ed. Georg Holz, Halle 1897, pp. 1–50; 96–182

[*Der Magezoge* =] *Der Tugendspiegel*. In *Kleinere mittelhochdeutsche Erzählungen*, ed. Rosenhagen, 21–9

Mai und Beaflor. Eine Erzählung aus dem dreizehnten Jahrhundert, ed. A. J. Vollmer, Leipzig 1848 (Dichtungen des Deutschen Mittelalters 7), repr. Hildesheim 1974

Vom mangelnden Hausrat. In *Samlung deutscher Gedichte*, ed. Myller, vol. iii. pp. XXXVII–XXXIX

'Mariengrüße', ed. Franz Pfeiffer, *ZfdA* 8 (1851), 274–98

[*Der Minne Freigedank* =] *Die zehn Gebote der Minne*. In *Miscellaneen zur Geschichte der teutschen Literatur* [. . .], ed. B. J. Docen, 2 vols., Munich 1806–7, ii. 171–88

Der Mönch als Liebesbote A. In *Novellistik*, ed. Grubmüller, 524–43

[*Der Mönch Felix* =] *Felix im paradise*. In GA iii. 613–23

[Der Zwingäuer.] *Des Mönches Not*. In *Novellistik*, ed. Grubmüller, 666–95

Moriz von Craûn, ed. Ulrich Pretzel, 4th revised edn. Tübingen 1973 (ATB 45)

Myller, Christoph Heinrich (ed.), *Samlung deutscher Gedichte aus dem XII. XIII. und XIV. Jahrhundert*, 3 vols., Berlin 1784–5

Das Nibelungenlied, edd. Karl Bartsch/Helmut de Boor, 22nd revised edn. by Roswitha Wisniewski, Mannheim 1988

Niewöhner, Heinrich (ed.), *Neues Gesamtabenteuer* [. . .] *Die Sammlung der mittel-hochdeutschen Mären und Schwänke des 13. und 14. Jahrhunderts*, Berlin 1937, 2nd edn. of vol. i. by Werner Simon, with variants noted by Max Boeters/Kurt Schacks, Dublin/Zurich 1967

Ortnit [AW]. In DHB iii. 1–77

Der Pfaffe mit der Schnur A. In *Maeren-Dichtung*, ed. Thomas Cramer, 2 vols., Munich 1979 (Spätmittelalterliche Texte 1/2), ii. 116–43

Der Pleier: Meleranz, ed. Karl Bartsch, Tübingen 1861 (StLV 60), repr., with an appendix by Alexander Hildebrand, Hildesheim/New York, NY 1974

Pseudo-Ovidius De vetula, ed. Paul Klopsch, Leiden/Cologne 1967 (Mittel-lateinische Studien und Texte 2)

Rabenschlacht. In DHB ii. 217–326

Rafold, Heinrich. *Der Nußberg.* In GA i. 445–7

Der Reiher. In NGA i. 100–7

Der heilige Georg Reinbots von Durne, ed. Carl von Kraus, Heidelberg 1907 (Germanische Bibliothek 3:1)

Reinfrid von Braunschweig, ed. Karl Bartsch, Tübingen 1871 (StLV 109)

Der Reinhart Fuchs des Elsässers Heinrich, ed. Klaus Düwel, Tübingen 1984 (ATB 96)

Rosengarten A; *Rosengarten* D. In *Die Gedichte vom Rosengarten zu Worms*, ed. Georg Holz, Halle 1893, pp. 1–67; 69–166

[*Rosengarten* C =] *Der Rosengarte*, ed. Wilhelm Grimm, Göttingen 1836

Rosenhagen, Gustav (ed.), *Kleinere mittelhochdeutsche Erzählungen, Fabeln und Lehrgedichte: III. Die Heidelberger Handschrift cod. Pal. germ. 341*, Berlin 1909 (DTM 17)

Rosenplüt, Hans. In *Die deutsche Märendichtung des 15. Jahrhunderts*, ed. Hanns Fischer, Munich 1966 (MTU 12)

Rüdeger der Hinkhofer. *Der Schegel.* In *Novellistik*, ed. Grubmüller, 112–77.

Rüdeger von Munre. [*Studentenabenteuer* B =] *Irregang und Girregar.* In GA iii. 43–82

Rudolf von Ems: Alexander. Ein höfischer Versroman des 13. Jahrhunderts, ed. Victor Junk, 2 vols., Leipzig 1928–9 (StLV 272/274), repr. Darmstadt 1970

Rudolf von Ems: Barlaam und Josaphat, ed. Franz Pfeiffer, Leipzig 1843 (Dichtungen des deutschen Mittelalters 3), repr., with an appendix by Heinz Rupp, Berlin 1965

Der guote Gêrhart von Rudolf von Ems, ed. John A. Asher, 3rd revised edn. Tübingen 1989 (ATB 56)

Rudolfs von Ems Weltchronik. Aus der Wernigeroder Handschrift, ed. Gustav Ehrismann, Berlin 1915 (DTM 20), repr. Dublin/Zurich 1967

Rudolfs von Ems Willehalm von Orlens. Aus dem Wasserburger Codex der fürstlich Fürstenbergischen Hofbibliothek in Donaueschingen, ed. Victor Junk, Berlin 1905 (DTM 2), repr. Dublin/Zurich 1967

Die sechs Farben. In *Samlung deutscher Gedichte*, ed. Myller, vol. iii. pp. XXIV–XXVI

Sekte der Minner. In *Samlung deutscher Gedichte*, ed. Myller, vol. iii. pp. XXX–XXXII

Sibote. [*Frauenerziehung =*] *Die Zähmung der Widerspenstigen.* In NGA i. 1–35

Siegfried der Dörfer. *Frauentrost.* In GA iii. 429–50

Der jüngere Sigenot, ed. A. Clemens Schoener, Heidelberg 1928 (Germanische Bibliothek 3:6)

Der Sperber. In *Novellistik*, ed. Grubmüller, 568–89 (cit.)

Der Sperber und verwandte mhd. Novellen, ed. Heinrich Niewöhner, Berlin 1913 (Palaestra 119)

Das Alexanderlied des Pfaffen Lamprecht (Straßburger Alexander), ed. Irene Ruttmann, Darmstadt 1974

Die Kleindichtung des Strickers, ed. Wolfgang W. Moelleken, 5 vols., Göppingen 1973–8 (GAG 107:1–5), vols. ii.–v. co-edited by Gayle Agler-Beck/Robert E. Lewis

Der Stricker: Verserzählungen I, ed. Hanns Fischer, 4th revised edn. by Johannes Janota, Tübingen 1979 (ATB 53)

Der begrabene Ehemann. In *Verserzählungen I*, ed. Fischer, 28–36

Die Buße des Sünders. In *Kleindichtung*, ed. Moelleken, v. 98–121

Der Stricker: Daniel von dem Blühenden Tal, ed. Michael Resler, 2nd revised edn. Tübingen 1995 (ATB 92)

Die drei Wünsche. In *Verserzählungen I*, ed. Fischer, 1–11

Der durstige Einsiedel. In *Verserzählungen I*, ed. Fischer, 143–55

Die eingemauerte Frau. In *Verserzählungen I*, ed. Fischer, 50–65

Strickers 'Frauenehre', ed. Klaus Hofmann, Marburg 1976

Der Gevatterin Rat. In *Verserzählungen I*, ed. Fischer, 66–91

Karl der Große von dem Stricker, ed. Karl Bartsch, Quedlinburg/Leipzig 1857 (BNL 35), repr., with an appendix by Dieter Kartschoke, Berlin 1965

Die Klage. In *Kleindichtung*, ed. Moelleken, v. 189–218

Der kluge Knecht. In *Verserzählungen I*, ed. Fischer, 92–109

Die Martinsnacht. In *Verserzählungen I*, ed. Fischer, 131–42

Der nackte Bote. In *Verserzählungen I*, ed. Fischer, 110–26

Der nackte Ritter. In *Verserzählungen I*, ed. Fischer, 126–31

'Der Stricker': Der Pfaffe Amis, ed. Michael Schilling, Stuttgart 1994 (Reclam Universal-Bibliothek 658)

Des Teufels Ächtung. In GA ii. 123–35

Thomasin von Zerclaere: Der welsche Gast, ed. Friedrich W. von Kries, 4 vols., Göppingen 1984 (GAG 425:1–4)

Der Wälsche Gast des Thomasin von Zirclaria, ed. Heinrich Rückert, Quedlinburg/Leipzig 1852 (BNL 30), repr., with an introduction and appendix by Friedrich Neumann, Berlin 1965 (cit.)

Ulrich von Etzenbach. *Alexander von Ulrich von Eschenbach*, ed. Wendelin Toischer, Tübingen 1888 (StLV 183)

Ulrich von Türheim: Rennewart, ed. Alfred Hübner, Berlin 1938 (DTM 39)

Ulrich von Türheim: Tristan, ed. Thomas Kerth, Tübingen 1979 (ATB 89)

[*Arabel* =] *Willehalm* [. . .] *von Meister Ulrich von dem Türlin*, ed. Samuel Singer, Prague 1893 (Bibliothek der mittelhochdeutschen Litteratur in Böhmen 4), repr. Hildesheim 1968

Lanzelet: Eine Erzählung von Ulrich von Zatzikhoven, ed. K. A. Hahn, Frankfurt a. M. 1845, repr., with an appendix by Friedrich Neumann, Berlin 1965

'Unser Vrouwen Klage', ed. Gustav Milchsack, *PBB* 5 (1878), 193–357

Virginal [v_{10}]. In DHB v. 1–200

Der Vriolsheimer. Der Hasenbraten. In NGA i. 108ff.

Walsingham, Thomas. *Gesta abbatum monasterii Sancti Albani a Thoma Walsingham, regnante Ricardo Secundo, ejusdem ecclesiae praecentore, compilata*, ed. Henry Thomas Riley, 3 vols., London 1867–9 (Rerum Britannicarum medii aevi scriptores 28. Chronica monasterii S. Albani 4)

Waltharius, ed. Karl Strecker, with a German translation by Peter Vossen, Berlin 1947

'Weiberzauber von Walther von Griven', ed. Moriz Haupt, *ZfdA* 15 (1872), 245f.

Walther von der Vogelweide: Leich, Lieder, Sangsprüche, ed. Karl Lachmann, 14th revised edn. by Christoph Cormeau, with contributions by Thomas Bein/Horst Brunner, Berlin/New York, NY 1996

Der Wartburgkrieg, ed. Karl Simrock, Stuttgart/Augsburg 1858

Wernher der Gartenaere: Helmbrecht, ed. Friedrich Panzer, 10th revised edn. by Hans-Joachim Ziegeler, Tübingen 1993 (ATB 11)

Wigalois der Ritter mit dem Rade von Wirnt von Grafenberc, ed. J. M. N. Kapteyn, Bonn 1926 (Rheinische Beiträge und Hülfsbücher zur germanischen Philologie und Volkskunde 9)

Wolfdietrich B. In DHB iii. 165–301

Wolfdietrich C. In DHB iv. 14f., 20ff., 137ff.

[*Wolfdietrich* D =] *Der große Wolfdietrich*, ed. Adolf Holtzmann, Heidelberg 1865

[*Wolfdietrich* Ka =] *The Wolfdietrich Epic in the Dresdener Heldenbuch (Wolfdietrich K)*, Louisville, Ky. 1935

Wolfdietrich y. In *Ortneit und Wolfdietrich nach der Wiener Piaristenhandschrift*, ed. Justus Lunzer, Tübingen 1906 (StLV 239), 58–310

Wolfram von Eschenbach: Parzival, ed. Karl Lachmann, 6th edn. Berlin 1926, repr., with [German] translation by Peter Knecht and an introduction by Bernd Schirok, Berlin/New York, NY 1998

Wolfram von Eschenbach: Willehalm. Nach der Handschrift 857 der Stiftsbibliothek St. Gallen, ed. Joachim Heinzle, Tübingen 1994 (ATB 108)

Zabulons Buch.—In: *Der Wartburgkrieg*, ed. Simrock, 184–229

Von zwei Blinden.—In: *Die Barlaamparabeln im Cod. Vindob. 2705: Studien zur Verfasserschaft kleinerer mhd. Gedichte*, ed. Ute Schwab, Naples 1966 (Quaderni della sezione germanica degli annali 3), 152–6

SECONDARY LITERATURE

Andersen, Elizabeth, *et al.* (eds.), *Autor und Autorschaft im Mittelalter: Kolloquium Meißen 1995*, Tübingen 1998

Appelhans, Peter, *Untersuchungen zur spätmittelalterlichen Mariendichtung: Die rhythmischen mittelhochdeutschen Mariengrüße*, Heidelberg 1970

Arndt, Paul Herbert, *Der Erzähler bei Hartmann von Aue: Formen und Funktionen seines Hervortretens und seiner Äußerungen*, Göppingen 1980 (GAG 299)

Asher, John A., 'Der übele Gêrhart: Einige Bemerkungen zu den von Gabriel Sattler geschriebenen Handschriften', *PBB* (Tüb.) 94 (1972), Sonderheft 416–27

Barthes, Roland, 'La Mort de l'auteur', in *Roland Barthes: Oeuvres complètes*, ed. Eric Marty, 3 vols., Paris 1993–5, ii. 491–5

Bartsch, Karl, *Die altdeutschen Handschriften der Universitäts-Bibliothek in Heidelberg*, Heidelberg 1887 (Katalog der Handschriften der Universitäts-Bibliothek in Heidelberg 1)

Bastert, Bernd, '*Dô si der lantgrâve nam*: Zur "Klever Hochzeit" und der Genese des Eneas-Romans', *ZfdA* 123 (1994), 253–73

Beckers, Hartmut, 'Brüsseler Bruchstücke aus Konrads "Trojanerkrieg"', *ZfdA* 124 (1995), 319–27

Beer, Ellen J., 'Die Buchkunst der Hs. 302 der Vadiana', in *Kommentar zu Ms 302 Vad.*, edd. Kantonsbibliothek (Vadiana) St Gallen *et al.*, 61–125

Bein, Thomas, 'Das Singen über das Singen: Zu Sang und Minne im Minne-Sang', in *'Aufführung' und 'Schrift'*, ed. Müller, 67–92

—'Mit fremden Pegasusen pflügen': Untersuchungen zu Authentizitätsproblemen in mittelhochdeutscher Lyrik und Lyrikphilologie*, Berlin 1998 (Philologische Studien und Quellen 150)

Bertau, Karl, 'Beobachtungen und Bemerkungen zum Ich in der "Goldenen Schmiede"', in *Philologie als Kulturwissenschaft: Studien zur Literatur und Geschichte des Mittelalters. Festschrift für Karl Stackmann zum 65. Geburtstag*, edd. Ludger Grenzmann/Hubert Herkommer/Dieter Wuttke, Göttingen 1987, pp. 179–92

—'Die "Goldene Schmiede" zwischen Rittern und Reuerinnen', in *Hof und Kloster*, edd. Palmer/Schiewer, 113–40

Beyer, Jürgen, *Schwank und Moral: Untersuchungen zum altfranzösischen Fabliau und verwandten Formen*, Heidelberg 1969 (Studia Romanica 16)

Biriotti, Maurice/Miller, Nicola (eds.), *What is an Author?*, Manchester 1993

Bleck, Reinhard, 'Eine Kleinsammlung mittelhochdeutscher Reimpaar-dichtungen (Nürnberg, Germanisches Nationalmuseum, Hs 42 531)', *ZfdA* 116 (1987), 283–96

Boesch, Bruno, *Die Kunstanschauung in der mittelhochdeutschen Dichtung von der Blütezeit bis zum Meistergesang*, Berne/Leipzig 1936

Bonath, Gesa, 'Nachtrag zu den Akrosticha in Gottfrieds "Tristan"', *ZfdA* 115 (1986), 101–16

de Boor, Helmut, *Die deutsche Literatur im späten Mittelalter: Zerfall und Neubeginn.*
Erster Teil: 1250–1350, Munich 1962 (= Helmut de Boor/Richard Newald
[eds.], Geschichte der deutschen Literatur von den Anfängen bis zur
Gegenwart 3:1), 5th revised edn. by Johannes Janota, 1997

—'Zum Häslein V. 1–4', *PBB* (Tüb.) 87 (1965), 200–3

—'Die Chronologie der Werke Konrads von Würzburg, insbesondere die
Stellung des Turniers von Nantes', *PBB* (Tüb.) 89 (1967), 210–69

Booth, Wayne C., *The Rhetoric of Fiction*, Chicago, Ill. 1961

Brackert, Helmut, *Rudolf von Ems: Dichtung und Geschichte*, Heidelberg
1968

Brandt, Rüdiger, *Konrad von Würzburg*, Darmstadt 1987 (EdF 249)

Brown, Cynthia J., 'Text, Image, and Authorial Self-Consciousness in Late
Medieval Paris', in *Printing the Written Word: The Social History of Books,
circa 1450–1520*, ed. Sandra Hindmann, Ithaca, NY 1991, pp. 103–42

Bulst, Walther, 'Zum *prologus* der *Natiuitas et uictoria Alexandri magni regis*: II.
Die Paraphrase im "Alexander" Rudolfs von Ems', *Historische Vierteljahrschrift* 29 (1935), 253–67

Bumke, Joachim, *Wolfram von Eschenbach*, Stuttgart 1964 (SM 36), 7th revised
edn. Stuttgart/Weimar 1997

—*Ministerialität und Ritterdichtung: Umrisse der Forschung*, Munich 1976

—*Mäzene im Mittelalter: Die Gönner und Auftraggeber der höfischen Literatur in
Deutschland 1150–1300*, Munich 1979

—*Höfische Kultur: Literatur und Gesellschaft im hohen Mittelalter*, 2 vols., Munich
1986 (dtv 4442)

—*Die vier Fassungen der 'Nibelungenklage': Untersuchungen zur Überlieferungsgeschichte
und Textkritik der höfischen Epik im 13. Jahrhundert*, Berlin/New York, NY
1996 (Quellen und Forschungen zur Literatur- und Kulturgeschichte 8
[242])

—'Autor und Werk: Beobachtungen und Überlegungen zur höfischen Epik
(ausgehend von der Donaueschinger Parzivalhandschrift G$^\delta$)', *ZfdPh* 116
(1997), Sonderheft 87–114

Bumke, Joachim (ed.), *Literarisches Mäzenatentum: Ausgewählte Forschungen zur
Rolle des Gönners und Auftraggebers in der mittelalterlichen Literatur*, Darmstadt
1982 (WdF 598)

Burke, Seán, *The Death and Return of the Author: Criticism and Subjectivity in
Barthes, Foucault and Derrida*, 2nd revised edn. Edinburgh 1998

Burke, Seán (ed.), *Authorship: From Plato to the Postmodern. A Reader*, Edinburgh
1995

Buschinger, Danielle (ed.), *Figures de l'écrivain au moyen âge: Actes du Colloque
du Centre d'Etudes Médiévales de l'Université de Picardie, Amiens 18–20 mars
1988*, Göppingen 1991 (GAG 510)

Butzer, Günter, 'Das Gedächtnis des epischen Textes: Mündliches und
schriftliches Erzählen im höfischen Roman des Mittelalters', *Euphorion*
89 (1995), 151–88

Cerquiglini, Bernard, *Eloge de la variante: Histoire critique de la philologie*, Paris 1989

Chartier, Roger, *Culture écrite et société: L'ordre des livres (XIVe—XVIIIe siècle)*, Paris 1996

Chenu, Marie-Dominique, 'Auctor, actor, autor', *Bull. du Cange* 3 (1927), 81–6

—*La Théologie au douzième siècle*, Paris 1957 (Etudes de philosophie médiévale 45)

Chinca, Mark, *History, Fiction, Verisimilitude: Studies in the Poetics of Gottfried's 'Tristan'*, London 1993 (MHRA Texts and Dissertations 35. Institute of Germanic Studies: Bithell Series of Dissertations 18)

Copeland, Rita, *Rhetoric, Hermeneutics, and Translation in the Middle Ages: Academic Traditions and Vernacular Texts*, Cambridge 1991 (Cambridge Studies in Medieval Literature 11)

Cormeau, Christoph, 'Quellenkompendium oder Erzählkonzept? Eine Skizze zu Konrads von Würzburg "Trojanerkrieg"', in *Befund und Deutung: Zum Verhältnis von Empirie und Interpretation in Sprach- und Literaturwissenschaft. (Hans Fromm zum 26. Mai 1979 von seinen Schülern)*, edd. Klaus Grubmüller *et al.*, Tübingen 1979, pp. 303–19

—'Überlegungen zum Verhältnis von Ästhetik und Rezeption', *JOWG* 5 (1988–9), 95–107

Cormeau, Christoph (ed.), *Deutsche Literatur im Mittelalter: Kontakte und Perspektiven. Hugo Kuhn zum Gedenken*, Stuttgart 1979

Cramer, Thomas, '*Solus creator est deus*: Der Autor auf dem Weg zum Schöpfertum', *Daphnis* 15 (1986), 13–28

Curschmann, Michael, 'Das Abenteuer des Erzählens: Über den Erzähler in Wolframs "Parzival"', *DVjs* 45 (1971), 627–67

—'The French, the Audience, and the Narrator in Wolfram's "Willehalm"', *Neophilologus* 59 (1975), 548–62

—'Zu Struktur und Thematik des Buchs von Bern', *PBB* (Tüb.) 98 (1976), 357–83

—'"Nibelungenlied" und "Nibelungenklage": Über Mündlichkeit und Schriftlichkeit im Prozeß der Episierung', in *Kontakte und Perspektiven*, ed. Cormeau, 85–119

—'Hören–Lesen–Sehen: Buch und Schriftlichkeit im Selbstverständnis der volkssprachlichen literarischen Kultur Deutschlands um 1200', *PBB* 106 (1984), 218–57

—'Zur Wechselwirkung von Literatur und Sage: Das "Buch von Kriemhild" und Dietrich von Bern', *PBB* 111 (1989), 380–410

—'Dichter *alter maere*: Zur Prologstrophe des "Nibelungenliedes" im Spannungsfeld von mündlicher Erzähltradition und laikaler Schriftkultur', in *Grundlagen des Verstehens mittelalterlicher Literatur: Literarische Texte und ihr historischer Erkenntniswert*, edd. Gerhard Hahn/Hedda Ragotzky, Stuttgart 1992 (Kröners Studienbibliothek 663), 55–71

—'*Pictura laicorum litteratura*? Überlegungen zum Verhältnis von Bild und volkssprachlicher Schriftlichkeit im Hoch- und Spätmittelalter bis zum Codex Manesse', in *Pragmatische Schriftlichkeit im Mittelalter: Erscheinungsformen und Entwicklungsstufen*, edd. Hagen Keller/Klaus Grubmüller/ Nikolaus Staubach, Munich 1992 (MMS 65), 211–29

Curtius, Ernst Robert, *Europäische Literatur und lateinisches Mittelalter*, Berne 1948

Dalby, David, *Lexicon of the Mediaeval German Hunt: A Lexicon of Middle High German terms (1050–1500), associated with the Chase, Hunting with Bows, Falconry, Trapping and Fowling*, Berlin 1965

Deighton, Alan, 'Studies in the Reception of the Works of Gottfried von Straßburg in Germany during the Middle Ages', D.Phil. thesis, University of Oxford 1979

Dinkelacker, Wolfgang, *Ortnit-Studien: Vergleichende Interpretation der Fassungen*, Berlin 1972 (Philologische Studien und Quellen 67)

Draesner, Ulrike, *Wege durch erzählte Welten: Intertextuelle Verweise als Mittel der Bedeutungskonstitution in Wolframs 'Parzival'*, Frankfurt a. M. 1992 (Mikrokosmos 36)

Drescher, Ulrich, *Geistliche Denkformen in den Bilderhandschriften des Sachsenspiegels*, Frankfurt a. M. 1989 (Germanistische Arbeiten zu Sprache und Kulturgeschichte 12)

Dronke, Peter, 'The Rise of the Medieval Fabliau: Latin and Vernacular Evidence', *RF* 85 (1973), 275–97

—*Poetic Individuality in the Middle Ages: New Departures in Poetry 1000–1150*, 2nd edn. London 1986 (Westfield Publications in Medieval Studies 1)

Düwel, Klaus, *Werkbezeichnungen der mittelhochdeutschen Erzählliteratur (1050– 1250)*, Göttingen 1983 (Palaestra 277)

Ehrismann, Gustav, 'Duzen und Ihrzen im Mittelalter [4]', *ZfdWf* 5 (1903–4), 127–220

—*Studien über Rudolf von Ems: Beiträge zur Geschichte der Rhetorik und Ethik im Mittelalter*, Heidelberg 1919 (Sitzungsberichte der Heidelberger Akademie der Wissenschaften. Philosophisch-historische Klasse 1919:8)

von Ertzdorff, Xenja, *Rudolf von Ems: Untersuchungen zum höfischen Roman im 13. Jahrhundert*, Munich 1967

von Euw, Anton/Plotzek, Joachim M., *Die Handschriften der Sammlung Ludwig*, 4 vols., Cologne 1979–85

Fasbender, Christoph, '*hochvart* im "Armen Heinrich", im "Pfaffen Amis" und im "Reinhart Fuchs": Versuch über redaktionelle Tendenzen im Cpg 341', *ZfdA* 128 (1999), 394–408

Finster, Franz, *Zur Theorie und Technik mittelalterlicher Prologe: Eine Untersuchung zu den Alexander- und Willehalmprologen Rudolfs von Ems*, Diss. Bochum 1971

Fischer, Hanns, *Studien zur deutschen Märendichtung*, Tübingen 1968, 2nd revised edn. by Johannes Janota, 1983

Flood, John L., 'Offene Geheimnisse: Versteckte und verdeckte Autorschaft im Mittelalter', in *Autor und Autorschaft*, edd. Andersen *et al.*, 370–96

Foucault, Michel, 'Qu'est-ce qu'un Auteur?', in *Dits et écrits: 1954–1988*, edd. Daniel Defert/François Ewald/Jacques Lagrange, 4 vols., Paris 1994, i. 789–821

Friedemann, Käte, *Die Rolle des Erzählers in der Epik*, Berlin 1910 (Untersuchungen zur neueren Sprach- und Literaturgeschichte NF 7), repr. Darmstadt 1965

Frühmorgen-Voss, Hella, *Text und Illustration im Mittelalter: Aufsätze zu den Wechselbeziehungen zwischen Literatur und bildender Kunst*, ed. Norbert H. Ott, Munich 1975 (MTU 50)

Gärtner, Kurt, 'Überlieferungstypen mittelhochdeutscher Weltchroniken', in *Geschichtsbewußtsein in der deutschen Literatur des Mittelalters: Tübinger Colloquium 1983*, edd. Christoph Gerhardt/Nigel F. Palmer/Burghart Wachinger, Tübingen 1985 (Publications of the Institute of Germanic Studies University of London 34), 110–18

Gally, Michèle, 'L'Amant, le Chevalier et le Clerc: l'auteur médiévale en quête d'un statut', in *Images de l'écrivain*, ed. José-Luis Diaz, Paris 1989 (Textuell 34/44: 22), 11–28

Ganz, Peter F./Schröder, Werner (eds.), *Probleme mittelhochdeutscher Erzählformen: Marburger Colloquium 1969*, Berlin 1972 (Publications of the Institute of Germanic Studies University of London 13)

Genette, Gérard, *Seuils*, Paris 1987

Gerhardt, Christoph, 'Überlegungen zur Überlieferung von Konrads von Würzburg "Der Welt Lohn"', *PBB* (Tüb.) 94 (1972), 379–97

—'Willehalm von Orlens: Studien zum Eingang und zum Schluß der strophischen Bearbeitung aus dem Jahre 1522', *WW* 35 (1985), 196–230

Gibson, Margaret T./Palmer, Nigel F., 'Manuscripts of Alan of Lille, "Anticlaudianus" in the British Isles', *Studi Medievali*, 3^A Series, 28:2 (1987), 905–1001

Glier, Ingeborg, 'Der Minneleich im späten 13. Jahrhundert', in *Werk–Typ–Situation*, edd. Glier et al., 161–83

—*Artes amandi: Untersuchung zu Geschichte, Überlieferung und Typologie der deutschen Minnereden*, Munich 1971 (MTU 34)

Glier, Ingeborg, et al. (eds.), *Werk–Typ–Situation: Studien zu poetologischen Bedingungen in der älteren deutschen Literatur. (Hugo Kuhn zum 60. Geburtstag)*, Stuttgart 1969

Goebel, K. Dieter, 'Der Gebrauch der dritten und ersten Person bei der Selbstnennung und in den Selbstaussagen mittelhochdeutscher Dichter', *ZfdPh* 94 (1975), 15–36

Green, Dennis H., *Irony in the Medieval Romance*, Cambridge 1979

—'On the Primary Reception of the Works of Rudolf von Ems', *ZfdA* 115 (1986), 151–80

—*Medieval Listening and Reading: The Primary Reception of German Literature 800–1300*, Cambridge 1994

Gröchenig, Hans, 'Ein Fragment einer mittelalterlichen Maerenhandschrift aus der UB Klagenfurt. Ein neu aufgefundenes Fragment zur Heidin "B" und zu Dietrich von Glesse: Der Gürtel', *Buchkunde* 1 (1984), 3–10

Gros, Gérard, *Le Poète marial et l'art graphique: Etude sur les jeux de lettres dans les poèmes pieux du Moyen Age*, Caen 1993

Grosse, Max, *Das Buch im Roman: Studien zu Buchverweis und Autoritätszitat in altfranzösischen Texten*, Munich 1994

Grunewald, Eckhard, 'Zur Handschrift A 94 der ehem. Straßburger Johanniterbibliothek', *ZfdA* 110 (1981), 96–105

Günther, Jörn-Uwe, *Die illustrierten mittelhochdeutschen Weltchronikhandschriften in Versen: Katalog der Handschriften und Einordnung der Illustrationen in die Bildüberlieferung*, Munich 1993 (tuduv-Studien: Reihe Kunstgeschichte 48)

Hartong, Maria-Magdalena, *Willehalm von Orlens und seine Illustrationen*, Diss. Cologne 1938

Haug, Walter, *Literaturtheorie im deutschen Mittelalter: Von den Anfängen bis zum Ende des 13. Jahrhunderts*, Darmstadt 1985, 2nd revised edn. 1992

—'Innovation und Originalität: Kategoriale und literarhistorische Vorüberlegungen', in *Innovation und Originalität*, edd. Walter Haug/Burghart Wachinger, Tübingen 1993 (Fortuna vitrea 9), 1–13

—'Mündlichkeit, Schriftlichkeit und Fiktionalität', in *Modernes Mittelalter*, ed. Heinzle, 376–97

—'Klassikerkataloge und Kanonisierungseffekte: Am Beispiel des mittelalterlichhochhöfischen Literaturkanons', in *Brechungen auf dem Weg zur Individualität: Kleine Schriften zur Literatur des Mittelalters*, Tübingen 1995, pp. 45–56

Haug, Walter/Wachinger, Burghart (eds.), *Autorentypen*, Tübingen 1991 (Fortuna vitrea 6)

Heger, Hedwig, *Das Lebenszeugnis Walthers von der Vogelweide: Die Reiserechnungen des Passauer Bischofs Wolfger von Erla*, Vienna 1970

Heinzle, Joachim, *Mittelhochdeutsche Dietrichepik: Untersuchungen zur Tradierungsweise, Überlieferungskritik und Gattungsgeschichte später Heldendichtung*, Munich 1978 (MTU 62)

—'Wann beginnt das Spätmittelalter?', *ZfdA* 112 (1983), 207–23

—'Altes und Neues zum Märenbegriff', *ZfdA* 117 (1988), 277–96

—'Die Entdeckung der Fiktionalität: Zu Walter Haugs "Literaturtheorie im deutschen Mittelalter"', *PBB* 112 (1990), 55–80

—*Das Nibelungenlied: Eine Einführung*, revised edn. Frankfurt a. M. 1994

—*Wandlungen und Neuansätze im 13. Jahrhundert (1220/30–1280/90)*, 2nd revised edn. Tübingen 1994 (= Joachim Heinzle [ed.], Geschichte der deutschen Literatur von den Anfängen bis zum Beginn der Neuzeit 2:2)

—'Literarische Interessenbildung im Mittelalter: Kleiner Kommentar zu einer Forschungsperspektive', in *Literatur im Lebenszusammenhang*, ed. Lutz, 79–93

—*Einführung in die mittelhochdeutsche Dietrichepik*, Berlin/New York, NY 1999

Heinzle, Joachim (ed.), *Literarische Interessenbildung im Mittelalter: DFG-Symposion 1991*, Stuttgart/Weimar 1993 (Germanistische Symposien Berichtsbände 14)

—*Modernes Mittelalter: Neue Bilder einer populären Epoche*, Frankfurt a. M./ Leipzig 1994

Hellgardt, Ernst, 'Anonymität und Autornamen zwischen Mündlichkeit und Schriftlichkeit in der deutschen Literatur des elften und zwölften Jahrhunderts. Mit Vorbemerkungen zu einigen Autornamen der altenglischen Dichtung', in *Autor und Autorschaft*, edd. Andersen *et al.*, 46–72

Herkommer, Hubert, 'Der St. Galler Codex als literarhistorisches Monument', in *Kommentar zu Ms 302 Vad.*, edd. Kantonsbibliothek (Vadiana) St Gallen *et al.*, 127–273

Höfler, Otto, 'Die Anonymität des Nibelungenliedes', in *Zur germanisch-deutschen Heldensage: Sechzehn Aufsätze zum neuen Forschungsstand*, ed. Karl Hauck, Bad Homburg 1961 (WdF 14), 330–92

Hoffmann, Werner, *Kudrun: Ein Beitrag zur Deutung der nachnibelungischen Heldendichtung*, Stuttgart 1967 (Germanistische Abhandlungen 17)

—*Mittelhochdeutsche Heldendichtung*, Berlin 1974 (Grundlagen der Germanistik 14)

Holznagel, Franz-Josef, *Wege in die Schriftlichkeit: Untersuchungen und Materialien zur Überlieferung der mittelhochdeutschen Lyrik*, Tübingen/Basle 1995 (Bibliotheca Germanica 32)

—'Autorschaft und Überlieferung am Beispiel der kleineren Reimpaartexte des Strickers', in *Autor und Autorschaft*, edd. Andersen *et al.*, 163–84

Honemann, Volker/Palmer, Nigel F. (eds.), *Deutsche Handschriften 1100–1400: Oxforder Kolloquium 1985*, Tübingen 1988

Howard, David Alexander, 'The Relationship between Poet and Narrator in Gottfried's "Tristan"', Ph.D. thesis, University of Cambridge 1973

Hult, David F., *Self-fulfilling Prophecies: Readership and Authority in the first 'Roman de la Rose'*, Cambridge 1986

Huot, Sylvia, *From Song to Book: The Poetics of Writing in Old French Lyric and Lyrical Narrative Poetry*, Ithaca, NY 1987

Ingold, Felix Philipp/Wunderlich, Werner (eds.), *Fragen nach dem Autor: Positionen und Perspektiven*, Constance 1992

—*Der Autor im Dialog: Beiträge zu Autorität und Autorschaft*, St Gallen 1995

Iwand, Käthe, *Die Schlüsse der mittelhochdeutschen Epen*, Berlin 1922 (Germanische Studien 16)

Jackson, Timothy R., 'Konrad von Würzburg's Legends: Their Historical Context and the Poet's Approach to His Material', in *Probleme mittelhochdeutscher Erzählformen*, edd. Ganz/Schröder, 197–213

—*The Legends of Konrad von Würzburg: Form, Content, Function*, Erlangen 1983 (Erlanger Studien 45)

Jackson, William H., 'Some Observations on the Status of the Narrator in Hartmann von Aue's *Erec* and *Iwein*', *FMLS* 6 (1970), 65–82

Jaeger, C. Stephen, 'Der Schöpfer der Welt und das Schöpfungswerk als Prologmotiv in der mhd. Dichtung', *ZfdA* 107 (1978), 1–18

Jaurant, Danielle, *Rudolfs 'Weltchronik' als offene Form: Überlieferungsstruktur und Wirkungsgeschichte*, Tübingen 1995 (Bibliotheca Germanica 34)

Jauß, Hans Robert, *Alterität und Modernität der mittelalterlichen Literatur: Gesammelte Aufsätze 1956–1976*, Munich 1977

Johanek, Peter, 'Höfe und Residenzen, Herrschaft und Repräsentation', in *Literatur im Lebenszusammenhang*, ed. Lutz, 45–78

Johnson, L. Peter, 'Die Blütezeit und der neue Status der Literatur', in *Literarische Interessenbildung*, ed. Heinzle, 235–56

Kahrmann, Cordula/Reiß, Gunter/Schluchter, Manfred, *Erzähltextanalyse: Eine Einführung in Grundlagen und Verfahren. Mit Materialien zur Erzähltheorie und Übungstexten von Campe bis Ben Witter*, 2 vols., Kronberg/Ts. 1977, 2nd revised edn. of vol. i. Königstein/Ts. 1981

Kantonsbibliothek (Vadiana) St Gallen, *et al.* (eds.), *Rudolf von Ems, Weltchronik. Der Stricker, Karl der Große. Kommentar zu Ms 302 Vad.*, Luzern 1987

Kartschoke, Dieter, '*in die latine bedwungin*: Kommunikationsprobleme im Mittelalter und die Übersetzung der "Chanson de Roland" durch den Pfaffen Konrad', *PBB* 111 (1989), 196–209

Kerby-Fulton, Kathryn, 'Langland and the Bibliographic Ego', in *Written Work: Langland, Labor and Authorship*, edd. Steven Justice/Kathryn Kerby-Fulton, Philadelphia, Pa. 1997, pp. 67–143

Kiening, Christian, *Reflexion—Narration: Wege zum 'Willehalm' Wolframs von Eschenbach*, Tübingen 1991 (Hermaea Germanistische Forschungen NF 63)

Kimmelmann, Burt, *The Poetics of Authorship in the Later Middle Ages: The Emergence of the Modern Literary Persona*, New York, NY 1996 (Studies in the Humanities 21)

Klein, Klaus, 'Ein "Barlaam"-Fragment in Herdringen', *ZfdA* 120 (1991), 202–9

Klein, Thomas, 'Ermittlung, Darstellung und Deutung von Verbreitungstypen in der Handschriftenüberlieferung mittelhochdeutscher Epik', in *Deutsche Handschriften 1100–1400*, edd. Honemann/Palmer, 110–67

—'Die Parzivalhandschrift Cgm 19 und ihr Umkreis', *Wolfram-Studien* 12 (1992), 32–66

Klopsch, Paul, 'Anonymität und Selbstnennung mittellateinischer Autoren', *Mittellateinisches Jahrbuch* 4 (1967), 9–25

—*Einführung in die Dichtungslehren des lateinischen Mittelalters*, Darmstadt 1980

Knape, Joachim, 'Geschichte bei Konrad von Würzburg?', *JOWG* 5 (1988–9), 421–30

Knapp, Fritz Peter, 'Historische Wahrheit und poetische Lüge: Die Gattungen weltlicher Epik und ihre theoretische Rechtfertigung im Hochmittelalter', *DVjs* 54 (1980), 581–635

—*Die Literatur des Früh- und Hochmittelalters in den Bistümern Passau, Salzburg, Brixen und Trient von den Anfängen bis zum Jahre 1273*, Graz 1994 (Geschichte der Literatur in Österreich von den Anfängen bis zur Gegenwart 1)

Kokott, Hartmut, *Konrad von Würzburg: Ein Autor zwischen Auftrag und Autonomie*, Stuttgart 1989

Koppitz, Hans-Joachim, *Studien zur Tradierung der weltlichen mittelhochdeutschen Epik im 15. und beginnenden 16. Jahrhundert*, Munich 1980

Kornrumpf, Gisela, 'Strophik im Zeitalter der Prosa: Deutsche Heldendichtung im ausgehenden Mittelalter', in *Literatur und Laienbildung im Spätmittelalter und in der Reformationszeit: Symposion Wolfenbüttel 1981*, edd. Ludger Grenzmann/Karl Stackmann, Stuttgart 1984 (Germanistische Symposien Berichtsbände 5), 316–40

Krása, Josef, *Die Handschriften König Wenzels IV.*, transl. from the Czech by Hans Gaertner and the author, Prague 1971

von Kraus, Carl, *Text und Entstehung von Rudolfs Alexander*, Munich 1940 (Sitzungsberichte der Bayerischen Akademie der Wissenschaften. Philosophisch-historische Abteilung Jahrgang 1940:8)

Kuhn, Hugo, *Minnesangs Wende*, Tübingen 1952 (Hermaea Germanistische Forschungen NF 1), 2nd expanded edn. 1967

Lachmann, Karl, 'Berichtigungen und zusätze zum sechsten bande', *ZfdA* 6 (1848), 580

Lämmert, Eberhart, *Reimsprecherkunst im Spätmittelalter: Eine Untersuchung der Teichnerreden*, Stuttgart 1970

Lenschen, Walter, *Gliederungsmittel und ihre erzählerischen Funktionen im 'Willehalm von Orlens' des Rudolf von Ems*, Göttingen 1967 (Palaestra 250)

Lienert, Elisabeth, 'Die Überlieferung von Konrads von Würzburg "Trojanerkrieg"', in *Die deutsche Trojaliteratur des Mittelalters und der Frühen Neuzeit: Materialien und Untersuchungen*, ed. Horst Brunner, Wiesbaden 1990 (Wissensliteratur im Mittelalter 3), 325–406

—'Der Trojanische Krieg in Basel: Interesse an Geschichte und Autonomie des Erzählens bei Konrad von Würzburg', in *Literarische Interessenbildung*, ed. Heinzle, 266–79

—*Geschichte und Erzählen: Studien zu Konrads von Würzburg 'Trojanerkrieg'*, Wiesbaden 1996 (Wissensliteratur im Mittelalter 22)

—'*Hoerâ Walther, wie ez mir stât*: Autorschaft und Sängerrolle im Minnesang bis Neidhart', in *Autor und Autorschaft*, edd. Andersen *et al.*, 114–28

—'Dietrich contra Nibelungen: Zur Intertextualität der historischen Dietrichepik', *PBB* 121 (1999), 23–46

Lofmark, Carl, *The Authority of the Source in Middle High German Narrative Poetry*, London 1981 (Institute of Germanic Studies: Bithell Series of Dissertations 5) de Looze, Laurence, 'Signing Off in the Middle Ages: Medieval Textuality and Strategies of Authorial Self-naming', in *Vox intexta: Orality and Textuality in the Middle Ages*, edd. Alger N. Doane/Carol B. Pasternack, Madison, Wis. 1991, pp. 167–78

Lutz, Eckart C., *Rhetorica divina: Mittelhochdeutsche Prologgebete und die rhetorische Kultur des Mittelalters*, Berlin 1984 (Quellen und Forschungen zur Sprach- und Kulturgeschichte der germanischen Völker NF 82 [206])

Lutz, Eckart C. (ed.), *Mittelalterliche Literatur im Lebenszusammenhang: Ergebnisse des Troisième Cycle Romand 1994*, Freiburg, Switzerland 1997 (Scrinium Friburgense 8)

Mayer, Günter, *Probleme der Sangspruchüberlieferung: Beobachtungen zur Rezeption Konrads von Würzburg im Spätmittelalter*, Diss. Munich 1974

Menhardt, Hermann, *Verzeichnis der altdeutschen literarischen Handschriften der Österreichischen Nationalbibliothek*, 3 vols., Berlin 1960–1 (Deutsche Akademie der Wissenschaften zu Berlin. Veröffentlichungen des Instituts für deutsche Sprache und Literatur 13)

Mertens, Volker, 'Konstruktion und Dekonstruktion heldenepischen Erzählens: "Nibelungenlied"–"Klage"–"Titurel"', *PBB* 118 (1996), 358–78

Meyer, Matthias, *Die Verfügbarkeit der Fiktion: Interpretationen und poetologische Untersuchungen zum Artusroman und zur aventiurehaften Dietrichepik des 13. Jahrhunderts*, Heidelberg 1994 (*GRM*-Beiheft 12)

Mihm, Arend, *Überlieferung und Verbreitung der Märendichtung im Spätmittelalter*, Heidelberg 1967

Minnis, Alastair J., *Medieval Theory of Authorship: Scholastic Literary Attitudes in the Later Middle Ages*, London 1984, 2nd edn. Aldershot 1988

Monecke, Wolfgang, *Studien zur epischen Technik Konrads von Würzburg: Das Erzählprinzip der 'wildekeit'*, with an introduction by Ulrich Pretzel, Stuttgart 1968 (Germanistische Abhandlungen 24)

von Moos, Peter, 'Gefahren des Mittelalterbegriffs: Diagnostische und präventive Aspekte', in *Modernes Mittelalter*, ed. Heinzle, 33–63

Müller, Jan-Dirk, 'Heroische Vorwelt, feudaladeliges Krisenbewußtsein und das Ende der Heldenepik: Zur Funktion des "Buchs von Bern"', in *Adelsherrschaft und Literatur*, ed. Horst Wenzel, Berne 1980 (Beiträge zur Älteren Deutschen Literaturgeschichte 6), 209–57

—'Zu einigen Problemen des Konzepts "Literarische Interessenbildung"', in *Literarische Interessenbildung*, ed. Heinzle, 365–84

—'*Ir sult sprechen willekomen*: Sänger, Sprecherrolle und die Anfänge volkssprachlicher Lyrik', *IASL* 19 (1994), 1–21

—'Auctor–Actor–Author: Einige Anmerkungen zum Verständnis vom Autor in lateinischen Schriften des frühen und hohen Mittelalters', in *Der Autor im Dialog*, edd. Ingold/Wunderlich, 17–31

—*Spielregeln für den Untergang: Die Welt des Nibelungenliedes*, Tübingen 1998

—'Aufführung–Autor–Werk: Zu einigen blinden Stellen gegenwärtiger Diskussion', in *Hof und Kloster*, edd. Palmer/Schiewer, 149–66

Müller, Jan-Dirk (ed.), '*Aufführung*' *und* '*Schrift*' *in Mittelalter und Früher Neuzeit*, Stuttgart/Weimar 1996 (Germanistische Symposien Berichtsbände 17)

Nellmann, Eberhard, *Wolframs Erzähltechnik: Untersuchungen zur Funktion des Erzählers*, Wiesbaden 1973

——'"Wilhelm von Orlens"-Handschriften', in *Festschrift Walter Haug und Burghart Wachinger*, edd. Johannes Janota *et al.*, 2 vols., Tübingen 1992, ii. 565–87

Nykrog, Per, *Les Fabliaux: Etude d'histoire littéraire et de stylistique médiévale*, revised edn. Geneva 1973 (Publications romanes et françaises 123)

Obermaier, Sabine, *Von Nachtigallen und Handwerkern: 'Dichtung über Dichtung' in Minnesang und Sangspruchdichtung*, Tübingen 1995 (Hermaea Germanistische Forschungen NF 75)

Ortmann, Christa/Ragotzky, Hedda, 'Zur Funktion exemplarischer *triuwe*-Beweise in Minne-Mären: "Die treue Gattin" Herrands von Wildonie, "Das Herzmaere" Konrads von Würzburg und die "Frauentreue"', in *Kleinere Erzählformen im Mittelalter: Paderborner Colloquium 1987*, edd. Klaus Grubmüller/L. Peter Johnson/Hans-Hugo Steinhoff, Paderborn 1988, pp. 89–109

Ott, Norbert H., 'Die Heldenbuch-Holzschnitte und die Ikonographie des heldenepischen Stoffkreises', in *Heldenbuch*, ed. Heinzle, ii. 245–96

——'Anmerkungen zur Barlaam-Ikonographie Rudolfs von Ems "Barlaam und Josaphat" in Malibu und die Bildtradition des Barlaam-Stoffs', in *Die Begegnung des Westens mit dem Osten: Kongreßakten des 4. Symposions des Mediävistenverbandes in Köln 1991 aus Anlaß des 1000. Todesjahres der Kaiserin Theophanu*, edd. Odilo Engels/Peter Schreiner, Sigmaringen 1993, pp. 365–85

Palmer, Nigel F., 'Eine Prosabearbeitung der Alexiuslegende Konrads von Würzburg', *ZfdA* 108 (1979), 158–80

——'Kapitel und Buch: Zu den Gliederungsprinzipien mittelalterlicher Bücher', *FMSt* 23 (1989), 43–88

——'Der Codex Sangallensis 857: Zu den Fragen des Buchschmucks und der Datierung', *Wolfram-Studien* 12 (1992), 15–31

——*German Literary Culture in the Twelfth and Thirteenth Centuries: An Inaugural Lecture delivered before the University of Oxford on 4 March 1993*, Oxford 1993

——'The High and Later Middle Ages (1100–1450)', in *The Cambridge History of German Literature*, ed. Helen Watanabe-O'Kelly, Cambridge 1997, pp. 40–91

Palmer, Nigel F./Schiewer, Hans-Jochen (eds.), *Mittelalterliche Literatur und Kunst im Spannungsfeld von Hof und Kloster: Ergebnisse der Berliner Tagung, 9.–11. Oktober 1997*, Tübingen 1999

Peters, Ursula, *Literatur in der Stadt: Studien zu den sozialen Voraussetzungen und kulturellen Organisationsformen städtischer Literatur im 13. und 14. Jahrhundert*, Tübingen 1983 (Studien und Texte zur Sozialgeschichte der Literatur 7)

—'Hofkleriker–Stadtschreiber–Mystikerin: Zum literarhistorischen Status dreier Autorentypen', in: *Autorentypen*, edd. Haug/Wachinger, 9–49

Pfeiffer, Franz, 'Über Konrad von Würzburg', *Germania* 12 (1867), 1–48

Poe, Elizabeth W., 'The *Vidas* and *Razos*', in *A Handbook of the Troubadours*, edd. F. R. P. Akehurst/Judith M. Davis, Berkeley, Calif. 1995 (Publications of the UCLA Center for Medieval and Renaissance Studies 26), 185–97

Pörksen, Uwe, *Der Erzähler im mittelhochdeutschen Epos: Formen seines Hervortretens bei Lamprecht, Konrad, Hartmann, in Wolframs Willehalm und in den 'Spielmannsepen'*, Berlin 1971 (Philologische Studien und Quellen 58)

Prillwitz, Siegmund, *Überlieferungsstudie zum Barlaam und Josaphat des Rudolf von Ems: Eine textkritisch-stemmatologische Untersuchung*, Copenhagen 1975

Ragotzky, Hedda, *Studien zur Wolfram-Rezeption: Die Entstehung und Verwandlung der Wolfram-Rolle in der deutschen Literatur des 13. Jahrhunderts*, Stuttgart 1971 (Studien zur Poetik und Geschichte der Literatur 20)

—'"Der Sperber" und "Das Häslein": Zum Gattungsbewußtsein im Märe Ende des 13., Anfang des 14. Jahrhunderts', *PBB* 120 (1998), 36–52

Richert, Hans-Georg, *Wege und Formen der Passionalüberlieferung*, Tübingen 1978 (Hermaea Germanistische Forschungen NF 40)

—'Die Literatur des Deutschen Ritterordens', in *Europäisches Spätmittelalter*, ed. Willi Erzgräber, Wiesbaden 1978 (Neues Handbuch der Literaturwissenschaft 8), 275–86

Ridder, Klaus, 'Autorbilder und Werkbewußtsein im "Parzival" Wolframs von Eschenbach', *Wolfram-Studien* 15 (1998), 168–94

Rikl, Susanne, *Erzählen im Kontext von Affekt und Ratio: Studien zu Konrads von Würzburg 'Partonopier und Meliûr'*, Frankfurt a. M. 1996 (Mikrokosmos 46)

Ritter, Richard, *Die Einleitungen der altdeutschen Epen*, Diss. Bonn 1908

Rosenfeld, Hellmut, 'Aristoteles und Phillis: Eine neu aufgefundene Benediktbeurer Fassung um 1200', *ZfdPh* 89 (1970), 321–36

Rychner, Jean, *Contribution à l'étude des fabliaux: variantes, remaniements, dégradations: I. Observations*, Neuchâtel/Geneva 1960 (Université de Neuchâtel: Recueil de travaux publiés par la Faculté des Lettres 28)

Sayce, Olive, 'Prolog, Epilog und das Problem des Erzählers', in *Probleme mittelhochdeutscher Erzählformen*, edd. Ganz/Schröder, 63–72

Schaefer, Ursula, 'Zum Problem der Mündlichkeit', in *Modernes Mittelalter*, ed. Heinzle, 357–75

Schirmer, Karl-Heinz, *Stil- und Motivuntersuchungen zur mittelhochdeutschen Versnovelle*, Tübingen 1969 (Hermaea Germanistische Forschungen NF 26)

Schirok, Bernd, *Parzivalrezeption im Mittelalter*, Darmstadt 1982 (EdF 174)

—'Zu den Akrosticha in Gottfrieds "Tristan": Versuch einer kritischen und weiterführenden Bestandsaufnahme', *ZfdA* 113 (1984), 188–213

Schmid-Cadalbert, Christian, *Der 'Ortnit' AW als Brautwerbungsdichtung: Ein Beitrag zum Verständnis mittelhochdeutscher Schemaliteratur*, Berne 1985 (Bibliotheca Germanica 28)

Schmidt-Wiegand, Ruth, 'Text und Bild in den Codices picturati des "Sachsenspiegels"', in *Text–Bild–Interpretation: Untersuchungen zu den Bilderhandschriften des Sachsenspiegels*, ed. Ruth Schmidt-Wiegand, 2 vols., Munich 1986 (MMS 55:1–2), i. 11–31

—/Milde, Wolfgang, '*Gott ist selber Recht*'. *Die vier Bilderhandschriften des Sachsenspiegels: Oldenburg, Heidelberg, Wolfenbüttel, Dresden*, 2nd revised edn. Wolfenbüttel 1993 (Ausstellungskataloge der Herzog August Bibliothek 67)

Schneider, Karin, *Gotische Schriften in deutscher Sprache: I. Vom späten 12. Jahrhundert bis um 1300*, 2 vols., Wiesbaden 1987

—'Cod. Bodmer 72', in René Wetzel, *Deutsche Handschriften des Mittelalters in der Bodmeriana* [. . .], Cologny-Genève 1994 (Bibliotheca Bodmeriana: Kataloge 7), 81–129

—*Die Fragmente mittelalterlicher deutscher Versdichtung der Bayerischen Staatsbibliothek München (Cgm 5249/1–79)*, Stuttgart 1996 (*ZfdA* Beiheft 1)

Schnell, Rüdiger, *Rudolf von Ems: Studien zur inneren Einheit seines Gesamtwerkes*, Berne 1969 (Basler Studien zur deutschen Sprache und Literatur 41)

—*Suche nach Wahrheit: Gottfrieds 'Tristan und Isold' als erkenntniskritischer Roman*, Tübingen 1992 (Hermaea Germanistische Forschungen NF 67)

—'"Autor" und "Werk" im deutschen Mittelalter: Forschungskritik und Forschungsperspektiven', *Wolfram-Studien* 15 (1998), 12–73

Scholes, Robert/Kellogg, Robert, *The Nature of Narrative*, New York, NY 1966

Scholz, Manfred G., *Hören und Lesen: Studien zur primären Rezeption der Literatur im 12. und 13. Jahrhundert*, Wiesbaden 1980

Schouwink, Wilfried, *Fortuna im Alexanderroman Rudolfs von Ems: Studien zum Verhältnis von Fortuna und Virtus bei einem Autor der späten Stauferzeit*, Göppingen 1977 (GAG 212)

Schröder, Edward, 'Studien zu Konrad von Würzburg I–III', *GGN* 1912, pp. 1–47

—'Studien zu Konrad von Würzburg IV–V', *GGN* 1917, pp. 96–129

—'Rudolf von Ems und sein litteraturkreis', *ZfdA* 67 (1930), 209–51

Schubert, Ernst, 'Die deutsche Stadt um 1300', *JOWG* (1988–9), 37–56

Schulze, Hans K., *Grundstrukturen der Verfassung im Mittelalter*, 2 vols., Stuttgart 1985–6 (Kohlhammer Urban-Taschenbücher 371–2)

Schulze, Ursula, 'Literarkritische Äußerungen im Tristan Gottfrieds von Straßburg', in *Gottfried von Strassburg*, ed. Alois Wolf, Darmstadt 1973 (WdF 320), 489–517

—'Konrads von Würzburg novellistische Gestaltungskunst im "Herzmaere"', in *Mediaevalia litteraria: Festschrift für Helmut de Boor zum 80. Geburtstag*, edd. Ursula Hennig/Herbert Kolb, Munich 1971, pp. 451–84

Schulz-Grobert, Jürgen, '"Autoren gesucht": Die Verfasserfrage als methodisches Problem im Bereich der spätmittelalterlichen Reimpaarkleindichtung', in *Literarische Interessenbildung*, ed. Heinzle, 60–74

Schwab, Ute, *Die bisher unveröffentlichten geistlichen Bispelreden des Strickers: Über-lieferung–Arrogate–Exegetischer und literarhistorischer Kommentar*, Göttingen 1959

Schweikle, Günther (ed.), *Dichter über Dichter in mittelhochdeutscher Literatur*, Tübingen 1970 (Deutsche Texte 12)

Schwietering, Julius, *Philologische Schriften*, edd. Friedrich Ohly/Max Wehrli, Munich 1969

—'Singen und Sagen', in *Philologische Schriften*, edd. Ohly/Wehrli, 7–58

—'Die Demutsformel mittelhochdeutscher Dichter', in *Philologische Schriften*, edd. Ohly/Wehrli, 140–215

Speckenbach, Klaus, *Studien zum Begriff 'edelez herze' im Tristan Gottfrieds von Straßburg*, Munich 1965 (Medium aevum 6)

Speyer, Wolfgang, *Bücherfunde in der Glaubenswerbung der Antike: Mit einem Ausblick auf Mittelalter und Neuzeit*, Göttingen 1970 (Hypomnemata 24)

Spitzer, Leo, 'Note on the Poetic and the Empirical "I" in Medieval Authors', in *Romanische Literaturstudien 1936–1956*, Tübingen 1959, pp. 100–12

Stanesco, Michel, 'Figures de l'auteur dans le roman médiéval', *Travaux de Littérature* 4 (1991), 7–19

Stanzel, Franz K., *Theorie des Erzählens*, Göttingen 1979 (Uni-Taschenbücher 904)

Stevens, Adrian K., 'Rudolf von Ems's "Barlaam und Josaphat": Aspects of its Relationship to Christian Rhetorical Tradition, With a Considera-tion of its Thematic Structure', Ph.D. thesis, University of Cambridge 1971

—'Zum Literaturbegriff bei Rudolf von Ems', in *Geistliche und weltliche Epik des Mittelalters in Österreich*, edd. David McLintock/Adrian Stevens/Fred Wagner, Göppingen 1987 (GAG 446. Publications of the Institute of Germanic Studies University of London 37), 19–28

Strasser, Ingrid, *Vornovellistisches Erzählen: Mittelhochdeutsche Mären bis zur Mitte des 14. Jahrhunderts und altfranzösische Fabliaux*, Vienna 1989 (Philologica Germanica 10)

Strohschneider, Peter, '"nu sehent, wie der singet!": Vom Hervortreten des Sängers im Minnesang', in *'Aufführung' und 'Schrift'*, ed. Müller, 7–30

Strunk, Gerhard, *Kunst und Glaube in der lateinischen Heiligenlegende: Zu ihrem Selbstverständnis in den Prologen*, Munich 1970 (Medium aevum 12)

Suchomski, Joachim, *'Delectatio' und 'utilitas': Ein Beitrag zum Verständnis mittel-alterlicher komischer Literatur*, Berne/Munich 1975 (Bibliotheca Germanica 18)

Thelen, Christian, *Das Dichtergebet in der deutschen Literatur des Mittelalters*, Berlin 1989 (Arbeiten zur Frühmittelalterforschung 18)

von Tippelskirch, Ingrid, *Die 'Weltchronik' des Rudolf von Ems: Studien zur Geschichtsauffassung und politischen Intention*, Göppingen 1979 (GAG 267)

Unger, Helga, 'Vorreden deutscher Sachliteratur des Mittelalters als Ausdruck literarischen Bewußtseins', in *Werk–Typ–Situation*, edd. Glier *et al.*, 217–51

Wachinger, Burghart, 'Zur Rezeption Gottfrieds von Straßburg im 13. Jahrhundert', in *Deutsche Literatur des späten Mittelalters: Hamburger Colloquium 1973*, edd. Wolfgang Harms/L. Peter Johnson, Berlin 1975 (Publications of the Institute of Germanic Studies University of London 22), 56–82

—— 'Autorschaft und Überlieferung', in *Autorentypen*, edd. Haug/Wachinger, 1–28

——'Wolfram von Eschenbach am Schreibpult', *Wolfram-Studien* 12 (1992), 9–14

Wailes, Stephen L., 'The Hunt of the Hare in "Das Häslein"', *Seminar* 5 (1969), 92–101

Warning, Rainer, 'Formen narrativer Identitätskonstitution im höfischen Roman', in *Identität*, edd. Odo Marquard/Karlheinz Stierle, Munich 1979 (Poetik und Hermeneutik 8), 553–89

——'Lyrisches Ich und Öffentlichkeit bei den Trobadors', in *Kontakte und Perspektiven*, ed. Cormeau, 120–59

Wattenbach, Wilhelm, *Das Schriftwesen im Mittelalter*, 3rd revised edn. Leipzig 1896, repr. Graz 1958

Wehrli, Max, *Literatur im deutschen Mittelalter: Eine poetologische Einführung*, Stuttgart 1984 (Reclam Universal-Bibliothek 8038)

Weidenkopf, Stefan, 'Poesie und Recht: Über die Einheit des Diskurses von Konrads von Würzburg "Schwanritter"', in *Kontakte und Perspektiven*, ed. Cormeau, 296–337

Weigele-Ismael, Erika, *Rudolf von Ems: 'Wilhelm von Orlens'. Studien zur Ausstattung und zur Ikonographie einer illustrierten deutschen Epenhandschrift des 13. Jahrhunderts am Beispiel des Cgm 63 der Bayerischen Staatsbibliothek München*, Frankfurt a. M. 1997 (Europäische Hochschulschriften Reihe 28: Kunstgeschichte 285)

Wenzel, Horst, 'Autorenbilder: Zur Ausdifferenzierung von Autorenfunktionen in mittelalterlichen Miniaturen', in *Autor und Autorschaft*, edd. Andersen *et al.*, 1–28

——'Die Beweglichkeit der Bilder: Zur Relation von Text und Bild in den illuminierten Handschriften des "Welschen Gastes"', *ZfdPh* 116 (1997), Sonderheft 224–52

Westphal-Wihl, Sarah, *Textual Poetics of German Manuscripts 1300–1500*, Columbia, SC 1993

Wilhelm, Friedrich, 'Antike und mittelalterl. Studien zur literaturgeschichte: I. Ueber fabulistische quellenangaben', *PBB* 33 (1908), 286–339

Wisbey, Roy, *Das Alexanderbild Rudolfs von Ems*, Berlin 1966 (Philologische Studien und Quellen 31)

Wittstruck, Wilfried, *Der dichterische Namengebrauch in der deutschen Lyrik des Spätmittelalters*, Munich 1987 (MMS 61)

Wolf, Alois, 'Die Verschriftlichung von europäischen Heldensagen als mittelalterliches Kulturproblem', in *Heldensage und Heldendichtung im Germanischen*, ed. Heinrich Beck, Berlin/New York, NY 1988 (Ergänzungsbände zum Reallexikon der Germanischen Altertumskunde 2), 305–28

Worstbrock, Franz Josef, 'Translatio artium: Über die Herkunft und Entwicklung einer kulturhistorischen Theorie', *AKG* 47 (1965), 1–22

Wyss, Ulrich, 'Rudolfs von Ems "Barlaam und Josaphat" zwischen Legende und Roman', in *Probleme mittelhochdeutscher Erzählformen*, edd. Ganz/Schröder, 214–38

Ziegeler, Hans-Joachim, *Erzählen im Spätmittelalter: Mären im Kontext von Minnereden, Bispeln und Romanen*, Munich 1985 (MTU 87)

—'Beobachtungen zum Wiener Codex 2705 und zu seiner Stellung in der Überlieferung früher kleiner Reimpaardichtung', in *Deutsche Handschriften 1100–1400*, edd. Honemann/Palmer, 469–526

Zink, Georges, 'Pourquoi la *Chanson des Nibelungen* est-elle anonyme?', *EG* 10 (1955), 247–56

Zumthor, Paul, *Essai de poétique médiévale*, Paris 1972

INDEX OF MANUSCRIPTS

Bold numbers denote reference to illustrations.

GENERAL INDEX